STRUCTURING EXPERT SYSTEMS

Selected Titles from the YOURDON PRESS COMPUTING SERIES
Edward Yourdon, Advisor

STRUCTURING
EXPERT SYSTEMS
Domain, Design, and Development

Edited by

Jay Liebowitz

and

Daniel A. De Salvo

YOURDON PRESS
PRENTICE HALL BUILDING
ENGLEWOOD CLIFFS, N.J. 07632

Library of Congress Cataloging-in-Publication Data

Structuring expert systems.

   Bibliography: p.
   Includes index.
   1. Expert systems (Computer science)
I. Liebowitz, Jay.   II. DeSalvo, Daniel A.
QA76.76.E95S87   1989   006.3'3   88-32485
ISBN 0-13-853441-1

Editorial/production supervision : Tally Morgan
Cover design: Ben Santora
Manufacturing buyer: Mary Ann Gloriande

© 1989 Prentice-Hall, Inc.
A Division of Simon & Schuster
Englewood Cliffs, New Jersey 07632

De Salvo, Glamm & Liebowitz from Barry Silverman, *Expert Systems for Business,* © 1987,
Addison-Wesley Publishing Co., Inc., Reading, Massachusetts. Chap. 3, pp. 40–77.
Reprinted with permission.

This book can be made available to businesses
and organizations at a special discount when
ordered in large quantities. For more information
contact:

   Prentice-Hall, Inc.
   Special Sales and Markets
   College Division
   Englewood Cliffs, N.J. 07632

Printed in the United States of America
10 9 8 7 6 5 4 3 2 1

ISBN 0-13-853441-1

Prentice-Hall International (UK) Limited, *London*
Prentice-Hall of Australia Pty. Limited, *Sydney*
Prentice-Hall Canada Inc., *Toronto*
Prentice-Hall Hispanoamericana, S.A., *Mexico*
Prentice-Hall of India Private Limited, *New Delhi*
Prentice-Hall of Japan, Inc., *Tokyo*
Simon & Schuster Asia Pte. Ltd., *Singapore*
Editora Prentice-Hall do Brasil, Ltda, *Rio de Janeiro*

To our families, Janet and Jason Liebowitz,
and Elaine, Dominick, and Robert De Salvo.

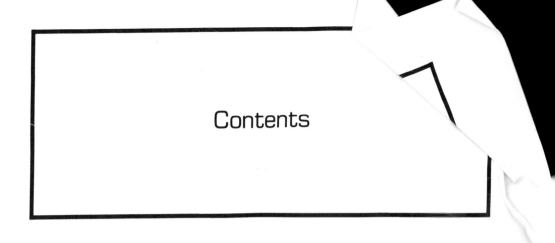

Contents

STRUCTURAL ELEMENTS OF EXPERT SYSTEMS DESIGN
User Interface Design Issues:

STRUCTURAL CONSIDERATIONS IN EXPERT SYSTEM DEVELOPMENT AND IMPLEMENTATION

Preface

The Expert systems field is young and promising. Commercial interest in Expert systems began in 1980, and now a variety of Expert systems for various applications are being developed and implemented. Expert systems are being used on a daily basis for diagnosing telephone cable problems, configuring computer systems, and even helping the police in solving burglaries. With this increase in interest in Expert systems, and in artificial intelligence in general, Expert system applications have blossomed in number and kind. But in the process, the development and usage of structured methodologies for selecting, building, testing, evaluating, and implementing Expert systems have been overlooked. A need thus exists to develop methodologies and structured approaches for building Expert systems. Perhaps some techniques and approaches from the disciplines of systems analysis and software engineering could be borrowed by the knowledge engineer, who is responsible for constructing the Expert system.

This book recognizes the need for structured methodologies for Expert systems development, and the book's focus is centered around that need. With contributions from leading authorities in the Expert systems field, the book addresses the use of structured approaches in each phase of the Expert system development life cycle. Each chapter surveys different methodologies for a particular part of that life cycle and then covers one or two favored methodologies in depth. Each chapter is filled with numerous examples and references for the reader's interest.

The book is divided into three parts: "Structuring the Expert System Domain," "Structural Elements of Expert System Design," and "Structural Considerations in Expert System Development and Implementation." It can be used primarily for two audiences: practitioners who are either currently working in

Expert systems or are interested in becoming involved with Expert system technology, and the university/college student who is interested in learning about Expert systems. The book can be used as either a reference book or a textbook.

Numerous individuals deserve recognition for their part in making this book become a reality. We are extremely grateful to the contributors to this book, who afforded their time, thoughtfulness, and sagest words throughout the book's development. We thank Ed Yourdon, Pat Henry, Ed Moura, Tally Morgan and the Yourdon Press/Prentice-Hall staff for their kind advice and commitment to the project. We are also grateful to the reviewers for their helpful comments. Our colleagues, parents, and family were continually supportive during the project; our wives and children deserve special acknowledgment for their patience throughout the period during which the book was written.

We hope this book will serve as an impetus for developing standards and using structured methodologies for Expert systems development.

April 1989   Jay Liebowitz
Washington, DC   Daniel A. De Salvo

Structuring the Expert System Domain

1

Problem Selection for Expert Systems Development

Jay Liebowitz

INTRODUCTION

Someone once said that there are three important rules in developing expert systems: "pick the right problem," "pick the right problem," and "pick the right problem." Thus, as in software development or scientific research, in expert systems development the most critical thing is choosing the right problem to work on. Selecting too large a problem or one with few test cases could lead to disastrous results when building an expert system. And picking too trivial a problem could leave managers and users unimpressed. If the problem is not properly identified and "scoped," complications will likely occur later in the knowledge engineering (i.e., expert systems development) process. By spending the time up front in identifying the problem, savings in time and money will ultimately accrue.

This chapter discusses some criteria to consider in selecting a problem for expert systems development. Some background on expert systems and their design is presented, and after the development of some characteristics regarding problem selection, some methodologies are set out that aid in the selection of a problem suitable for expert systems development. Finally, several application areas in which expert systems have been built and used are reviewed.

BACKGROUND

Expert systems is an area that is gaining worldwide interest in industry, government, and academia. From telephone cable maintenance to medical diagnosis to tax and legal planning, expert systems are being applied increasingly and ever more proficiently. The field of expert systems is a subset of artificial intelligence and draws upon many disciplines, including cognitive psychology, linguistics, philosophy, and computer science. Although more research is needed to improve expert systems technology, expert systems are beginning to have a strong impact on all kinds of decision making.

An expert system is a computer program that emulates the behavior of a human expert within a specific domain of knowledge. The major characteristics of an expert system are (1) the ability to perform at the level of an expert, (2) the representation of domain-specific knowledge in the manner in which the expert thinks, (3) the incorporation of explanatory mechanisms and ways of handling uncertainty into the repertoire of the system, and typically (4) a predilection for problems that can be symbolically represented. In effect, an expert system differs from a conventional computer program mainly by being more tolerant of errors and imperfect knowledge and by separating the expert knowledge from the general-reasoning mechanism. Because the knowledge base is thus separated from the control structure, the knowledge base can be incrementally developed and the same general system can be used for different applications by substituting one knowledge base for another.

Expert systems are helpful in verifying one's knowledge, as well as in documenting or preserving knowledge. Before an individual retires, quits, or moves on to a different project within a company, it would be helpful to preserve the knowledge and professional experiential learning that the individual has accumulated over the years. By capturing this expert's knowledge, the institutional memory of the organization could be built and maintained and new employees would be able more easily to learn from the successes and failures of the expert in his or her area of expertise. Expert systems are also helpful in situations where an expert is unavailable, where expertise is scarce or expensive, or where the decision maker is placed under time and pressure constraints.

An expert system consists of three parts: a dialogue structure, an inference engine, and a knowledge base. The dialogue structure is the language interface which allows the user to interact with the expert system, query it, obtain explanations from it, and challenge its results. The inference engine is the control structure which allows various hypotheses to be generated and tested. The knowledge base is where the real power of an expert system lies. The old adage, "knowledge is power," applies here because if an expert system has incomplete knowledge, then the answer obtained from the system will most likely be incomplete no matter how well the inference engine searches and efficiently generates hypotheses.

The knowledge base is a set of facts and heuristics (rules of thumb) about the particular domain. It is important for the expert system to consist of both facts and rules of thumb derived from an expert's experience. This can be seen especially in the legal field. Bellord [1] points out the falsity of the assumption that where the law is concerned the source of information is books alone. He shows that another form of relevant legal knowledge may be tactics. Thus, the knowledge of who is going to judge a particular case and what the judge's reaction usually is to a particular kind of murder may be of far greater importance than anything to be found in a book [1]. This suggests that besides having "book knowledge" (facts in the expert system), it is just as important to have heuristics obtained from the expert lawyer. The knowledge base of the expert system thus has both facts and heuristics.

BUILDING AN EXPERT SYSTEM

The time taken for the construction of early expert systems was on the order of 20 to 50 man-years. More recently, simple expert systems have been built in 3 man-months, but a complex system is still apt to take as long as 10 man-years to complete. With the advent of shells, development time is approaching 5 man-years per system. (An expert system *shell* contains a generalized dialogue structure and inference engine; a knowledge base can be designed for a specific problem domain and linked to the expert system shell to form a new expert system for a particular application.)

The first step in building an expert system is to select the problem, define the expert system goal(s), and identify the sources of knowledge. The task must have a well-bounded domain of knowledge to avoid the combinatorial explosion of alternatives. Additionally, there must be at least one expert willing to develop the expert system.

Once this step is accomplished, knowledge from the expert must be acquired in order to develop the knowledge base. It is also helpful to develop a framework for representing the acquired information. Knowledge acquisition is an iterative process in which many meetings with the expert are needed to gather all the relevant and necessary information for the knowledge base.

After the knowledge is acquired, an approach to its representation must be chosen. Such approaches include using predicate calculus, frames, scripts, semantic networks, or production rules. According to Software A&E [2], rule-based deduction is an appropriate method for knowledge representation if (1) the underlying knowledge is already organized as rules, (2) the type of classification is predominantly categorical, and (3) there is not a large amount of context-dependence. Frames, scripts, or semantic networks are best used when the knowledge preexists as a set of descriptions.

Next, the knowledge must be programmed into the system by using a text editor in an expert system shell or by using LISP, Prolog, or some other appropriate programming language. The last step is to validate, test, and evaluate the expert system.

Validation is necessary to check the knowledge base and the expert system as a whole. Validation can be achieved by running the knowledge base on past problems whose solutions are known or accepted. It can also be confirmed by other experts knowledgeable in the problem domain.

Testing is important because, when the expert system finally runs, it typically produces a variety of unexpected results. These are summarized by Hayes-Roth et al. [3] as follows:

- *Excess generality*—Special cases are overlooked.
- *Excess specificity*—Generalizations remain undetected.
- *Concept poverty*—A useful relationship is not detected and exploited.
- *Invalid knowledge*—Facts are misstated or stated only approximately.
- *Ambiguous knowledge*—Implicit dependencies are not adequately articulated.
- *Invalid reasoning*—The programmer incorrectly transforms knowledge.
- *Inadequate integration*—Dependencies among multiple pieces of information are incompletely integrated.
- *Limited horizon*—Consequences of recent, past, or probable future events are not exploited.
- *Egocentricity*—Little attention is paid to the probable meaning of others' actions.

In order to correct these "bugs," the knowledge base must be refined and then maintained. Toward these ends, iterative refinements of the knowledge base through knowledge acquisition, knowledge representation, knowledge programming, and knowledge testing are conducted until user goals and expectations are met. An evaluation of the expert system can then be made by both users and experts working in the problem domain.

PROBLEM SELECTION CRITERIA

The selection of a problem for expert system development can be discussed in terms of the type of problem at issue, the experts available, and the users requiring the system.

Type of Problem

The following criteria are relevant to the knowledge engineering team's selecting an appropriate type of problem to work on [4–15]. The team should consider what kinds of problems are subsumed under each criterion, or, for a given problem, which criteria it falls under and which rule it out.

- The task requires primarily symbolic reasoning.
- The task requires the use of heuristics, e.g., rules of thumb or strategies.
- The task may require decisions that are based upon incomplete or uncertain information.

- The task does not require knowledge from a very large number of areas.
- The system development has its goal either to develop a system for actual use or to make major advances in the state of the art of expert system technology, but does not attempt to achieve both of these goals simultaneously.
- The task is defined very clearly, i.e., at the project outset there is a precise definition of the inputs and outputs of the system to be developed.
- A good set of test cases exists.
- Some small systems will be developed to solve problems that are amenable to conventional techniques simply because the users need the systems quickly and have decided that they can develop workable solutions by themselves using shells rather than waiting for their data processing groups to help them with their problems.
- There are a few key individuals required for the project, but they are in short supply.
- Corporate goals are compromised as a result of scarce human resources.
- Competitors appear to have an advantage because they can consistently perform the task better.
- The domain is one where expertise is generally unavailable, scarce, or expensive.
- The task doesn't depend heavily on common sense.
- The task has outcomes that can be evaluated.
- The task is decomposable, allowing relatively rapid prototyping for a small closed subset of the task and then slow expansion to the complete task.
- The system solves a problem which has value, but is not on a critical path.
- The task is neither too easy (taking a human expert less than a few minutes) nor too difficult (requiring more than a few days for an expert).
- The amount of knowledge required for the task is large enough to make the knowledge base to be developed interesting.
- The task is sufficiently narrow and self-contained; i.e., the aim is not for a system that is expert in an entire domain, but for a system that is expert in a limited subdomain within the domain.
- The number of important concepts (e.g., rules) required is limited to no more than several hundred.
- The domain is characterized by the use of expert knowledge, judgment, and experience.
- Conventional programming (i.e., algorithmic) approaches to the task are not satisfactory.
- There are recognized experts that solve the problem in question today.
- The experts are probably better than amateurs in performing the task.

- Expertise in the domain is not or will not be available on a reliable and continuing basis, i.e., there is a need to "capture" the expertise.
- The completed system is expected to have a significant payoff for the corporation.
- The domain selected is the one that best meets overall project goals regarding payoff versus risk of failure.
- The system can be phased into use gracefully, i.e., some percentage of incomplete coverage can be tolerated (at least initially), and the determination whether a subproblem is covered by the system existing at a given time is not difficult.
- The task is not all-or-nothing, i.e., some percentage of incorrect or non-optimal results can be tolerated.
- The skill required by the task is taught to novices.
- There are books or other written material discussing the domain.
- The task's payoff is measurable.
- Experts would agree on whether the system's results are satisfactory (correct).
- The need for the task is projected to continue for several years.
- The domain is fairly stable; i.e., the system may require changes that utilize the strengths of expert systems (e.g., ease of updating or revising specific rules in a knowledge base), but it will not require major changes in reasoning processes.
- At the outset of the project, the expert is able to specify many of the important concepts relating to the domain.
- Management is willing to commit the necessary human and material resources to the project.
- The task requires only cognitive skills.
- The task is not poorly understood.
- Expert systems could have great payoffs in mundane tasks, as well as in heroic ones.
- The task is thought of as too small to handle; even in this case, in all likelihood it will have to be narrowed even further.
- The task is performed frequently.

The Expert

An essential part of expert systems development is having an expert to work with the knowledge engineering team. Here are some criteria used in selecting an expert [4–15]:

- There exists an expert to work with the project.
- The expert's knowledge and reputation are such that if the expert system is

able to capture a portion of the expert's expertise, the system's output will have credibility and authority.

- The expert has built up expertise over a long period of time.
- The expert will commit a substantial amount of time to the development of the system.
- The expert is capable of communicating his or her knowledge, judgment, and experience, as well as the methods used to apply them to the particular task.
- The expert is cooperative.
- The expertise for the system, or at least that pertaining to one particular subdomain, is to be obtained primarily from one expert.
- If multiple experts contribute in a particular subdomain, one of them should be the primary expert with final authority.
- A backup expert is desirable and available.
- The expert is the person the company can least afford to do without.
- The expert has a strong vested interest in obtaining a solution.
- The expert understands what the problem is and has actually solved it quite often.
- Experts agree on the solutions to the problem.

Domain-Area Personnel

Besides the knowledge engineer and the expert, there are also the needs and desires of domain-area personnel to consider when selecting a problem for expert systems development. The domain-area personnel are the users of the system together with their management. The following are some criteria relating to the domain-area personnel that may be used in selecting a problem [11]:

- Personnel in the domain area are realistic, understanding not only the potential but also the limitations of an expert system for their domain.
- The domain-area personnel understand that even a successful system will likely be limited in scope and, like a human expert, may not produce optimal or correct results 100 percent of the time.
- There is strong managerial support for the project from the domain area, especially regarding the large commitment of time by the expert(s) and their possible travel or temporary relocation, if required.
- The specific task within the domain is jointly agreed upon by the system developers and the domain-area personnel.
- Managers in the domain area have previously identified the need to solve the problem the system attacks.
- The project is strongly supported by a senior manager, so that it can be protected and followed up.

- Potential users would welcome the completed system.
- The system can be introduced with minimal disturbance to current practices.
- The user group is cooperative and patient.
- Introduction of the system into the domain area will not be politically sensitive or controversial.
- The knowledge contained by the system will not be politically sensitive or controversial.
- The system's results will not be politically sensitive or controversial.

METHODOLOGIES FOR EXPERT SYSTEM PROBLEM SELECTION

To increase the likelihood of proper problem selection for expert system development, the criteria just presented should be carefully considered. One methodology that can help the knowledge engineer in selecting and scoping a problem is the *Analytic Hierarchy Process* (AHP), developed by Saaty [16–18]. This technique is useful for quantifying subjective judgments used in decision making. A microcomputer software package called Expert Choice [19] embodies the method.

AHP has been successfully applied to numerous problems, from selecting an appropriate expert system shell [20] to choosing the best house to buy. AHP breaks down a problem into its constituent parts and then calls for only simple pairwise comparison judgments to develop priorities in each hierarchy [16]. The steps of AHP are as follows [16]:

1. The problem is defined.
2. The hierarchy is structured from the top level (the objectives from a general viewpoint) through the intermediate levels (criteria on which subsequent levels depend) to the lowest level (usually a list of the alternatives).
3. A set of pairwise comparison matrices is constructed for each of the lower levels—one matrix for each element in the level immediately above.
4. After all the pairwise comparisons have been made and the data entered, the consistency of the judgments is determined using the eigenvalue.
5. Steps 3 and 4 are performed for all levels in the hierarchy.
6. The hierarchical composition is now used to weight the eigenvectors by the weights of the criteria, and the sum is taken over all weighted eigenvector entries corresponding to those in the next lower level of the hierarchy.
7. The consistency of the entire hierarchy is found by multiplying each consistency index by the priority of the corresponding criterion and adding them together.

Mathematically speaking, priorities are calculated by the process of principal eigenvector extraction and hierarchical weighting [21]. Suppose we have a matrix of pairwise comparisons of weights that has n objects $A_1, \ldots, A_n$ whose vector of corresponding weights is $w = (w_1, \ldots, w_n)$. Then the problem $A_w =$ (maximum eigenvalue) (w_i) should be solved to obtain an estimate of the weights w_i. A pairwise-comparison reciprocal matrix is used to compare the relative contribution of the elements in each level of the hierarchy to an element in the adjacent upper level [21]. The principal eigenvector of this matrix is then derived and weighted by the priority of the property with respect to which the comparison is made [21]. That weight is determined by comparing the properties among themselves with respect to their contribution to the criteria of a still higher level [21]. The weighted eigenvectors can then be added componentwise to obtain an overall weight or priority of contribution of each element to the hierarchy. Bazaraa and Jarvis [22] provide a further explanation, in terms of linear algebra, of the derivation of an eigenvalue.

AHP has been robustly tested and successfully applied to numerous diverse problems [17,18]. Its results have been remarkably accurate in situations where numerical measures are known [23]. In one experiment, four chairs were arranged in a straight line from a light source, and pairwise verbal judgments from subjects were then made about the relative brightness of the chairs [16,23]. The results, when analyzed, showed a remarkable conformity to the inverse square law of brightness as a function of distance, as can be seen in the following table [23]:

Trial 1	Trial 2	Inverse Square Law
0.61	0.61	0.61
0.24	0.22	0.22
0.10	0.10	0.11
0.05	0.06	0.06

Another validation experiment involved estimating the relative areas of two-dimensional figures by using pairwise verbal judgments [19,23]. Subjects were asked to estimate the relative areas of five geometrically shaped objects by using Expert Choice, an automated AHP. The accuracy of the results of different subjects' verbal judgments was truly amazing [23]:

Figure	Actual Percentage	Expert Choice Estimate
A	0.47	0.45
B	0.05	0.07
C	0.23	0.24
D	0.15	0.15
E	0.10	0.09

Expert Choice

Expert Choice [24,25] represents a significant contribution to the decision-making process, as it is able to quantify subjective judgments in complex decision-making environments [23]. Expert Choice enables decision makers to visually structure a multifaceted problem in the form of a hierarchy [23]. Employing AHP, the system is one methodology which is helpful in selecting an appropriate expert system problem.

In using Expert Choice, the user (i.e., decision maker) first constructs a hierarchy of the goal, criteria, and alternatives for the Expert Choice application. At the top level of the hierarchy, the goal is defined—in this case, to select an expert system problem. At the next level, the criteria used in selecting the problem are defined. The problem-selection criteria, which are based on those discussed earlier, are categorized as follows:

> PRO TYPE—Type of problem criteria
> EXPERT—Expert criteria
> DOM PERS—Domain-area personnel criteria

Subcriteria under each of these headings can be defined at the next level of the hierarchy and are as follows:

PRO TYPE

> SYMBOLIC—Task involves mostly symbolic processing
> TEST CAS—Test cases are available
> WELL-BND—Problem task is well bounded
> FREQUENT—Task is required to be performed frequently
> WRIT MAT—Written materials exist explaining the task
> COG SKLS—Task requires only cognitive skills
> EXP AGRE—Experts agree on the solutions to the problem

EXPERT

> EXP EXST—An expert exists
> COOPERTE—The expert is cooperative
> ARTICULT—The expert is articulate
> EXPERNCE—The expert's knowledge is based on experience, facts, and judgment
> OTHER EX—Other experts exist

DOM PERS

> NEED EXI—A need exists for developing an expert system for the problem
> FIN SPRT—The task will be provided with the necessary financial support
> TOP MGMT—Top management supports the project
> REAL EXP—The domain-area personnel have realistic expectations regarding the use of an expert system
> USERS WL—Users would welcome the expert system
> NOT POL—The knowledge used in the expert system is not politically sensitive or controversial

The last level of the hierarchy contains the alternatives, i.e., the possible problems (or tasks) to be worked on for expert systems development. For the sake of illustration, we shall consider the following three alternatives:

MACROECO—Develop an expert system for determining macroeconomic policy in the U.S.

NUCLEAR—Develop an expert system for determining what the U.S. should do in case of a nuclear war

BID/NO—Develop an expert system for determining whether to bid on a request for proposal

Figure 1–1 shows the Expert Choice hierarchy before pairwise comparisons are made (i.e., before weighting takes place) for the application in question.

After constructing the hierarchy, the evaluation process begins in which Expert Choice will ask questions to the user in order to assign priorities (i.e., weights) to the criteria. Expert Choice allows the user to provide judgments verbally so that no numerical guesses are required. (It also allows the user to answer numerically if desired.) Thus, the first question is, "With respect to the goal of selecting an expert system problem, is criterion one (i.e., PRO TYPE) equally as important as criterion two (i.e., EXPERT)?" If the user's answer to this question is "yes," then criterion one is compared to criterion three (PRO TYPE vs. DOM PERS). If the answer is "no," then, as shown in Figure 1–2, Expert Choice will ask, "Is PRO TYPE more important than EXPERT," and it will ask for the level of importance. The number of pairwise comparisons is shown in a triangle of dots, as displayed in the right-hand corner of the figure. The relative importance, also shown in the figure, is categorized into equally as important, moderately more important, strongly more important, very strongly more important, extremely more important, or a degree within this range. Based upon the user's verbal judgments, Expert Choice will calculate the relative importance according to the following scale [16–18]:

1	Of equal importance
3	Moderate importance of one alternative over another
5	Essential or strong importance
7	Very strong importance
9	Extreme importance
2,4,6,8	Intermediate values between the two adjacent judgments

This procedure is followed to obtain relative priorities for the criteria, for which eigenvalues are calculated based upon pairwise comparisons of one criterion versus another, as discussed earlier. These pairwise comparisons are made for each of the criteria and subcriteria. Figures 1–2 and 1–3 show the priorities after the pairwise comparisons are made. Also, an inconsistency index is calculated after each set of pairwise comparisons to show how consistent the user's judgments are. An overall inconsistency index is calculated at the end of the synthesis as well. This

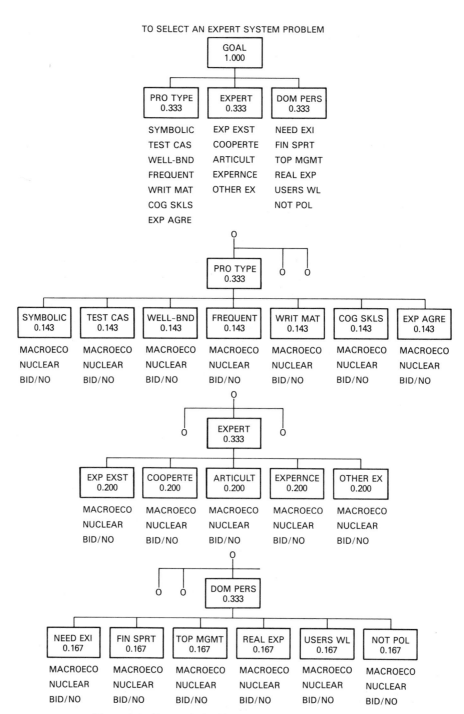

Figure 1–1 Expert choice hierarchy before pairwise comparisons.

GOAL: TO SELECT AN EXPERT SYSTEM PROBLEM

With respect to
GOAL OF TO SELECT AN EXPERT SYSTEM PROBLEM

PRO TYPE
is EQUAL to MODERATELY MORE IMPORTANT THAN
EXPERT

EXTREME ------------------------------------

VERY STRONG -----------------------------

STRONG --------------------------------

MODERATE ------------------------------

EQUAL ------------------------------------

PRIORITIES OF IMPORTANCE OF . . . WITH RESPECT TO
GOAL OF TO SELECT AN EXPERT SYSTEM PROBLEM

0.500
PRO TYPE

0.250
DOM PERS

0.250
EXPERT

INCONSISTENCY RATIO = 0.000

Figure 1–2 Weighting of first-level criteria.

measure is zero when all judgments are perfectly consistent with one another and becomes larger when the inconsistency is greater [23]. The inconsistency is considered tolerable if it is 0.10 or less [23].

After the criteria and subcriteria are weighted, pairwise comparisons are made between the alternatives and the subcriteria. For example, one question would be "With respect to SYMBOLIC, are MACROECO and NUCLEAR equally preferable?" After all the pairwise comparisons have been entered, Expert Choice performs a synthesis, adding the global priorities (global priorities indicate the contribution to the overall goal) at each level of the tree hierarchy. Figure 1–4 shows the hierarchy after all the pairwise comparisons are made. Figure 1–5 shows the synthesis of the results and, finally, the ranking of the alternatives. For the example presented, after taking all the pairwise comparisons into account, the best problem to select for expert systems development is BID/NO (i.e., develop an expert system for determining whether a company should bid on a request for proposal). Its priority is 0.578, followed by MACROECO (0.266), and then NUCLEAR (0.156). The overall inconsistency index is 0.06, which is within the tolerable range. Expert Choice also allows for sensitivity analysis if the user desires.

Other Approaches to Expert System Problem Selection

Another technique for selecting an expert system problem is to have a checklist of important problem criteria, based on those set out earlier, and see how many of the criteria fit the problem under consideration. This is an unsophisticated approach, but is effective and probably what most knowledge engineers use when selecting a possible problem task for expert systems development.

A cost-benefit analysis should also be conducted to determine whether it is technically, economically, and operationally feasible to develop an expert system

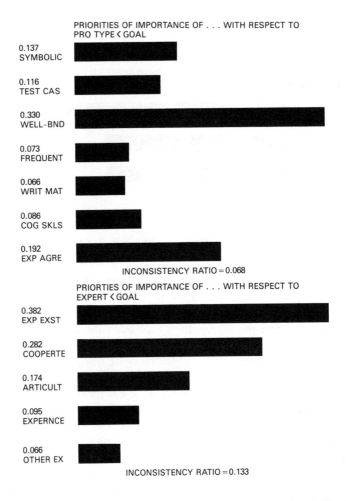

(Cont'd.)

Figure 1–3   Weighting of second-level criteria.

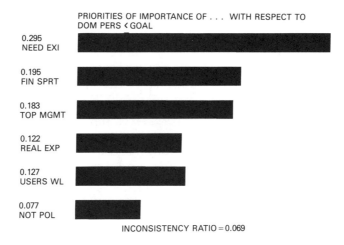

Figure 1–3   (*Cont'd.*)

for a particular problem. Costs include the expert's time as well as that of the knowledge engineer [4]. Additional costs may include the acquisition of hardware, the acquisition of software like expert system shells, overhead, the expert's travel and lodging expenses, and computing time. The benefits of an expert system may include reduced costs, increased productivity, increased training productivity and effectiveness, preservation of knowledge, enhanced products or services, and even the development of new products and services [4,26]. A comparison of the costs and benefits between the current system and the proposed expert system could be conducted. Expert Choice could even be used for this cost-benefit analysis to see whether the expert system would be more cost-effective than the current system.

APPLICATIONS FOR WHICH EXPERT SYSTEMS HAVE ALREADY BEEN DEVELOPED

Over the years, expert systems have been developed and applied to numerous endeavors. Waterman [5], Rauch-Hindin [27], and Liebowitz [14,28,29] list the following as fields to which expert systems have been successfully applied:

- Interpretation
- Prediction
- Diagnosis
- Fault isolation
- Design
- Planning

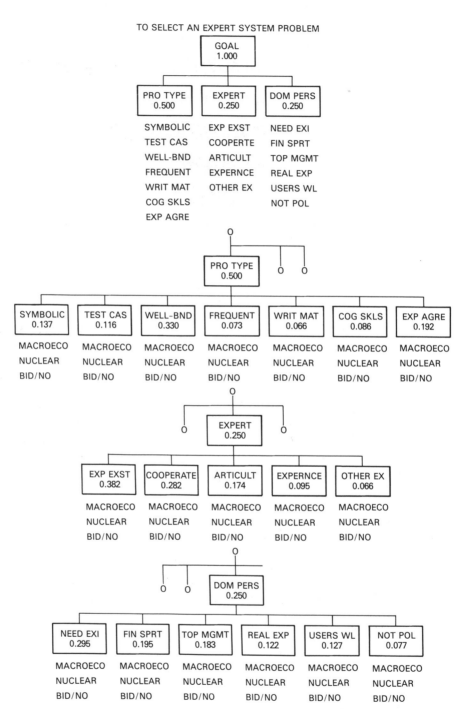

Figure 1–4 Hierarchy after pairwise comparisons.

LEVEL 1	LEVEL 2	LEVEL 3	LEVEL 4	LEVEL 5
PRO TYPE = 0.500				
.	WELL-BND = 0.165			
.	.	BID/NO = 0.125		
.	.	MACROECO = 0.027		
.	.	NUCLEAR = 0.012		
.	EXP AGRE = 0.096			
.	.	BID/NO = 0.075		
.	.	MACROECO = 0.013		
.	.	NUCLEAR = 0.008		
.	SYMBOLIC = 0.069			
.	.	BID/NO = 0.042		
.	.	NUCLEAR = 0.018		
.	.	MACROECO = 0.008		
.	TEST CAS = 0.058			
.	.	MACROECO = 0.039		
.	.	BID/NO = 0.015		
.	.	NUCLEAR = 0.004		
.	COG SKLS = 0.043			
.	.	MACROECO = 0.017		
.	.	BID/NO = 0.017		
.	.	NUCLEAR = 0.009		
.	FREQUENT = 0.036			
.	.	BID/NO = 0.025		
.	.	MACROECO = 0.009		
.	.	NUCLEAR = 0.002		
.	WRIT MAT = 0.033			
.	.	BID/NO = 0.021		
.	.	MACROECO = 0.010		
.	.	NUCLEAR = 0.002		
EXPERT = 0.250				
.	EXP EXST = 0.096			
.	.	BID/NO = 0.071		
.	.	MACROECO = 0.017		
.	.	NUCLEAR = 0.007		
.	COOPERTE = 0.070			
.	.	BID/NO = 0.050		
.	.	MACROECO = 0.015		
.	.	NUCLEAR = 0.006		
.	ARTICULT = 0.044			
.	.	MACROECO = 0.015		
.	.	NUCLEAR = 0.015		
.	.	BID/NO = 0.015		
.	EXPERNCE = 0.024			
.	.	MACROECO = 0.011		
.	.	BID/NO = 0.011		
.	.	NUCLEAR = 0.002		
.	OTHER EX = 0.017			
.	.	BID/NO = 0.011		
.	.	MACROECO = 0.004		
.	.	NUCLEAR = 0.001		
DOM PERS = 0.250				
.	NEED EXI = 0.074			
.	.	BID/NO = 0.036		
.	.	MACROECO = 0.023		
.	.	NUCLEAR = 0.014		
.	FIN SPRT = 0.049			
.	.	NUCLEAR = 0.028		
.				

(Cont'd.)

Figure 1–5 Synthesis of results.

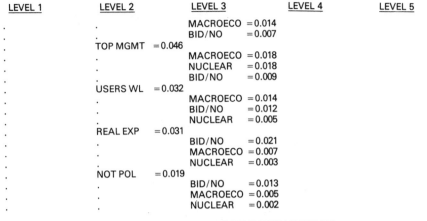

LEVEL 1	LEVEL 2	LEVEL 3	LEVEL 4	LEVEL 5
.	.	MACROECO = 0.014		
.	.	BID/NO = 0.007		
.	TOP MGMT = 0.046			
.	.	MACROECO = 0.018		
.	.	NUCLEAR = 0.018		
.	.	BID/NO = 0.009		
.	USERS WL = 0.032			
.	.	MACROECO = 0.014		
.	.	BID/NO = 0.012		
.	.	NUCLEAR = 0.005		
.	REAL EXP = 0.031			
.	.	BID/NO = 0.021		
.	.	MACROECO = 0.007		
.	.	NUCLEAR = 0.003		
.	NOT POL = 0.019			
.	.	BID/NO = 0.013		
.	.	MACROECO = 0.005		
.	.	NUCLEAR = 0.002		

TO SELECT AN EXPERT SYSTEM PROBLEM

LEAF NODES SORTED BY PRIORITY

OVERALL INCONSISTENCY INDEX = 0.06

BID/NO   0.578

MACROECO 0.266

NUCLEAR   0.156
       1.000

Figure 1–5   (*Cont'd.*)

- Monitoring
- Debugging
- Repair
- Scheduling
- Instruction
- Control
- Analysis
- Legal analysis
- Maintenance
- Configuration
- Targeting (i.e., resource allocation)

Expert systems that have been built in these application areas include the following [5,9]:

INTERPRETATION

PUFF—Interprets pulmonary function tests

PREDICTION

PLANT/cd—Predicts the damage to corn due to the black cutworm

DIAGNOSIS

MYCIN—Diagnoses bacterial infections in the blood
CATS—Diagnoses problems in diesel-electric locomotives

FAULT ISOLATION

ACE—Troubleshoots telephone lines

DESIGN

MOTOR BRUSH DESIGNER—Constructs the design of brushes and springs for small electric motors

PLANNING

CSS—Aids in planning the relocation, reinstallation, and rearrangement of IBM mainframes
PlanPower—Aids in financial planning

MONITORING

YES/MVS—Monitors the IBM MVS operating system

DEBUGGING

BUGGY—Debugs students' subtraction errors

REPAIR

SECOFOR—Advises on drill-bit sticking problems in oil wells

SCHEDULING

ISA—Schedules orders for manufacturing and delivery
ISIS—Schedules manufacturing steps in a job shop

INSTRUCTION

TVX—Tutors users about an operating system

CONTROL

PTRANS—Helps control the manufacture and distribution of Digital Equipment Corporation's computer systems

ANALYSIS

DIPMETER ADVISOR—Analyzes oil well logging data

LEGAL ANALYSIS

LDS—Assists legal experts in settling product liability cases

MAINTENANCE

COMPASS—Analyzes telephone switching systems' maintenance messages and suggests maintenance actions to perform

CONFIGURATION

XCON—Configures VAX computer systems
VT—Configures orders for new elevator systems

TARGETING (RESOURCE ALLOCATION)

BATTLE—Allocates weapons to targets

Of course, these are only a small sample of the expert systems that have been developed and used over the years. In the coming years more business expert systems will be developed, and as hardware and expert system shell prices drop, more widespread expert system applications will be facilitated.

CONCLUSION

Problem selection is a critical step in the expert system development process. By not selecting the "right" problem or not scoping the problem down to a manageable size at the start, complications will ultimately occur in the subsequent construction of the system.

The criteria for problem selection presented in this chapter should be followed closely when considering the type of problem, domain expert, and domain-area personnel pertinent to the design of an expert system. The Analytic Hierarchy Process (AHP) is a useful structured methodology for implementing these criteria. The software system called Expert Choice easily facilitates the use of AHP. In any event, whether this structured methodology or some other approach is used in problem selection, the important point to remember is to make sure that the method used will help to identify the "right" problem for expert systems development.

REFERENCES

1. Bellord, N.J. "Information and Artificial Intelligence in the Lawyer's Office." *In Artificial Intelligence and Legal Information Systems.* Amsterdam: North-Holland, 1982.
2. Software A&E. *Knowledge Engineering System—Knowledge Base Author's Reference Manual.* Arlington, VA.
3. Hayes-Roth, F., Klahr, P., and Mostow, D.J. *Knowledge Acquisition, Knowledge Programming, and Knowledge Refinement.* Washington, DC: Rand Report R-2540-NSF, May 1980.
4. Harmon, P., and King, D. *Expert Systems: Artificial Intelligence in Business.* New York: Wiley, 1985.
5. Waterman, D.A. *A Guide to Expert Systems.* Reading, MA: Addison-Wesley, 1986.
6. Liebowitz, J. *Introduction to Expert Systems.* Santa Cruz, CA: Mitchell Publishing, 1988.
7. Liebowitz, J., ed. *Expert System Applications to Telecommunications.* New York: Wiley, 1988.

8. Goyal, S.K., Prerau, D.S., Lemmon, A.V., Gunderson, A.S., and Reinke, R.E. "COMPASS: An Expert System for Telephone Switch Maintenance." *Expert Systems* 2 (July 1985).

9. Buchanan, B.G. "Expert Systems: Working Systems and the Research Literature." *Expert Systems* 3 (January 1986).

10. Prerau, D.S. "Knowledge Acquisition in Expert System Development." *AI Magazine* 8 (Summer 1987).

11. Prerau, D.S. "Selection of an Appropriate Domain." *AI Magazine* 6 (Summer 1985).

12. Bobrow, D.G., Mittal, S., and Stefik, M.J. "Expert Systems: Perils and Promise." *Communications of the ACM* 29 (September 1986).

13. Liebowitz, J. "Expert Systems and Telecommunications." *Telematics and Informatics* 2 (1985).

14. Liebowitz, J. "Expert Systems in Law: A Survey and Case Study." *Telematics and Informatics* 3 (1986).

15. Freiling, M., Alexander, J., Messick, S., Rehfuss, S., and Shulman, S. "Starting a Knowledge Engineering Project: A Step-by-Step Approach." *AI Magazine* 6 (Fall 1985).

16. Saaty, T.L. "Priority Setting in Complex Problems." *Proceedings of Second World Conference on Mathematics,* Las Palmas, Canary Islands, 1982.

17. Saaty, T.L. *The Analytic Hierarchy Process.* New York: McGraw-Hill, 1980.

18. Saaty, T.L. *Decision Making for Leaders.* Belmont, CA: Wadsworth Publishing, 1982.

19. Decision Support Software, Inc. *Expert Choice Manual.* McLean, VA.

20. Forman, E.H., and Nagy, T.J. "EXSYS vs. TOPSI/OPS 5 vs. MICRO-PS: A Multi-criteria Model to Select an Expert System Generator." *Telematics and Informatics* 4 (1987).

21. Wind, Y., and Saaty, T.L. "Marketing Applications of the Analytic Hierarchy Process." *Management Science* 26 (1980), pp. 641–658.

22. Bazaraa, M.S., and Jarvis, J.J. *Linear Programming and Network Flows.* New York: Wiley, 1977.

23. Forman, E.H. "The Analytic Hierarchy Process as a Decision Support System." In *IEEE Compcom 83 Proceedings.* Washington, DC: IEEE, 1983, pp. 101–111.

24. Liebowitz, J. "A Useful Approach for Evaluating Expert Systems." *Expert Systems* 3 (April 1986).

25. Liebowitz, J. "Structured Decision Making in Classroom Teaching: The Use of Expert Choice." *Collegiate Microcomputer* 4 (August 1986).

26. Jones, W.T., and Samuell, R.L. "Strategic Assessment of Expert System Technology: Guidelines and Methodology." In *Expert System Applications to Telecommunications,* edited by J. Liebowitz. New York: Wiley, 1988.

27. Rauch-Hindin, W.B. *Artificial Intelligence in Business, Science, and Industry: Volume I—Fundamentals.* Englewood Cliffs, NJ: Prentice-Hall, 1986.

28. Liebowitz, J., and Lightfoot, P. "Training NASA Satellite Operators: An Expert System Consultant Approach." *Educational Technology* 27 (1987).

29. Liebowitz, J., and Lightfoot, P. "Expert Systems for Scheduling: Survey and Preliminary Design Concepts." *Applied Artificial Intelligence Journal* 1 (1987).

2

A Specific Knowledge Acquisition Methodology for Expert Systems Development: A Brief Look at Precision Knowledge Acquisition™

M. James Naughton

INTRODUCTION

In spite of the enormous potential of expert systems, millions of dollars in developmental funds have been lost because expenditures on expert systems software and hardware have often been made without proportional resources being put into knowledge acquisition. Knowledge acquisition methods [3, 4] now exist that guide developers in acquiring the right kinds of knowledge from the expert(s) in the right amounts, in mapping that knowledge into a coherent organizational structure, and in translating the mapped knowledge into the inference engine software to replicate important and valuable parts of the expert's knowledge. One such knowledge acquisition approach, Precision Knowledge Acquisition™ [1], provides, at a moderate cost, a documented and auditable system which has successfully solved a wide range of applied problems for businesses and the government.

The Precision Knowledge Acquisition™ (PKA) approach developed and used by Expert Knowledge Systems, Inc. (EKS), is the culmination of more than 18 years of professional work in integrating domain knowledge from cognitive psychology and computer science with domain knowledge from the clinical behavioral sciences and that branch of business administration called operations and systems analysis (also known as production and operations management). The purpose of this integration is to produce knowledge-based systems which can be used to solve applied problems through the application of scarce expertise packaged in a form which multiplies its impact. In an extremely simplified form, the applicable focus on each domain can be described as follows:

Cognitive psychology deals with how humans think—particularly, how humans solve problems.

Computer science of the sort used in knowledge-based systems deals with the symbolic processing of information.

The clinical behavioral sciences deal with helping people put into words internal mental events and states that may be of profound importance to the individual yet may never be adequately described by that individual to another.

Operations and systems analysis deals with the organization of work processes, both mental and physical, to maximize both efficiency and effectiveness.

Selected knowledge from these domains, and additional knowledge from several other domains, comprises the PKA approach. The system of knowledge acquisition, mapping, and implementation that EKS has developed is consistent with the quality philosophy of the Deming theory of management and the methods that have been derived from that theory [2].

OVERVIEW

Precision Knowledge Acquisition™ is aimed at efficiently and effectively using the time and energy of everyone on a project to produce applied knowledge-based systems. This means that the development of knowledge-based systems using PKA goes beyond a mere attempt at replicating the expert's thoughts and actions under a particular circumstance. Rather, it depends on working with the expert and using suitable knowledge from operations and systems analysis and from the clinical behavioral sciences to utilize the inherent reactivity of the knowledge acquisition process in guiding the rapid evolution of the expert's knowledge into the most efficient and effective form of knowledge attainable regarding work processes.

The basic structure of PKA is exhibited in the *Knowledge Engineering Blackboard*™ (KEB). The KEB* reflects all of the strategic elements that must be addressed and balanced within a project to maximize the likelihood that an operational applied knowledge-based system will be developed and deployed (see later).

The aim of the KEB is to make explicit all of the major areas which must be recognized and addressed if a knowledge engineering project for solving applied problems is to have a high likelihood of success (see Figure 2–1). The relative heights of the various categories are proportional to the relative levels of effort in

---

*The term "blackboard" is *not* used here in the sense in which it is customarily used in the field of artificial intelligence (AI), i.e., to refer to a system architecture that uses multiple accessible processes, called knowledge sources, in its data base. Rather, in this chapter "blackboard" is a part of the name of a *methodology*, e.g., knowledge engineering.

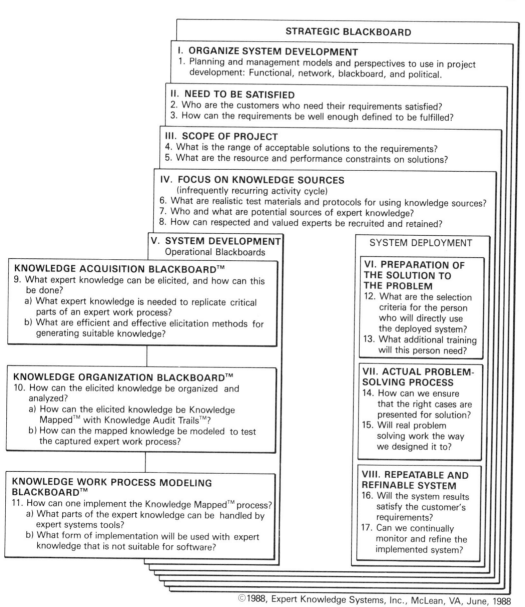

Figure 2–1   The knowledge engineering blackboard™.

each area. Acquiring, mapping, and implementing knowledge are clearly the dominant activities; yet they depend on sufficient work being performed in all the other areas of the blackboard that the acquisition, mapping, and implementation are firmly anchored to the realities of the knowledge domain.

PKA depends on brief, yet thorough, groundwork for guiding the development of knowledge-based systems in satisfying customers' requirements. The anchor for all the effort in the project is the clarity of understanding those requirements. The customers include the end user as well as those involved in the stage of the production process after the stage for which we are developing the knowledge-based system. Additional key information includes the identification of the key requirements to be fulfilled, the establishment of the project scope including any constraints, the definition of the focus of the project, and (both during and after the development of the knowledge-based system) the results of the system deployment and subsequent efforts at refinement of the system.

THE PROMISE OF EXPERT SYSTEMS

The promise of expert systems is that knowledge acquired from experts can be packaged in appropriate software and delivered to suitable nonexpert system users who will then have some part of the expert's capability at hand for solving problems. The basic notion is that the expert's knowledge is acquired and then programmed, using an appropriate inferencing strategy. An approach called rapid prototyping is popularly believed to be the best way to go about acquiring and programming the expert's knowledge. The purported capability of the rapid-prototyping knowledge engineer and the systematic processing of work of Precision Knowledge Acquisition™ (PKA) are shown in Figure 2–2.

The PKA approach directly challenges the attractive, but unobtainable, simplicity of rapid prototyping. PKA does this by providing mechanisms for rapidly acquiring and developing the important parts of the expert's knowledge into a prototype and then the completed system. Knowledge acquisition interviews range from 8,000 to 12,000 words per hour. Some way other than memory and notes is needed to process this volume of information. One knowledge-mapping approach is to record and transcribe the interview and work from the transcript to analyze the expert's responses to the knowledge engineer's questions. Many knowledge en-

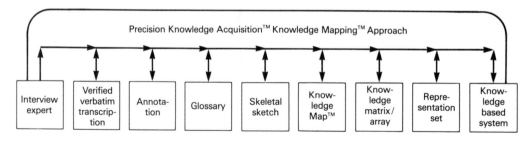

© 1988, Expert Knowledge Systems, Inc., McLean, VA

Figure 2–2 Steps involved in converting the expert's words into a knowledge-based system (claimed capability of "rapid-prototyping" approach).

gineers claim that they do not need to work from interview transcripts, however, since they use the rapid-prototyping approach of note taking and then develop a prototype which the expert and the knowledge engineer incrementally improve.

Experiments with over 140 people with the job title of knowledge engineer or its equivalent have demonstrated that the rapid-prototyping approach has a fatal flaw. Knowledge engineers were asked to listen to an audio tape of a knowledge acquisition interview and to take notes as though they were going to develop a rapid prototype from the notes. On average, the knowledge engineers only noted 30% of the topics the expert mentioned, and in respect to these, about 80% of the accompanying detailed notes contained one or more common analysis errors. The results show that only about 6–7% of what the expert said was captured correctly in the knowledge engineers' notes [1].

THE PARROT OWNER'S ADVISOR—AN EXAMPLE OF PKA

As a brief illustration of the PKA approach, consider a small portion of a knowledge-based advisory system regarding home veterinary care called the Parrot Owner's Advisor. In general, the PKA approach consists of a series of actions, each of which contributes significantly to the overall development of an efficient and effective system and at the same time is clear enough and small enough that it can be performed by "ordinary mortals." (Virtuoso hackers generally find PKA too methodical for their tastes.) In seeing how the PKA approach is applied to the Parrot Owner's Advisor, we shall compress and combine a number of these elementary actions.

To begin with, a veterinarian who has received national recognition for his ability to care for large pet birds such as parrots, macaws, and cockatoos is interviewed about factors that a bird owner should consider in safeguarding his or her large pet bird. The expert is James F. Gaines, D.VM., of Chantilly, Virginia. A small portion of that interview, which deals with cat attacks on large birds, reveals the major steps in acquiring, mapping, and implementing the expert's knowledge in this application.

Transcript of an Expert Veterinarian Describing Hazards that Threaten Pet Birds

The interview transcript is a verified verbatim transcript made from an audio recording. The interview was conducted to elicit specific kinds of information from the expert veterinarian. Researchers have established that it is effectively impossible through interviewing alone to accurately learn procedural and descriptive knowledge from an expert in real time. Rather, an apprenticeship lasting years is required to reap the benefits of the expert's knowledge. Accordingly, the knowledge acquisition interviewer must him- or herself be an expert at guiding the content expert in describing key knowledge. Then, the analysis and assimilation of that knowledge takes place "off-line."

Most knowledge engineers who have studied PKA initially find verified verbatim transcripts shocking. Like most of us, these knowledge engineers believe that they speak in the same manner in which they write. However, the grunts, groans, and choppy half-completed statements and questions ever present in a transcript, occasionally interspersed with patches of coherent statements, attest to the distinctive flavor of spoken English, particularly in an exploratory context such as knowledge acquisition interviews. The need for verbatim transcripts, as well as their verification, is that the transcript is the source document for all the analysis and system development which is to follow. If the expert's knowledge, as presented in the transcript, is contaminated through editing by the transcriber, it can no longer be trusted to be the expert's knowledge.

In the following segment of interview with the veterinary expert, EE is shorthand for the interviewee (the veterinarian) and ER is shorthand for the interviewer. The numbering of each block of text is the interview number, 1 in this case, and the block of text within the interview. Thus, block 10 of the first interview is coded 1.10.

Verbatim transcript of elements from the first Parrot Owner's Advisor's study

1.10 EE . . . Of course, occasionally they have been attacked by a dog or a cat.

1.11 ER Uh huh.

1.12 EE If it's attacked by a cat, don't even try to treat it yourself...get it to a veterinarian. You'll lose it every time, because they always get this one particular bacterial infection; if you don't get on it, it takes a couple of weeks for them to die from it, but it'll get them every time.

1.13 ER Uh huh (long pause). So, that's an absolute? You'd better get that cat, cat attacked bird, into the vet.

1.14 EE Absolutely, absolutely.

1.15 ER Uh huh. So that, let's see, uh, sanitation leading into trauma, we got water dish, air movement, lead, stove in the kitchen, half-full glasses of liquid, uh, fans running, uh, trauma like broken legs, uh, from things falling on the bird that you have to be very careful if the bird's loose that you don't have things that the bird can disturb to fall under.

1.16 EE Right.

```
1.17 ER OK. And occasionally attacks by dogs and cats, or cats.

1.18 EE Uh huh.

1.19 ER And cat attacks in particular.

1.20 EE Yeh...they...because of the...it's the bacteria that
        the cat transmits,

1.21 ER Uh huh.

1.22 EE And, it, it'll, it'll kill them every time.

1.23 ER Uh huh. From the claws, or the teeth., or...?

1.24 EE The teeth.
```

As it stands in the interview, no one could use the veterinarian's knowledge effectively; the valuable procedural and descriptive knowledge presented by the expert must be organized if it is to provide usable advice.

The Dialogue between a Bird Veterinary Advisor and a User

The veterinarian's knowledge contained in the preceding interview was developed into a computer program which, when tested with a prospective user, resulted in the following dialogue between system and user:

```
>This is a coaching session for owners of large birds in the
parrot family on the prevention of accidents as well as the
detection and treatment of trauma injuries to the bird. Are
there particular areas of bird care in the list below that you
want to explore?

_Sanitation?
_Water dish?
_Air movement?
_Bird loose in house? Etc.
```

The user selects "bird loose in house."

```
>Is the bird able to fly around the house without any
restrictions?

Yes.

>There are a number of sources of risk to the bird from trauma.
Select the topic you would like to study.
```

```
_Biggest danger for loose birds.
_Thing falling on the bird.
_Stove in the kitchen.
_Half-full glasses of water.
_Attack by animals. Etc.
```

The user selects "attack by animals."

```
>Please select the animal you fear might attack your bird.
```

```
_Dog.
_Cat. Etc.
```

"Cat" is selected.

```
>Occasionally a bird is attacked by a cat. If it is attacked by
a cat, do not treat the bird yourself but get it to the veterinarian,
because bacteria that the cat transmits via its teeth are fatal.
The bird will always get a particular bacterial infection; if
you do not treat the infection, the bird will die within a couple
of weeks.
```

The user learns, from the expert system, of the high risk posed by having a cat and a bird together should the cat attack the bird. (An attack on the bird is too irresistible for most cats to pass up—even though the large bird usually wins the battle before succumbing to the infection from any bite received.)

THE REPRESENTATION OF THE VETERINARY KNOWLEDGE IN SOFTWARE

There is an enormous gap between the expert's words on the transcript and the dialogue with the potential user. The step immediately preceding the actual dialogue is the programming of the expert's knowledge into the inference engine software. This occurs after a series of earlier stages in which the expert's words are analyzed. The representation of the knowledge which must be contained in the system for the preceding dialogue to take place is as follows.

Knowledge Mapped™ expert knowledge directly translated into the inference engine

The knowledge base used as the illustration in this section is shown implemented in Texas Instrument's Personal Consultant Plus inference engine:

```
ROOT FRAME
INJURY [FRAMETYPES]
   TRANSLATION: (A coaching session about some common injuries
```

that birds suffer and some insight into their prevention or
treatment)
OFFSPRING: (ATTACK SANIT HOUSE)
IDENTIFIER: "INJURY"
RULEGROUP: (INJURY-RULES)
PARMGROUP: INJURY-PARMS
PROMPTEVER: (This is a coaching session about the common
  injuries that birds suffer and some insight into their
  prevention or treatment)_
GOALS: (COACHED IN)
INITIALDATA: (TOPICS)

ROOT FRAME PARAMETERS
ANIMAL [INJURY-PARMS]
  TRANSLATION: (Whether an animal was selected as attacking
    the bird)
  TYPE: YES/NO
  USED-BY: RULE001
  UPDATED-BY: RULE005
= =

ROOT FRAME RULES
ROOTRULES
  RULE001 [INJURY-RULE]
   IF: TOPICS = ATTACKED BY-   ANIMALS AND ANIMAL
   THEN: COACHED-IN = SUBJECT2 AND
   PRINT "Ending coaching in animal attack"
= =

CHILD FRAME
ATTACK [FRAMETYPE]
  TRANSLATION: (The hazards suffered by the bird because of
    being attacked by an animal
  IDENTIFIER: "ATTACK-"
  RULEGROUPS: (ATTACK-RULES)
  PRAMGROUP: ATTACKPRAMS
  PARENTS: (INJURY)
  GOALS: (ANIMAL-GOAL)
  PROMPT1ST: (Animals occasionally attack birds. If a bird
    is attacked by an animal, a serious injury might result.
    Do you want to study this type of hazard to your bird?)
  PROMPT2ND: (Do you want to study the attacks by animals
    again?)
  INITIALDATA: (ANIMAL-TYPE)

CHILD FRAME PARAMETERS
  ANIMAL-ATTACK [ATTACK-PARMS]
    TRANSLATION: (The type of animal that might attack your
      bird)

```
PROMPT:          (Please select the animal you fear might
  attack your bird)
TYPE:            ASK-ALL
EXPECT:          (CAT DOG)
USED-BY:         RULE002 RULE003      RULE004


TREATMENT [ATTACK-PARMS]
TRANSLATION: (Whether or not to take a bird injured by a
  cat to the veterinarian)
TYPE:            YES/NO
USED-BY:         RULE002     RULE003
UPDATED-BY:      RULE016     RULE018


ANIMAL-GOAL [ATTACK-PARMS]
TRANSLATION:     (A dummy value that indicates successful
  frame instantiation)
LEGALVALUES:     (ANIMAL1    ANIMAL2    ANIMAL3)
TYPE:            MULTIVALUED
USED-BY:         RULE005
UPDATED-BY:      RULE002     RULE003     RULE004


  CHILD FRAME RULES

    RULE002 [ATTACK-RULES]
     IF:       ANIMAL-TYPE = CAT
     THEN:   ANIMAL-GOAL = ANIMAL1 AND PRINT "This is the
     best decision. Treating a bird which has been
     injured by a cat attack is the solution in order to
     save the bird's life."

    RULE004 [ATTACK-RULE]
     IF:       ANIMAL-TYPE = DOG
     THEN:   ANIMAL-GOAL = ANIMAL3 AND PRINT "Dogs
     occasionally attack birds {EE 1.10, 1.18, ER 1.17}...
     This knowledge system does not know much about this
     problem yet."

    RULE005 [ATTACK-RULE]
     IF:       ANIMAL-GOAL = ANIMAL1 OR ANIMAL-GOAL = ANIMAL2
      OR ANIMAL-GOAL = ANIMAL3
     THEN:   ANIMAL
```

Clearly, there is no coherent way to directly convert the dialogue with the expert, contained in the verified verbatim transcript, into the rule-and-frame structure programmed into the computer to make the dialogue with the would-be user possible. Instead, intermediate transformation of the expert's words must take place before the acquired expert knowledge can be implemented. This stage is the Knowledge Mapping™ stage.

THE KNOWLEDGE MAP™ FROM WHICH THE REPRESENTATION IS DERIVED

The Knowledge Map™ stage of knowledge engineering consists of a number of steps. Only the direct Knowledge Map™ stage, together with its programming into the inference engine, is considered here. The Knowledge Map™ has several notable features. First, it is intended, in its fully developed form, as a powerful visual display of how much, and what kind, of the expert's knowledge we have codified. This visual form helps in planning subsequent interviews with the expert. The Knowledge Map™ guides the planning and conduct of the knowledge acquisition interviews. Without a map to steer by, knowledge acquisition interviews deteriorate into expensive and time-consuming sessions. The nesting of topics, shown in Figure 2–3, reflects the layering of the knowledge accumulated from the expert. The ellipsis following a keyword signifies the subsequent elaboration of a particular topic, and the ellipses below each topic serve a critical control function. The ellipses are used to review the Knowledge Map™ with the expert. The expert is asked a question, and if he or she answers, "No additional information is needed," we fill in the bullets and make no further routine inquiries about that topic. If, on the other hand, the answer is "Yes, additional information is needed," we then ask for a few key prompts on that topic to use in subsequent knowledge acquisition interviews with the expert. Thus, the expert has definite control over the depth to which we pursue a particular topic, rather than the knowledge engineer deciding by whim which topics to pursue and which not to pursue.

The expert is asked similar questions on encountering the ellipses below each layer in the Knowledge Map™. Again, the critical element is the expert's having control over the relative importance of each topic and how much attention each deserves. Without this positive control mechanism directed by the expert, the knowledge acquisition interviews would become no more than random walks.

An additional feature to note on the Knowledge Map™ is the Knowledge Audit Trail™ shown to the right of the elements in the blackboard. Thus, {EE1.10, 1.18} refers to the interviewee's (the expert's responses in blocks of dialogue numbers 10 and 18 of interview 1 on the verified verbatim transcript. A direct trace back through all prior analytic steps to the exact statement where the expert expressed this knowledge is accordingly possible. Requiring traceability as to the source of information in the knowledge-based system is aimed at reducing the contamination of the expert's knowledge.

TRANSLATION OF THE KNOWLEDGE MAP™ INTO COMPUTER REPRESENTATION

The translation of the Knowledge Map™ is directly transformed into programmed expert knowledge, ready for the system user. The form of the translation, in a structure called Personal Consultant Plus, is as follows on p. 37.

```
▢ Trauma Injuries
  ▢ (Causes)
  = = = = = = = = = = = = = = = = = = = =
      ▢ (Being loose in the house)
      = = = = = = = = = = = = = = = = = = = = = = = = = =
          ▢ (Attack by animals)
              ▢ Dogs                            {EE 1.10, 1.18}{ER 1.17}
                  ▢ (Frequency)
                      ▢ Occasional ...>         {EE 1.10, 1.18}{ER 1.17}
                        •
                        •
                        •
                  •
                  •
                  •
              ▢ Cats
                  ▢ (Frequency)
                      ▢ Occasional ...>         {EE 1.10, 1.18}{ER 1.17}
                        •
                        •
                        •
                  ▢ IF   Bird is attacked by a cat;       {EE 1.12}
                    THEN Don't even try to treat it
                         yourself,                        {EE 1.12}
                         (But) get it to a veterinarian
                  ▢ (Reason)
                      ▢ Bacteria that the cat can transmit
                        (through its) teeth {EE 1.20, 1.24}{ER 1.23}
                          ▢ Will always cause one particular
                            bacterial infection           {EE 1.12}
                              ▢ IF Don't treat infection  {EE 1.12}
                                THEN Death will occur in a
                                     couple of weeks      {EE 1.12}
                              ▢ (Frequency)
                                  ▢ Every time
                                    {EE 1.12, 1.14, 1.22}{ER 1.13}
                                    •
                                    •
                                    •
                                  •
                                  •
                                  •
      = = = = = = = = = = = = = = = = = = = = = = = = = = = = = = = = = = = =
        •
      •
      •
      •
```

Figure 2–3 Knowledge Map™ for Parrot Owner's Advisor.

KNOWLEDGE MAP TRANSLATION TO A PERSONAL CONSULTANT PLUS™ STRUCTURE

`ROOT FRAME AND PARAMETERS:` 1st level of knowledge map and its definition could be obtained from this level [trauma injuries in k̲-map.

`RULES AND GOALS/RT FRAME:` 2nd level within k̲-map. [These are the causes in the k̲-map, i.e., any injury is caused by any of the following factors: ...]

`CHILD FRAME AND PARAMETERS:` 3rd level within k̲-map [sanitation, water dish, air movement, b̲eing loose in house, attacks by animals].

`CHILD RULES/CHILD FRAME:` 4th level within k̲-map [prevention, danger, etc.].

The complexity of the implemented expert knowledge reflects the difficulty inherent in capturing and replicating any substantial body of knowledge.

ANNOTATION: THE TRANSLATION FROM TRANSCRIPT TO KNOWLEDGE MAP™

The Knowledge Map™ itself is the result of a translation of the verified verbatim transcript into an annotated form and then into the map. The annotation of the transcript for the Parrot Owner's Advisor is as follows:

(attacks by animals)

1.10 EE ...Of course, <u>occasionally they have been attacked by a dog **or** a cat.</u>

1.11 ER Uh huh.

1.12 EE **If** <u>it's attacked **by** a cat,</u> |[**then**] <u>don't even try to treat it yourself...get it to a veterinarian...You'll lose it every time,</u> **because** <u>they always get this one particular bacterial infection;</u> **if** <u>you don't get on it, it takes a couple of weeks for them to die from it,</u> **but** <u>it'll get them every time.</u>

1.13 ER Uh huh (long pause). <u>So</u>, <u>that's an absolute? You'd better get</u> that cat, cat <u>attacked bird, into the vet</u>.

1.14 EE <u>Absolutely, absolutely</u>.

1.15 ER Uh huh. <u>So</u> that, <u>let's see</u>, uh, <u>sanitation leading into</u>
<u>trauma</u>, we <u>got water dish, air movement, lead, stove in the</u>
<u>kitchen, half-full glasses of liquid</u>, uh, <u>fans running,</u>
uh, <u>trauma like broken legs</u>, uh, <u>from things falling on the</u>
<u>bird that you have to be very careful</u> **if** <u>the bird's loose</u>
<u>that you</u> [**then**] <u>don't have things that the bird can disturb</u>
<u>to fall under</u>.

1.16 EE <u>Right</u>.

1.17 ER OK. **And** <u>occasionally attacks by dogs</u> and cats, <u>or cats</u>.

1.18 EE Uh huh.

1.19 ER **And** <u>cat attacks in particular</u>.

1.20 EE Yeh...they...**because** of the...its the <u>bacteria that</u>
<u>the cat transmits</u>.

1.21 ER Uh huh.

1.22 EE **And**, it, it'll, <u>it'll kill them every time</u>.

1.23 EE Uh huh. <u>From the claws</u>, **or** <u>the teeth</u>., or...?

1.24 EE <u>The teeth</u>.

THE RESULTS OF THE INTERACTION BETWEEN THE USER AND THE SYSTEM

Building an expert system is an incremental activity which involves the development, critiquing, and subsequent refinement of a succession of prototypes. The successive approximation of the final expert system to the desired system depends on the results of user trials with the prototypes. Following is the result of one user session with the prototype Bird Owner's Advisor:

The prototype users dialogue helped him to understand a risk that he was completely unaware of, the fatal bacterial infection transmitted by cat bite. Yet he now has many additional questions. For the system developer, defining what these user questions are and how they might be responded to helps describe the scope of additional knowledge needed from the expert. For instance, the user asked the developer, "What if the cat attacks the bird when I'm not home? What if the bird and cat scuffle while I'm in the next room? What if I'm in the same room with them, I see them scuffle, and I notice that the cat threatens the bird with bared teeth. I hear a lot of hissing and cawing, they spar with each other, the cat rushing the bird, the bird beats his wings at the cat, yet I'm not sure there has been an actual cat bite?''

This feedback from the user of the prototype is part of the ongoing reinterpretation of a number of issues which will have to be resolved through further knowledge acquisition:

What are the boundaries of the problem I am trying to solve?
What capability and prior knowledge do I require of the user?
What additional preparation will I require of the user?
What additional domain knowledge shall I acquire from the expert?
What additional commonsense knowledge must be acquired?
How will I acquire this knowledge?
How will I integrate the acquired knowledge into the knowledge base?
How will I know when I have enough additional knowledge?

In sum, this illustration of the Expert Knowledge Systems, Inc., approach to the Knowledge Mapping™ of expert knowledge elicited through a Precision Knowledge Acquisition™ interview shows that complex expert knowledge can be elicited, mapped, and implemented in a verifiable, documentable, and auditable manner.

THE STRATEGIC PERSPECTIVE OF PRECISION KNOWLEDGE ACQUISITION™

Precision Knowledge Acquisition™ and the Knowledge Engineering Blackboard™ are the outgrowth of the management of, participation in, and reviewing of numerous projects that had as their purpose the acquisition, organization, packaging, and dissemination of expert knowledge. These programs have ranged in budget from the thousands to the tens of millions of dollars and in length from weeks to nearly a decade.

Over the years, Expert Knowledge Systems, Inc., has participated in a number of project bailouts. In such projects, the development of a knowledge-based system was undertaken and at some point the sponsor of the project brought Expert Knowledge Systems in because the project was failing. It is partially as a result of this type of activity that the KEB and PKA were developed.

To put the problems that naive knowledge-based systems developers create for themselves and their sponsors in perspective, consider the following brief portion of a review of a one-year project costing hundreds of thousands of dollars that had produced *nothing* useful:

Based on the evidence I have seen, my impression is that the project has been an enormous random walk by the contractor. It is as if a hacker had kludged together fragments of information to produce a voluminous, rather than useful, information compilation. It is not a knowledge base in the sense that we use those words. Many words have been produced. And, those many words have the appearance of having a frame- and rule-like structure. Yet, again based on the documents I have seen, there is *no* evidence that the project was conducted in a way that could be reasonably expected to produce a useful product. If I were asked to testify in court as an expert witness in knowledge acquisition, and I were asked to evaluate just what I have seen, I would state that the written product I have reviewed presents *no evidence whatsoever of being the result of the systematic acquisition of an expert's knowledge for the purpose of using that knowledge to develop and deploy an operational knowledge-based system of any sort that I have knowledge of.*

I have used the Knowledge Engineering Blackboard™ as a framework for evaluating the extent to which the material examined reflects the development of a viable applied expert knowledge solution to an applied problem of great [deleted] importance. This evaluation is not based on whether or not the work was performed the way EKS would perform it. Rather, the evaluation is based on whether the critical applied knowledge-based systems development issues addressed in the KEB are dealt with in a competent manner. A summary of the review of the material follows:

The material presented for examination shows no evidence of being the result of a competently planned and executed project management system for building applied problem-solving systems.

The material presented for examination shows no evidence of being the product of a knowledge acquisition process that was planned to meet explicit customer requirements.

There is no evidence of the establishment of explicit customer needs to be satisfied.

Nor is there evidence that the scope of work was established and used to ration project effort among all of the project elements which must be competently completed if a system is to be actually delivered.

Nor is there evidence that the knowledge acquisition had an explicit focus through which to guide the development of the system.

Nor is there evidence that any of the alleged expert knowledge in the (multiple hundreds of)-page document examined came from anywhere other than the knowledge engineer's imagination.

There is, in particular, no evidence that systematic knowledge acquisition was conducted by a competent interviewer who was trained in the acquisition of the requisite knowledge of cognitive work processes held by the expert. That is, there is no evidence that the interviewer knew what specific kinds of information he needed to elicit from the expert, and in what amounts, to meet the needs, scope, and focus of the project, And there is no evidence that the interviewer knew how to formulate and ask the specific kinds of questions of the expert that would yield the requisite information.

There is no evidence of a systematic Knowledge Mapping™ type of procedure to organize acquired knowledge against the requirements and which serves as a planning tool to define what additional knowledge must be acquired to fill knowledge gaps. In addition, there is no type of Knowledge Audit Trail™ to provide traceability from the rules and frames in the system back to their actual source in the expert's words.

There is no systematic evidence that the knowledge implementation was carried out in a manner that would allow a usable system to be developed and deployed.

There is no evidence that the developers of the collection of rule- and frame-like information I have examined had any concept of who would be the actual users of the system and how the system would actually operate when it was deployed.

There is no evidence of any means by which the repeatability of the system could be evaluated, nor of how refinements could be incorporated.

In summary, I find the material I have examined grossly deficient as a product of a knowledge acquisition effort designed to develop a deployable knowledge-based system which could play a significant part in [nature of the organization deleted]. I have grave reservation as to the salvageability of the material I have examined. The actual (hundreds of hours of) interview tapes may be a useful source of information generally which could be used to make the most of last year's work. However, given the deficiencies I have noted in the material that I have examined, I expect that the overall actual interviewing has been no more competently handled than the development of what is claimed to be the project knowledge base.

The project had been carried out by a major expert systems oriented organization. The problems that had occurred are all of a common nature, and are all ones that competent project planning and management can handle and minimize.

The Establishment of a Strategic Perspective for the Development of Knowledge-Based Systems Projects

The strategic plan of a knowledge-based systems development project needs to tie together the customer's requirements, all the activities undertaken to develop the system to fulfill those requirements, and the actual results of the system deployed in fulfillment of the requirements. A statement of work needs to address each of the elements in the KEB in some manner in order for the developers to attain and demonstrate a good grasp of the complex, and highly interactive, applied knowledge-based systems development requirements. Failure to successfully deal with any one element in the KEB almost ensures a failed project. Few developers can deal effectively with even one of the elements in the KEB; many, if not most, of the hack developers could be eliminated by requiring the developers to define and show examples of how they will deal with each of the critical 17 elements shown on the blackboard.

Developing a Balanced Knowledge Engineering Capability

The development of a balanced knowledge engineering capability requires a strategic perspective on the entire system of knowledge engineering. It is beyond the capability of any one individual to be knowledgeable in and proficient at all of the 17 elements in the blackboard. At the beginning of the formation of a knowledge engineering group, most, if not nearly all, of the 17 elements in the blackboard will be ignored. The first project a new knowledge engineering group accomplishes will usually be a proof-of-concept demonstration project.

After the proof-of-concept demonstration, when the knowledge engineering group is called on to provide tangible results for the organization, great difficulties occur. Nearly always, the bulk of the resources for the development of a knowledge engineering capability has been spent on hardware, software, and people who are highly specialized in the hardware and software. By contrast, there has been little or no investment in knowledge acquisition, Knowledge Mapping™, or any of the other 16 essential areas of knowledge that are necessary for knowledge implementation.

THE STRATEGIC KNOWLEDGE ENGINEERING BLACKBOARD™

An abbreviated form of the KEB, shown in Figure 2–4, highlights the interdependent and interactive nature of this planning and management tool. The KEB is used iteratively for the acquisition and management of information and skills in defining the need the project addresses and within what scope and with what focus the need is addressed. The development of a knowledge-based system through knowledge acquisition, Knowledge Mapping™, and knowledge implementation is based on the project needs, scope, and focus. The development is aimed at deploying a knowledge-based system that is used by a competent problem solver to satisfactorily fulfill the customer's need and that undergoes continual refinement.

REFINEMENT: REPEATABLE AND REFINABLE SYSTEM

Refinement requires a comparative standard. We must have a model of what it is that we are trying to achieve and an understanding of what we are actually doing. The comparison between our goal and our current performance provides us with

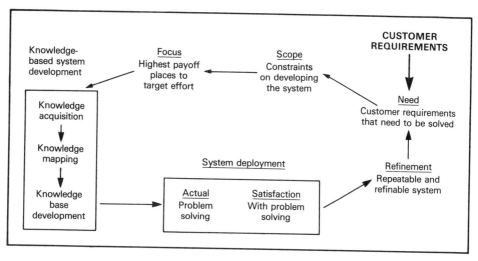

Figure 2–4   Elements of the Knowledge Engineering Blackboard™.

information on the direction and extent of change that need to be brought about in the system. Our deep understanding of the degree to which the deployed system fulfills the customer's need provides us with corrective feedback to direct the system refinements to bring about improved customer satisfaction.

A strategic perspective such as that provided by the KEB requires that the 17 interdependent and interactive elements in the blackboard (see Figure 2–1) be iteratively refined through cycles of progress in the project. Explaining the iteration process, however, requires a linear process. As is the custom in project planning and project management, the explanation begins at the end and works backwards to the beginning.

Step 17. Can we continually monitor and refine the implemented system?
What are the key parameters that we will monitor and use to form the basis of our refinement efforts? And how will we structure the monitoring and refinement so that they are built into the system? That is, from the very first cycle of project development, how can we ensure that we are tracking the parameters that are the most relevant to fulfilling the customer's requirements?

Step 16. Will the system results satisfy the customer's requirements?
Are the needs of the customer, so carefully defined in the second and third elements of the strategic blackboard, still valid when the system is deployed and in action? What unanticipated changes must we make to our definition of the customer's requirements given what we observe when the system is in actual operation?

Figure 2–5 incorporates steps 16 and 17 into the KEB.

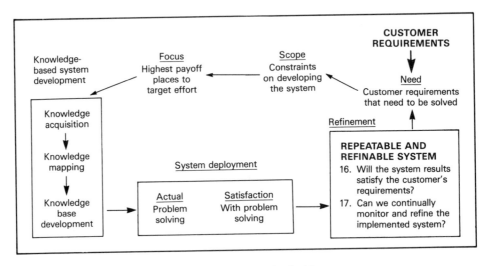

Figure 2–5   Repeatable and refinable system.

SYSTEM DEPLOYMENT: ACTUAL PROBLEM-SOLVING PROCESS

No developmental process can anticipate all of the problems that will be encountered in system deployment. Nor should effort be expended in development on solving every possible problem that will be encountered in deployment. The question becomes, How can we economically develop a system that solves, to customer satisfaction, certain problems that the customer needs solved?

Step 15. Will real problem solving work the way we designed it to? How do we anticipate the inevitable difference between the performance of the system in development and its actual performance in deployment? What structure will we create to anticipate, detect, and satisfactorily resolve differences in actual performance from developmental performance of the knowledge-based system?

Step 14. How can we ensure that the right cases are presented for solution?   Is the stream of actual problems presented to the system to solve like the set of case materials used in the development of the system? Are the differences between the developmental material and the actual applied problems presented for solution merely differences in exceptional cases, are they essential differences in the actual problems as compared with the developmental test problems? How can the stream of problems be stabilized so that refinements can bring system performance into a state more likely to fulfill the customer's need?

Figure 2–6 incorporates steps 14 and 15 into the KEB.

SYSTEM DEPLOYMENT: PREPARATION OF THE PROBLEM SOLVER

Someone, somehow, must apply the deployed system. Who will do this? And how will they be prepared to carry this out?

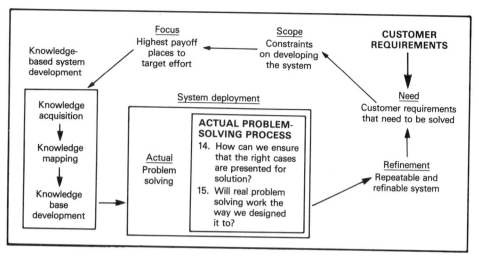

Figure 2–6   Actual problem-solving process.

Step 13. What additional training will this person need?   Given a suit-able candidate problem solver, what training will such a person need to become a competent problem solver? How will the achievement of competence be recognized?

Step 12. What are the selection criteria for the person who will directly use the deployed system?   The person who operates the knowledge-based system may or may not be the end user of the system. Will the person doing the problem solving that the knowledge-based system is designed to support be the one that is actually operating the system? If so, what characteristics must this person possess? If there is an intermediary between the problem solver and the direct manipulator of the knowledge-based system what characteristics must the problem solver possess? In short, what are the requirements to become a problem solver for this knowledge-based system?

Figure 2–7 shows steps 12 and 13 in the KEB process.

OPERATIONAL BLACKBOARD: KNOWLEDGE WORK PROCESS MODELING BLACKBOARD™

All of the acquired knowledge that has been organized into a logical and useful form must somehow be further organized into a form that will allow the knowledge-based system, the problem solver, and whoever is the user of the knowledge-based system to satisfactorily fulfill the customer's needs.

Step 11. How can one implement the Knowledge Mapped™ cognitive work process?   The domain of cognitive work process analysis and design

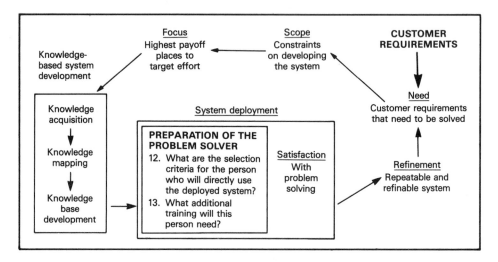

Figure 2–7   Preparation of the problem solver.

provides the foundation for transferring the organized acquired knowledge into a work process. The transformation effected will create a predictable and repeatable pattern for the replication of the expert's work in solving the customer's applied problem.

a) What parts of the expert's knowledge can be handled by expert systems tools? Only some forms of cognitive work process knowledge lend themselves to implementation in a knowledge-based system. Accordingly, what components of this knowledge-based system will we use within expert systems technology? And how will we go about identifying and organizing those components?

b) What form of implementation will be used with expert knowledge that is not suitable for software?   A major part of the development of any knowledge-based system for solving applied problems involves the delivery of major components of the system in other than an expert system format. What components of the knowledge-based system, then, will we develop and deliver other than as software? How will we identify those components? How will we package them for delivery?

Figure 2–8 shows step 11 as part of the Knowledge Implementation Blackboard.™

OPERATIONAL BLACKBOARD: KNOWLEDGE ORGANIZATION BLACKBOARD™

Step 10. How can the elicited knowledge be organized and analyzed?

Interviews yield, on average, about 10,000 words per hour. How can we then manipulate the suitable knowledge gathered as a result of competent interviewing into a usable format?

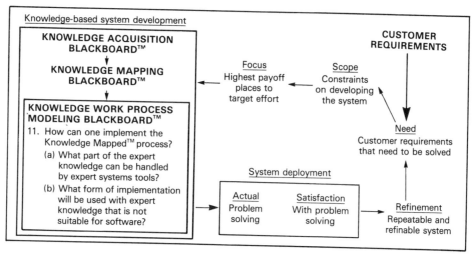

Figure 2–8   Knowledge Implementation Blackboard™

a) How can the elicited knowledge be Knowledge Mapped™ with Knowledge Audit Trails™?   What cognitive work processes will we use to transform the results of interviews into a usefully structured format? How can this work be reliably performed? How can we track all manipulations of the information through an auditing procedure?

b) How can the mapped knowledge be modeled to test the captured expert work process?   What model of the cognitive work process can we provisionally adopt to further knowledge acquisition and at the same time provide for the in-depth development of the modeling phase of the cognitive work process?

Figure 2–9 shows the mapping process.

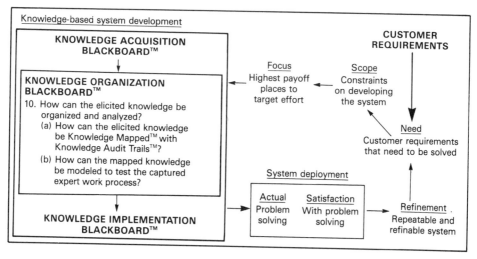

Figure 2–9   Knowledge Mapping Blackboard™.

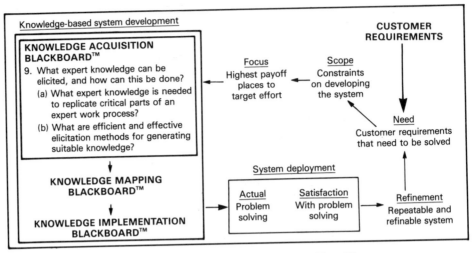

Figure 2–10   Knowledge Acquisition Blackboard™.

OPERATIONAL BLACKBOARD: KNOWLEDGE ACQUISITION BLACKBOARD™

Step 9. What expert knowledge can be elicited, and how can this be done?   What expert knowledge can be elicited, and how can this be done?

a) What expert knowledge is needed to replicate critical parts of an expert work process?   From among the many things that the expert knows, what is the essential knowledge needed to develop a knowledge-based system that will allow others to obtain results comparable to the expert's? How can we begin to sort out the superstitious and harmful knowledge of the expert?

b) What are efficient and effective elicitation methods for generating suitable knowledge?   What cognitive work process of interviewing will allow the efficient and effective acquisition of the essential parts of the expert's knowledge? How can this work process provide a high yield of useful information?

Figure 2–10 shows the Knowledge Acquisition Blackboard™.

FOCUS: FOCUS ON KNOWLEDGE SOURCES (THE INFREQUENTLY RECURRING ACTIVITY CYCLE)

Focusing is another term for targeting. Who and what will we target as sources of, or about, expert knowledge?

Step 8. How can respected and valued experts be recruited and retained?   What can we offer an expert to make participation in the development of

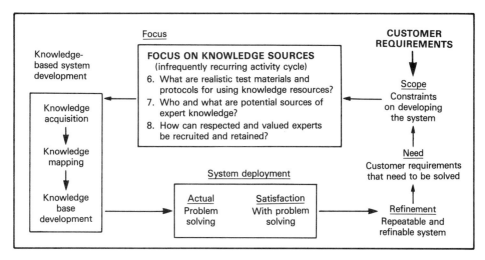

Figure 2–11   Focus on knowledge sources.

the knowledge-based system a high priority for him or her? In exchange for the scarce and valuable time of the expert, what can the expert expect to get from us?

Step 7. Who and what are potential sources of expert knowledge? Who are the key organizational gatekeepers who can, in a strong project advisory role, tell us whether the problems we are trying to solve are (1) solvable, (2) worth solving, and (3) problems such that there is an identifiable expert who can solve them.

Step 6. What are realistic test materials and protocols for using knowledge sources? What set of problems will we select from the actual stream of applied problems to give us a set of strongly realistic mainstream instances of the problems we want to solve with the knowledge-based system?

Figure 2–11 shows the focus part of the blackboard.

SCOPE: THE SCOPE OF THE PROJECT

What constraints on resources and acceptable solutions do we face?

Step 5. What are the resource and performance constraints on solutions? What is most important on this project? Time? Money (resources)? Performance? We can at best control for one. Which one shall it be? How can we prevent the less important constraints from interfering with the realization of the controlled constraint?

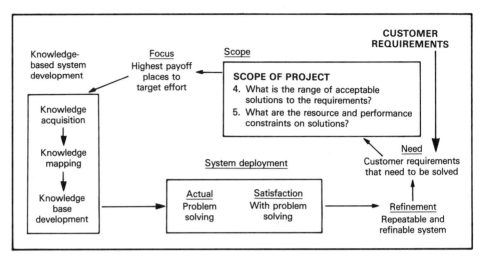

Figure 2–12   Scope of knowledge-based system development effort.

Step 4. What is the range of acceptable solutions to the requirements?

What are the legitimate solutions as far as the sponsors and other stakeholders are concerned? What benefit would accrue to the project from helping to shift the stakeholders' perceptions of what constitutes a legitimate solution?

Figure 2–12 portrays the scope section of the blackboard.

NEED: SATISFACTION OF THE REQUIREMENTS

Solving applied problems requires that we have customers whose needs we are aiming to satisfy.

Step 3. How can the requirements be well enough defined to be fulfilled?   What are the customer's requirements? How can these requirements be put into a form that allows the project team, the expert, and the customers to agree that the requirements are the focus of the project?

Step 2. Who are the customers who need their requirements satisfied?

Who is it we are serving through development of a knowledge-based system that replicates expert knowledge solutions to the customer's requirements?

Figure 2–13 shows the "need" part of the blackboard.

PLANNING AND MANAGEMENT: ORGANIZING AND MAINTAINING BALANCED KNOWLEDGE ENGINEERING

Step 1. Models and perspectives to use in project development: Functional, network, blackboard, and political.   What explicit cognitive work processes does a developer have for dealing with each of the 17 elements in the KEB?

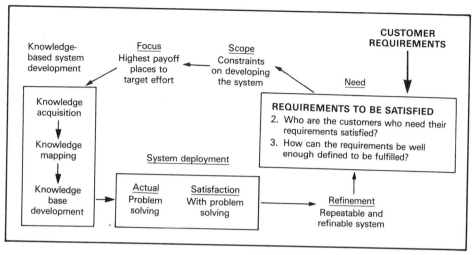

Figure 2–13 Need: Requirements to be satisfied.

For instance, how does the developer propose to capture and utilize the approximately 10,000 words produced in each hour of interview? A developer who can present the foundation knowledge—that is, the functional knowledge—for each element in the blackboard and who can provide evidence of the procedures, or an activity network, that reflects how he or she will deal with each element still has more information to provide. Just how does the execution of the procedures depend on and interact with the other elements of the blackboard? This interactivity is the essence of the concept of the blackboard architecture. In addition, the developer needs to be clear how he will deal with the second-order, third-order, etc., effects of each project activity.

Figure 2–14 portrays step 1 in the KEB.

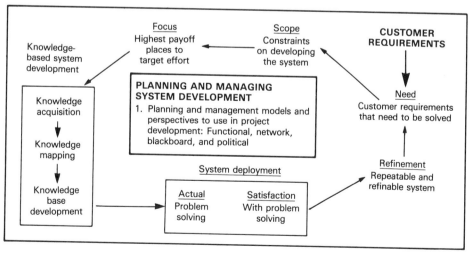

Figure 2–14 Planning and managing system development.

SUMMARY

The carrying out of a knowledge-based systems development project for the solution of customers' applied problems requires far more than just knowledge of expert systems hardware and software. A complex set of interdependent and interactive information must be developed to guide all of the activities of acquiring, organizing, and implementing scarce and valuable expert knowledge. The Strategic Knowledge Engineering Blackboard™ provides a framework for the development of a balanced set of activities that have a reasonable likelihood of achieving the project aim.

REFERENCES

1. Expert Knowledge Systems, Inc. Precision Knowledge Acquisition Course, PO Box 6600, McLean, VA 22106: 1988.
2. Deming, W.E. *Out of the Crisis.* Cambridge, MA: MIT Press, 1986.
3. Boose, J.H. *Expertise Transfer for Expert System Design.* New York: Elsevier, 1986.
4. DeSalvo, D.A. "Knowledge Acquisition for Knowledge-Based Systems." In *Expert System Applications to Telecommunications,* edited by J. Liebowitz. New York: Wiley, 1988.

3

Structured Design of an Expert System Prototype at the National Archives*

Daniel A. De Salvo
Amy E. Glamm
Jay Liebowitz

This chapter presents a case study of a software development project, during which American Management Systems, Inc. (AMS) built a prototype expert system for the National Archives and Records Administration (NARA). Some of the highlights of this project include the following:

- The final product was a medium scale (about 300 rules) expert system. The software acts as a "front end" which helps users retrieve information from a data base on an IBM-PC/AT microcomputer. It does this by implementing as "rules of thumb" the methods that archivists use to search for information.
- The project team either adapted or developed new structured software design techniques for this project. They used model building as their major design paradigm.
- The project team applied project planning and management techniques to deliver this system on time and within strict budget constraints.

INTRODUCTION

This project started in the last half of 1985, when AMS had just begun to design a large-scale information storage and retrieval (ISAR) system for the Archives. The Archives had already started several other projects to see how digital imaging,

*From Barry Silverman, *Expert Systems for Business,* © 1987, Addison-Wesley Publishing Co., Inc., Reading, MA. Chap. 3, pp. 40–77. Reprinted with permission.

high-accuracy optical character recognition, and other new information technologies might contribute to the ISAR.

The Archives' goal was to apply the findings from these various projects to the ISAR's design. The overriding concern was to find out if these new technologies were practical, reliable, and appropriate.

There were, therefore, two major constraints on this project. First, the project team had to produce definitive answers to some key questions. In particular, the Archives had to know if expert systems were practical at all, before committing scarce resources to investigating them further. Second, the information gathered from this project had to be available in time to influence the early stages of the ISAR system design. Because the first stages of the ISAR design were already underway, the project had to produce a system within about four and one-half months, complete an evaluation of it by the end of approximately five months, and document the project by the end of about six months total elapsed time.

This project therefore was a practical example that supports the following premise:

> Knowledge systems will never be commercially acceptable until we can develop them on time and within a budget, just as we do with the more conventional systems.

Structured systems development methods are the keys to doing this, just as they are in more traditional systems implementations. Many of the structured design tools we need are available from two closely related disciplines: *systems analysis,* the study and design of "traditional" algorithmic computer systems, and *knowledge engineering,* the study and design of knowledge-based or inferential computer systems.

Structured methodologies have already been put to good use in the development of both algorithmic and knowledge-based systems. However, project planning, knowledge acquisition, and system verification/validation are areas that still present significant challenges to the developer of commercial or government expert systems.

The National Archives encouraged a carefully structured systems development approach. The main elements of the system development strategy and some of the tools that have proven useful include the following:

- Requirements analysis—This was the first step in the system's development, during which the system's environment was fully described using narratives and data flow diagrams (De Marco 1979). This step was actually performed during the larger system design effort from which this project arose.

- Knowledge acquisition—During this phase, information was collected about the information handling process as performed by the domain experts—highly skilled archivists. This phase was highly dependent on the use of logical models of the system's behavior and knowledge-level analysis of the heuristics employed by the archivists (Clancey 1984).

- System development—During this phase, the system software was developed using structured programming techniques (Ziegler 1983; Page-Jones 1980; and Powers, Adams, and Mills 1984) adapted from algorithmic systems design methods.

- System assessment—This is the phase during which the system's behavior was evaluated for (1) its ability to emulate the domain experts and (2) what the project experience suggests about the usefulness of employing expert systems at the Archives.

In this chapter, we discuss three specific techniques that were applied to the development of the system. They are (1) the use of a "traditional" requirements analysis, (2) the use of system models as a key element in the knowledge acquisition process, and (3) the application and results of a quantitative system evaluation process.

Other techniques included in the discussion, but not addressed here in detail, are the use of structured programming, multiple experts, and techniques for managing the multiple tasks associated with the project.

ENVIRONMENT AND WORKING HYPOTHESIS FOR THE PROTOTYPE

The Archives comprises a large and complex, mostly manual, information system, which the archivists manage and maintain. We believed an expert system should be able to capture and use at least some of the expertise of the archivists. Therefore, we determined to test that hypothesis by building a prototype that would emulate at least some key parts of the archivist's expert behavior. Since the need to retrieve records is the key factor in determining how they will be arranged and handled, we determined to try to emulate the retrieval process.

The Archives is charged with preserving historically significant records of the federal government and with making those records available to the public for research. The types of records include photographs, microfilm, machine-readable records, cartographics, bound volumes, and standard documents.

These holdings are arranged *hierarchically* to reflect the work done by the agencies. Therefore, the Archives' records are currently organized into an artificial set of groupings that reflect the Archives' view of how the government functions. For example, the *record groups,* or artificial collections, of the Bureau of Land Management (BLM) reflect such things as geography or accounting functions, whereas the original records were organized to reflect the internal organization of the various parts of BLM. The archivist or researcher must therefore go to the *series,* or basic level of the Archives' record structure, to see how the records were actually arranged by the agency.

This method was originally developed in order to make a large and complex records system manageable in several ways, including (1) to establish a certain *intellectual control* over the records by defining a common view that could be shared among archivists, (2) to establish some kind of stable records structure that did not have to be changed every time an agency was reorganized, and (3) to reflect the activities of the government in such a way that the archivists could effectively relate the records organization to the sometimes broad or unfocused inquiries posed by researchers.

While this kind of arrangement ensures that the records are preserved in historical context, it narrows somewhat the means for accessing those records. For example, the primary *finding aid,* or directory, to the records is the *records description,* the main component of which traces the origin, or *provenance,* of the records. The content of the records is outlined in the records description, but again, the descriptions are organized to reflect the work done by the author agencies, rather than by topic or subject.

Various finding aids have been prepared for research purposes, including some very good topical finding aids. However, there is no comprehensive set of finding aids that provides researchers with subject or topical access to all of the Archives' holdings. This is largely due to the fact that archival holdings comprise mostly source documents (e.g., original working papers, memoranda, etc.). Establishing subject indexes to these kinds of records is more difficult (unless the subject of the query is the creator of the records) than for published works, which are inherently topical. Even after the advent of the Archives' large-scale information system, comprehensive and effective subject access will probably take years to develop, if only because there is such a massive amount of information to be drawn out of the billions of pages of Archives' documents.

Yet, archivists have developed a series of methods for (1) abstracting from researchers' inquiries the subjects that may be contained in federal government records and (2) efficiently searching those records in order to retrieve information.

It is clear that the archivist must understand the function of the agency that created the records, in order to know what kind of information would be contained in its records. For this kind of information, the archivist must rely on the *administrative histories* of the federal agencies that created the records. For example, to know that information about water rights is available in the BLM records, it is necessary to know that the BLM was charged with conducting several major programs concerning water rights.

The archivist's knowledge of the administrative histories thus comprises a view of the records, organized according to the activities of the federal agencies and mapped to the hierarchical records structure. This view is dynamic, changing as the archivist learns more about the records, about the administrative histories, or about how different parts of the view relate to specific kinds of inquiries.

We had two reasons for believing that an expert system could successfully imitate the archivist's record search techniques:

1. Interviews with archivists showed that they can describe their work and the knowledge they use to do it as a set of discrete judgments with known inputs and outputs. This made it much simpler to describe the work of archivists within a logical structure and thus to turn that logical structure into a straightforward computer program.

2. The average time an archivist takes to answer an inquiry, based on a quick sample of cases, appeared to vary from less than one minute to no more than one-half hour (discounting the time it may take to physically handle records). This is a good indication that the archivist is pulling information directly out of memory, rather than performing logical calculations of great depth. The ability to pull information directly from memory ("if you want to answer this question, look here") indicates that the archivist has reduced the complex retrieval process to a set of highly organized and crystallized rules of thumb or heuristics, which may be applicable for use in an expert system.

As Figure 3–1 shows, the archivists rely heavily on their shared knowledge about (1) the Archives' organization, (2) the existing finding aids such as administrative histories and records descriptions, and (3) rules of thumb about how best to search the records to find specific kinds of information. This knowledge comprises an invaluable *institutional memory*.

The knowledge acquisition process revealed that archivists use heuristics to (1) control the search strategy, and (2) manipulate and communicate specific facts about the records. For example, specific topics that are abstracted from the researcher's broad inquiry may be heuristically matched to what the archivist knows about the content of specific records. Inherent in this is the archivist's empirical and tactical selection and management of specific search techniques (e.g., best-first).

Knowledge acquisition further indicated that the archivist uses internal lists (e.g., facts about records) and a knowledge indexing scheme that accommodates several views of the Archives' data in order to formulate search paths. These views include a network of predetermined, generalized search paths related to specific classes of topics; hierarchical views of the recrods, which correspond to their arrangement and description; and views of the functional topics contained in the records. The last views correspond to the activities engaged in by the agency (e.g., water conservation) and are derived from both the administrative histories and the archivist's knowledge of the record contents.

THE NEED TO APPLY SYSTEMS ANALYSIS TECHNIQUES TO THE STRUCTURED DEVELOPMENT OF EXPERT SYSTEMS

The regular use of expert systems in practical business environments will not happen until potential commercial or government buyers are confident that expert systems fit in with other systems, other projects, limited budgets, and their or-

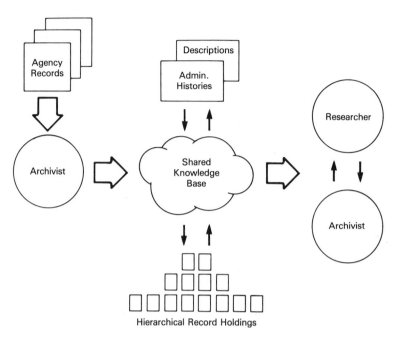

*The Archives' records management environment is conceptually straightforward. Agencies release their records to the Archives, where an archivist generates records descriptions. Rolled into those descriptions, and available from other sources such as the *Government Handbook,* are the administrative histories of the agencies. Administrative histories describe what the agency responsibilities were—for example, the programs they administered, what larger agencies they were a part of, and so on.

The records descriptions contain a little of that same information and a lot of data on the *provenance* of the records: who created them, when they were created, what kind of records they were (e.g., correspondence) and so on. The records themselves are arranged hierarchically to reflect the organizational structure of the government entity that created them.

Archivists also help researchers use the records, since the archivists share a body of knowledge between them about what kinds of information are located in what kinds of records. Much of the shared knowledge that archivists develop over time goes toward knowing how to interpret a researcher's questions in terms of the administrative histories. For example, because an archivist knows the program areas administered by a certain agency, that archivist can interpret what kinds of information should be contained in the agency files.

Figure 3–1 Archivist's use of shared knowledge and reference data.*

ganizations' schedules. Systems analysis already comprises a well-developed discipline of techniques for structuring, planning, and implementing "traditional," or deterministic, software. At least some of those techniques can be combined with knowledge-engineering techniques to improve our ability to plan, manage, and execute knowledge systems and buyer confidence in the process.

This project, in a small scale, successfully applied conventional systems analysis to the development of an expert system. We found the same general approach to be applicable to both kinds of project: (1) define the concept and role of the system, usually through a requirements analysis; (2) use available analytical tools such as models to express and refine that concept through the various stages of the project; and (3) define each step of the project as a collection of smaller, logically discrete operations.

Some Potentially Applicable Systems
Development Approaches

Several systems development approaches have been designed and used over the years. Some of these, pertaining to software life cycles, were written by Davis (1974), Quade and Boucher (1978), Mandell (1979), Freeman and Wasserman (1977), Peters (1981), Metzger (1973), Boehm (1976), Silverman (1985), and Liebowitz (1984). These methodologies are outlined in Figures 3–2 and 3–3.

While each of these methodologies is different, each does allow for some form of stepwise progression from concept to finished product. Yet many expert systems are still being developed in a fashion consistent with academic or research projects, in which the exercise is often more important than the final product.

For example, Figure 3–3 shows Silverman's (1984) suggested stepwise, structured approach to expert systems development. This approach clearly recognizes the need to identify key steps in the project management process that can be tied to specific stages in the expert systems development cycle. For example, step 2 of his approach shows that an idealized view of a knowledge system can be developed and then brought into line with practical constraints.

As noted above, the National Archives' project had four main activities: (1) a preliminary requirements analysis, (2) knowledge acquisition, (3) system develop-

Davis	Quade and Boucher	Mandell	Freeman**
1. Definition a. Feasibility assessment b. Information analysis 2. Physical design a. System design b. Program development c. Procedure development 3. Implementation a. Conversion b. Operation and maintenance c. Postaudit	1. Problem 2. Formulation 3. Search 4. Evaluation 5. Interpretation 6. Verification 7. Suggested action	1. Design situation a. Problem recognition b. Determination of objectives c. Study present system d. Design new system e. Propose solution 2. Implementation a. Detailed system design b. File design c. Develop programs d. Develop documentation e. Develop test data f. System test g. Conversion 3. Evaluate a. Efficiency analysis b. System modification c. Postaudit	1. Needs analysis 2. Specification 3. Architectural design 4. Detail design 5. Implementation 6. Maintenance

*See reference list for complete source of these methodologies.

**In addition to the reference see Peters, L.J., *Software Design: Methods and Techniques* (New York: Yourdon Press, 1981).

Figure 3–2 Stepwise systems analysis methodologies.*

Metzger**	Boehm	Silverman (1985)	Liebowitz
1. (System) definition	1. System requirements	1. Requirements identification	1. Problematic state of affairs
2. Design	2. Software requirements	2. Design, development, test and integration a. Analogous programs	2. User a. Value hierarchies b. World views
3. Programming	3. Preliminary design		3. Problem identification
4. System test			4. Motivation
5. Acceptance	4. Detailed design	3. Operation and maintenance	a. Novel, innovative methodologies
6. Installation and operation	5. Code and debug		5. Analogical reasoning
	6. Test and preoperations	4. Collection	a. Existing methodologies
		5. Disposal	6. Chosen methodology
	7. Operation and maintenance		7. Design
			8. Validation
			9. Testing and evaluation
			10. Forecasted results
			11. Implementation
			12. Critique/Postaudit

*See reference list for complete source of these methodologies.

**In addition to the reference see Peters, L.J., *Software Design: Methods and Techniques* (New York: Yourdon Press, 1981).

Figure 3–2   (*Cont'd.*)

ment, and (4) system assessment. The approach we took to the Archives' project does not contradict Silverman's. For example, the requirements analysis led, at a lower level, to the activities described in step 2 of his approach; our use of logical system models was a key tool in a two-way communication between the project team and the archivists, which corresponded to step 3 of his approach; and steps 6, 7, and 8 of his approach correspond to the system assessment scheme used in the Archives' project.

However, there are some differences between the approach we took on the

1. Initiate knowledge-engineering project.
2. Explore the domain for a knowledge-engineering view.
   a. Construct idealized view.
   b. Describe actual activity.
   c. Pinpoint needs/bottlenecks in the project.
3. Recommendations
   a. Formulate knowledge-based system related recommendations.
   b. Make other recommendations.
   c. Act on other recommendations (i.e., accommodate suggestions).
4. Obtain approval and guidance to proceed.
5. Design and integrate knowledge-based system into the domain.
6. Verify knowledge-based system.
7. Validate knowledge-based system.
8. Evaluate knowledge-based system.
9. Resulting knowledge-based systems (spin-offs)

Figure 3–3 Silverman's suggested approach.

Archives' project and Silverman's approach. For example, as shown in Figure 3–3, his outline highlights the need to gain approval from the client at each step of the development cycle. At each step of the development process in the Archives' project, the team was required to document what they intended to do with a work plan and to demonstrate that they had completed the work, either by producing written documentation or working software. This is common operating procedure for most governmental or commercial clients outside of the research arena.

The process of getting the client's approval for each completed project task was dictated by long experience and governmental requirements. Therefore, the project team could concentrate on evaluating the interactions between those tasks, one with the other. This is illustrated in Figure 3–4.

We have not included the functional requirements process in Figure 3–4. There are two reasons for this: (1) the functional requirements analysis was done as

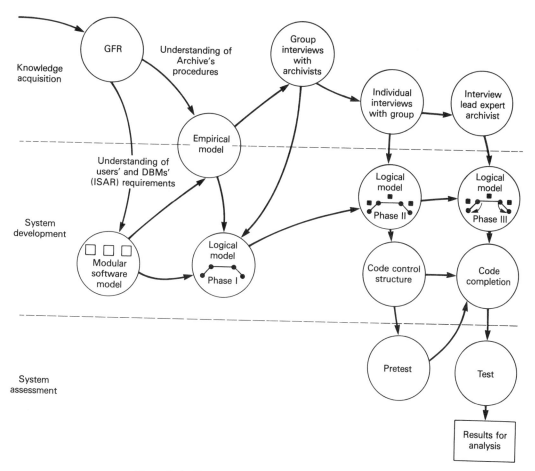

Figure 3–4 Development of the expert system prototype.

part of a different, large-system design, and (2) it is a preliminary step to the other three processes and would have been represented as a logically separate function. However, Figure 3–4 does show the development cycle beginning at the completion of the requirements analysis. This is represented by the oval at the top left of the figure labeled "GFR" for "general functional requirements," which is the document that describes the requirements analysis.

Figure 3–4 is a modified program evaluation and review technique (PERT) chart. For this illustration, we have removed some of the lower level detail regarding documents that had to be delivered, approval steps, and the numerous code-test-debug-test cycles.

Subsequently we shall address the use of models as an analytical tool. However, as Figure 3–4 shows, the use of models helped tie the entire project together. For example, the GFR provided the basic information from which the project team developed two models: (1) an *empirical model* of the archivist's activities and (2) a simple *modular software model,* which noted that the final software could be completed with three major modules. The project team then worked with those two models and interviewed archivists in order to develop a series of progressively more complex *logical software models,* which defined the basic logical and functional relationships between each of the software modules. Work on the software itself did not begin until the logical model had been fairly well developed—enough so that we named it the "phase II" version.

As with the models, software development was a top-down process. Most of the software was written in M.1, a Prolog-based expert system shell. Like most AI development environments, it facilitates top-down implementation as well as the top-down design employed by most systems developers. In that respect, the use of an AI language enhanced the traditional, top-down conceptualization techniques that are usually recommended for all programming projects.

Current Approaches to the Structured Programming of Expert Systems

Rapid prototyping has recently gained wide acceptance as a systems development technique for both traditional and expert systems. The underlying approach is to quickly build working models or emulations of important system components, let users work with and comment on the results, and refine the final system concept to accommodate those comments. Usually, work starts on one or more of the following key systems components:

- The user interface, which is often the part of a system that gets the most immediate and critical attention
- Primary logic, such as accounting calculations, which have to be built into the system in order to demonstrate that it works at all
- Preliminary data structures, so that the project team can start to load initial test data into the system.

Rapid prototyping is a structured technique, in the sense that (1) there are definable, repeatable steps in the process and (2) a higher level design, such as the primary system logic and user interface, drives the lower level programming process, such as data file or knowledge base manipulation. However, rapid prototyping has often been the only system development technique used to build expert systems, without the extensive preliminary planning and design so familiar to traditional systems developers. This is acceptable or even desirable in a laboratory environment but not in the business world.

We suggest that rigorous examples exist in conventional systems analysis for systems planning and that these proven approaches can be adapted to developing expert systems without constraining either the creativity of the development process or the usefulness of its products. For example, *data flow diagrams*—a "traditional" systems analysis tool (De Marco 1979)—were used to describe the problem domain and perform a functional requirements analysis of the proposed system during the Archives' project; as discussed below, this preliminary analysis provided a number of benefits to the planning and development processes.

Tools that have proven useful in other projects include characteristic charts, attribute hierarchies, and "and/or" graphs, all derived from the knowledge-engineering arena. Decision tables, "borrowed" from systems analysis, have aided knowledge engineers in understanding and showing which rules are being fired, and the expert system's line of questioning in response to a given user input. Other tools, derived from "traditional" systems analysis, which are useful in the programming process include the following (see Davis 1974; Page-Jones 1980; Powers, Adams, and Mills 1984; and Glass 1982):

- Visual table of contents (VTOC)
- Warnier-Orr diagrams
- System flowcharts
- Synchronized flowcharts
- PERT charts
- Petri nets
- Hierarchy-input-processing-output (HIPO) charts
- Decision trees
- Threads
- Builds
- Data flow diagrams
- Top-down design
- Structured design
- Data dictionary
- Structured English/pseudocode

The Archives' project benefited from a structured approach that (1) "borrowed" tools from conventional systems analysis, such as the use of data flow diagrams, and (2) applied some knowledge-engineering tools, such as Clancey's (1984) knowledge level analysis techniques, in a fashion that would be familiar to "traditional" systems builders.

We therefore believe the knowledge-engineering process can be improved through formalization and standardization of expert system building methods. This may allow developers of expert systems to repeat the experience of "traditional" systems builders and increase the amount of reusable software they write, thereby reducing the level of effort and resources required to implement their systems.

THE USE OF A FUNCTIONAL REQUIREMENTS ANALYSIS IN BUILDING THE EXPERT SYSTEM

A great deal of a knowledge engineer's time in building a system goes toward understanding both the environment and the client's expectations for the system. A "traditional" functional requirements analysis can shorten this process significantly and provide a sound basis for defining the major components of the system design.

The functional requirements analysis was, in this case, performed during a previous project. The major data flows and archival processes were evaluated during interviews with archivists and other Archives staff. The resultant documents provided an empirical view of the archival information handling process, graphically depicted in data flow diagrams (De Marco 1979).

One of the major advantages of this approach is that it produces a set of specifications—narrative and graphic—for the empirical performance of the system. Knowledge engineering is, after all, a creative science, wherein we try to build systems that imitate the behavior of a human expert, even though the underlying computer system is vastly different from the human mind in its form, functions, and capabilities.

As DeMarco (1979) says:

> In classical [systems] analysis, we first try to see the operations from the user's viewpoint; i.e., we interview him and try to learn from him how things work. Then we spend the rest of our time trying to document the working of modified operations *from the system's viewpoint.* (Notice that this approach is pervasive in unstructured technology; a flowchart, for instance, is design documentation from the system's point of view.)

> The inversion of viewpoints occasioned by Structured Analysis [data flow diagramming] is that we now present the workings of a system as seen by the data, not as seen by the data processors. The advantage of this approach is that the data sees the big picture, while the various people and machines and organizations that work on the data see only a portion of what happens.

In this project, our understanding of how data moved and changed within the host environment helped greatly in the following ways:

- The initial requirements analysis provided a high-level understanding of the system's major processes, thereby allowing the project team to establish the major software modules early in the project.

- Once the software modules and functions were defined, structured programming was possible, because (1) major system functions could then be consistently identified with specific parts of the software, (2) logically discrete functions could be identified for each part of the software, (3) those logically discrete functions could be broken down into pseudocode, and (4) programming could begin. All of this required that some initial order be placed on the structure of the system, which is often very difficult for expert systems.

- Understanding the flow and forms of data allowed the team to clearly define the format for encoding facts into the system. For example, archivists work with multiple series of lists that follow specific formats; by accommodating the same forms, the system inherited (1) an ability to work congenially with an underlying, list-based information storage and retrieval system and (2) a form of knowledge representation that is both understandable to and maintainable by the archivists.

The formal benefits of doing an initial functional requirements analysis are difficult to estimate. However, our experience indicates that at least two or more complete overhauls of the knowledge base were avoided as a result. One of the reasons for this was the amount of information the project team gained about the information that is exchanged between archivists. Once the project team had identified what knowledge was used and exchanged during the inquiry and search processes, it was possible to classify and organize that knowledge. Therefore we suggest that:

> A preliminary functional requirements analysis is appropriate in the design of both conventional and knowledge-based systems.

THE USE OF MODELS AS AN INTEGRAL ANALYTICAL TOOL

An important strategy in this system development effort was the use of models to (1) codify, and thereby help maintain a coherent view of the system throughout the project, and (2) save time and resources by using the models as a vehicle for iteratively constructing, changing, and refining the system design.

Several kinds of systems representations were used over the course of the project:

- During the requirements analysis—the initial stage—of the project, data flow diagrams, narratives, an empirical model, and a modular software model were developed. Figures 3–5, 3–6, and 3–7 show or describe data flow diagram models. Figures 3–8 and 3–9 show at a high level the empirical and modular

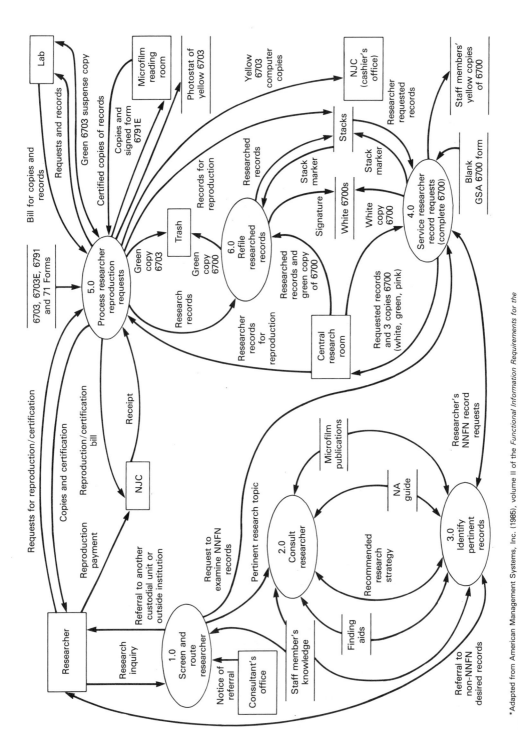

Figure 3–5 High-level data flow diagram of the research process in the Archives' scientific and natural resources branch.*

*Adapted from American Management Systems, Inc. (1985), volume II of the *Functional Information Requirements for the Office of the National Archives.*

● *Processes* are represented by an oval. A process is any activity that acts on information to produce an output. Each process is given a name describing the operation that it performs. In cases in which an operation is extremely complex, a discussion of the precise steps or subprocesses that combine to make up that process will be included.

● *Data flows* are packets of information in motion, represented by arrows. Each arrow is labeled with a descriptive name explaining the data that it represents. Each process has inputs (information that it requires) and outputs (information that it produces). From the viewpoint of the data flow diagram there is no distinction between inputs and outputs. An output from one process is often an input to another process. Collectively, inputs and outputs are called data flows.

● *Files* represent data at rest. A file is any temporary or permanent repository of information. Any location where data is temporarily stored between processes or any set of information that is part of the system and provides different data to more than one process is a file. For example, a collection of manuscripts qualifies as a file under this definition.

● *Sources* or *destinations* for data are represented by a box. A box represents any person or organizaation, lying outside the context of the system being examined, that is a net originator of information input to the system or a receiver of information output from the system. Any person, agency, or external system that is not part of the system being examined but contributes inputs to or receives outputs from the system being examined is represented by a box.

*Adapted from American Management Systems, Inc. (1985), volume II of the *Functional Information Requirements for the Office of the National Archives.*

Figure 3–6   Data flow diagram conventions as used here.*

software models, respectively. The data flow diagrams and narrative representations provided significant insights into the system's inputs, its outputs, its representation of facts, and its working environment.

● During the knowledge acquisition phase, the empirical model and modular software models contributed to the development of a logical model of the system. The logical model is derived from (1) Clancey's (1984) method for knowledge level analysis and (2) the notational method employed by Teknowledge, Inc. in their Knowledge Engineering Methodology program. The logical model provided the foundation for a coherent view of both the project and the emerging system.

How Data Flow Diagrams Were Used in Building the Expert System

Data flow diagrams are a tool of conventional systems analysis. The systems analyst can use them to improve his or her understanding of (1) how an organization or system handles information, and (2) how the final system will have to behave. Just as with all good design tools, data flow diagrams should also help the analyst

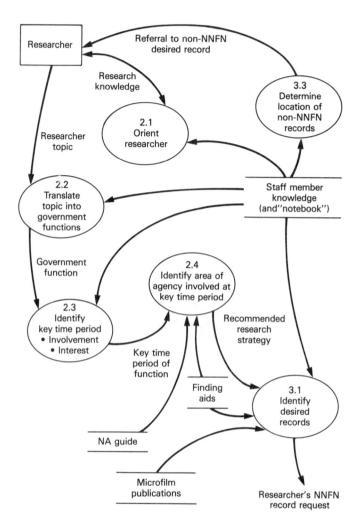

*Adapted from American Management Systems, Inc. (1985), volume II of the *Functional Information Requirements for the Office of the National Archives.*

Figure 3–7   The research topic translation process.*

develop a reasonably objective and comprehensive view of some situation, which is necessary in knowledge engineering as in any analytical discipline.

During the initial stages of the Archives' project, the design team used a set of data flow diagrams that had been prepared as part of the Archives' long-term information systems development effort. These provided a capsule summary of the Archives' environment that was very useful to the knowledge-engineering process.

For example, Figure 3–5 shows a high-level view of what happens when a researcher—a member of the public—asks for information from the Scientific and

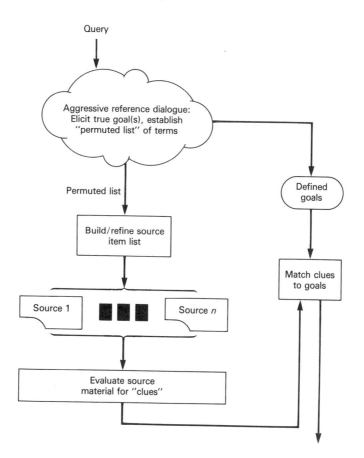

Query

Aggressive reference dialogue:
Elicit true goal(s), establish
"permuted list" of terms

Permuted list

Defined
goals

Build/refine source
item list

Match clues
to goals

Source 1 ▮▮▮ Source *n*

Evaluate source
material for "clues"

*On a high level, the retrieval process consists of the following steps: (1) an interview is set up whereby the archivist engages the researcher in a dialogue to extract from the researcher's broad subject those topics that can be answered by information found in federal government records; (2) the archivist—by relating those topics to government program areas or his or her own knowledge of record content—sets up a list of records that might satisfy the topics, which in expert systems parlance can be referred to as *query goals*; and (3) the archivist helps the researcher work through the process of finding and using the appropriate records.

Figure 3–8   Empirical software model.*

Natural Resources Branch of the National Archives. Figure 3–6 gives a brief explanation of data flow diagram technique. Note that, in order to follow De Marco most closely, the diagram in Figure 3–5 should be broken into a series of simpler diagrams. However, we have included this one because (1) it is the one actually used on the project, and (2) it is reasonably comprehensive.

The Scientific and Natural Resources Branch (which the Archives identifies with the NNFN mail code seen in Figure 3–5) was the primary site of the prototype. The project's primary domain expert works with records of the Bureau of Land Management (BLM), which are under the control of the Branch.

As Figure 3–5 shows, there are several major points at which the researcher's inquiry stimulates the movement of information. At each of those points, one or

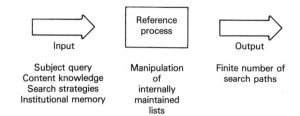

Input	Reference process	Output
Subject query Content knowledge Search strategies Institutional memory	Manipulation of internally maintained lists	Finite number of search paths

*This is the modular software model developed for the expert system prototype. It shows the reference process used by the archivist as a "black box" that accepts input to create an output. The input is the query, and the output is a list of records that will provide an answer to the query.

Figure 3–9 Modular software model.*

more archivists or members of the staff have to evaluate that information and may confer with other archivists or members of the staff.

For example, when a researcher makes an inquiry (see oval 1.0 of Figure 3–5), it is screened and routed to a particular archivist with knowledge of some particular set of records. In order to perform just this one function, at least the following knowledge must change hands:

- The subject of the original inquiry
- Potential topics addressed in federal records that may pertain to the inquiry
- The [names of] archivist(s) or other members of the staff who may know more about the topics and where they may be found
- At least the basic protocol for handling an inquiry

Figure 3–7 is drawn one level of detail deeper into the interaction between researcher and archivist. It shows the exchange of information and knowledge that occurs when the researcher presents an inquiry to an archivist, who then "translates" the often-ambiguous question into a set of discrete topics that might be addressed in federal government records.

An examination of Figure 3–7 will show that at least the following types of knowledge, in addition to those noted previously, must change hands among one or more individuals:

- The researcher's specific areas of interest, such as the time period (oval 2.3) of the event or activity in which the researcher is interested
- A knowledge of how to go about translating the researcher's inquiry into appropriate topics
- The applicability of the inquiry to other sets of records than those to be found in the Scientific and Natural Resources Branch (NNFN)
- The specific parts of government agencies that may have been involved in activities pertaining to the inquiry at the time of their occurrence

- A knowledge of the contents and use of various search tools, such as published guides, microfilm, or archivists' notebooks

Therefore we suggest that:

The data flow diagrams provided two important kinds of information to the design team: (1) a conceptual view of the data that the underlying information system would have to process and (2) an initial inventory of the different kinds of knowledge that might be embodied in the system. Subsets of the data and the knowledge were then more easily selected for inclusion into the actual system. A conventional systems analysis technique helped bound the domain of the expert system and, in so doing, helped solve one of the more difficult problems of expert system design.

The Empirical, Modular, and Logical Software Models

The differences between the empirical, modular, and logical software models are as follows:

- The *empirical software model* (see Figure 3–8) represents the way the archivist's job appears to the outside observer (in this case, a previous project team). It was developed as a convenient, generalized, high-level representation of the archivist's use of lists. As the figure shows, it is a somewhat richer model, even at this high level, than the modular software model, but it still embodies the same three major components.
- The *modular software model* (see Figure 3–9) was used during the initial knowledge acquisition phase as a convenient framework for describing the system's inputs and outputs. As Figure 3–9 shows, it is a simple "black box" model, with modules that correspond to the main parts of the empirical model.
- The *logical software model* (see Figure 3–10), and its succeeding refinements, show the major functional modules of the system. Again, as Figure 3–10 shows, its major modules correspond to the empirical model's.

During the knowledge acquisition phase, the logical model was used in two ways:

1. The model served as a visual representation of what the archivists were saying during the interviews. Initially, the project team conducted group and individual interviews with five archivists, and the model provided a common view of the way they made inferences. With the model as a backdrop, the project team was able to obtain concrete lists of facts and heuristic rules and associate them with specific, logical parts of the retrieval process.

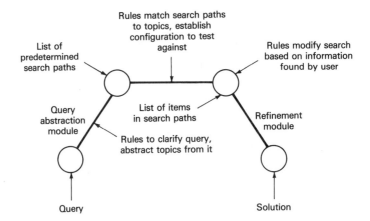

Resolution module

Rules match search paths
to topics, establish
configuration to test
against

List of
predetermined
search paths

Rules modify search
based on information
found by user

Query
abstraction
module

List of items
in search paths

Refinement
module

Rules to clarify query,
abstract topics from it

Query

Solution

*After talking with the archivists about this model of the retrieval process we worked it into a model developed by Dr. William Clancey for what are called *classification-type expert systems*. Classification systems, which include diagnostic and catalog selection systems, are designed to recursively refine the definition of a subject area or question until it becomes small and limited enough to match to some real object.

In this model, the notational graphics—courtesy of Teknowledge, Inc.—serve much as a HIPO chart would in giving a conceptual view of a process as it goes from general to specific. The three parts of the model are named here to correspond to the specific applications.

Abstraction produces a list of potential topics out of a general query. Resolution maps those to program areas and then to specific sets of records. In the process, it works from the highest, or *record group* level of the records organization, to the lowest practical level, the record *series*. The refinement part of the model logically represents the place where the archivist and the researchers progressively review and discard the records they retrieve.

The model was used during interviews with the archivists to help determine (1) where each module's functions should begin and end and (2) the parameters that have to be passed between modules, in this case in the form of lists.

It is worth noting that the models helped us in working with multiple experts. Although the bulk of the work was done with one expert archivist, Renee Jaussaud of the Office of the National Archives, we did a substantial amount of work with as many as five experts at one time. The ability to pull together a large design team is, we feel, essential to successfully developing commercial software.

Figure 3–10 Logical software model.*

2. The model served as the conceptual design of the physical system. The inferences represented by the model were made progressively more detailed during the project—well after the project team had actually started to write software. At one point, a large schematic of the logical model was drawn on a blackboard, and 4-by-5-inch index cards with pseudocode rules written on them were stuck to it in order to help evaluate the interdependencies of the rules.

Both group and individual interviews were used during knowledge acquisition, with the models serving as the focus of discussion. Initially, five archivists, each of whom are responsible for a different area of records within the Archives, were interviewed in a group setting, were a consensus could be reached on the proper form for the model. Each of the five was then interviewed separately, in order to ascertain which group of records was the best target site for the prototype. Finally, in-depth knowledge acquisition was carried out with one archivist—Renee Jaussaud—when it was determined that the records for which she is responsible were the best subject for the prototype.

The group interviews provided an opportunity to do two things: (1) carefully examine, with the help of an expert, each of the five records areas in order to select the most appropriate one and (2) obtain a consensus of opinions and advice on the logical system model from a group of experts.

By obtaining a consensual agreement from all of the archivists on the form of the logical model, the project team (1) was assured that the basic form of the model was correct and (2) was provided with important insights into how and to what extent the practices of the five archivists differed.

The individual interviews served to further refine the logical model. The process of examining and revising the logical model provided both the archivists and the project team with valuable insight into the design and operations of the future system.

With the model as a framework, key decisions made by the archivist during the search process were located conceptually in the program's structure. For example, the model helped clarify where query abstraction—the process of analyzing the inquiry for its content—ends and where resolution—the process of mapping query content to the record structure—begins.

The facts and heuristics associated with each logical process could then be much more clearly defined and placed within the proper software module prior to any code being written. For example, the query abstraction process contains a wealth of heuristics to match, to the researcher's query, topics that may be addressed by federal government records. The resolution process, however, uses a much more generalized set of heuristics to manipulate detailed facts (e.g., about the records, the administrative histories, etc.) as it maps the topics to specific sets of records.

Therefore we suggest that:

The expert tends to view what he or she does as a cohesive process. . . . However, the use of models (1) allowed rules to be grouped efficiently, thereby improving software efficiency, and (2) allowed much more compact software routines to be written to manipulate a small data base in which the majority of facts and lists are maintained.

APPLICATION OF A SCHEME FOR SYSTEM ASSESSMENT

Overview of the System Assessment

The purpose of the system assessment was to test three aspects of the system's performance:

1. The system's *recall.* This test was based on the answers to sample research questions. The expert archivist, Renee Jaussaud, drew up a list of the record series that she would recommend as places to look for answers to the sample

questions. The system's answers were then compared to hers, to see what percentage of the series recommended by the archivist were also recommended by the system. That percentage reflects the system's ability to recall, from its data base, the names of all *record series* that might contain information pertinent to a particular query. A *record series* is normally the smallest set of records that the Archives handles. A series might contain a group of individual documents, file folders, and so forth. The Archives has catalogued the individual files in some series, but by and large the series is the basic element of archival control.

2. The system's *precision*. This test was based on the same sample questions as the test for system recall. Here the system's answers were compared to the archivist's to see if the system suggested any records that the archivist would not have recommended. That is, the more of these "wrong" answers given by the system, the higher the degree of imprecision in its responses.

3. The system's *behavior*. This test was based on a hands-on review of the system by the expert archivist, members of an Archives' project review committee, and the project team. It is a partially subjective review of what the system is like to use. For example, the archivist must ask the researcher questions in the right order, in order for the researcher to understand the reasoning behind the questions. The system's ability to mimic this kind of behavior was evaluated during this test. Other factors, such as how quickly it performed certain tasks, were also evaluated.

The assessment process was conducted as follows:

1. An *assessment team* was established to conduct the test. Members included the software design team, the primary domain expert, and several members of a project review committee, which the Archives had established to monitor the progress of the project.

2. A set of *sample inquiries* was developed by the project team and the primary domain expert. The domain expert then answered the inquiries by suggesting records series that might be appropriate to each of the queries.

3. The same inquiries were run through the system.

4. The *responses* of both the archivist and the system were researched to determine how many correct, wrong, or missed answers had been made. The research identified 100 record series that were pertinent to the test questions. The archivist failed to identify some on the first pass but recalled them easily while researching the answers. The system failed to identify some of the series, primarily because some keyword indexing data had not been entered into the data base, although one case was wrongly identified because of a software problem. Interestingly enough, the system identified some of the cases the archivist had missed and, when the proper data was entered into the data base, the system successfully recalled the cases it had missed before.

5. The expert archivist and the review committee worked with the system for several days and determined that its behavior was appropriate. As a good example of the value of letting an organization actually work with a prototype of a system, the review committee suggested a number of features that a production version of the system should have.

The Quantitative Tests for Recall and Precision

As Figure 3–11 shows, the archivist and the system together identified 100 series as possible places to look for answers to the sample inquiries. The sample cases are all unique, although the same series may appear more than once if it is applicable to more than one research inquiry.

The key factors in the system's recall and precision scores were: (1) the system logic, which performed well, although 1 series out of the 100 was misidentified because we did not write software to specifically compare the geographic areas of the inquiry and the records; (2) the system's data base, in which not all of the series were completely described, therefore causing the system to pass over 21 and misidentify 1 more of the 100 cases (this was later corrected); and (3) the limited

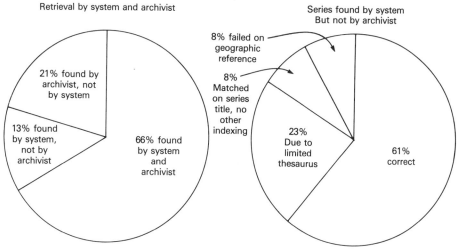

*This figure shows the relative performance of the system and the archivist in identifying records that might apply to the sample inquiries. The system missed some retrievals altogether, as did the archivist, when both of the identified series were examined after the test. Significantly, the system was able to retrieve some series that the archivist missed on the first pass. The right-hand chart defines the series that the system found but the archivist did not. A significant portion (61%) turned out to be correct. The others were wrong for one of three reasons: (1) the series was retrieved based on subject but was in the wrong geographic area, because no specific geographic data were included in the index; (2) the temporary thesaurus created in the system made a weak match between terms (in this case, "hydroelectric power" was matched to the term "water-power" which, because of the limited text search capabilities in the prototype, matched on the subject index term "water"—out of four series retrieved that way, only one had information on hydroelectric power; and (3) a plain lack of indexing (in this case, predecessor records to the Bureau of Fisheries were retrieved on the title line reference to "fish").

Figure 3–11   100 series retrieved by the archivist and the system.*

thesaurus built into the system (it did not have a match for 1 search term), which resulted in 3 series being wrongly identified.

The system's recall and precision were calculated as follows:

$$\text{Recall} = [(R2 - RS)/R2]*100$$

where $R2$ is the number of series identified by the archivist, and RS is the number identified by the archivist that are not in the system's data base.

This is a *limited technical definition of recall but sufficient to compare the system to the archivist as benchmark.* Therefore

$$\text{System Recall} = [(81 - 21)/81]*100 = 74\%$$

This is a fairly low level of recall. To increase this, the expert system would have to be married to a powerful conventional information retrieval system. Conventional systems often recall several times more records than a highly experienced human would have. The expert system would thus act to counterbalance this effect.

$$\text{Precision} = (S1/S)*100$$

where S is the set of records series identified by the system, and $S1$ is the set of records that both the system and the archivist identified.

Therefore

$$\text{Initial System Precision} = (66/100)* 100 = 66\%$$

This is a *limited definition of precision* but, as with the recall calculation above, it is sufficient to compare to the archivist as a benchmark. It is also a much lower score than we had anticipated. After examining the data, however, we adjusted the score for inaccuracies in the raw data. The calculation then becomes

$$\text{Precision(Adjusted)} = [S1/(S - Sc)]* 100$$

where Sc is the number of series that we felt were retrieved because of the data errors.

Therefore

$$\text{Precision(Adjusted)} = [66/(100 - 31)] = 96\%$$

This would be a very good score. In practice, after updating the data base, the score hovered around 91 to 92% during several postassessment trials. That is still a good score, but it indicates that the quality of data in any system directly affects its value—no less so with an expert system.

A BRIEF REVIEW OF THE SYSTEM

As Figure 3–12 shows, the system's construction is very straightforward. Most of the software was built using the M.1 expert system "shell" or development environment, as a series of knowledge bases, each of which is a collection of heuristics that the system uses to direct the information retrieval process.

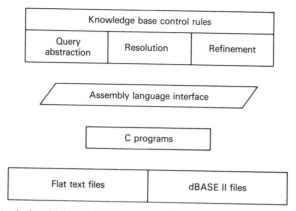

*The system's construction is straightforward. Most of the programming effort went into building the knowledge base as a series of IF-THEN rules in the M.1 system shell. M.1 is an expert system shell from Teknowledge for the IBM-PC built on Prolog and assembly language. It has good support for recursive functions—something we needed with all the list manipulations we were doing.
     The system manipulates some dBASE II files, via external M.1 calls to C. We used the Computer Innovations' C86 compiler, because it provides almost all of the DBMS functions we needed. The bulk of the files the system uses comprise flat data files that contain facts about the records, cues the system, picks up during the search process, and so on.

Figure 3–12   The system components.*

The system is implemented on an IBM-PC/AT, with 640KB of main memory and currently occupies something less than 400KB of disk space. The software is menu-driven, as a natural language processor would have reduced the memory available for the knowledge bases and would have increased the cost of the prototype. It currently comprises about 300 rules and 1,200 lines of C and assembly language source code.

The System Components

The system has five main components. They are:

1. The *knowledge bases.* These are subdivided into four functional modules, each of which operates part of the retrieval process. The knowledge bases are written in the M.1 expert system shell and contain four modules of backward-chaining rules: (1) *control rules,* which control the flow of the program; (2) *query abstraction,* which uses rules and certainty factors to determine the most important topics contained in a set of general subjects that the user identifies; (3) *resolution,* which first matches topics to the general types of documents (e.g., personnel records) that may have answers to an inquiry and then identifies specific sets of records in the underlying data base; and (4) *refinement,* which allows the user to cycle back through the process if desired.

2. An *assembly language interface.* This allows the M.1 software to call and execute other programs. For example, an M.1 rule can contain the following command to open a data file:

```
IF external (150, [open, series, series]) =["ok"]

THEN data base is open.
```

The assembly language interface picks up the command and passes it to a program—"150"—written in C. This opens the particular file—"series"—which is indexed on a field named "series." The C program then sends "ok" back through the interface to M.1 to indicate that the file is open.

3. *C language programs.* This prototype uses C language programs to do most file handling chores. For example, dBASE II files contain information on the record series, which are the common units of records in the Archives' files. The knowledge base software, using C programs through external calls, searches the dBASE II files to find topic indices series titles, or other information. In some cases, the C program, as in the preceding example, sends information from the dBASE II file directly back to M.1. In other cases, the data are temporarily stored in simple text files, which the M.1 software can then read directly from disk. Passing data directly through the assembly language interface is much faster than creating and reading a disk file. However, the software is implemented in version 1.2 of M.1, which unlike the current version can only pass 80 characters at a time to a C program. Therefore, whenever large quantities of information have to be picked up by the knowledge bases, text files are used.

4. *Flat text files.* The M.1 shell can read and interpret certain kinds of flat text files. In this prototype, text files are used primarily to store the various lists that the system makes use of during processing, including facts and information about the records or the search process. For example, Figure 3–13 shows a sample of a file called "subjects.txt." This file contains a list of the research subjects the system can address. As the figure shows, these files are in a very straightforward form; they can be used in much the same way that data tables would be in a conventional system. Therefore the system can be expanded and maintained by changing or enlarging the lists with which it works, since the knowledge base contains generalized rules for interpreting the lists.

5. *dBASE II files.* dBASE II files are used in much the same way as the flat text files. However, data are extracted from them using C language routines, which are under the control of the knowledge base and search and sort files much more efficiently than the M.1 software could. The titles of record series, for example, are contained and indexed into dBASE II files.

As noted previously, control rules guide the general flow of processing within the system. For example, to paraphrase the top-level control rule:

```
IF the introduction has been presented to the user

AND query_abstraction is done
```

```
subs = subject-water__resources.
subs = subject-land__resources.
subs = subject-territories.
subs = subject-economic__development.
subs = subject-transportation.
subs = subject-environment__conservation.
subs = subject-alaska.
subs = subject-indians.
subs = subject-national__resources.
subs = persons.
subs = documents.

subj__infos = water-resources.
subj__infos = land-resources.
subj__infos = territories.
subj__infos = transportation.
subj__infos = environment__conservation.
subj__infos = alaska.
```

*This figure shows a sample of a flat text file, "subject.txt." The file represents two kinds of information. The top section shows research subjects ("subs") that the system will present to the user in a menu. The bottom section defines which of those subjects ("subj__infos") the system can provide an explanation, or "help" menu, for. This scheme is somewhat redundant, but it is quicker for the system to read these facts directly than to have the M.1 shell manipulate them internally. This kind of data redundancy would be eliminated in a production system.

Figure 3–13   Example of a flat text file.*

```
AND resolution is done

AND refinement is done

THEN consultation is over.
```

The software attempts to evaluate each of the arguments to the IF-THEN statement in order. For example, there is a rule that ends with the statement "THEN query__abstraction done." The system must evaluate each argument of the second rule before it can determine whether query__abstraction is indeed done. Some of the rules analyze data, some drive a process such as menu generation, and so on. By chaining backward through the rules in this fashion, the system imitates a simple, mechanistic form of deductive logic with which it narrows down the possible set of records that pertain to the researcher's inquiry.

Building the System

The actual software took about 11 weeks to build, as Figure 3–14 shows. A good part of the effort, however, was devoted to analyzing and documenting what the team had learned about the Archives, about applying expert systems in the archival environment, and about designing and building expert systems on microcomputers.

Therefore, although Figure 3–15 shows the knowledge engineer's time tapering off toward the end of the project, it is because the graph reflects only that time spent by the expert archivist, Renee Jaussaud, and the lead knowledge engi-

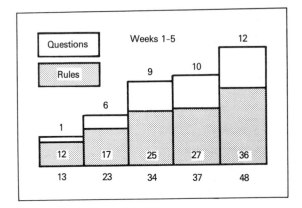

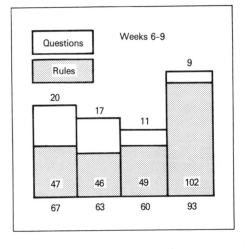

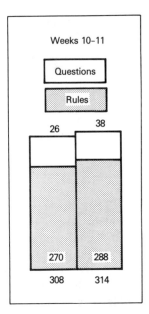

*"Questions" indicates the number of program routines devoted directly to dialogue: "rules" shows the number of rules used either for inferring search strategies or handling data. The first five weeks were spent building "core" software. During the last six weeks, the user interface was refined (the number of dialogue routines actually decreased) and the number of rules more than tripled.

Figure 3–14   Growth of software during project.*

neer (systems analyst), Amy Glamm, on either (1) actually writing the software or (2) performing the system assessment tests. In fact the level of effort stayed quite steady over the entire five months of the project.

Ultimately, the test of analytical techniques comes in our ability to use them to deliver what we promised. The project was completed within its schedule and budget constraints. That was not a surprise. However, we were interested to note

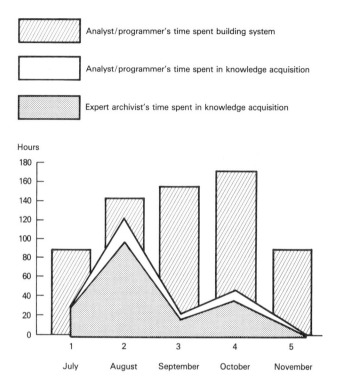

*This figure compares the amount of time spent by the expert archivist and the AMS systems analyst programmer. Not shown are the lesser amounts of time spent by oversight committee members from the Archives, lead systems and management personnel from AMS, etc. As the figure shows, the archivist's involvement (black plot) was heaviest at the beginning of the project, while the systems analyst/programmer's time involvement was fairly steady, when both the amount of time spent working on the system (background bars) and time spent in knowledge acquisition sessions with the expert (gray plot) are taken into account.

Figure 3–15 Hours spent by the expert archivist and system analyst/knowledge engineer.*

that the pattern of software growth and the number of hours spent writing the software did not follow some previous patterns found in many expert systems projects.

For example, our previous experience indicates that program size may grow and shrink several times during an expert system development. This occurs as the knowledge bases are (1) tossed together during knowledge acquisition and (2) refined and optimized afterward. This cycle can repeat itself several times.

By taking a structured approach, we were able to avoid this. As Figure 3–14 shows, we reduced our knowledge base by approximately four questions during the seventh week of the project, when we decided not to install a function to trap the results of inquiry pattern matching to a disk file.

We also found that the use of models made a tremendous difference in our ability to work independently of the domain expert. Ms. Jaussaud, the primary domain expert, would work for several half-day sessions on a new part of the rules.

Then, she could use the model as a guideline for making comments on the behavior of the system.

For example, during the first six weeks of the project, as Figure 3–15 shows, the domain expert spent an increasing amount of time working directly with the knowledge engineer. Then, for about the next four weeks, they worked apart except for one or two meetings per week of a half day each. As the system neared its completion during the fourth month of the project, they worked more closely together again, primarily refining the system's dialog and the order in which it asks questions. As Figure 3–14 shows, the number of questions the system could ask increased dramatically between the ninth and eleventh weeks of the project.

Finally, Ms. Jaussaud participated in the hands-on evaluation of the system, as well as several follow-on meetings that were devoted to discussing and analyzing the results of the project.

Based on this experience, we suggest that:

> The use of structured design and analysis techniques can permit expert systems development to proceed with essentially the same regularity of effort and predictability that exemplify conventional systems developments.

CONCLUSIONS

Structured systems development methods from both "conventional" systems analysis and knowledge engineering have been successfully applied to this prototype expert system. This and other evidence (Boehm 1976; Silverman 1984, 1985; Liebowitz 1984; and Clancey 1984) suggest (1) that other, more rigorous, structured techniques from classical systems analysis may be merged to develop expert systems and (2) that there should be cost savings and other benefits associated with doing so.

Certainly, a prime goal in managing any software development effort is to avoid wasted effort. To that end, two key elements are required (1) good communications among the project team members and (2) a cohesive view of the role, purpose, and functions of the emerging system that is shared by both users and developers of the system (Davis 1974; Quade and Boucher 1978; Powers, Adams, and Mills 1984; and American Management Systems, Inc. 1985).

We believe that management goal was met during this project through the application of three key techniques:

1. The use of an initial requirements analysis, which established the system's role, its purpose within a defined environment, and the functions required of it

2. The use of various system models that (1) provided a means for the users and developers of the system to agree on the design of the emerging system and (2) eliminated at least some of the initial false steps associated with a rapid prototyping effort

3. Quantitative measurement of the system's behavior—in this case a measure of how completely and accurately it retrieved information—that (1) helped the system users put their own hands-on evaluation of the system into perspective and (2) helped clarify the differences between this system and one built for a similar purpose with conventional technology.

This was a limited project to build a small computer system. Therefore our experiences and the results of our efforts cannot be construed to be too far reaching. We hope, however, that this provides useful information for those who wish to develop expert systems while taking advantage of the body of knowledge developed during conventional systems developments.

ACKNOWLEDGMENT

We wish to acknowledge the kind advice and assistance of Frank Burke, Archivist of the United States, William Yoder, American Management Systems, Inc., and Ted Weir of the National Archives. We would also like to thank the five archivists who participated in the initial knowledge acquisition, Robin Cookson, Sara Jackson, James Rush, Richard Myers, and the archivist who spent much time on the project, Renee Jaussaud.

REFERENCES

AMERICAN MANAGEMENT SYSTEMS, INC. *Functional Information Requirements for the Office of the National Archives, Volumes I–III.* Washington, D.C.: IEEE, 1985.

BOEHM, B.W. "Software Engineering." Paper read at IEEE Computer Society, December 1976.

CLANCEY, W.J. "Knowledge Acquisition for Classification Expert Systems." Palo Alto, CA: Stanford University Heuristic Programming Project working paper (HPP 84-18), July 1984.

DAVIS, G.B. *Management Information Systems: Conceptual Foundations, Structure, and Development.* New York: McGraw-Hill, 1984.

DE MARCO, TOM. *Structured Analysis and System Specifications,* New York: Yourdon Press, 1979.

FREEMAN, P., AND WASSERMAN, A.I. "Tutorial on Software Design Techniques," Paper read at IEEE Computer Society, Washington, D.C.: IEEE, April 1977.

GLASS, R.L. *Modern Programming Practices: A Report from Industry.* Englewood Cliffs, NJ: Prentice-Hall, 1982.

LIEBOWITZ, J. "Determining Functional Requirements for NASA Goddard's Command Management System Software Design Using Expert Systems." Ph.D. dissertation, George Washington University, 1984.

MANDELL, S.L. *Computers and Data Processing: Concepts and Applications.* St. Paul, MN: West Publishing, 1979.

METZGER, P.W. *Managing a Programming Project*. Englewood Cliffs, NJ: Prentice-Hall, 1973.

PAGE-JONES, M. *The Practical Guide to Structured Systems Design*. New York: Yourdon Press, 1980.

PETERS, L.J. *Software Design: Methods and Techniques*. New York: Yourdon Press, 1981.

POWERS, M.J., ADAMS, D.R., AND MILLS, H.R. *Computer Information Systems Development: Analysis and Design*. Cincinnati, OH: South-Western Publishing, 1984.

QUADE, E.S., AND BOUCHER, W.I. *Systems Analysis and Policy Planning: Applications in Defense*. New York: Elsevier, 1978.

SILVERMAN, B.G. "Nature of an Expert's Knowledge." Chapter 1 in *Institute for Artificial Intelligence Technical Report*. Washington, D.C.: George Washington University, 1984.

SILVERMAN, B.G. "Software Cost and Productivity Improvements: An Analogical View." Paper read at IEEE Computer Society, Washington, D.C.: IEEE, May 1985.

ZIEGLER, C.A. *Programming System Methodologies*. Englewood Cliffs, NJ: Prentice-Hall, 1983.

Structural Elements of Expert System Design

4

Man-Machine Interface Design for Expert Systems

Mike Jones

INTRODUCTION

Artificial intelligence (AI) is a field of study that encompasses computational techniques for performing tasks that apparently require intelligence when performed by humans [1]. An expert system is "a computer system or program which incorporates one or more techniques of artificial intelligence to perform a family of activities that traditionally would have to be performed by a skilled or knowledgeable human" [2]. The finest expert system in existence is of little use if no one can communicate with it. In this chapter, we are concerned with the design of interfaces to computers, and in particular to expert systems.

Few people get through a day without encountering and having to communicate with computers. In many cases, the interfaces to these machines are so cleverly designed as to distance the user from the whole idea that he or she is dealing with a computer at all. For example, you might start your day by pouring a cup of coffee that you programmed your automatic brewer to produce the night before. In driving to work, your automobile's engine (and, increasingly, other automotive systems) is under the control of a microprocessor. If you stop at the automatic bank teller on the way to pick up lunch money, you will use a numeric keypad to traverse a number of menus and enter a dollar amount, with the whole interface designed to model a traditional "cash a check" transaction.

Taken at face value, the concept of interfacing human beings to computing machines would seem relatively straightforward and easy to define. One could easily overlook the years of analysis and design that have led to current models for man-machine communication. In each of the examples just cited, the user interface has been carefully conceived, designed, and implemented to present a sparse but complete functional palette to a user that minimizes the probability of errors.

Man-computer interfaces vary widely, depending on their intended function and their intended audience. A computer programmer requires a much different interface to a system than does the prospective user of that system. In this chapter, we shall examine the work and art that comprise current thinking on user interfaces and show how this can be applied to designing user interfaces for new systems.

This discussion is intended to be of primary applicability to developers of expert systems. It will quickly become apparent, however, that the intelligence of the interface is related more to the intended system function and level of expertise of the user than it is to artificial intelligence per se. Therefore, many of the techniques and approaches presented here are borrowed from and can be applied to conventional data processing systems as well.

PEOPLE VS. MACHINES

People do not, as a rule, deal naturally with computers. Computers are very narrow, specialized devices. Their inputs have to be precise and parameterized, or the machine cannot understand them. People, on the other hand, are slower but are also very flexible and broad in their avenues of communication. We use virtually every sensible attribute associated with ourselves to aid in communicating with other people. We are certainly not precise from the viewpoint of a computer.

Because of these differences, we have a problem to solve when we set out to build a computer-based system which must communicate effectively with a community of users. We must bridge the gap between the machine and the user. One possibility is to make the user more like the computer. This is what computer scientists and programmers are constrained to do when learning their trade. A better choice is to make the machine more like the user. The machine is under our control, the user isn't. Once the machine has a friendly, usable interface, the interface can be instantly transferred to other machines. This process is slightly less simple when it comes to transferring expertise from user to user.

Our approach will be to take some of the computer capacity we have allocated for whatever application we are building and use it to present a user with a "face" that is better suited for use by a person who is not a computer programmer, but is instead interested in using our application to solve a problem. The computer should drop out of the picture as much as possible. It is the tool, the means to the end, and not the end itself.

TRADITIONAL SELECTION OF USER INTERFACES

Sadly, there have been few canons involved in the selection of user interfaces for many systems to date. In most cases, either the developmental environment, the nature of the development community, the traditions of the shop, or some combination of these has dictated the user interface for a new system. For example:

1. In a certain bank, transactions are presented to a user via formatted screens with fields to be supplied with content. Reports are returned as further formatted screens. This interface is used universally in all banking applications, even when the application and user community might be better served with a friendlier interface. The rules for designing and using screens are well documented and incorporated in bank data processing policy and procedures. When a new system is to be added, the local developer decides with cause that a windowing environment with some use of graphics input would make the application friendly and easy to use. This idea is rejected by management, and the application is developed with traditional screens.

2. A programmer whose previous assignment was to port X-Windows to a selected personal computer is assigned to a payroll project with simple, parameterized input and output. He rejects the idea of formatted screens as dated and uninteresting and builds a Ferrari of a software system complete with pop-up help screens, numeric selection from a "soft" keypad, and other features that are fun to write. The user community is up in arms, and the programmer is traded to Apple for a disk drive.

3. An AI system developer who has spent years working in LISP and creating conversational models is asked to write an introduction to a user's guide for her latest application. The company has to hire word-processing support to remove all the parentheses from the delivered text.

The first example is probably achingly familiar to most data processing professionals in large companies. Tradition dictates the user interface, without regard for the introduction of new technology. Management usually has a point: once the user community is accustomed to a certain user interface, reeducation is generally a major headache. This fact, combined with a strong and valid unwillingness to have a cornucopia of user interfaces across the company's applications, generates a conservative attitude. The only problem is that a genuinely better way, with a potentially positive impact on the company's bottom line, may be missed and the company's competitive edge lost. However, data processing personnel would be well advised to remember that the latest and greatest technology is rarely even half as interesting to management as the profit-and-loss statement and the continued contentment of the user community.

In the second example, the principle of parsimony has been violated. A traditional screen interface is all that is needed or desirable, and the effort put into making a straightforward application fit an advanced user interface has been wasted.

In the third example, the developer has become so accustomed to the LISP environment that the use of LISP has superseded the normal rules of English. This developer probably needs a vacation. However farcical the example is, however, reading the interface to SHRINK described elsewhere in this section should suffice to show that developers can lose sight of the fact that the user community does *not* know LISP, and should not have to know it.

If, in their development, traditional applications have been assigned user interface techniques willy-nilly, it has been largely because those same applications have driven the current research into user interfaces. We shall show in this section that there is a better way.

ART AND USER INTERFACES

In the very early days of computing, programs were entered into the system and invoked via such crude mechanisms as toggle switches and plug panels. The user was required to know the machine "code" that was understood by the computer, a language of binary numbers. This interface gave way to punched cards and then to hard-copy terminals and CRTs. With the latter, interactive or conversational communication became a possibility. With decreasing technology costs and increasing technical sophistication, the use of variable character size, computer graphics, and such niceties as windows has become more common. The palette available to the designer of a user interface is richer than it has ever been and will continue to expand as computational evolution continues.

So what defines an ideal user interface? This is a topic of considerable debate and involves art as well as science. Any time aesthetic considerations are involved, however, it becomes very difficult to say with certainty what is "good" and what is "bad." As if this weren't enough, tastes change: what is considered ideal today probably won't be tomorrow. Nonetheless, there are some characteristics of user interfaces that can be shown to be consistently valuable. For example:

- The user interface should be targeted to the intended user community. Thus, an infant's computer game should have an interface that is conceptually much simpler than that required for a tax-preparation program.
- The symbols and terms used in the interface should be consistent with those accepted in the area the application is intended to support. For example, using architectural symbols in a system supporting the operation of a nuclear power plant might lead to the transfer of some unintended and unfortunate concepts. (The toilet symbol, in particular, should be avoided.)
- The general type of interface should be tailored to the type of application. For example, a menu tree will work very well for an environment where a series of multiple-choice questions will lead to a single answer. (Think of the previously mentioned bank teller machine.) By contrast, in an application where the computer is simulating a human conversation, menus would be hopelessly misapplied.
- Symbols and graphics should be used where, and only where, they can add value to the interface.
- Clutter should be avoided. Only related data should be shown or requested at any one logical part of the user interface.

USER INTERFACE OPTIONS

There are two general types of application user interface. The first is an interactive conversation. Here, the computer and user both ask questions, and both issue atomic answers on a question-by-question basis. A metastructure describing an entire problem or class of problems is thereby built by both the computer and the user. The second type of interface consists of the user entering a large amount of data or control information and then receiving an answer in return. This answer might consist of a number, or a picture of some sort. The option that distinguishes the second type from the first is that much of the information to be entered can be arranged as multiple-choice questions with parameterized answers, and thus can be structured as entries on forms. The first type of interface is much more free-form, and thus more flexible, but may be harder to learn. Both are commonly used in interfacing to expert systems.

TOOLS

A host of tools are available to the current designer of an application user interface. The most common ones are the following:

- *The interactive cathode-ray terminal (CRT).* This is the hardware that supports the remaining tools. It is available in huge variety and remains the workhorse of user interfaces in one form or another.
- *Q & A (conversational) input and output.* This sort of interface is used when the keyboard and CRT are simulating a human conversation.
- *Text processing.* This is one of the most common areas in use in application interfaces. In it, the CRT and user communicate via the written word. Symbols are limited to those held in common among the application developers and users and are presented as words or phrases.
- *Natural language processing (NLP).* In this interface, computational linguistics is used to support conversational input and output, permitting a flexible and human-like conversation. More sophisticated NLP systems support the preservation of context across the conversation chronology and use parsing to support various sentence structures.
- *Computer graphics.* This is the capability of drawing pictures on a CRT or other graphics device and not be limited to alphanumeric input and output. The pictures can be either symbolic or analytical graphs.
- *Cursors.* These are images, icons, or other symbols presented on a screen to denote logical "location." They can be mapped onto underlying structures, such as logical objects or symbols presented on the screen.
- *Graphics input (GIN) device.* This is a device, such as a mouse or track ball,

that permits movement of a cursor on a screen and corresponding selection of a location and underlying structures from the data presented on that screen.

- *Color.* This is the facility whereby images and choices are presented in color, and the user is not limited to monochrome.
- *Animation.* Animation is an increasingly popular part of many user interfaces. It consists of the dynamic movement of symbols and other structures around on the screen and is used to relay information and hold user interest.
- *Menus.* Menus provide the ability to structure a series of questions so as to obtain information in various semantic structures, including almost any structure which can be represented as a digraph.
- *Windows.* Windows provide the ability to open "virtual terminals" or additional sessions on a given CRT. They support the type of parallel thinking that people are so good at and permit the context of one path of thought to be preserved while the user pursues another.
- *Icons and symbols.* These are generally an offshoot of computer graphics and permit the user's thought processes and interactions to be modeled and assisted by the use of associative symbols or metaphors.

The preceding tools are not mutually exclusive: any combination can be incorporated into an effective interface design. The remainder of the chapter is concerned with the selection and use of these tools to produce a good interface.

TOOL SELECTION AND USAGE

We have briefly described each of the tools available for implementing a user interface. While we do not have the space to completely describe all issues related to the current state of the art where these tools are concerned, it is important that each be presented together with some related issues. With the understanding gained thereby, we can proceed to design an interface for a given application.

The CRT

The development of the CRT as an element of the user interface has been an evolutionary one, made possible by the great reduction in cost of the components that make up the device. As previously mentioned, in one form or another it is the hardware of choice of virtually all computer system interfaces. However, it is important to remember that the CRT is not an end in itself, but is instead part of the continuing evolution of computer systems. As a reminder, interfaces based on voice processing are already in existence and are likely to be more prevalent in the future.

Q & A Conversations

Discussion.   The question-and-answer conversational type of interface is widely encountered in systems utilizing artificial intelligence. It consists of a series of questions and answers coming from and to the user from the application. The text will have an English-like structure and may in fact utilize even more natural language in newer applications. This interface is a very powerful mechanism in expert systems. It emulates what might happen if a lay individual came to ask questions of a human expert in a field of interest.

Examples

SHRINK.   SHRINK [1–3] is a psychoanalysis program that uses Q & A as its interface. As far as interfaces are concerned, it is interesting to note that the use of LISP to implement SHRINK has allowed several language quirks to trickle through to the user. The user responses must be enclosed in parentheses, and the use of the apostrophe is not allowed.

```
(shrink)
WELCOME TO MY SOFA
PLEASE ENCLOSE YOUR INPUT IN PARENTHESES
(hello)
TELL ME MORE
(i have a small problem)
HOW LONG HAVE YOU HAD A SMALL PROBLEM
(ever since my girl friend discovered my true love)
ALL IS FAIR IN LOVE AND WAR
(i see)
YOU SEE
(yes)
HOW CAN YOU BE SO SURE
(because i understand your comment)
IS THAT REALLY THE REASON
(perhaps not)
I SEE
(she wants me to give up computers)
SHE WANTS YOU TO GIVE UP COMPUTERS
(you got it)
WHAT DOES THAT INDICATE
(i cant see you anymore)
YOU CANT SEE ME ANYMORE
(no but)
DONT BE SO NEGATIVE
(but i will dream of you)
FOR DREAM ANALYSIS SEE FREUD
(bye)
GOODBYE
```

PUFF.   PUFF [4] is a pulmonary diagnostic assistance tool. The questions asked it are more inclined to use technical terminology, or jargon, than, say, SHRINK, and the interface has been designed to fit the user community. Note that PUFF accepts all input before applying rules and printing a diagnosis. Also, the conversational context does not change as a result of the nature of the answer. In other words, giving an answer does not result in a choice of the subsequent question.

```
*PUFF*

(PUFF asks the user for pulmonary function test results
and patient data and then executes rules to reach con-
clusions in interpreting the tests.)

PATIENT-7

   1)  Patient's identifying number:
       **7446

   2)  Referral diagnosis:
       **ASTHMA

 (RV, TLC, FVC, etc., are the lung test measurements.)

   3)  RV/RV-predicted:
       **261

   4)  TLC(body box)observed/predicted:
       **139

   5)  TLC(DLCO)observed/predicted:
       **111

   6)  FVC/FVC-predicted:
       **81

   7)  FEV1/FVC ratio:
       **40

   8)  The slope F5025:
       **9

   9)  The FEV1/FVC threshold:
       **77

  10)  MMF/MMF-predicted:
       **12
```

```
11)  The DLCO/DLCO-predicted:
     **117

12)  Change in FEV1 (after dilation):
     **31

13)  The change in resistance(after dilation):
     **2.0

14)  The severity of coughing:
     **NONE

15)  The number of pack-years of smoking:
     **17

16)  The degree of dyspnea:
     **NONE
```

At the conclusion of the dialogue, PUFF first types a summary of the most important pulmonary function data:

```
            SUMMARY OF DATA

            The degree of dyspnea: NONE
            The severity of coughing: NONE
            The number of pack-years of smoking: 17
            Referral diagnosis: ASTHMA
            RV/RV-predicted: 261
            FVC/FVC-predicted: 81
            TLC(body box) observed/predicted: 139
            FEV1/FVC ratio: 40
            MMF/MMF-predicted: 12
            The DLCO/DLCO-predicted: 117
            The slope F5025: 9
```

Finally, PUFF gives its interpretation of the data and its pulmonary disease diagnosis:

```
INTERPRETATION

Obstruction is indicated by curvature of the flow-
  volume loop.
Forced vital capacity is normal but the FEV1/FVC ratio
  is reduced, suggesting airway obstruction.
Low mid-expiratory flow is consistent with severe
  airway obstruction.
```

```
Change in expired flow rates following bronchodilation
  shows that there is reversibility of airway
  obstruction.
Improvement in expired flow rates following dilation
  indicates reversibility of airway obstruction, and
  this is confirmed by improvement in airway resistance.
Good response to bronchodilators is consistent with an
  asthmatic condition, and their continued use is
  indicated.
The high diffusing capacity is consistent with asthma.
Elevated lung volumes indicate overinflation.
Airway obstruction is consistent with the patient's
  smoking history.
The pulmonary diffusing capacity for carbon monoxide is
  normal.
Obstructive airways disease of the asthmatic type.
```

Issues.   The issues and questions associated with the selection and use of the Q & A conversational type of interface are as follows:

- Is the application well served by a conversational interface? Is it intended to guide a relatively unsophisticated user through a complicated network of choices and to present increasingly sophisticated analyses of the conversation as it progresses? Does the conversational context change as the result of the nature of the answer? If the answer to these questions is yes, then Q & A is a good candidate for a user interface. Even if the result of the session is a display of quantitative information using computer graphics, this can be combined with the conversation as a whole for a very effective result.

  Note that the system PUFF presented before does not require, and might even be better off without, a conversational interface. Its questions are static and are answered in order. Moreover, the nature of the answer does not either change the order of the questions or result in new or different questions. Consequently, a traditional form or screen for entering data would be sufficient for it and might even be a faster way to get the relevant information into PUFF.

- Is "meaning" in the conversation both precise and important? Keyword matching, such as that done in SHRINK, is fine as far as it goes and makes interesting conversations, but an expert system needs to do significantly more than that. It may be that a combination of Q & A and more rigid text-processing input is called for, if limiting options can grant greater precision to the input stream the application has to work with without causing the user undue pain.

- Is line-by-line interaction required, or is it more efficient to obtain a large amount of input from the user before presenting a sparse response? Interaction can be useful for short or even extended conversations, but may get in the way of the application's function if misapplied. For example, consider the following hypothetical situation, in which SHRINK is misused as a fire department dispatching program:

```
(shrink)
WELCOME TO MY SOFA
PLEASE ENCLOSE YOUR INPUT IN PARENTHESES
(hello)
TELL ME MORE
(i have a small problem)
HOW LONG HAVE YOU HAD A SMALL PROBLEM
(does not matter)
TELL ME MORE
(i have a fire)
ALL IS FAIR IN LOVE AND WAR
(i need a fire truck)
DONT BE SO NEGATIVE
(here is my address)
HOW CAN YOU BE SO SURE
(because i live there!)
IS THAT REALLY THE REASON
(yes)
TELL ME MORE
(101 elm street)
WHAT DOES THAT INDICATE
(i need a fire truck)
BE MORE DECISIVE
(will you send one?)
I THINK YOU SHOULD ANSWER THAT YOURSELF
(argh)
BE MORE DECISIVE
(bye)
GOODBYE
```

It is immediately obvious that the needs of this user would have been much better served by an application which asked the relevant questions about the nature and location of the event and dispatched a fire truck. The benefits of a Q & A session are lost in this crisis situation.

Text and Natural Language Processing

Discussion.   Virtually all user interfaces use some form of text processing. Text is presented to describe choices, to transfer information, to solicit input, and to accept user commands. In more primitive interfaces, the text used is rigidly parameterized, and incorrect responses generate interesting and (usually) pathological results. As the field of computational linguistics has progressed, however, language interfaces to computers have become much more flexible and powerful, permitting a more natural path of communication to be implemented between the user and the expert system or other application than has traditionally been the case. In the following example, we shall assume the existence of a natural language processor.

Examples.   The following are examples of the use of text processing in a user interface:

- In our by now well-worn paradigm of the automatic bank teller, the user is presented with a set of menus whereby an action, account, and dollar amount are selected and a report is issued, possibly with money in return. The report presents the results of the action against the target account. This type of transaction-oriented interface is very common in data processing in general, but may have limited applicability in expert systems. If we know all of our inputs and outputs to the extent where a completely menu-driven interface can be implemented, we are probably dealing with a traditional data processing application. This should not be taken as a limiting factor: however, if the designer of an expert system finds an area where this type of interface can be effective, it certainly should be considered. At a minimum, it can be used to fill data tables and other control structures.
- In the case of a data retrieval system such as a database query language, there is a rich environment available for the use of NLP. Traditionally, database access has been parameterized and rigid, and it has been necessary for complex front-end programs to be written to do relatively simple searches and reports. Early work in less rigid query languages has helped, but has still required detailed knowledge on the part of the user as to the structure and names of the elements that comprise the database. With the evolutionary development of NLP, however, the user has become increasingly able to phrase English-like commands with a flexible format and to have the system understand and produce a reply without requiring application development each time a new look at the database is required.

Issues.   There are a number of questions and issues related to the selection and use of text processing in a user interface. These apply either to the entire user interface or selectively to parts of it.

- Are the inputs known and can they be parameterized? If so, the use of a descriptive text string on menus is an attractive option. If the inputs are not known, or if a greater degree of flexibility is required, then an NLP may be more appropriate.
- Gobbledygook is not any easier to read on a computer screen than it is in a book or manual. Keep the language simple and straightforward, and follow accepted rules of good style.
- Generally, avoid jargon. Remember, the "expert" is in an expert system and

is intended to supplement or replace the activities of a human expert. It follows, then, that the user's level of expertise will be lower than that of the expert. If a term has a specialized and specific meaning, use it only if there is not an acceptable equivalent term in common usage.

- On a powerful graphics system, a number of fonts and character sizes are available. Avoid the temptation to let this get out of control. A report presented to the user in Gothic font with letters varying in color may appeal to the instincts and creativity of the programmer, but it isn't going to help the business much. Again, keep it simple.

- Obey the principle of parsimony on output: output to the user should be minimal and succinct.

- Tolerate the violation of the principle of parsimony on input—i.e., on the part of the user. This has become increasingly possible as the field of NLP has progressed. Minimize the impact of a violation that the interface can't handle through the use of interactive Q & A sessions designed to "fill in the blanks" where parsing is not possible. Consider using the parse tree built by the interface as a way to rephrase the user input and repeat it back for confirmation.

Computer Graphics

Discussion.   Computer graphics has been expanding explosively in recent years. High-performance color CRTs are now available at costs that rival those of conventional monochrome tubes. It is unlikely that any computer-based system will lack graphics in the near future. The particular strengths of graphics include the following:

- The ability to present symbols rather than the words that describe symbols. This permits the development of models or metaphors as front ends to applications. There is a much higher degree of associativity for most users with a model than there is with a string of text. (See Figure 4–1.)

- The ability to show relationships among symbols using other symbols rather than words. (See Figure 4–2.)

- The ability to represent voluminous and multivariate data in a manner that intuitively and immediately relays its meaning. For example, the data describing the day-to-day performance of the stock prices of several competing companies in the field of artificial intelligence might take a lengthy report. The same data could be easily presented with immediate transfer of information and far lower probability of error through the use of a multivariate bar graph. (See Figure 4–3.)

- The ability to present continuous data in a continuous manner. For example, suppose we want to know the state of congestion at any point in time on a road we commute upon. A textual account might report to a terminal each time the

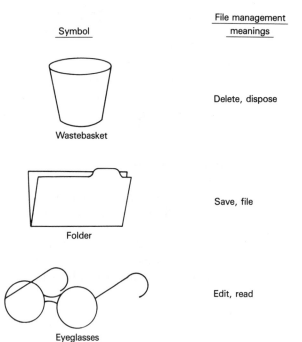

Symbol   File management
                  meanings

Wastebasket   Delete, dispose

Folder   Save, file

Eyeglasses   Edit, read

Figure 4–1   Concepts presented as symbols.

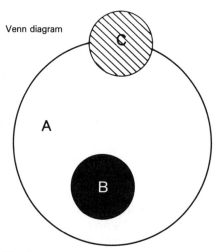

Venn diagram

A

B

C

Meaning

Set *A* contains set *B* (*B* is a subset of *A*).
Set *A* partially contains set *C* (Venn intersect).
Set *B* and set *C* are mutually exclusive.

Figure 4–2   Graphic depiction of relationship among symbols.

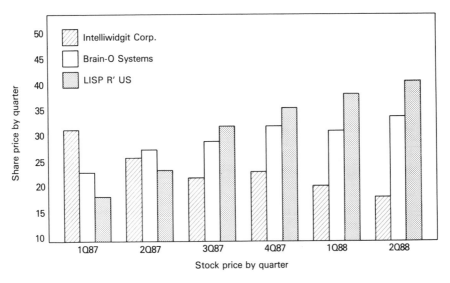

Figure 4–3   Graphic presentation of multivariate information.

level of congestion passed through a predefined threshold. Then, in order to determine the current state, we would have to remember the most recent one that appeared. On the other hand, varying the color or line thickness and style on a map of the road could give immediate, at-a-glance knowledge of the road's state. The problem becomes more apparent when we observe that what our road-surveying program would more likely be doing would be watching every road in a geographic area. In that case, we would not only have to remember the most current state, but remember it for a particular road. (See Figure 4–4.)

Along with its strengths and power, graphics carries some heavy responsibility. It is possible to lie very convincingly utilizing graphic presentation. It is also very easy to trap oneself into overusing the medium. Graphics should be used where appropriate, and not made to fit the wrong-shaped hole just to put a flashy interface on a system. Designs should be aesthetic. Some basic principles for using graphics are as follows [5]:

- The graphic should present interesting data with "substance, statistics, and design."
- The graphic should consist of "complex ideas communicated with clarity, precision, and efficiency."
- The graphic should convey the "greatest number of ideas in the shortest time with the least ink in the smallest space."
- The graphic should tell the "truth about the data."

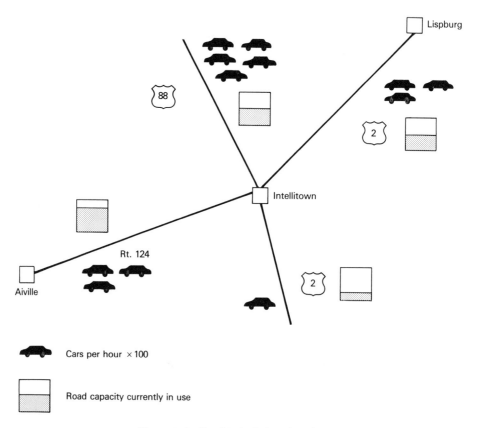

Figure 4–4   Graphic depiction of road use.

The following five basic principles covering aesthetic design were obtained from behavioral research [6]:

- *Balance.* If we understand that the eye gives different "weights" to objects in a picture, then we can readily see that balance in a picture means the same thing that it does on a scale. (See Figure 4–5.)

- *Sequence.* The eye moves easily from bright to subdued, from large to small, from color to gray scale, and from chaos to order. The picture should take this into account.

- *Proportion.* This has to do with the relationship of shapes to themselves and to each other. Two rules which help to produce good images are the rule of thirds and the golden section. (See Figure 4–6.)

- *Unity.* The objects in a picture should look as though they fit together, with similar visual attributes.

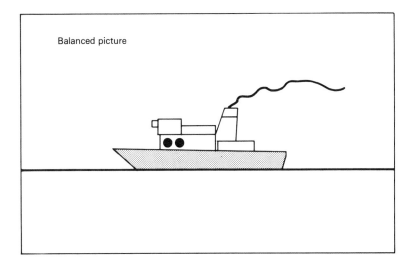

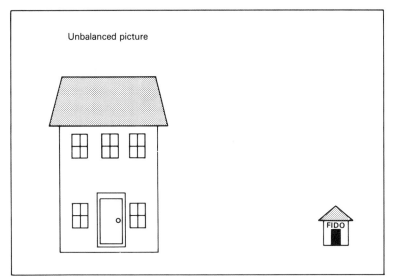

Figure 4–5 Picture balance.

- *Emphasis.* The most important objects in a picture should catch the user's attention first.

Aesthetic considerations should not be overlooked. Following them can make a large difference in the eventual usability of the overall user interface, and that is the whole idea behind designing and implementing such an interface in the first place.

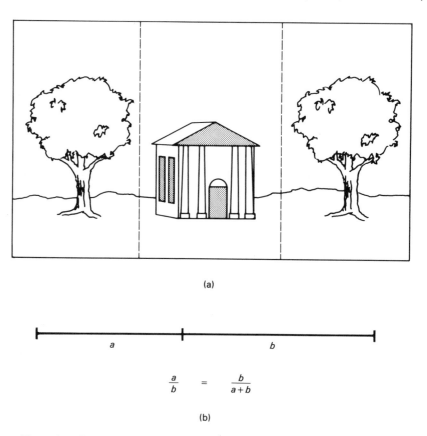

(a)

$$\frac{a}{b} \quad = \quad \frac{b}{a+b}$$

(b)

Figure 4–6   Rule of thirds and golden section. (a) Rule of thirds: Distribute the major objects of a picture among the three thirds of the graphic area. (b) Golden section or golden rectangle: The height of a graphic area or shape is related to the width as $A = 1$ is to $B = 1.618$.

Examples.   The following are examples of the use of computer graphics:

- The operators of a telephone network are interested in the state and usage of the lines that make up the network. The network is presented as a geographic map, and color coding or changing line style is used on the links to display the current status while line width is used to show capacity. The control system which drives the graphic receives real-time information regarding the network status from various reporting points within the network. (See Figure 4–7.)
- The users of an artificial intelligence system that does complex analysis on the telecommunications industry want to show relative company performance via a report. The designers include a graphic which is a multivariate line chart.
- The developers of an expert system which uses frames wish to make available

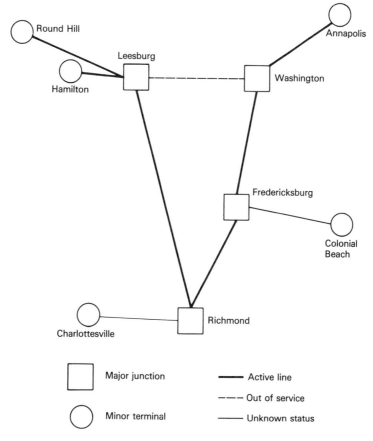

Figure 4–7 Graphic depiction of telephone net topology.

the reasoning process by which a decision was reached. They include a graphic which draws the frame as it might be drawn on a sheet of paper and show the contents of the frame as text. (See Figure 4–8.) They include a hierarchy of frames traversed for each decision, presented as a graph.

- One of the results of an expert system which calculates the relationships among various elements in a pattern-matching system is a graphic which presents the elements as nodes and the relationships among them as lines. (See Figure 4–9.)

- Part of the developer's workbench within an expert system shell shows semantic networks as nodes and relations. There is a hierarchical numbering scheme within the nodes such that subordinate semantic networks can be selected with a GIN device and brought up or exploded into the foreground of the display area.

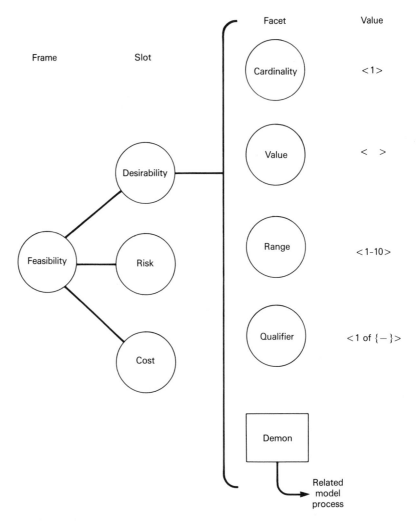

Figure 4–8   Graphic depiction of a frame (courtesy of Dan DeSalvo).

Issues.   As discussed earlier, there are a number of issues and questions related to the use of computer graphics, including the following:

- Is the use of graphics appropriate? Have the rules governing aesthetic considerations been consulted? Is the application in question better served by the use of text?
- "Junking up" screens should be avoided. Trying to present too much or unrelated data runs the risk of nullifying the intended purpose of graphics—to clarify. (See Figure 4–10.)
- Will graphics be available on all workstations on which the application is to

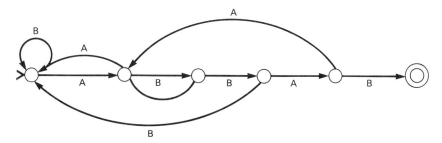

Figure 4–9 Graphic depiction of pattern-matching automation to find string 'ABBAB'.

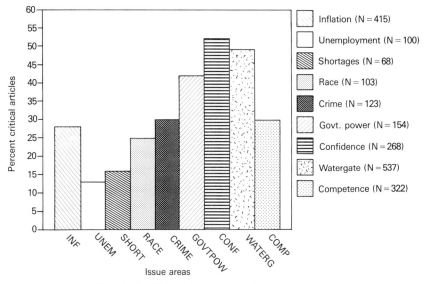

Figure 4–10 Chart junk. "This substance, clotted, crude lettering all in upper case sans serif; the pointlessly ordered crosshatching; the labels written in computer abbreviations, the optical vibration . . . " [7]

run? If not, then two separate user interfaces, one utilizing graphics and one making up for its absence, are required, along with the attendant overhead incurred in writing the extra interface.

Graphics Input Devices

Discussion

Examples. Graphic input (GIN) devices (see Figure 4–11) and cursors are numerous and are certainly not limited to expert systems. In fact, they can be used as a mechanism for "hooking" expert systems into other systems. Some examples are the following:

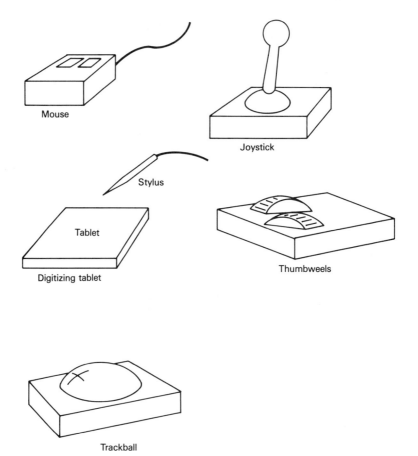

Figure 4–11   Graphic input (GIN) devices.

- A computer-aided design/computer-aided manufacturing (CAD/CAM) system uses a digitizing tablet with a template to allow a user to select symbols and locate them on a screen. The tablet also permits function selection to designate an orientation and size for the symbols.

- A personal computer drawing program uses a mouse and a symbolic metaphor for a cursor to aid the user in producing graphics. The user selects a function from a menu of options represented as icons. For example, to "paint," the user selects a paint brush icon and a color and paints lines, all using the mouse. The cursor is represented as a paint brush. (See Figure 4–12.)

- A developer's front end for an artificial intelligence shell system uses a GIN device and cursor to guide the system developer through the process of setting up a rule base and establishing an independent user interface. The GIN device and cursor are used to select functions from icon menus. For example, frames

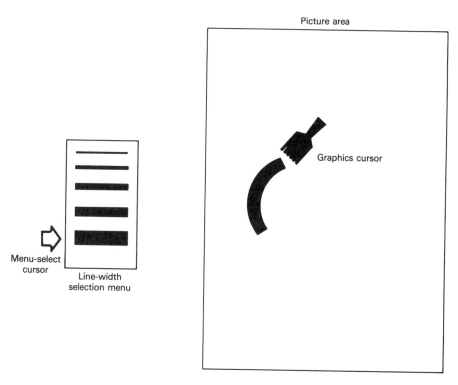

Figure 4–12   Paint brush metaphor.

are brought up as graphic structures. The developer uses the GIN device to select the portion of the frame to be filled in and uses the keyboard to enter the related text.

Issues.   The following issues apply to the selection and use of GIN devices in user interfaces:

- There is a tendency on the part of new devotees of GIN devices to get carried away. GIN devices are probably not the best choice for cursor position control on purely textual and traditional screens, for example. The TAB key works just fine and doesn't require sophisticated programming to control the speed with which the cursor races through form screens. The rule of thumb to follow is that if the field the cursor operates in is continuous (i.e., the cursor moves from pixel to pixel, not from field to field), then GIN is appropriate; if the field is purely discrete (the cursor moves from field to field, with textual content required), then GIN is probably a poor fit. In instances where both seem to apply, such as occurs many times in a PC drawing package, both keyboard input and a GIN device may be legitimately supported.

- Consideration should be given to the user community in GIN device selection. If the environment where the system is to be used is intense, noisy, and/or dirty, a breakable mouse on the end of an inconvenient piece of wire is a poor choice. A joystick would probably be broken in such an environment as well. Interested observers will note that many video games, designed for just such environments, limit themselves to the use of trackball GIN devices.

Color

Discussion.   Color is at once one of the most promising and one of the most abused tools available to the designer of a user interface. The problem seems to be that the novelty of color on computers, especially when related to its use in graphics, warps the otherwise sound judgment of system and application developers. There are a number of decisions to be made when considering the use of color as part of a human interface. The first, and in many cases the primary, decision is whether or not to use color at all. There are strong arguments that color confuses the user interface rather than facilitating its function. We will come upon this issue again later in this section.

Color is generally expressed in one of two ways: RGB or HST. RGB (red, green, blue) is a system in which any given color is a point within the unit cube defined with red, blue, and green axes. This system is fading in popularity due to its poor congruence with human color association. However, it was an early method for color expression on computers and is still fairly widely encountered, especially on personal computers. The HST (hue, saturation, intensity) system has a stronger human association. It can be drawn as a double cone with the upper cone inverted. Intensity is the vertical axis of the cone; saturation, or difference from a gray scale, is the horizontal distance from the vertical axis; and hue is the angular rotation of a point about the vertical axis, with blue, red, and green (the primary colors) at 120 degree angles from each other. (See Figure 4–13.)

Examples.   Examples of the use of color here will not be limited to those that are aesthetically pleasing. Both good and poor usage of color are illustrated, to reinforce the ideas expressed in the next section on issues.

- A bar chart is created showing the relative sales for four divisions of a company by quarter. Each region is depicted via a different color on the chart, thereby making it very easy to make sense of the chart.
- A graphics-produced map is used by a telecommunications company to depict the topology of the company's transmission network, as well as to show the dynamic status of links in the network. The said status is color-coded, red used to show blocked links, yellow for links that are experiencing difficulty, and green for links which are operating properly. Using this map, an operator can intuitively and quickly grasp the current status of the network, whereas it

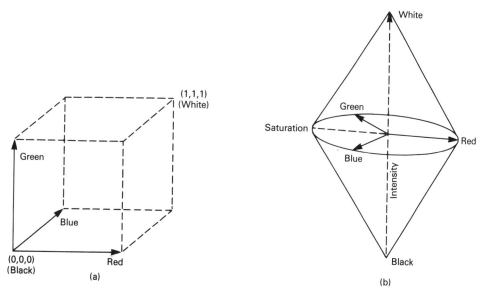

Figure 4–13 (a) RGB (red, green, blue) system, unit cube. (b) HSI (hue, saturation, intensity) color cone.

might take hundreds of pages of report sifting and many hours to comprehend the situation without the use of color.

• The developer of an application-building system for personal computers is using a window-management and graphics package which supports the use of color. On each screen, any element that differs logically from any other is shown in a different color. Customers asked to test the new interface, which is largely concerned with text entry and editing along with some control flows, complain about the "busy" nature of the screen, saying that their applications are harder to develop now than they were with an earlier monochrome version of the package.

• A graphic artist obtains a powerful personal computer with equally capable graphics and begins to explore various geometric forms as part of a presentation she is putting together. The package has enough colors that shades within a family of colors are readily supported. The customer sees the presentation and is surprised and delighted to learn that it was produced quickly and cheaply using the computer.

Issues.   Some issues related to the use of color are as follows:

• Does the interface need color? Interface developers should ask this question repeatedly and often. Does color add anything material to the interface? If the interface is primarily a model of a text processing system, what purpose can color serve other than to confuse? Following are some questions and rules to remember governing the selection of color as a tool:

—Will color add function or clarity to the interface?

—By contrast, will color make the interface harder to use?

—Are there parts of the interface for which color is inappropriate, even though its use is dictated for some of the interface?

—The operative rule for color selection should be "Use color only in those cases where it can add value to the interface." The default should be not to use color.

—Finally, color costs money with current technology, and more and better colors cost more money. Accordingly, target the use of color to the size of the checkbook of the customer.

● Use color according to human associations with it. One useful way of looking at color in this context is in terms of "warmth" and "coolness" [8]. Using color in this way allows emotional context to be put into a presentation. For example, "warm" colors such as red, yellow, or orange imply excitement and emotional involvement and ask for attention, while "cool" colors such as gray or blue present a more detached emotional content. Warm colors should be used where the user's attention is desired, such as in the displaying of alarms in a graphic depiction of an assembly line. Cool colors should be used where an item can be ignored by the user. In the earlier example of the window-management and graphics package, the use of garish and contrasting colors works against the interests of the package. The thing that should be of primary interest is the application being developed, not the support system.

● If color is to be employed, use it effectively. Some useful guidelines for the effective use of color are the following [9]:

FOR ADJACENT COLORS

● Use colors that differ significantly in hue (unless you are deliberately creating a shading effect). Yellows, greens, oranges, browns, and reds often go quite well together.

● Use complementary or "opposite" color pairs such as yellow and blue, red and green, or cyan and magenta.

● Avoid pairing intense colors that lie at or near opposite ends of the spectrum (e.g., intense red and purple). The eye has to refocus for the different wavelengths, and this can cause eyestrain. If you must display red with blue or violet, use unsaturated shades of each. (Your eyes will tell you when it hurts!)

● Avoid adjacent colors that differ only in the amount of blue in them. Because of blue's short wavelength, such colors may be difficult to distinguish from each other.

FOR LARGE SOLID AREAS AND BACKGROUNDS

- Use colors that are comfortable to the eye—blues, light grays, greens, yellows, and browns. Use other colors in unsaturated forms.
- Avoid highly saturated colors such as intense reds, blues, or purples, as well as "loud" colors such as magenta, chartreuse, or mustard yellow.

FOR EDGES AND OUTLINES OF LARGE AREAS

- Distinguish edges by both hue and brightness; it is difficult to distinguish edges on the basis of hue alone.
- Use white, yellow, blue, or green in less intense shades. Or use black as an outline color on pastel or unsaturated backgrounds.

FOR EMPHASIS OR TO GET ATTENTION

- Use bright, saturated colors such as reds, yellows, oranges, or greens.
- Use colors that differ significantly in hue and brightness from the surrounding areas.

FOR LESS IMPORTANT INFORMATION

- Use subdued tones with less than full saturation.

Animation

Discussion.   Simply put, animation is the ability to show the motion of an object or objects over time. A car can graphically be shown to be driving, a conveyor belt can be depicted in operation, and the gauges in a flight simulator can model the operation of actual gauges in an aircraft.

Because of this capability of showing motion, animation is another tool for the designer of a human interface that is gaining wider acceptance as personal computers and workstations become less expensive and more powerful. It is generally used to grab and hold user attention or to show the passage of time. It can be very effective in showing a process modeled in terms of time. Animation probably has the same capacity for eventual abuse as does color, but it has not been available long enough and it is currently too hard to use to have suffered extensively just yet.

Examples.   Some examples of the use of animation as part of a user interface are the following:

- As part of a presentation, a company logo is made to grow in size and spin on an axis as it is brought to an eventual site on the display screen. (See Figure 4–14.)
- Video games.

- Television advertisements showing characters and geographical movement as part of the product pitch.
- Process models, such as conveyor belts, robot arms, and control gauges.

Issues.   Issues related to the use of animation include the following:

- There is a strong sense of novelty associated with computer animation at the moment. In addition, the capabilities of computers to perform and assist animation are growing rapidly. As a result, there is a tendency to use animation to take advantage of this sense of novelty rather than for a specific and

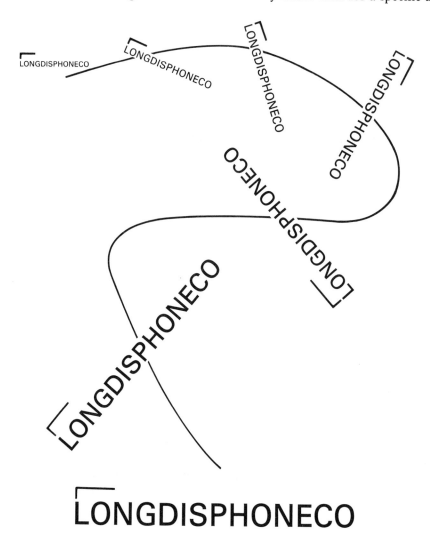

Figure 4–14   Animated company logo.

definable purpose. The developer should take care to apply the same principles of parsimony to the use of animation as he or she would to the use of color. Does the use of animation add anything of value to the user interface?

● Animation, even more than color, costs money. The more complex the animation, the more computer power is required. In addition, animation is difficult and expensive to program in many cases. Is it worth it?

Menus

Discussion.   Menus are formatted screens that are used to present information and specify commands to an application or system. They also have the capability of being linked logically into trees or networks of menus. This capability can provide a powerful and simple mechanism to a user for exercising a system. Menus can also be used within a windowing user interface management system (UIMS) to provide a very effective user interface for almost any system.

Examples.   Some examples of menu use in a user interface are the following:

● An application is divided into two subsystems, which in turn have several parameters to define their exact function. A user has a top-level menu which permits the choice of subsystem by numeric entry, as well as menus for each of the subsystems with field specification areas. (See Figure 4–15.)

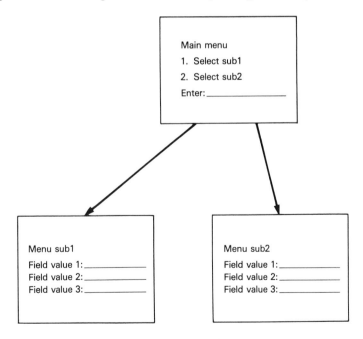

Figure 4–15 Subsystem selection via menus.

- A windowing system permits the creation and deletion of new windows within a current workstation session. This function is provided via pulling up a menu in an area of the screen and selecting a window type via a GIN device. (See Figure 4–16.)

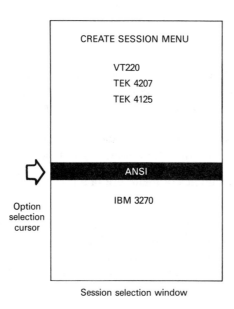

Session selection window

Figure 4–16 Window creation via window menu.

- A graphics editor available on a workstation has a function selection menu which consists of icons depicting various shapes available for use. Selection of a shape, such as a circle, curve, or polygon, is by using a GIN to move a cursor to the icon and then using the GIN input button to select the shape. (See Figure 4–17.)

Issues.   Issues related to the use of menus in a user interface include the following:

- While menus can greatly simplify both command entry and user presentation, they can also slow the interface down greatly. They are most useful when a user is first learning the ins and outs of a system, but they can bog a more experienced user down. When they are used in a hierarchical interface, the user should be provided an alternative form of command entry and menu selection, such as direct command entry or menu selection by name/number.
- Menus can also limit the flexibility to enhance or otherwise change a user interface. Not only is this true for the specific elements on the menu, but it is also true once the existence of certain menus is defined. If the functionality of the application dictates the creation of a new menu, the deletion of an old one,

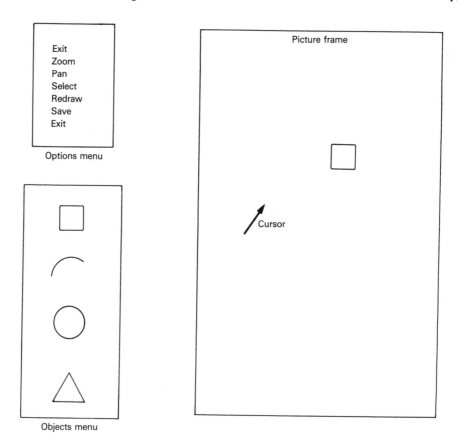

Figure 4–17   User interface for graphic drawing package.

or a different sequence of commands for invoking a menu, then a fair amount of work can be involved.

- Menus should have a strong set of functional associations. Indeed, in a manner analogous to modules in program development, they should be functionally bound. In other words, a single menu should perform the entirety of one function. Many transaction processing systems in fact limit the number of menus which may be associated with a single transaction to one. This limitation can be stifling, but should be considered nonetheless when developing a user interface.

- Subareas within a menu should be grouped together rather than placed at random on the screen. Also, similar functions should have similar input techniques. (For example, if command selection is by numeric key entry for a menu within a system, it should be by numeric key entry for all menus within that system.)

Many of the limitations governing the use of menus go away if a windowing system with a screen-location or icon menu-selection context is used. This allows the developer to avoid getting the user trapped at some level in the menu hierarchy without knowing where that level is.

Windows

Discussion.   Windows and window management are relatively recent developments in data processing. They were developed as part of continuing research in user interfaces and are some of the most powerful user interface tools available today for applications development.

A window is simply a logical area for information entry and display that maps to some portion of the display screen. It is generally invoked by a user input, an application context, or some other phenomenon such as a trap within an application. Windows may be linked to each other in hierarchical or network fashion in a manner similar to that used with menus. Windows vary in size, can be shrunk to and used as icons in many UIMS packages, and often support the use of graphics within the window environment. There is usually a programmer interface package for the developer to make window management a simple part of applications development.

A number of window management systems are available today with varying degrees of power and flexibility, and standards are only slowly emerging. The developer who uses a given system runs the risk of thereby becoming bound to a given hardware and/or software architecture. In most cases, however, the advantages supplied by windows outweigh any such risks.

Examples.   Some examples of window management and use are the following:

- A personal-computer-based drawing package permits the selection of options and assignment of characteristics for each option through the selection of menus by a GIN device and icon as part of the drawing process. The procedure is asynchronous in that it can occur at any point in the execution of the package.

- A network management system uses windows to present various aspects of the current network state. For example, one window contains a topological map depicting the network status, while other windows present an alarm content based on user selection of a node on the mapping window. (See Figure 4–18.)

- A UIMS permits associating windows with each element on a menu. Setting the cursor on a field and selecting a help function provides an informational window describing field use which does not affect the contents or context of the menu itself. (See Figure 4–19.)

Issues.   Some issues related to the use of windows are as follows:

- Selecting a UIMS often binds the developer to a hardware and/or software platform. If the benefits of this outweigh any risks, then the UIMS is generally used anyway.

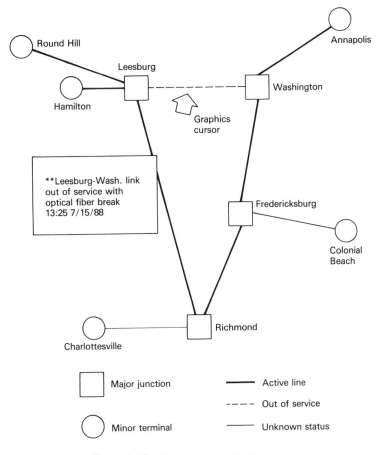

Figure 4–18   Network status via window.

- Windows are like menus in that any one window should do one task in its entirety; that is, the window should be functionally bound.
- Windows should be movable and sizable. They are a superset of menus in this context.
- If windows are used as part of a user interface, then they should be used consistently throughout the interface.

Icons and Symbols

Discussion.   Icons and symbols are simple programmatic ways to associate a function with ideas that are more commonly accepted. In the popular "office metaphor" environment available on the Apple MacIntosh computer, for example, file disposal is accomplished via a wastebasket icon, and other functions are accomplished in a similar manner.

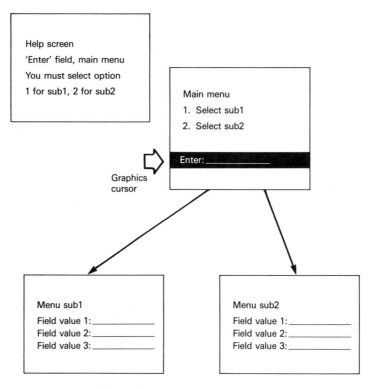

Figure 4–19   UIMS "Help" function.

Symbols can be built that fit almost any model. They are generally intended to be a simple representation of an element within the model.

Examples.   Some examples of icon and symbol use are the following:

- *Function and attribute selection within a graphics editor.* For example, the user may select to "spray" a line on the picture surface. This is accomplished via the selection of a spray-paint can icon and a line icon and then using the GIN device to make the line.

- *Function selection on a file-control menu.* For example, as mentioned earlier, file disposal can be selected with a wastebasket symbol, and archiving via a file cabinet symbol.

- *Showing network status via a symbol.* For example, a failed link can be shown by a symbol depicting a rope snapping or a fire burning.

- *Walking a menu tree.* In a system with a large number of selectable menus, walking the menu tree is accomplished via selection of a menu icon with the name of the menu within it. In this manner, a large number of menus can be presented to the user in a simple fashion.

Issues.   Issues related to icon and symbol use include the following:

- If symbols or icons are used, they should be used consistently. Thus, disposal should always be via the wastebasket metaphor if it is used anywhere at all for this purpose.
- There should be a strong intuitive association with a symbol or icon. This is not always easy to accomplish. If you examine the metaphors in your automobile, for example, it is not always easy to tell that the strange symbol on the temperature gauge represents a thermometer in water. Icons should not be force-fed to a system: if it is impossible to develop an icon that makes sense, do not use one.
- A catalog of symbols and icons should be developed across a family of systems to be used—not just because it's fun to make them.

Expert Systems and the User Interface

Expert systems are just a special case of a computer-based system or application in general. There are very few cases in which any one element of a user interface for an expert system cannot be used effectively in other types of systems, and vice versa. Computer platforms that support expert systems in many cases are powerful enough to provide a broad catalog of user interface tools, and indeed in many cases an expert system "shell" may go a long way toward defining the user interface itself. This simply means that the developer should pay great heed to the warnings throughout this section about letting the user interface drive the system.

Breaking Down the Interface

The specification of the user interface for a system should occur just after the system functions and flow are defined. This does not mean that a user interface model such as screens and menus cannot be used as a tool for system specification; rather, it means that the user interface model should not be permitted to define the actual user interface.

At a point in the system development, functions will have been bound into modules. These modules can be considered *nodes* in the user interface system. They can be invoked sequentially (as the result of context obtained from another node) or asynchronously (as the result of user specification or a program interrupt). This flow must also be considered as the user interface takes form.

Once user interface nodes are defined, the developer should document the characteristics of each node. Is the result quantitative information that can be effectively represented as a graph? Can and should it be shown using a picture? (For example, a reasoning frame can be shown very effectively with the use of graphics.) Does command entry apply, and what tool best supports it?

At the end of this process, all elements within the user interface should have been identified and described, and links between nodes should be identified and mapped to states in the superior or peer node.

Selection Tools

Selection tools can be easy or difficult, depending on the complexity of the system to be supported. Questions to be asked and answered as part of this process include the following:

- Which tools are supported on the system platform? If, for example, the developer is limited to the use of an ANSI CRT, then consideration of graphics, windows, icons, etc., is academic. Define the palette that is available. To what degree are these tools supported? Tool selection must proceed from the results of this sort of analysis.
- What are the simplest tools beyond which use does not add value to the system? Use these tools. If text entry or conversation is the simplest interface, use it. Use graphics and other tools selectively and only if they add value to the interface.
- What tools are consistent with other interfaces associated with the system? Try to keep interfaces reasonably consistent across generations of similar systems. (*Note:* This should not be taken to mean that a menu-driven system should always stay that way; instead, it means that a replacement for a menu-driven system that works well should map the user interface as strongly as makes sense into the functional breakdown of the menus.
- What tools are consistent with the available programming talent? Training people is fine, but the use of animation requires a different set of skills than does the use of menus and forms. Will you be entering a maintenance nightmare by adding "sizzle" to the user interface?

Defining the Interface

Once the system developer is at a point where the user interface can be designed, it is quite likely that the system functions are defined and well understood. The modules or nodes within the user interface selected can then be mapped to these system functions. In fact, this is usually the simplest and most straightforward way to proceed.

Once the user interface nodes are identified, the developer should use the criteria detailed in this chapter to choose tools to associate with the interface. The developer should bear in mind that at all levels the interface should be as consistent as possible and that the simplest tools and invocation of those tools will provide the easiest interface to use.

Rules for selecting the interface are as follows:

- Pick the simplest interface that applies. If command entry will do and is effective, use it.
- Use tools consistently. Do not, for example, use a menu at one level and command entry at another.

- If it will simplify the interface, use graphics. If it will help present the data, use graphics. If it will not help, do not use graphics.
- Under the same set of rules, use color, menus, windows, and/or icons. Use these consistently across all elements within the user interface.
- Ensure that the user interface provides for both novice and experienced users.
- Once you have a user interface that works well on a system, consider applying the work you have done to subsequent systems. You can only get better with time.
- Last but not least, be prepared to get rid of techniques that get poor user acceptance, regardless of how much they appeal to your personal taste. The interface is not for the developer; it is for the user of the system.

SUMMARY

This chapter afforded the following information to the reader:

1. A summary of user interface work and thought that have driven the industry to the present time.
2. A catalog of tools and techniques available to the developer of a user interface.
3. Some of the perils and pitfalls associated with those tools and techniques.
4. Some ideas about how those tools and techniques can be used in systems in general and in expert systems in particular.

It should be obvious at this point that much of the work in user interfaces to date has been technology-driven rather than dependent on hard sociological and psychological research. Presumably, as the catalog of tools grows, this will begin to change. There is wide disagreement on the effectiveness of many tools and techniques in use today. The pragmatic system developer will obey the principle of parsimony in all cases: the simplest interface is almost invariably the best interface. To gainsay MacLuhan [10], regardless of its power and ease of use, the medium (or interface) is *not* the message.

REFERENCES

1. Tanimoto, Steven L. *The Elements of Artificial Intelligence.* Rockville, MD: Computer Science Press, 1987, p. 6.
2. Ibid., p. 461.
3. Ibid., p. 69.
4. Hayes-Roth, F.; Waterman, D. A.; Lenat, D. B., *Building Expert Systems,* Reading, MA: Addison-Wesley, 1983, pp. 33–34.

5. Tufte, J. *The Visual Display of Quantitative Information,* Graphics Press, 1983, p 51.

6. Reilly, T. and Roach T., "Improved Visual Design for Graphics Display," *IEEE* Computer *Graphics and Applications,* Feb. 1984.

7. Tufte, *op. cit.,* p. 120.

8. Hobbs, *An Introduction to Computer Graphics,* Tektronix, 1985, p 54

9. Ibid., pp. 54–55.

10. MacLuhan, *The Medium is the Message.*

5

Applying Artificial Intelligence Techniques to Human-Computer Interfaces[1]

Diane H. Sonnenwald
C. Lynn Dolan

INTRODUCTION

The operations systems at Bellcore are applications that maintain, test, and configure customer telephone and data networks. Because current computer technology does not provide a single environment that satisfies all requirements for all operations systems, the applications must execute in different hardware and software environments. Even within homogeneous environments, interface commonality may not exist. This problem will continue to grow as the applications become more sophisticated and use new technology, such as Integrated Services Digital Network (ISDN) and fiber optics, and as intelligence migrates from host computers.

The diversity of hardware and software implies that users who need to access multiple systems may be required to use a diverse set of access devices[2] and that they may have to learn, and effectively remember, multiple interfaces. High access-device costs, high end-user training costs, and high end-user dissatisfaction with multiple interfaces provide motivation for exploring universal interface techniques.

Our proposed solution is a knowledge-based user interface management system (UIMS) that functions as an intelligent intermediary between applications and users. The exploratory UIMS provides consistent views across applications and systems and supports multiple presentation styles and knowledge acquisition tools that allow customization of the interface. Because these features are knowledge-

---

[1] A previous version of this chapter appeared in [1].

[2] The term *access devices* includes synchronous and asynchronous terminals, personal computers, workstations, printers, touch-tone telephone sets, and portable, hand-held devices.

intensive and data-driven processes, artificial intelligence (AI) techniques were used. These techniques include frame representation, object-oriented programming, and rule-based programming. Future work includes making the UIMS prototype suitable as a product and expanding the prototype to dynamically adapt to the changing experience levels of multiple users. Logic programming, truth maintenance systems, and hypothetical reasoning are techniques considered to support these enhancements.

In what follows, first the AI techniques used in UIMS are defined. Second, the UIMS architecture is introduced. Third, each functional component in the UIMS and the AI techniques used in the component are described. Finally, future enhancements and their possible implementation using AI techniques are discussed.

ARTIFICIAL INTELLIGENCE TECHNIQUES

To familiarize the reader with the concepts relating to AI and mentioned in the Introduction, each technique is described in this section.

Frame Representation

Frame representation languages provide a rich structural metaphor to capture the way experts typically think about their domains [2]. They also provide efficient, special-purpose reasoning techniques that are based on representational structures. These reasoning techniques are more direct than general methods such as logic. In addition, frames allow descriptive information to be shared among multiple objects and semantic integrity constraints to be maintained. This can reduce redundant and incorrect data in a system.

A *frame* is a data structure construct that can be used to describe the attributes, constraints, and type of a conceptual or physical object or object class. *Frame attributes* (also referred to as *slots* or *properties*) provide storage for variables that describe an object or object class represented by a frame. Attributes can have multiple values (the Choices slot on the object Menu could have seven values) and are used to describe further relational properties between objects. For example, an inverse slot is used to show that a subclass is the inverse of its class. In some frame languages, transitive, symmetric, and reflexive slots are also supported.

Links that represent class/member relationships between frames are used to build a prototype description of a complex object. The prototype description is used to generate descriptions of instances of the object. Links that represent class/subclass relationships between frames support definitions by specialization. That is, a general class definition is created, and then it is specialized by multiple subclass definitions. The types of class and attribute decompositions supported in most frame representation languages include disjoint decomposition (an object is either a User, Window, or Rule) and complete composition (an object is a User and a Domain Expert).

Facets are annotations on attributes. A facet can represent constraints on slot values, such as cardinality (the number of possible values) and value class (the permissible data types, data values, or Boolean values). A facet can also represent properties such as units of value, comments, date added, owner, and defaults.

Frame languages provide multiple *reasoning services*. Reasoning services are deductive retrievals that use inference techniques to deduce the values of an attribute when necessary. In frame systems, reasoning services are based on the structural properties of frames and their taxonomies. The types of inference supported through inheritance include the following:

- Structure and value inheritance: provided by class/subclass and class/member links.
- Integrity maintenance/constraint checking: provided by constraints coded in facets.
- Relational inference that includes
  —Complementation, e.g., $>$ is a complement of $< =$; at most one of these relationships holds between any two given objects. If $X > Y$, then X NOT $< = Y$.
  —Reflexivity: X is always, or never, related to Y.
  —Transitivity: if X is related to Y and Y is related to Z, then X is related to Z.
  —Symmetry: X is related to Y if and only if Y is related to X.

Object-oriented Programming Languages

Object-oriented programming languages enhance frame representation languages by supporting procedural attachment to objects (or frames) [3]. *Methods* are procedures that are attached directly to objects. Action is initiated by sending messages that request an action on objects. When an object receives a message, the appropriate method attached to the object implements the response. For example, a presentation object, such as a window, may be sent a display message from a program. The calling program does not have to make assumptions about the implementation and internal representation of the window; the display method attached to the window object provides the correct function execution to display the window. This principle is referred to as *data abstraction*. Messages are usually designed in sets that define a standard interface to objects. This allows different types of objects to respond to exactly the same protocols, in turn enabling programs to uniformly access objects in different classes. For example, display messages can be sent to windows, menus, and dialogue boxes. This concept is referred to as *polymorphism*.

Object-oriented languages often have rich behavioral properties. Methods can be shared through inheritance similar to the sharing of slots and slot values in frame languages. Methods attached to instances or subclasses will override methods attached to superclasses. Inherited methods also support a standard behavioral framework. When an object inherits a method, the variables in the inherited method are bound to local values in that object. In addition, methods support procedural specialization since programmers can specify when methods in sub-classes or instances should be executed before or after inherited methods. Methods are functions themselves and can send messages to objects.

In object-oriented languages, objects are defined in terms of classes that determine their structure *and* behavior. This is helpful when it is necessary to represent collections of things that interact. It also simplifies program testing and maintenance (in comparison to conventional languages) since all information about an object is physically located in one place. Through the use of standard message protocols, programs sending messages do not have to know about the classification, structure, or behavior of an object. Programs do not have to change, or even be recompiled, when methods are modified or when class relationships are changed. The standard messages are always uniformly interpreted. In some systems, only methods can change instance variables, thereby supporting data integrity.

Rule-based Systems

Rule-based, rule-oriented, or *production systems* consist of an unordered set of basic units, called *rules, production rules,* or *productions* [4, 5]. The rules express symbolic processing acts in *if* **X**, *then* **Y** structures. The left-hand side (LHS, pattern, or antecedent) of a rule describes a situation, and the right-hand side (RHS, action, or consequent) describes an action to be taken in that situation. Rules are stored, unordered, in production memory.

Structures representing physical objects in the problem domain and facts (i.e., declarative statements) about the objects are stored in data memory. Conceptual objects, such as goals, are also stored in data memory.

Control in a rule-based system is managed by an inference engine that deter-mines which rules are relevant to a given data memory configuration. The proces-sing cycle is referred to as a recognize-act cycle. In *forward-chaining systems,* the inference engine first matches the LHS of rules to current objects in data memory. When only one match is found, the RHS of the matched rule is executed. When more than one match is found, the inference engine performs conflict resolution to determine which rule should be executed. Conflict resolution is often based on the following:

- Order: execute the rule matched first.
- Recency: execute the rule most recently added to production memory.
- Generality: execute the most specific or least general rule.

In *backward-chaining systems,* the same cycle is performed, except that the RHSs are viewed as subgoals and are matched against data memory. The LHSs are instantiated when a match occurs. Thus, backward-chaining systems are referred to as goal-directed, whereas forward-chaining systems are referred to as data-driven.

Logic Programming

In *logic programming* logic is used to represent domain knowledge, and deduction is the problem-solving mechanism that acts on the knowledge [6–9]. The programmer's task is to describe a domain, not to define a set of instructions to compute an answer. Logic programming, therefore, is frequently referred to as *programming by description*. The description is comprised of a set of clauses from *first-order logic* that specify domain objects and relationships among them.

First-order logic includes the predicate calculus, which allows for objects and relationships to be expressed and manipulated. The predicate calculus has the following components:

- Sentential connectives (AND, OR, NOT, IMPLIES, and IS EQUIVALENT TO) that are used with simple propositions
- Inference rules for the propositional calculus
- Predicates (e.g., is strong, is wise)
- Quantifiers (universal and existential)
- Variables
- Constants
- Inference rules for the quantifiers

Besides the predicate calculus, first-order logic includes functions that return objects (e.g., sister of, record of) and the predicate EQUALS. The rules of inference are needed to manipulate the various components of the predicate calculus. Deduction is one type of inference. The most frequently used rule of deduction is *modus ponens,* which states that $(x$ AND $(x$ IMPLIES $y))$ IMPLIES $y)$. Deduction allows for the generation of new facts that can be used to infer more information. Another inference mechanism is *resolution*. Resolution states that given a clause C1 with a term P on the left-hand side, and a clause C2 with the term P on the right-hand side, a new clause C3 may be created that has as its left-hand side the union of the left-hand sides of C1 and C2 without the term P and has as its right-hand side the union of the right-hand sides without the term P.

In the logic programming language PROLOG, clauses have a left-hand side referred to as the consequent and a right-hand side consisting of antecedents. Facts are represented as consequents with no antecedents. Relations are described as an antecedent or group of antecedents that, when true, imply or invoke the consequent. If there is a clause with antecedents and no consequent, then at least one of the antecedents is false.

Resolution refutation assumes the negation of a theorem and tries to derive an empty clause using *unification*. Unification is the process of finding instantiations of variables that cause two atoms to be identical so that clauses can be resolved. This method guarantees that any conclusions drawn are correct, assuming that the premises are correct.

The PROLOG interpreter is a theorem prover. It is used with the domain description to draw conclusions and answer queries when presented with requests in predicate calculus format. The interpreter's basic strategy is exhaustive backtracking, which is accomplished by unification. As a result, multiple solutions to a query can be generated.

Using logic to represent knowledge allows the latter to be understood declaratively, while using deduction on the knowledge lets it be understood procedurally. In logic programming, new objects and relationships can be added without disturbing existing objects and relationships. Predicate logic is seen by many individuals as being a very natural and powerful knowledge representation language.

Truth Maintenance Systems

A *truth maintenance system* (TMS) is a justification-based belief revision system that supports problem-solving systems by providing *nonmonotonic reasoning* capabilities [10–13]. Nonmonotonic reasoning permits conclusions to be based on the absence of information to the contrary. Nonmonotonic proofs can be invalidated by the addition of new axioms, resulting in the need for conflict resolution. While the problem solver deals with the rules of the domain and generates new assertions, it is the responsibility of the TMS to record the assertions and the inferences that lead to them; i.e., the TMS updates the knowledge base of current beliefs based on the new information.

The data elements of a TMS are *nodes* and *justifications*. A node represents an assertion, rule, procedure, or other program belief. A justification is a list associated with a node that records the inference process used to derive the node. A justification is comprised of two sublists: the IN-list and the OUT-list. A node is considered valid (believed) when all propositions contained in the IN-list are IN (believed) and all propositions contained in the OUT-list are OUT (not believed).

There are two types of justifications: a *support list* (SL) justification and a *conditional-proof* (CP) justification.[3] The TMS uses only SL-justifications to provide *well-founded support* for a node. Well-founded support ensures that no node is believed because of circular reasoning. SL-justifications are used to represent the following types of deduction:

- A premise that is always believed is represented by a node with a justification that has an empty IN-list and an empty OUT-list, e.g.,

```
((premise-1)(SL()()))
```

---

[3] CP-justifications are comprised of a consequent node and two sublists. The nodes of these sublists are assumptions; thus, for the proof to be valid, the consequent must be IN whenever the nodes of the IN-hypotheses list are IN and OUT-hypotheses are OUT. CP-justifications are used as the justifications for contradiction nodes created in order for the TMS to remove an erroneous assumption. CPs also provide a control mechanism for developing structured explanations.

- A monotonic deduction has a nonempty IN-list and an empty OUT-list, and it is believed as long as all propositions of the IN-list are IN. E.g.,

$$((node-\underline{r})(SL\ (node-\underline{c},\ node-\underline{n})(\ )))$$

- In a nonmonotonic deduction, the justification of the node requires that all IN-list items be valid and all OUT-list items be OUT (not believed). The IN-list items can be viewed as the reasons for making an assumption, while the OUT-list represents the incomplete knowledge that authorizes the assumption. For example,

$$((node-\underline{a})(SL\ (node-\underline{c})(node-\underline{l},\ node-\underline{d})))$$

The TMS uses dependency-directed backtracking as the control strategy for conflict resolution. It is invoked when an assumption is proved false and the assumption was used as a justification that led to a contradiction. Dependency-directed backtracking has two significant advantages over the chronological backtracking that is used in PROLOG. The first advantage is that irrelevant assumptions are not considered. This is because only those assumptions that are part of the dependency trace of a node involved in the contradiction are considered. The second advantage is that the cause of the contradiction becomes part of the system knowledge, so that the contradiction is never rederived.

In sum, the following steps occur during dependency-directed backtracking:

1. A contradiction is identified.
2. The assumptions that resulted in the contradiction are collected. The backtracker assumes that the cause of the contradiction is the belief in a node that is based on incomplete knowledge. The backtracker assumes that all monotonically justified nodes are correct and searches only the set of nonmonotonic justifications.
3. This set of assumptions is summarized as a *NOGOOD SET* so that it can be used to prevent deriving the same contradiction again.
4. The NOGOOD SET is used to retract one of the inconsistent assumptions, thus eliminating the contradiction but retaining the knowledge about the inconsistent derivation.

TMSs are important to expert systems development because of the additional inference capabilities they provide, i.e., they allow an expert system to reason using assumptions and relieve the expert system inference engine from the burden of maintaining a consistent knowledge base. For example, default assumptions can be structured in the TMS by forming a proposition that is IN, where the support of the node is simply that alternative propositions are OUT. When any OUT-list propositions become IN, the default value is OUT and the alternative value is IN. When the default value causes a contradiction, the backtracker can cause the default proposition to be OUT by justifying at random one of the alternatives because its validation is simply the lack of belief in the other alternatives.

The TMS also provides an explanation facility for expert systems. Many times there is a need for an expert system to explain its conclusions in a well-structured and detailed manner for developers and expert and nonexpert users, and TMS justifications provide the knowledge needed to build explanations.

Hypothetical Reasoning

Hypothetical reasoning is the capability to reason simultaneously about multiple alternative solutions to problems. The *Assumption-based Truth Maintenance Systems* (ATMSs) were designed to support hypothetical reasoning [14–17]. An ATMS, like a TMS, is a component subsystem that works in conjunction with the problem solver. It creates, compares, and modifies alternative solutions simultaneously, allowing for inconsistency between the alternative solutions. In an ATMS, each node has a justification and an *assumption set* associated with it. The justification is the record of the inference process used to derive the node and is composed of an IN-list and OUT-list. An assumption set is set of beliefs or facts believed to be true based on the absence of contradictory facts. When a node has multiple derivations, each justification and its corresponding assumption set are recorded. A *context* also referred to as a *world* or *belief space* is the set of all nodes, primitive and derived, that are valid for a particular environment, or set of non-conflicting assumptions. Thus contexts represent the alternative solutions to a problem.

In hypothetical reasoning the problem solver informs the ATMS of each new derivation, and the ATMS then creates a new ATMS node for the derived fact. The ATMS node is then added to the appropriate contexts. The ATMS achieves efficiency by organizing the search for valid contexts in such manner as to begin with the most general inferences first. Thus, the number of rules executed and the contexts examined are minimized. Since the node justification retains the derivation process, nodes do not need to be rederived for each context in which they exist, and keeping environmental information in the node ensures that facts are shared across multiple contexts.

An ATMS does not explore any inconsistent nodes, i.e. nodes that do not share an environment. Thus, dependency-directed backtracking, the conflict resolution mechanism in a TMS, is not necessary in an ATMS. Also, the ATMS does not need to modify or add any node justifications in order to retract a contradiction, as is done in a TMS. The inconsistent information remains in the knowledge base, and the facts can be used for reasoning in other contexts.

ATMSs have proved to work well on design, planning, and scheduling problems because of their hypothetical reasoning capabilities. The properties of an ATMS that enhance hypothetical reasoning include the following:

- The ATMS can efficiently work on simultaneous solutions to a problem, thus making the comparison of possible solutions easy.
- The ATMS can quickly identify an assumption that causes a contradiction because it just does a direct comparison of environment sets. In a TMS a contradiction is actually derived.

- An ATMS has the ability to change quickly among belief sets. There is no need to create and insert justifications to negate current assumptions, and contradiction resolution does not need to be invoked.

UIMS ARCHITECTURE

The UIMS architecture is an open, modular architecture based on the separation of presentation and applications issues [18] and consists of the following three components:

- *Virtual user information (VUI).* Application-generated information to be presented to the user
- *Physical user information (PUI).* The actual, or physical, presentation of application information to and from the user
- *Interface agent (IA).* The intelligent intermediary that transforms VUIs to PUIs

Operations systems send VUI messages to the UIMS. The VUI messages contain application-specific data to be presented to the user and semantic attributes describing the data, but they do not contain information regarding *how* the data should be presented to the user. This is given in the physical presentation primitives, which are part of the PUI. Some examples of PUI primitives are yes/no dialogue boxes, multiple-choice menus, and single-choice menus. The IA maps VUI messages into PUI primitives. The UIMS architecture is illustrated in Figure 5–1.

The VUI-PUI mapping is based on knowledge about the type of application data that is to be presented to the user and on knowledge about the user skill level

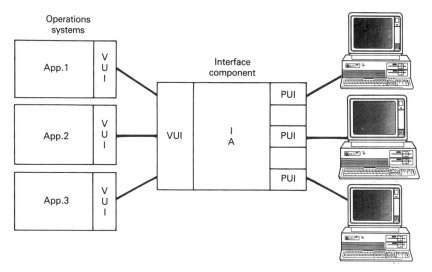

Figure 5–1   UIMS architecture. Applications communicate with the UIMS via a high-level protocol, the VUI. The IA interface component translates the VUI into PUI, a protocol used by access devices, e.g., terminals.

and task category. This allows presentation of consistent interfaces across multiple applications and multiple, consistent interfaces tailored to user-specific goals. The centralization of the interface design process in the IA allowed the Bellcore team to build a toolkit that domain experts can use dynamically, and directly, to manipulate the end-user interface.

Several advantages of the architecture are as follows:

- External and internal customers are provided with a standard interface (implemented in software) to multiple applications.
- An application interface standard that allows easier product integration is provided.
- The embedded base of applications and access devices is supported.
- The interface can be customized to meet unique needs of users.

IMPLEMENTATION OF THE VUI, PUI, AND IA

The VUI, PUI, and IA were implemented using the AI techniques described earlier. The prototype executed on a Symbolics workstation[4] and used the KEE[5] software package.

The VUI: Virtual User Information

Applications communicate with the UIMS via the VUI protocol, a high-level application-to-application protocol. The VUI protocol is a variable-length tag-value protocol that contains the application data to be presented to the user, together with semantic attributes describing the functionality of the data. It does not, of course, contain specifications for the presentation of application data. Figure 5–2 illustrates the protocol with a sample message. For purposes of simplicity, date-time stamps and other housekeeping tags have been omitted. This kind of message would customarily be displayed to users as illustrated in Figure 5–3.

```
(senders (ABC.APP), receivers (FRED),
    choices (selections (transactions (FIND.TN.STATUS,
                                        FIND.CP.STATUS,
                                        FIND.OE.STATUS),
             commands))))
```

Key	
Symbol	Meaning
Lowercase	Tags
Uppercase	Values

Figure 5–2 Sample VUI message. The VUI message is in a tag-value format. This message, sent from the "ABC" application to the user "FRED", indicates that the user may choose between several transaction selections or commands.

[4] The Symbolics workstation is manufactured by Symbolics, Inc.
[5] KEE is a trademark of Intellicorp.

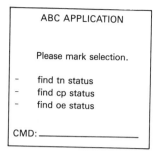

Figure 5–3 Customary screen display. The message in Figure 5–2 is customarily formatted by the application as a menu.

In the UIMS, tags and important values are permanently stored as frames and frame classes in a VUI.KB knowledge base. This knowledge base serves as a template for manipulating messages. When the UIMS receives a message, it creates temporary objects out of the data values and stores the objects in the VUI.INSTANCE.KB knowledge base. These objects are created as instances of the nearest tag in the message, or the value itself if it exists as an object in the VUI.KB. If the nearest tag does not already exist in the VUI.KB, the tag is created as a subclass of its higher level tag in the message. In addition, since concurrent messages are possible, all objects from a message are linked together. Figures 5–4 and 5–5 show the relevant portions of the VUI.KB and VUI.INSTANCE.KB.

The message objects in the VUI.INSTANCE.KB inherit slots and slot values from their parents in the VUI.KB. Typical slots on value classes include display names and data validation rules. Slots on tag classes vary. Slots on CURRENT.MSGS include time stamps and other housekeeping data, while slots on USERS include skill and task categories and security-related data. Other tag classes, such as TRANSACTIONS, do not have slots at this time. The role these slots and slot values play are described later.

Creating active message objects in a separate knowledge base allows us to delete messages easily when they are no longer needed. It also allows us to support multiple users, through the creation of user-specific VUI.INSTANCE.KBs.

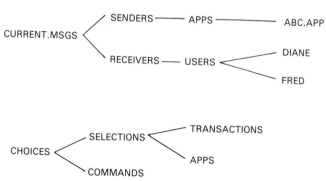

Figure 5–4 VUI.KB knowledge base. Information about VUI tags and values are stored in frames and frame classes, and the knowledge is used to manipulate messages.

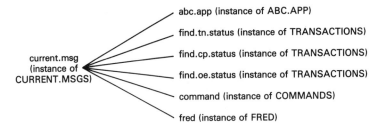

abc.app (instance of ABC.APP)

find.tn.status (instance of TRANSACTIONS)

find.cp.status (instance of TRANSACTIONS)

current.msg
(instance of
CURRENT.MSGS)

find.oe.status (instance of TRANSACTIONS)

command (instance of COMMANDS)

fred (instance of FRED)

Figure 5–5   VUI.INSTANCE.KB knowledge base. This knowledge base stores
VUI messages. Message values are instances of frames in the VUI.KB.

The PUI: Physical User Information

Presentation primitives and related knowledge are stored as frames in the physical user information knowledge base, called the PUI.KB. The objects in the
PUI.KB are high-level interface primitives such as data entry forms, yes/no dialogue boxes, and multiple-choice menus. The primitives are stored in a hierarchy
that allows efficient inheritance of attributes and methods. For example, all primitives[6] include generic window manipulation functions (methods), such as open,
close, scroll, shrink, reshape, and move. These are defined once on the parent class,
WINDOWS. In some instances, these basic functions are overridden by local functions attached to a specific primitive, or basic functions are enhanced by local
functions that execute before or after them. Figure 5–6 illustrates several primitives
currently defined in the PUI.KB.

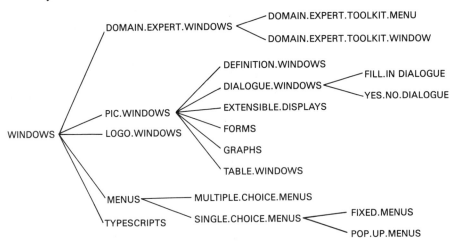

Figure 5–6   The PUI.KB interface primitives. The PUI.KB contains interface
objects, each of which has methods to construct and modify itself.

[6] Throughout this chapter, the terms *interface primitive* and *window* are used interchangeably.
This is motivated by hardware and software environments used in our work in which all interface
primitives are implemented as windows.

After a VUI message has been received and processed, the IA determines how the VUI information should be displayed to the end user. (See next subsection.) After the determination has been made, the IA sends a *create!* message to the selected interface primitive. Pointers to the appropriate VUI knowledge are also sent with the message. Each primitive has a *create!* method that processes the message. Each *create!* method is specialized for the interface primitive it is attached to, but conceptually each does the following:

- Creates an instance of the primitive using the appropriate VUI knowledge and data to fill in the window.
- Displays the new instance to the user.

The new instance is stored in a temporary knowledge base, called the PUI.INSTANCE.KB. The use of this knowledge base is analogous to the use of the VUI.INSTANCE.KB.

The IA: Interface Agent

The IA is the component that determines how the current VUI should be displayed to the user. It does not build the actual display, but passes that task via messages to the PUI knowledge base. The IA consists of the following components:

- Interface design rules.
- A knowledge acquisition toolkit.
- A control component

Interface design rules. The interface design rules in the IA knowledge base (IA.KB) determine how current VUI data are to be displayed to the end user. Each rule consists of an antecedent, or LHS, that checks the classification of the VUI, the end-user expertise level, and the end-user task category. Based on the results, it sends a *create!* message to an appropriate PUI primitive. The *create!* method attached to the PUI object is responsible for correctly building the display for the user. This arrangement enables knowledge about presentation selection to be separate from knowledge about presentation construction.

Figure 5–7 shows an interface design rule. Figure 5–8 illustrates several possible different presentations for the sample VUI. In the example, presentations are based on end-user expertise [19] and task category [20]. User expertise and skill levels are determined statically through user input, and may be changed at any time

If (there is a CURRENT.MSG)
   and (the components of the CURRENT.MSG are SELECTIONS)
   and (the SKILL.LEVEL of the RECEIVER of the CURRENT.MSG
     is 'intermediate)

Then (sendmsg 'multiple.choice.menus 'create!
   CURRENT.MSG .....)

Figure 5–7 Interface design rule (paraphrased). Interface design rules determine how current VUI data are to be displayed based on end-user expertise and task category.

```
┌────────────────────────────┐    ┌──────────────────────────────────┐
│    SELECT TRANSACTIONS     │    │     SELECT QUERY TRANSACTIONS     │
│                            │    │                                   │
│                            │    │                                   │
│       Find TN status       │    │                                   │
│       Find CP status       │    │                                   │
│       Find OE status       │    │                                   │
│                            │    │                                   │
│                            │    │                                   │
└────────────────────────────┘    └──────────────────────────────────┘
```

```
┌─────────────────────────────┐
│  CMD: _____   │
└─────────────────────────────┘
```

Figure 5–8 Multiple presentations for one VUI message. These presentations were built from one VUI message and vary due to different user expertise and task categories.

during a session. In Figure 5–8, a single-choice, textual menu with help messages is created for the novice clerical user, a command-line window is created for the expert clerical user, and an icon menu is created for the plant engineer.

The centralization of interface knowledge and design processing has allowed Bellcore to support multiple, consistent presentations across multiple applications. This centralization also means that the design knowledge can be more readily maintained and enhanced.

Knowledge acquisition tools. Separating knowledge about VUI messages, presentation selection rules, and presentation construction algorithms enables a knowledge-acquisition toolkit to be placed in the IA that allows authorized users, e.g., domain experts, to directly manipulate the end-user presentation by

- Modifying VUI attributes, such as display names.
- Updating interface design rules.
- Building new PUI primitives.

The VUI attributes that domain experts may update include field names, window titles, and help messages. The domain expert logs into the toolkit and selects the desired option from menus. The current field names, etc., are displayed, and the domain expert can interactively enter new names and save them. The updated data are stored in appropriate attribute-value pairs in the VUI.KB. From that point on, end users will see the new field name displayed in their windows. The update takes place immediately, without programming or compilation, and applies to all applications.

Domain experts may also modify interface design rules. After invoking the toolkit, the domain expert can simulate the running of any valid application at any particular end-user skill level or in any particular end-user task category. Actual processing windows are created for the domain expert, allowing the expert to modify the window and objects in the window using a mouse. Objects may be rearranged, reshaped, or deleted. For example, suppose it is not necessary for novice clerical users to execute the "find oe status" transaction shown in Figure 5–8. Then the domain expert could bring up the appropriate menu for novice clerical users and simply delete the presentation of that menu option. Note that neither the option itself nor knowledge about the option have been deleted; only the presentation of the option on the given menu type has been affected. After the domain expert saves the modified menu, novice clerical users will no longer be presented with the "find oe status" option.

The domain expert may also modify the presentation style by replacing an interface primitive selected by the interface design rules with another primitive. For example, a single-choice menu could be replaced by a multiple-choice menu. The domain expert can create instances of primitives dynamically, and then move items from other primitives to the new primitives.

When the domain expert saves the modified or new primitive, it is stored in the PUI.KB in a specialized class, indicating that a domain expert created the primitive. Information about the context of the original message, its intended audience, and the new primitive, is stored as a rule in a specialized rule class. This rule class is always activated before the general interface design rules are activated. Thus, the customized presentation always takes precedence over the standard interface presentation.

Control Component

Processing in the IA is controlled by sets of LISP functions that exist separately from the knowledge bases and rules. One set of functions controls user login and logout tasks. A second set controls interface design and rule processing by activating the rule set when VUI messages are received. A third set controls toolkit processing. The sets of functions do not execute in a hierarchical manner, but are activated in response to requests (mouse clicks) from the user. For example, the user may decide to log into another application, or to log in as a domain expert (to get into the toolkit). These are done by clicking on a UIMS icon and making the appropriate selection from the resulting menu. When the menu selection is made, the appropriate login function is activated. In this way, the user controls the system (instead of the system controlling the user through a fixed sequence of tasks.)

FUTURE DIRECTIONS

An implementation goal is to expand the UIMS prototype into a software product. Product implementation issues include software product portability and processing efficiency. Portability is important because customers have an installed base of mainframe, mini, and personal computers, and they may not want to purchase new hardware to support the UIMS product. Processing efficiency is necessary to meet customers' response-time standards. To address these issues, Bellcore is investigating the implementation of a VUI parser and IA interface design rules in PROLOG.

PROLOG is generally available on many mainframe, mini, and personal computers, and although there are some differences between PROLOG implementations, rules written in PROLOG could be ported among these types of processors.

To provide processing efficiency, VUI parsing rules and IA interface design rules could be combined into PROLOG clauses. Since VUI messages sent from applications have a hierarchical tag-value format, they can be viewed and processed as PROLOG facts. PROLOG clauses can then parse the facts and determine the best PUI interface primitive to display the VUI message. Figure 5–9 illustrates a PROLOG clause that processes the VUI message illustrated in Figure 5–2. Combining VUI parsing and IA interface design rules into PROLOG clauses eliminates the need to separately parse VUI messages, create temporary frames to store the parsed messages, and apply interface design rules. As a result, processing requirements may be reduced.

```
create.pui.object (multiple.choice.menus, Y, Z):-

    msg (sender (X), receiver (Y), choices (selection (Z))),

    user (Y (skill.level (intermediate))).
```

Figure 5–9 PROLOG parse and interface design clause. The PROLOG clause parses a VUI message and determines how the message should be displayed based on end-user expertise.

A research goal is to expand the UIMS prototype into an adaptive interface system that is able to dynamically select the "best" interface to the user [21]. At any given time, operations systems are accessed by users at a variety of experience levels, including parrot, novice, intermediate, advanced, and expert. As users gain experience with an application, their experience level changes. However, when a user's job function changes, or when a new version of an application is deployed, a user's effective experience level again changes. The challenge is to provide an interface that can dynamically adapt to changing experience levels to maximize end-user productivity and decrease user training costs.

To support a dynamic and adaptive UIMS, Bellcore is investigating using a truth maintenance system. A TMS would allow the UIMS to make assertions about the user's skill level and task category based on observed and unobserved user actions. But when the observation set changed, the assertions would change accordingly. Figure 5–10 illustrates a possible assertion and justification list that could be generated in the UIMS. The assertion and justification list state that the assertion "Fred's skill level is intermediate" is believed because Fred has used the system for thirty hours, does more than one task in the system, and has not requested detailed task explanations. But should Fred start requesting detailed task explanations, the assertion "Fred's skill level is intermediate" will be withdrawn—i.e., marked NOGOOD—and an earlier assertion that "Fred's skill level is novice" will be

Assertion: Fred's skill level is intermediate

Support-List Justification:

    IN-list:
        • Fred has 30 hours of system experience
        • Fred does more than one task

    OUT-list:
        • Fred requests detailed task explanations

Figure 5–10 Sample TMS node. The node illustrates why Fred's skill level is believed to be intermediate.

reinstated. This knowledge would then immediately be used by the IA interface design rules to select the appropriate interface presentation for Fred.

This example illustrates a simple reasoning process to determine a user's skill level. However, we envision that a more complex reasoning process that considers observed and unobserved user actions, user characteristics, operation systems semantics, system status, and management objectives will be needed to best determine a user's skill level and task category. Therefore, when a contradiction is observed, a TMS may have to do extensive (and time-consuming) backtracking to determine a new skill level or task category. Since the backtracking process could significantly increase user response time, we are investigating using an ATMS in addition to a TMS. The ATMS would create alternative solutions simultaneously; when one solution was found inconsistent, another solution could be immediately provided. This would eliminate costly backtracking, but it also introduces a new cost, i.e., the cost of creating and actively maintaining multiple solutions. Further investigation is needed to determine which implementation is most cost effective for the UIMS.

CONCLUSIONS

This chapter has presented an architecture for a universal interface to multiple systems. The architecture is characterized by the following features:

- The separation of presentation issues from application issues.
- A modular user interface management system that consists of virtual user information (VUI), physical user information (PUI), and an interface agent (IA).

The AI techniques used to build the prototype UIMS include frame representation, object-oriented programming, and rule-based programming. These techniques allowed us to maintain consistent interfaces across multiple applications and multiple, consistent interfaces tailored to user-specific needs. Future work includes the expansion of the UIMS into a product and into an adaptive interface management system that dynamically selects the best presentation style for users.

The AI techniques that may be used to implement these enhancements include logic programming, truth maintenance systems, and hypothetical reasoning.

ACKNOWLEDGMENTS

We would like to thank the reviewers of this chapter, including David Copp, for their helpful suggestions.

REFERENCES

1. Sonnenwald, D. H. "Applying Artificial Intelligence Techniques to Human-Computer Interfaces." *IEEE Communications* 26 (March 1988): 14–20.
2. Fikes, R. and Kehler, T. "The Role of Frame-based Representation in Reasoning." *Communications of the ACM* 28 (September 1985): 904–920.
3. Stefik, M. and Bobrow, D. "Object-Oriented Programming: Themes and Variations." *AI Magazine* 7 (Fall 1986): 40–62.
4. Brownston, L., Farrell, R., Kant, E., and Martin, N. *Programming Expert Systems in OPS5.* Reading, MA: Addison-Wesley, 1985.
5. Hayes-Roth, F. "Rule-Based Systems." *Communications of the ACM* 28 (September 1985): 921–932.
6. Genesereth, M. R., and Ginsberg, M. L. "Logic Programming." *Communications of the ACM* 28 (September 1985): 933–941.
7. Kowalski, R. A. "The Early Years of Logic Programming." *Communications of the ACM* 31 (January 1988): 38–43.
8. Cohen J. "A View of the Origins and Development of Prolog." *Communications of the ACM* 31 (January 1988): 26–37.
9. Colmerauer, A. "Prolog in 10 Figures." *Communications of the ACM* 28 (December 1985): 1296–1310.
10. Doyle, J. "A Truth Maintenance System." *Artificial Intelligence* 12 (1979): 231–272.
11. De Kleer, J., Doyle, J., Steele, G. L., and Sussman, G. J. "Explicit Control of Reasoning." In *Artificial Intelligence: An MIT Perspective,* vol 1, edited by P. H. Winston and R. H. Brown, pp. 93–116. Cambridge: MIT Press, 1979.
12. Martins, J. P. and Shapiro, S. C. "Reasoning in Multiple Belief Spaces." *Proceedings of the Eighth International Joint Conference on Artificial Intelligence,* Palo Alto, CA: Morgan Kaufman, 1983, pp. 370–372.
13. Martins, J. P. and Shapiro, S. C. "Theoretical Foundations for Belief Revision." In *Theoretical Aspects of Reasoning about Knowledge,* edited by Joseph Y. Halpern, pp. 383–398. Palo Alto, CA: Morgan Kaufmann, 1986.
14. De Kleer, J "Choices without Backtracking." in *Proceedings, AAAI-84.* Palo Alto, CA: Morgan Kaufman, 1984, pp. 79–85.
15. De Kleer, J. "An Assumption-based Truth Maintenance System." *Artificial Intelligence* 28 (January 1986): 127–162.

16. De Kleer, J. "Problem Solving with the ATMS." *Artificial Intelligence* 28 (January 1986): 197–223.

17. Filman, R. E. "Reasoning with Worlds and Truth Maintenance in a Knowledge-based System Shell." *Communications of the ACM* 31 (April 1988): 382–400.

18. Coutaz, J. "Abstractions for User Interface Design." *Computer* 18 (September 1985): 21–34.

19. Schneider, M. L. "Models for the Design of Static Software User Assistance." In *Directions in Human/Computer Interaction,* edited by Albert Badre and Ben Schneiderman, pp. 137–148. Norwood, NJ: Ablex Publishing Corp., 1982

20. Feldman, M. B. and Rogers, G. T. "Toward the Design and Development of Style-independent Interactive Systems." *Proceedings of Human Factors in Computer Systems Conference.* Gaithersburg, MD: March 1982, pp. 111-116.

21. Sonnenwald, D. H. "A Universal Interface to Multiple Operations Systems." *Proc. 1986 IEEE International Conference of Systems, Man, and Cybernetics,* New York: IEEE, 1986, pp. 732–736.

6

Building Expert Databases

Roy Rada

INTRODUCTION

An expert database system is a combination of a database management system (DBMS) and an expert system. In one simple view, the expert system performs intelligent processing on data stored in the DBMS. In a more complicated view, the DBMS and expert system are united so that large amounts of knowledge and data are stored and processed in an intelligent way.

A DBMS provides multiple users access to the same information for purposes of update and retrieval. It provides consistency, recovery, concurrency, and security control. Most DBMSs are tailored for large amounts of information—exceeding a gigabyte—and necessarily, the information resides on secondary storage. Expert systems apply expert knowledge to the solution of problems. There is a one-to-one correspondence between the human chunk of expertise and the rule or frame in the expert system which encodes that chunk. This relationship makes the expert system better able to present explanations to users as to why a conclusion was reached and helps experts update the knowledge in the system through time.

The distinction between databases and knowledge bases is based on the distinction between data and knowledge (see Table 6–1). "Data" tends to imply large volumes, while "knowledge" tends to imply small volumes. Data are typically valid or invalid, while knowledge is less precise. Data are atomic, but knowledge deals with large groups of atoms. From an operational point-of-view [7]:

> If you would let a clerk update it, then it is data. If you let experts update it, then it is knowledge.

Data	Knowledge
Large volumes	Small volumes
Verifiable	Imprecise
Atomic	Aggregative
Clerical	Expertise

Table 6–1   Data versus Knowledge.

For example, the statement that "a person is 50 years old" is data, as it can be verified and entered by a clerk. On the other hand, the statement that "50-year-old people are prone to heart attacks" is an evaluative statement that applies to large numbers of people and should be made by an expert. More abstractly, the distinction between data and knowledge can be related to extensional versus intensional information [53]. Extensional information is atomic intensional information schematic.

The knowledge level goes beyond the symbol or data level to deal with competence rather than representation (see Table 6–2). The knowledge level [49] has an agent that takes actions towards goals. The medium is knowledge, and the behavioral law is that agents will choose whatever actions take them towards their goals. There is no law of composition that would apply at the knowledge level for combining components into systems.

Knowledge level	
System	Agent
Components	Actions and goals
Medium	Knowledge
Composition law	None
Behavior law	Principle of rationality

Table 6–2   The Knowledge Level.

Expert databases are likely to be distributed systems and to require a level of analysis that goes beyond that of the knowledge level. One view of this level beyond knowledge is the organization level [26]. At the knowledge level an agent must conform to the principle of rationality, whereas the behavior of an organization is not bound to follow that principle. At the organization level (see Table 6–3), the contracts between agents and protocols of communication are important. This is in contrast to the knowledge level, which has no law of composition. At the knowledge level, functional performance is critical and time considerations are secondary; at the organization level timeliness is very important.

Organizational level	
System	Organization
Components	Agents
Medium	Transactions
Composition law	Contracts
Behavior law	Many

Table 6–3   The Organization Level.

PROGRAMMING AND HARDWARE ISSUES

Logic Programming and Databases

The interface between logic programming and databases is substantial [51]. Logic programming permits the storage of complex information structures as well as records, blends deduction and procedural constructs into information management, and unites intensional and extensional information. Logic programming extends relational databases via deduction, storage of non-record-oriented information, and the ability to combine schema, metadata, and constraints with database facts. However, a number of important database features, such as concurrency and indexing, are not typically available in logic programming systems. The selection of Prolog by the Japanese Fifth Generation project has stimulated interest in logic programming as a way to deal with both knowledge-base issues and database issues [14].

New primitives in Prolog could support various database activities, such as improved query handling, data modeling, and integrity constraints. It is hard to write programs declaratively, and large Prolog programs often depend on procedural features. But the apparent declarative and procedural interpretations of a Prolog statement may vary. Accordingly, a modification to Prolog, called Syllog, has been developed which lessens this declarative-procedural disparity [65]. Syllog forms a syllogistic, expert-system-like user interface to a relational database. Syllog uses a mixed backward-and-forward chaining approach and can handle a spectrum of recursive queries over a relational database.

Database systems and logic programs handle facts and their retrieval well. To deal with differences in time, however, new modal operators must be introduced. Modal logic deals with necessity and possibility. A modal proposition is called *necessary* if it is satisfied in all worlds, and *possible* if it is satisfied in some. A collection of worlds is hypothesized, and accessibility relations connect the worlds.

The unbound variable of logic programming provides many of the properties one wants in modeling the unknown value in a database. While the notion of generalization in databases is frequently restricted to "is-a" hierarchies, in logic programming a variety of concepts relate to generalization. Generalization reduces the distinction between extension and intension. Consider, for example, some different degrees of specification about universities:

> university (name, city, number of students, endowment)
> university (name, College Park, 40,000, endowment)
> university (Harvard, Boston, 10,000, millions)

Logic programming supports this spectrum naturally, so that intensional and extensional information can coexist.

Logic programming does not handle some fundamental database activities very well, e.g., secondary storage. DBMS techniques, like tree-based structures for range queries and hashing techniques for exact-match queries, are being applied to Prolog work in order to improve the storage capabilities of Prolog systems. Prolog systems were not designed to support multiple users, but this is also being investigated.

The connection between an existing logic language and a DBMS helps solve the storage problem. One simple example of such an architecture is the PROSQL interface between Prolog and SQL/DS [51]. SQL/DS resides on its own virtual machine, as does Prolog. A query in PROSQL is a special Prolog predicate of the form sql(sql-command). When the predicate is encountered during Prolog execution, the SQL command is executed on the virtual machine, and the results are made available to Prolog. Another example is the Logic Workbench, which includes Prolog, a database manager for Prolog clauses, and an interface between Prolog and a DBMS [51]. The interface supports the translation of Prolog queries into DBMS commands. Special features allow for pattern retrieval, nested transactions, and flexible dynamic indexing.

Object-Oriented Databases

Object-oriented programming offers the opportunity to unify approaches taken with databases and logic languages. Object-oriented systems allow the treatment of data and metadata in a common way and may represent a unifying paradigm in the design of expert databases [67]. Simula 67 manifests the data abstraction and encapsulation which are at the core of the object-oriented approach.

In Simula 67 every object has a set of operators which operate upon the state of the object. Objects communicate and perform all computations via messages. Smalltalk is the best known of the object-oriented programming languages [29]. In Smalltalk a message identifies a target object, a method, and arguments. Objects are organized into classes that specify the methods which an object uses to respond to a message. Classes are organized hierarchically and inherit the methods of their superclasses. Object-oriented programming allows operator overloading, so that the same symbols can denote different operations on different data. The late binding of methods means that programs can be augmented without recompilation.

While in relational systems tuples can only be distinguished on the basis of their values, in object-oriented systems a unique identifier is assigned to each entity. By referring to entity identifiers, relationships among entities can be easily supported. Thus, object-oriented programming can be used to implement the semantic data models of entity-relationship models. The paradigm provides referential transparency because any change in an entity value is automatically seen by all entities which refer to it. Version management is also facilitated: old versions of objects can be archived with a time stamp, and the old environment can be reestablished by calling forward the objects from a certain past time.

The object-oriented approach fits nicely with the frame-based approach of artificial intelligence. In a frame system the properties of an object are described through slots in a frame. Each slot may contain factual data, pointers to other objects (frames), or procedures which are invoked when certain messages come to the frame. Of particular importance are the "is-a" relationships between frames which define a hierarchy and allow the inheritance of slot values from one frame to another.

While most application programming languages are procedural, data manipulation languages are usually declarative because being so facilitates indexing and secondary storage management. In the object-oriented language OPAL, the syntax is extended with a declarative notation [67]. The syntax is

< bindings > < result expression > < selection condition >

For example, the statement

< professor:p, student:s > < p name, s name >
< (s of p) and (s publications > p publications) >

might be posed to a database about students and professors to find out whether any student has more publications than his professor.

To develop expert databases, the data dictionary has to be manipulated in a more dynamic way than has usually been possible with DBMSs. In an object-oriented database the atomic data and the data dictionary can both be captured as objects. Properties of the objects are used to describe both the characteristics of classes of data structures and the characteristics of specific instances of a class. The properties of objects also specify how they will behave when manipulated by database operations. These behavioral properties can be seen as constraints, not only static ones on integrity and security, but also dynamic constraints that change objects due to update operations. Since constraints can be specified explicitly, they can be interpreted and themselves manipulated. PRISM is a constraint-based, object-oriented system [67], the specification of which is stored in a knowledge base of constraints. When PRISM is initiated, the constraints are loaded and a knowledge kernel is constructed. The user can interact with PRISM so as to specify a database schema, populate a database, and specify new constraints.

Hardware

A number of computers have been developed with expert systems as a target application, as have machines with databases as a target application. Some examples of an expert system machine are:

- The Symbolics 3600, which supports the programming language Zeta-lisp, the knowledge-engineering environment KEE, and the mathematics expert system MACSYMA, and
- the Xerox Dandelion, which runs the Interlisp-D programming environment and the object-oriented programming language LOOPS.

Neither Symbolics nor Xerox have paid much attention to database problems. One of the more commercially successful database machines has been the Britton-Lee IDM 500. The IDM has a central processor and a large disc. The IDM relational database language can interface to an expert system that runs on another computer but which regularly sends queries to the IDM. To allow large expert databases to run more efficiently, new hardwares are being tested. For example, in one type of semantic network hardware, each node in a network is maintained by a dedicated microprocessor [22]. Queries are addressed simultaneously to all nodes, and the nodes respond with answers.

Database languages based on the relational calculus have significant attributes in common with symbol manipulation languages like LISP. Each relational calculus operator can be put in an almost one-to-one correspondence with a LISP operator. This perspective encourages examination of the intersection between artificial intelligence and databases and may help both fields exploit existing parallel-processing hardware. With content-addressable memories, for instance, a query could be sent to all of memory in parallel. If a null answer to the query was returned, then the program could issue another query to determine what rules (also represented as relations in the content-addressable memory) might apply to the query. The appropriate rules could then be processed in various parallel ways [57].

A systolic array machine differs from a content-addressable machine in that processor-memory units are connected only to neighboring units. The systolic array implementation particularly lends itself to problems in which a stream of data comes off some device and can be funneled through the array. Several systolic arrays could be attached to a disc and allow rapid processing of all the data on the disc for certain types of problems.

EXPERT SYSTEMS VERSUS DATABASES

Evolutionary Approach

At a recent international workshop on expert databases there was a discussion about four ways to connect artificial intelligence (AI) with DBMS methodologies [7]:

1. Loosely couple an existing AI system with a DBMS.
2. Extend a DBMS by enhancing it with AI functionality.
3. Extend an AI system so that is has DBMS functionality.
4. Tightly integrate DBMS and AI capabilities.

The first three of these approaches are evolutionary, whereas the fourth is revolutionary. In the discussion at the workshop, John Mylopoulos said,

I prefer a revolutionary approach that would address issues at the knowledge level. We need to jump from the more computational level of DBMSs to the higher knowledge level, just as we needed to jump from assembler language to higher level languages many years ago.

The strong response from the other participants in the workshop was that the revolutionary approach is ill-advised at this time. Ron Brachman noted that DBMS developers wanted to make their systems more user friendly and intelligent, but that their solutions must be computationally practical and the best techniques for them may not even come from the AI field. Michael Brodie said that we don't know enough about AI to start a revolution, and Gio Wiederhold added, "The revolutionary approach is currently impossible since there are still significant problems with large databases."

Database management systems based on the relational approach have gained wide popularity due to their ease of use and data independence. The main limitation of the relational model is its semantic scantiness, which inhibits the natural expression of some relationships. This problem has motivated the introduction of semantic data models. Some approaches to semantic data models entirely abandon the relational database approach, but adding semantic data model characteristics to relational systems takes advantage of the many successes of relational technology [63].

In DBMS terms, the database administrator is responsible for maintaining data quality. Expert systems do not have a direct analogue to the database administrator. Systems like MYCIN and INTERNIST partially automate the data quality function of the database administrator. The maintenance of certainty factors enables a system to interpret the quality of its own data. A system which has beliefs about the external world can apply those beliefs to an evaluation of the credibility of new data. DBMSs pay great attention to the physical integrity of data, while expert systems focus on the logical integrity of data. Accordingly, database systems are more advanced in implementation, while expert systems may have more sophisticated data semantics. While developers of DBMSs pay attention to data security and privacy, developers of expert systems are concerned about legal liability for incorrect decisions by their systems.

Inference Efficiency

In expert systems searching serves making inferences, but in DBMSs searching is for the purpose of query evaluation. While expert system methodologies allow for many different types of inference, one of the most common is deductive inference. In deductive inference, axioms represent the current knowledge, and a formula with a free variable is to be deduced from the axioms with certain values for the free variables. Thus, consider the two axioms

owner(toy, John) or owner (toy, Sue)   (1)
and
not(owner (toy, John))   (2)

Given the problem of determining who owns the toy, which may be expressed as owner(toy, x), deductive inference can determine that x is Sue. While demonstrating that owner(toy, Sue) is true is straightforward in this case, in the general case deductive inference can be very costly. When the axioms contain variables, then a proof that a formula holds under the axioms requires that all possible interpretations of the axioms be considered. The number of interpretations is an exponential function of the number of variables. For instance, for a set of axioms that includes owner(x,y), every instantiation of x has to be tried with every instantiation of y in the course of finding sets of instantiations (or models) which would hold true for all the axioms and against which every proof must be tested. For inferential search, it is not sufficient to demonstrate that a formula holds for one specific interpretation, because it must hold true for *all* valid interpretations. While there are heuristics for expediting the proofs, these second-level demonstrations make inferential search potentially very costly.

The companion to inferential search in expert systems is query evaluation in database systems. But query evaluation is based on a database which is fully instantiated. Thus, it is not necessary to test all possible worlds under which the axioms might hold. For instance, if the database simply says owner(toy, John) and the querist asks for the owner of toy, then the response is constrained by the value of owner(toy, John). In general, query evaluation is orders of magnitude faster than deductive inference. In one approach to building expert databases expert systems are used only for tasks that require deductive inference, although the expert system modules may access information from the databases. In either case, where feasible, computational burdens are moved to the database systems [1].

Interfaces

Given a model with an expert database (EDP), an interface, and a person, we can vary any of these three components so as to get a different view of the issues confronting designers of EDBs. The people using a given EDB have different goals. The content expert wants to interact with the EDB in the course of updating its knowledge, the client or end user wants to benefit from the knowledge stored in the computer, and the clerks interact with the EDB so that they can enter various kinds of routine data into it.

The interfaces to the EDB should vary according to the type of user. The expert wants to see a different aspect of the system than does the clerk; a natural language interface might help naive end users; graphical interfaces help encode information at various levels.

The convenience with which a user can express his or her requests to a system is a key factor in determining the user's satisfaction with the system [19]. One of the chief challenges to the improvement of these systems is to make the front end accept queries posed in something close to natural language. The natural language processing approaches typically require a dictionary, a grammar, and a semantics. By using the semantics of a database, a query processor can be relatively robust without the development of other extensive knowledge bases [31]. In some cases this semantics is a separate set of rules built onto the database [20]. In general, the domain-specific information should be isolated from the universal syntactic and semantic information [40], and an expert system plus a database from a certain domain may provide this domain-specific information.

In relational DBMSs the formats for displaying data are usually rigid—rows and columns. In knowledge-based systems, the data or knowledge is more complex and deserves display strategies that go beyond the tabular. A system has been constructed atop Smalltalk to permit varied graphical views of complex objects. The system is called SIG, for *Smalltalk Interaction Generator* [67]. SIG produces displays based on descriptions encoded in class types (a class characterizes a set of objects). A class can have multiple display types which are separately invoked, depending on the state of the objects which are to be displayed. One example of a display type for a tree is indented, outline form, while another example is a graph.

HYPERDOCUMENTS

The knowledge acquisition bottleneck hinders expert system builders. One of the attractions behind expert databases is that existing databases may provide information to fuel the expertise of the system. Alternatively, database techniques offer to expert system developers ways to structure and access large amounts of expertise— assuming the bottleneck of acquiring the knowledge can be overcome. But these two links, namely, one where vast expertise is encoded and the other where data become knowledge, are both tenuous—i.e., the link between data and expertise or between experts and explicit rules is weak. For these reasons, hyperdocuments become an attractive approach to expert databases. The amount of document material on computers is enormous; the word processing and publishing booms have seen to this. Text is more meaningful to people than raw data. Expertise, to the extent that it is "encoded," is more likely to be represented in documents than in computer rules. By putting extra links between portions of documents so that readers can get special views of the knowledge in the documents, writers or editors create hyperdocuments and something akin to expert databases.

Support Software

Hyperdocuments are defined as having the following three key components [16]:

- A database of document material.
- A semantic net that connects document components.
- A mechanism for traversing the document via its semantic net.

The term "hypertext" is a synonym for "hyperdocument," with the interpretation that the text can include graphics. Researchers have been testing prototypes of hypertext for over two decades, but only in the past few years have commercial versions of hypertext support software become widely available. Two of the first widely distributed hyperdocument systems, Hypercard and Guide, are intended to be used in homes. KMS and HAM are examples of systems that are targeted for business audiences.

Hypercard is delivered automatically with every new purchase of a MacIntosh microcomputer from Apple Corporation. Hypercard takes advantage of the user-friendly interface of the MacIntosh and also incorporates most of the features of MacWrite and MacPaint [30]. Thus, the average user has simple tools for text and graphics. Portions of a document are created on cards, each of which fills the screen of the MacIntosh. So-called buttons may be inserted in a card to connect it to another card.

When a Hypercard button is activated, another card is usually brought to the screen. However, the designer of a Hypercard document has the option of attaching a procedure to a button. Procedures are written in an object-oriented programming language which treats each card as an object and allows inheritance along links created by the buttons. Apple Corporation has put considerable emphasis on a connection between Hypercard and video discs.

Guide began as a research project at the University of Kent in Canterbury, England, in 1982 [9]. The aim of the Guide developers was to display documents on computer screens in as ideal a way as feasible. The first implementations were on UNIX workstations, but subsequently Office Workstations Limited translated key features of the original system so that it worked on microcomputers, including the MacIntosh and IBM-PC.

Guide has several types of buttons:

- *Replacement* buttons implement embedded menus [36] which, when selected with a mouse, lead to an in-line replacement of the material linked with them. The intent is that the replacement material will expand on material around the button.

- *Note* buttons are an extension of replacement buttons, but display the additional material to which they point in a separate window of a split screen and keep it there only as long as the mouse is activated over them.

- *Reference* buttons cause a jump to a different point of the document or point to a new document. They have a goto effect unlike that of replacement and note buttons (both of which keep the original material surrounding the button on the screen).

The Guide developers feel that goto-type buttons may lead readers into dark corners and would like to know how readers could be guided so as not to get lost as they follow the gotos.

KMS is a commercial hyperdocument system for networks of heterogeneous workstations. It is a successor to the ZOG system developed at Carnegie Mellon University from 1972 to 1985 [3]. For simplicity of presentation, in this section ZOG will be considered an early version of KMS). The 1972 version of KMS provided a uniform menu-selection interface to various computer programs. By 1983 a version of KMS was launched with the USS Carl Vinson, a nuclear-powered aircraft carrier.

This version supported an interactive management system for analyzing and tracking complex tasks and an interface to an expert system. KMS is based on frames which incorporate units of text and pointers to other frames [42]. The database consists of interlinked, screen-sized workspaces. While any kind of link can be used, KMS particularly supports hierarchical links. Users interact with the database by navigating from frame to frame, manipulating the contents of frames, creating new frames, and invoking frames. KMS's quickness depends on the graphics performance of the window system and the speed of the storage device, but response times under one second are typical. KMS provides to a community a single, logical database, physically distributed across multiple workstations and file servers on a network. The author/reader transition is automatic, and any changes to a frame are saved as soon as the frame is exited. Tools also exist for allowing characteristics of one frame to be inherited by another and for importing material from other sources, such as text files, into frames.

The Hypertext Abstract Machine (HAM) from Tektronix is a general-purpose hypertext storage system [11]. HAM can be used as a base engine for other hypertext systems. While most hypertext systems emphasize the application and user interface layers, HAM addresses the storage model. HAM stores its database in a centralized file server and doesn't interfere with the other distributed file system functions of a network. The HAM storage model is based on five objects: graphs, contexts, nodes, links, and attributes. A graph is the highest-level object and, in its turn, contains contexts. Each context has one parent context and zero or more children contexts. This type of hierarchical structure is fundamental to both HAM and KMS. Contexts contain nodes and links, and attributes can be attached to contexts, nodes, or links. Also, HAM provides filtering mechanisms that allow predicates on contexts, nodes, links, and attributes to specify what objects from the database should be viewed. A version history is maintained such that earlier versions of an object can be viewed. The version history for a HAM object is updated each time the object is modified.

There is great interest in methods of translating documents which have been stored on the computer for linear publication into hyperdocument form. Some way to automatically impart structure to documents is needed. The Thumb system is designed to work with existing documents but to have them appear as hypertext to the user [52]. The text is represented by a passage tree and a passage-dependent network. An expert in the domain of the document must read the document and interact with Thumb in the course of building the passage-dependent network. In the Prototype Electronic Encyclopedia, and encyclopedia has been converted into a hypertext system [66].

Collaborative Creation of a Hyperdocument

Honeywell's Los Angeles Development Center (LADC) for documenting the Control Program-Six operating system allows access to documentation by several methods, including demand printing, electronic distribution, and direct querying of the database [34]. It would be impossible to make timely updates of documentation available to the readership without the document database. Furthermore, the document database simplifies the maintenance of documentation. At LADC, from the moment a software product is conceived, the responsible programmer records thoughts in a file and a message is broadcast to other programmers that the file exists. Then, once a consensus has been reached on the design of the software, writers begin working with the programmers to determine the content of the documentation. As the product solidifies, the writers transfer existing information from programmers and customers into the documentation. As assessment of various technical publication departments of computer and industrial firms has shown that the average cost to produce camera-ready masters for technical publications is about 250 dollars per page. At LADC the average cost for the same product is about 80 dollars per page. For reasons such as these, collaborative document creation is an important topic. At Xerox PARC, an experimental meeting room called the Colab has been created to study computer support of collaborative problem solving in face-to-face meetings [60]. The system supports simultaneous entry of text by arbitrarily many people and attempts to facilitate group face-to-face construction of outlines and documents from scratch.

An electronic textbook was implemented for the information systems course taught at George Washington University. Since the textbook was directly related to the course topic, the intent was to have the students experiment with it in their assignments, as well as use the textbook content for their reading assignments. The system was implemented as a relational database under SQL/DS. One of the goals was to have multiple users access and update the semantic net for the book. The student was expected to

1. Read a textbook online.
2. Improve the textbook by inserting and evaluating segments.
3. Create the semantic net through which the book could be browsed.
4. Experiment with the hypertext.

So the student was reader, writer, reviser, publisher, and scientist all at the same time—call this kind of user a *participator.*

In one experiment, half the participators indicated paragraphs that they didn't like by entering the unique identifier of the paragraph and typing "bad". The other half of the participators not only chose paragraphs which they didn't like but also explained on the computer why they didn't like each paragraph. The simple "bad" votes were not as helpful as the more detailed comments. Almost all the comments fell into one of two types: the paragraph is poorly written, and the content of the paragraph is inappropriate. A poorly written paragraph could of course be reworded: if the content of a paragraph was inappropriate, more radical changes were needed.

One of the major goals of the experiment was to have the participators create a semantic net as an index to the textbook. The four relations in the semantic net were:

- Hierarchical(term, hier_term), representing a hierarchical relationship between term and hierterm.
- Synonym(term, syn_term), meaning that term is a near-synonym to syn_term.
- Otherwise-related(term, other_term), meaning that other_term is associated in a nonhierarchical way with term.
- Point(term, Unique_Identifier), meaning that the text paragraph identified by Unique_Identifier is about the term.

Through a combined view of two or more relations, such as hierarchical and point, a user could follow a semantic net concept to the text about that concept.

Each participator's contribution to the hierarchical, otherwise, and synonym relations was evaluated on a three-point scale:

- +1, or good, if the relation was clearly appropriate.
- −1, or bad, if the relation was clearly inappropriate.
- 0, or ambiguous, if what the participator meant could be good or bad, depending on context.

The hierarchical and synonym relations had approximately the same number of good and bad answers, and their number of good answers was greater than that of the otherwise relation and their number of bad answers was less. These results can be interpreted by saying that the definitions of the hierarchical and synonym relations are relatively well established and the participators are better able to understand and implement them. The hierarchical relation often carries the property of inheritance or set inclusion.

The preceding suggests two major directions of research. The first concerns the guidelines which are needed to help people create semantic nets for documents. The second requires people to interact with one another through comments in the hypertext and expert databases. The general principle is that knowledge on the computer can be used to stimulate people in the course of their interactive elaboration of that knowledge.

The writing of hypertext may be more time-consuming than the writing of ordinary text because it requires the development of a semantic net which is not required for ordinary text. But the same tool, namely the computer, which makes hypertext desirable for the end user can also be turned into a labor saver for the development of hypertext. While the use of hypertext systems for office paperwork is important, the appropriateness of such systems for education and software engineering also merits attention. The principles and products which are developed should be applicable to a variety of problems concerning knowledge creation. This is true whether the knowledge is represented in a computer program prepared by a software firm, a scholarly paper written by a group of students, a patient record developed by a medical staff, or a financial analysis developed by an investment firm. Since all these knowledge-generation activities may be currently done with the assistance of the computer, it is reasonable to expect that an improvement in methodology might be commercially exploitable in the short run.

BUILDING A MEDICAL DOCUMENT EXPERT DATABASE

Investigations into what is wanted of office computer systems have revealed that knowledge bases are required to meet many of the tasks that the office workers would like the system to perform [32, 66]. Furthermore, the most common use of office computer systems involves documents. Accordingly, an intelligent interface to a document retrieval system requires knowledge about both the documents and the users [12, 64]. How to build, store, and retrieve this knowledge is itself a major problem. This section explores the role of relational database management systems in building and storing knowledge bases that may serve as indices to other information.

Thesauri and Merging

A popular approach to research in document storage and retrieval involves the use of word frequencies to characterize documents [56]. However, the concensus is that more than word frequency can be useful in helping to manage document information systems [5]. An alternative method of storing and retrieving documents relies of the indexing of those documents into terms of a thesaurus [37].

A thesaurus is a set of terms that point to *hierarchical, synonymous,* and *otherwise-related* terms [18]. The effectiveness of a retrieval system is largely dependent upon the document classes in it, and these classes are determined by the labels assigned to them from the thesaurus. A thesaurus is thus a type of knowledge base, although it exists primarily to provide a vocabulary and a hierarchical structure [55].

Thesauri use the elements, sets, and associations of some semantic data models [8]. The inheritance properties [62], which are seen as critical to a robust office information system [2], are fundamental to the character of thesauri. The taxonomies behind thesauri have been used in one form or another in artificial intelligence, programming languages, and databases for over a decade because their generalization/specialization hierarchies facilitate description and prediction [6]. In an organization with many different collections of information, ways to connect this information should allow each group in the organization to retain substantial autonomy, while permitting the various groups to share data as easily as possible [33]. Given different information retrieval systems, each with a thesaurus as part of its front end, the linking of these retrieval systems requires the linking of the different thesauri [48].

Thesaurus integration is a process in which multiple thesauri are merged or linked together by common terms. Merging allows a searcher to locate the proper search terms for a concept within multiple databases [59]. Thus, a user can enter a term or concept and move from that term to the appropriate descriptors for each database. The objectives of database management systems include [27]

1. Making an integrated collection of data available to a wide variety of users,
2. Providing for quality and integrity of the data, and
3. allowing centralized control of the database.

Merging thesauri or knowledge bases involves the following similar features:

1. The objective of merging knowledge bases which index data is to make data available to a wide number of users.
2. One of the difficulties in this merging is to resolve the conflicts which can occur when two different systems disagree on the relationship which should exist between two terms.
3. The merged knowledge base can be controlled from a centralized site.

As database work becomes more complex, more sophisticated methods for ensuring integrity and maintaining central control are needed. For instance, in the modeling of time in databases, it becomes important to decide when two versions of data created at different times are equivalent [35]. This problem is connected to that of determining when two concepts in different knowledge bases are equivalent.

A Particular Thesaurus

The National Library of Medicine (NLM) has long been concerned with the development, maintenance, and improvement of document retrieval systems [38]. NLM is responsible for MEDLINE, a computerized bibliographic listing of over six million documents from the biomedical periodical literature [41]. Each bibliographic reference to a document is associated with a set of indexing terms from a thesaurus or knowledge base called the Medical Subject Headings (MeSH) [43]. A trained indexer scans a document and assigns indexing terms from MeSH based on a set of rules. MeSH brings the vocabulary of the indexer and searcher into coincidence. A search on MEDLINE can be performed for documents represented by indexing terms satisfying any Boolean combination of terms in a query. Thousands of queries are hand-encoded into MeSH each day from users around the world. MeSH contains about 100,000 concepts in a nine-level hierarchy. Near the top of the hierarchy are terms like "anatomy," "disease," and "chemicals."

NLM is trying to extend the use of MeSH by connecting it to other thesauri and information systems. The Library of Congress maintains a massive thesaurus, called the Library of Congress Subject Headings, and a mapping has been made between that thesaurus and MeSH. This mapping is to allow people searching for documents through either the computerized Library of Congress system or MEDLINE to be able to access material simultaneously from the other system

[44]. NLM is also trying to connect the genetics database, called GenBank, to MEDLINE. Part of this connection has involved a mapping between the keywords of GenBank and MeSH.

At Harvard Medical School the students are being introduced to a new mode of education that focuses on tutoring, self-pacing, and computers. Each student is provided with a personal workstation that facilitates communication with other students, with faculty, and with databases. The students are expected to take advantage of the computer to help themselves organize the vast amount of information that goes along with a medical education. MeSH is being explored as a tool to help this organization of information. Researchers at Harvard have developed a program that runs on a microcomputer and provides an environment wherein the user may explore the MeSH vocabulary by browsing its hierarchical structure [4]. The system is being augmented with terminology and techniques that make it increasingly useful to students who want to learn about medical care and organize their own library. The medical school staff indexes all lectures, laboratory exercises, and patient cases with a controlled vocabulary based on MeSH.

Knowledge-building Experiments

The strategies for semiautomatic augmentation of MeSH have focused on finding the similarities between MeSH and other thesauri and then exploiting the differences [25]. Thesauri are rich in hierarchical relationships but poor in other kinds of relationships. In the medical domain there are several computerized knowledge bases which are rich in nonhierarchical relationships. One such knowledge base, called "Current Medical Information and Terminology" (CMIT), gives the etiology, signs, symptoms, laboratory findings, and more for each of about 4,000 diseases [24]. The addition of such information to MeSH could be useful in many computer tasks, such as expectation-based parsing. If a parser first detects terms relating to the etiology and symptoms of a disease in a paper, then the parser might expect that that disease will be discussed in the paper.

Algorithm.   An attempt to store MeSH in a frame-based [23] language on the VAX 11/780 running UNIX bsd4.2 failed due to memory overflow problems. Database management systems were then considered as a way to overcome the memory management problem. In constructing a large knowledge base, one may establish a data model, and then estimate the final size, of the knowledge base [50]. With these estimates in hand, one may then determine the basic hardware and software resources that are needed. The medical knowledge base used in such an experiment requires at least 25 megabytes of storage. The relational data model seemed adequate to represent the knowledge bases [15]. To facilitate transportability to other development environments, and to avoid building a new relational DBMS, a commercially available system was chosen.

The Systematized Nomenclature of Medicine (SNOMED) is a 50,000-term thesaurus that is used in the indexing of patient records [17]. The contents of MeSH,

CMIT, and SNOMED were analyzed for both the kinds of information present and the relationships between pieces of information. Then, a relational data model was developed to reflect the information and relationships contained within each of the three knowledge bases. The data models are in a form such as

(Disease | Disease Name, Etiology, Symptom, Sign)

which states that the **Disease** relation has as its attributes *Disease Name, Etiology, Symptom,* and *Sign.*

To combine the knowledge bases, components of one knowledge base are mapped to components of another. The mapping is accomplished by representing the component knowledge bases as semantic nets and then mapping the edges in the semantic net to entity-attribute relationships in the relational model. Merging is initially accomplished by identifying the edges and nodes that the component knowledge bases have in common, based on lexical matches. Disease attributes or semantic primitives are determined, and then inheritance properties are used to find additional points of connection among the knowledge bases.

The hardware for this experiment included

- A VAX 11/780 superminicomputer running the UNIX bsd4.2 operating system, with a Britton-Lee Intelligent Database Machine attached as a back-end processor, and
- An Apollo DN3000 workstation, running the UNIX bsd4.2 operating system with an experimental relational DBMS.

Many routines were built with the high-level software tools available within the UNIX operating environment. MeSH, SNOMED, and CMIT were read from flat files into the two relational DBMSs with these tools alone. Although both relational DBMSs used somewhat different query languages, the data models were the same. As expected, the back-end database machine responded to requests significantly faster. On the other hand, the software utilities ran much faster on the Apollo workstation than on the multiuser VAX 11/780 superminicomputer. With a UNIX-based front end to the IDM, complex database operators are expressed easily, but even the simplest procedural function becomes impossible to compute. This limitation forces much of the computation to be done on the host, thus reducing the benefits of off-loading and creating unnecessary communication costs [63]. The Apollo workstation and relational DBMS approach had several advantages over the IDM approach for a single user—namely, that there was no time- or space-sharing and the interface supported better graphics. To graphically depict the hierarchical structure of diseases in MeSH, CMIT, and SNOMED, a modification of a program originally posted on USENET [28] was developed.

Results.   The merging algorithm maps many of the MeSH terms to CMIT diseases based on lexical matching alone. It is able to iteratively suggest another set of diseases which may be mapped into the knowledge base, based on the inheritance properties of nodes. At this point, intervention of a human expert becomes necessary in choosing which CMIT diseases to add to the knowledge base. However, the algorithm becomes increasingly sophisticated in its suggestion of which diseases to add to the hierarchy, as each additional disease added to the knowledge base increases the average number of semantic primitives which can be viewed as inheritance properties for each node. Thus, the system "learns" from a human expert which diseases might be most appropriately mapped to a specific root-to-leaf path [54].

From the clinical standpoint, the construction of a robust medical knowledge base is a key issue for medical expert systems [10], the development and maintenance of which are labor intensive. Given a set of attributes describing a patient, the preceding system is able to provide a list of diseases which are related to those attributes but is not able to make a specific diagnosis. This sort of system is most useful in establishing a differential diagnosis for an unusual constellation of patient complaints, but not in the diagnosis of a patient with a set of common complaints. For example, the unusual triad of "diarrhea," "dyspnea," and "headache" is only associated with the rare kyanasur forest disease. However, each of the attributes "diarrhea," "dyspnea," and "headache" taken alone is common.

Directions.   MeSH is based on the occurrence of terms in the documents being indexed. Since it is reasonable to suppose that querists would tend to use the same terms as the authors of the documents, grounds exist for driving the parser of queries from MeSH. With some simple parsing rules and a heavy reliance on the thesaurus from which indexing was done, one may obtain a simple but highly portable natural language–processing front end to a document system. This approach of simplicity together with a purposefully highly restricted natural language domain has been applied successfully elsewhere [21].

The first knowledge-base merging strategy was to merge two subtrees with synonymous roots by connecting the two synonyms to the same concept and bringing the children of each root under one root. What should happen, though, when one of the children has a synonymous uncle after the merge? If one thesaurus says that x is broader than y, but another thesaurus says that x and y are siblings, then an inconsistency has occurred. Heuristics to properly handle such situations are not necessarily straightforward.

The algorithm for merging may be viewed as an intensional database, with the thesauri themselves being the extensional database [46]. In this way, one can build databases of rules for merging databases [45]. Ultimately, these databases might be applied to themselves so as to obtain a true learning program [58]. The principles underlying semiautomatic construction of medical knowledge bases may be portable to other knowledge domains. Other efforts at medical knowledge acquisition have had the computer interact with experts to collect rules or analyze patient data to deduce patterns [39]. The effort reported in the preceding paragraphs takes advantage of existing computerized knowledge bases that are used in medicine and asks how they can be put together [25].

A TRANSPORTATION EXPERT DATABASE

The control of ship harbor operations involves large amounts of information and intelligent processing [57]. Useful information about a ship includes the ship's name, radio call signal, size, shape, weight, maximum speed, harbor location, cargo, and sailing schedule. Furthermore, the database may associate textual and photographic information with each ship, and details of the harbor, such as its location and the status of piers and work crews, must be available. Not only should queries to the harbor system be answered straightforwardly from information in the databases, but the system should be able to make intelligent inferences. For instance,
IF

1. The location of a ship is requested,
2. The system doesn't have the current location explicitly stored, and
3. The system knows that yesterday the ship left a certain harbor and maintains a certain average speed,

THEN the system should, with some knowledge of travel and a map of the seas, be able to compute where the ship is likely to be today.

One proposed approach to facilitating the assessment of the harbor involves the daily collection of aerial photographs of the harbor. In this way, reported schedules of travel and cargo could be compared to what was shown in the photographs. Each day several ships enter and leave the harbor. To identify each ship in the photograph involves first detecting the ship from the background and then comparing that ship with a file of ships. This operation would require many man-hours each day, and the possibility of automation is appealing. To store a high-resolution harbor image on the computer would require about a megabyte of memory. Over a thousand photographs could be stored on an optical disc. The matching of parts of one photograph with parts of another photograph (such as that of a ship in one photo against a ship in another photo) would be improved by spatial reasoning. Spatial reasoning uses the spatial properties of objects to deal with such visual phenomena as lighting and rotation [57]. Other knowledge-based approaches would take advantage of the constraints introduced by what is known about the photographs to reduce the search for a correct match.

The harbor expert database system might store information about ships in predicates such as "docked(Titanic, pier 13)". Rules may also be represented in the system, to allow the answering of queries by deductive inference. For example, a rule might say "if (arrived(ship y) and empty (pier z) and type-pier(ship y, pier z), then pier-assignment (ship y, pier z)," which basically says that a ship will be assigned to the appropriate vacant pier. Since the rules may not always hold, certainty factors could be attached.

In the traditional approach to representing this database, there might be a photograph file, a ship file, and an event file, and complete inverted indices would be created for each of these files. These inverted files are large and can be converted into more efficient structures by introducing ship classes and event scripts. Several ship classes, such as pleasure ships, tankers, and tugboats, could be distinguished by physical characteristics and behavior rules. A particular ship would inherit all the characteristics of the class of which it was a member. An event script would represent a time sequence of reported events. Such an augmented index offers major savings in memory costs.

CONCLUSION

An expert system contains knowledge for a domain and mechanisms to process that knowledge. The knowledge in expert systems is typically represented by rules and frames, and an inference engine is built into the system. A database management system records the extension, or detailed data points of reality. Transitions across states of time are performed by application procedures. Since both general knowledge as in expert systems and detailed knowledge as in databases are needed to solve complex problems in specific domains, a unified approach is highly desirable.

Researchers in database systems are now focusing on ways to capture more semantics in their schemata. Expert system researchers are struggling with ways to handle applications that require large numbers of existential facts. The incorporation of concepts from both the database and expert systems sides can occur at different levels. At the symbol level, structures are advocated which can handle both data and rules and which can be extended to the knowledge level. However, the advantage of combining knowledge about facts with facts also has disadvantages. In reality, different types of people deal with facts than with knowledge, and this distinction might be meaningfully extended to the corresponding computer programs. Data are handled by clerks, while knowledge is manipulated by experts. The goal should be not only to build a large and fast system, but also one whose components take advantage of the natural divisions in the world.

The traditional relational DBMS can be used in a more knowledge-intensive way. Rather than dealing strictly with data, the DBMS can be designed to emphasize knowledge. Thus, many of the objectives of DBMS methodology can be reinterpreted and used in artificial intelligence work [13]. There is also much interest in the augmentation of database schemes for the handling of large knowledge bases [61].

A typical homogeneous approach to the database-cum–expert system challenge uses logic programming, particularly Prolog. Prolog permits easy management of facts as well as knowledge. Its pattern-matching and inferencing mechanisms are well suited to applications with small amounts of information. But for large applications, Prolog alone is unsuitable because it does not handle data on external devices and because it makes tailoring of the data versus knowledge processing awkward [47].

In the heterogeneous approach, the expert system interfaces with the database system. The difficulty with this approach is just that the two methodologies are presently very different. The putting together of database and expert system technology should include the development of highly effective storage structures on the one hand and a hierarchy of abstractions about data and knowledge on the other hand. Progress in the arena of merged database–expert system tools will also require a better semantics of how facts and rules should be processed in fast, expert ways.

The fact that databases and expert systems are fundamentally information-rendering systems makes feasible a bridge between the two. To build expert databases, one can

1. Start with a database and augment what happens to the data by connecting the database to an expert system,
2. Start with an expert system and broaden its applicability by attaching it to a database, or
3. Start from scratch and design a unified database-cum–expert system.

The third approach is of greatest interest to researchers. But the first two take advantage of the very important information that has already been collected on the computer and lead to systems that can quickly play a role in the everyday world.

ACKNOWLEDGEMENTS

Thanks to Dan de Salvo for inviting me to submit this chapter. My appreciation also to the many students who contributed to some of the hyperdocument and knowledge-base merging experiments described here.

REFERENCES

1. Smith, John Miles. "Expert Database Systems: A Database Perspective." In *Proceedings from the First International Workshop on Expert Database Systems,* edited by Larry Kerschberg, pp. 3–15. Menlo Park, CA: Benjamin/Cummings, 1986.
2. Ahlsen, Matts, Bjornerstedt, Anders, Britts, Stefan, Hulten, Christer, and Soderlund, Lars. "An Architecture for Object Management in OIS." *ACM Transactions on Office Information Systems* 2, (1984): 173–196.
3. Akscyn, Robert, McCracken, Donald, and Yoder, Elise. "KMS: A Distributed Hypermedia System for Managing Knowledge in Organizations." *Hypertext '87.* Chapel Hill, NC: University of North Carolina Press, 1987, pp. 1–20.
4. Barnett, G. O. "An Interactive MeSH Environment." *NLM Contract Report PO #467-MZ-600562,* August 1986.
5. Blair, David, and Maron, M. E. "An Evaluation of Retrieval Effectiveness for a Full-text Document-retrieval System." *Communications of the Association for Computing Machinery* 28 (March 1985), pp. 289–299.

6. Borgida, Alexander, Mylopoulos, John, and Wong, Harry K. T. "Generalization/ Specialization as a Basis for Software Specification." In *On Conceptual Modelling*, edited by J. Schmidt, pp. 333–356. New York: Springer-Verlag, 1984.

7. Brodie, Michael, Balzer, Robert, Wiederhold, Gio, Brachman, Ron, and Mylopoulos, John. "Knowledge Base Management Systems: Discussions from the Working Group." In *Proceedings from the First International Workshop on Expert Database Systems*, edited by Larry Kerschberg, pp. 19–33. Menlo Park, CA: Benjamin/Cummings, 1986.

8. Brodie, M. L. "Association: A Database Abstraction for Semantic Modeling." In *Entity-Relationship Approach to Information Modeling and Analysis*, edited by Peter Chen, pp. 577–602. Amsterdam: North Holland, 1983.

9. Brown, P. J. "Turning Ideas into Products: The Guide System." *Hypertext '87*. Chapel Hill, NC: University of North Carolina Press, 1987, pp. 33–34.

10. Buchanan, B. and Shortliffe, E. "Major Lessons from This Work." In *Rule-Based Expert Systems: The MYCIN Experiments of the Stanford Heuristic Programming Project*, edited by E. Shortliffe, pp. 669–702. Reading MA: Addison-Wesley, 1984.

11. Campbell, Brad, and Goodman, Joseph M. "HAM: A General-purpose Hypertext Abstract Machine." *Hypertext '87*. Chapel Hill, NC: University of North Carolina Press, 1987, pp. 21–32.

12. Michael Caplinger, "Graphical Database Browsing." *Proceedings of the Third ACM-SIGOIS Conference on Office Information Systems*, October 1986, pp. 113–121. Also published as SIGOIS Bulletin 7, 2.

13. Cercone, Nick, and McCalla, Gordon. "Accessing Knowledge through Natural Language." In *Advances in Computers*, vol. 25, edited by M. Yovits, pp. 1–99. New York: Academic Press, 1986.

14. Clocksin, W. F. and Mellish, C. S. *Programming in Prolog*, New York Springer-Verlag, 1981.

15. Codd, E. F. "A Relational Model of Data for Large Shared Data Banks." *Communications of the Association for Computing Machinery* 13 (1970): 377–387.

16. Conklin, Jeff. "Hypertext: An Introduction and Survey." *Computer* (September 1987): 17–41.

17. Cote, R. A. "Architecture of SNOMED: Its Contribution to Medical Language Processing." *Proceedings of the Tenth Annual Symposium on Computer Applications in Medical Care*. Washington: IEEE Computer Society, 1986, pp. 74–80.

18. National Library and Information Associations Council. *Guidelines for Thesaurus Structure, Construction, and Use*. New York: American National Standards Institute, 1980.

19. Culnan, Mary. "The Dimensions of Accessibility to Online Information: Implications for Implementing Office Information Systems." *ACM Transactions on Office Information Systems* 2, (1984): 141–150.

20. Damerau, Fred. "Problems and Some Solutions in Customization of Natural Language Database Front Ends." *ACM Transactions on Office Information Systems*, 3 (1985): 165–184.

21. Epstein, Samuel. "Transportable Natural Language Processing through Simplicity—the PRE System." *ACM Transactions on Office Information Systems* 3 (1985): 107–120.

22. Fahlman, S., Hinton, G., and Sejnowski, T. "Massively Parallel Architectures for AI: NETL, THISTLE, and Boltzmann Machines." *Proceedings of the American Association for Artificial Intelligence* (1983): 109–113.

23. Fikes, Richard, and Kehler, Tom. "The Role of Frame-based Representation in Reasoning." *Communications of the Association for Computing Machinery* 28 (Sept 1985): 904–920.

24. Finkel, A., Gordon, B., Baker, M., and Fanta, C. *Current Medical Information and Terminology.* Chicago: American Medical Association, 1981.

25. Forsyth, Richard, and Rada, Roy. *Machine Learning: Expert Systems and Information Retrieval.* London: Ellis Horwood, 1986.

26. Fox, Mark S. "Beyond the Knowledge Level." In *Expert Database Systems,* edited by Larry Kerschberg, pp. 455–463. Menlo Park, CA: Benjamin/Cummings, 1987.

27. Fry, J., and Sibley, E. "Evolution of Database Management Systems." *Association of Computing Machinery Computing Surveys* 8 (1976): 7–42.

28. Gillam, April. "Tidy Tree Plotting." *Article 4775 of Net.sources,* El Segundo, CA: The Aerospace Corporation, 1986.

29. Goldberg A., and Robson, K. *SMALLTALK-80: The Language and Its Implementation.* _____: Addison-Wesley, 1983.

30. Goodman, Danny. "Hypercard." *MacIntosh Today,* 11 August 1987, pp. 60–64.

31. Hafner, Carole, and Godden, Kurt. "Portability of Syntax and Semantics in Datalog." *ACM Transactions on Office Information Systems* 3 (1985): 141–164.

32. Harris, Sidney, and Brightman, Harvey. "Design Implications of a Task-driven Approach to Unstructured Cognitive Tasks in Office Work." *ACM Transactions on Office Information Systems* 3 (1985): 292–306.

33. Heimbigner, Dennis, and McLeod, Dennis. "A Federated Architecture for Information Management." *ACM Transactions on Office Information Systems* 3 (1985): 253–278.

34. James, Geoffrey. *Document Databases.* New York: Van Nostrand Reinhold, 1985.

35. Katz, Randy, Chang, Ellis, and Bhateja, Rajiv. "Version Modeling Concepts for Computer-aided Design Database." *Proceedings SIGMOD '86, International Conference on Management of Data.* New York: Association for Computing Machinery, 1986, pp. 379–386.

36. Koved, Larry, and Shneiderman, Ben. "Embedded Menus: Selecting Items in Context." *Communications of the Association for Computing Machinery* 29, (1986): 312–318.

37. Lancaster, F. W. *Vocabulary Control for Information Retrieval.* Washington, DC: Information Resources Press, 1972.

38. MEDLARS Management Section of the National Library of Medicine. *Online Services Reference Manual.* Bethesda, MD: National Library of Medicine, 1982.

39. Mars, Nicolaas, and Miller, Perry. "Tools for Knowledge Acquisition and Verification in Medicine." *Proceedings of the Tenth Annual Symposium on Computer Applications in Medical Care.* Washington: IEEE Computer Society, 1986, pp. 36–42.

40. Marsh, Elaine, and Friedman, Carol. "Transporting the Linguistic String Project System from a Medical to a Navy Domain." *ACM Transactions on Office Information Systems* 3 (1985): 121–140.

41. McCarn, D. B. "MEDLINE: An Introduction to On-Line Searching." *Journal of the American Society for Information Science* 31 (May 1980): 181–192.

42. McCracken, Donald, and Akscyn, Robert. "Experience with the ZOG Human-Computer Interface System." *International Journal of Man-Machine Studies* 21 (1984): 293–310.

43. Medical Subject Headings Section of the National Library of Medicine. *Medical Subject Headings, Annotated Alphabetical List,* Springfield VA: National Technical Information Service, 1986.

44. National Library of Medicine. "Unified Medical Language System." *National Library of Medicine News* 41 (November 1986): 1–4.

45. Mili, Hafedh, and Rada, Roy. "Merging Thesauri: Principles and Cases." *IEEE Transactions on Pattern Analysis and Machine Intelligence* 10 (1988): 204–220.

46. Minker, Jack. "An Experimental Relational Data Base System Based on Logic." In *Logic and Data Bases,* edited by J. Minker, pp. 107–148, New York: Plenum Press, 1978.

47. Missikoff, Michele, and Wiederhold, George. "Towards a Unified Approach *for Expert* and Database Systems." In *Expert Database Systems,* edited by Larry Kerschberg, pp. 383–400. Menlo Park, CA, Benjamin/Cummings, 1986.

48. Mukhopadhyay, Uttam, Stephens, Larry, Huhns, Michael, and Bonnell, Ronald. "An Intelligent System for Document Retrieval in Distributed Office Environments." *Journal of the American Society for Information Science* 37 (1986): 123–135.

49. Newell, Allen. _____. *AI Magazine* 2 (1981).

50. Pangalos, G. J. "Design and Implementation of an Integrated Hospital Database." *Medical Informatics* 11 (1986): 159–166.

51. Parker, D. Stott, Jr., Carey, Michael, Golshani, Forouzan, Jarke, Matthias, Sciore, Edward, and Walker, Adrian. "Logic Programming and Databases." In *Expert Database Systems,* edited by Larry Kerschberg, pp. 35–48. Menlo Park, CA: Benjamin/Cummings, 1986.

52. Price, Lynne A. "Thumb: An Interactive Tool for Accessing and Maintaining Text." *IEEE Transactions on Systems, Man, and Cybernetics* 12 (March/April 1982): 155–161.

53. Quillian, M. R. "Semantic Memory." In *Semantic Information Processing,* edited by M. Minsky. Cambridge MA: MIT Press, 1968.

54. Rada, Roy, and Martin, Brian. "Augmenting Thesauri for Information Systems." *ACM Transactions on Office Information Systems* 5 (1987): 378–392.

55. Sager, J. C., Somers, H. L., and McNaught, J. "Thesaurus Integration in the Social Sciences, Part 1: Comparison of Thesauri." *International Classification* 8 (1981): 133–137.

56. Salton, Gerard. "Another Look at Automatic Text-Retrieval Systems." *Communications of the Association for Computing Machinery* 29 (July 1986): 648–656.

57. Schutzer, Daniel. "Artificial Intelligence-based Very Large Data Base Organization and Management." In *Applications in Artificial Intelligence,* edited by Stephen Andriole, pp. 251–277. _____: Petrocelli Books, 1985.

58. Simon, Herbert. "Why Should Machines Learn?" In *Machine Learning,* edited by T. Mitchell, pp. 25–38. Palo Alto, CA: Tioga, 1983.

59. Soergel, Dagobert. *Indexing Languages and Thesauri: Construction and Maintenance.* New York: Wiley, 1974.

60. Stefik, Mark, Foster, Gregg, Bobrow, Daniel, Kahn, Kenneth, Lanning, Stan, and Suchman, Luch. "Beyond the Chalkboard: Computer Support for Collaboration and Problem Solving in Meetings." *Communications of the Association of Computing Machinery* 30 (1987): 32–47.

61. Stonebraker, Michael. "Adding Semantic Knowledge to a Relational Database Sys-

tem." In *On Conceptual Modelling,* edited by J. Schmidt, pp. 333–356. New York: Springer-Verlag, 1984.

62. Touretzky, David. "The Mathematics of Inheritance Systems." Ph.D. dissertation, Carnegie-Mellon University, 1984.

63. Tsur, S., and Zaniolo, C. "An Implementation of GEM—Supporting a Semantic Data Model on a Relational Back-end." *Proceedings SIGMOD '84, International Conference on Management of Data.* New York: Association for Computing Machinery, 1984, pp. 286–295.

64. Tyler, Sherman, and Treu, Siegfried. "Adaptive Interface Design: A Symmetric Model and a Knowledge-based Implementation. *Third ACM-SIGOIS Conference on Office Information Systems,* October 1986, pp. 53–60. Also published as *SIGOIS Bulletin* 7, 2.

65. Walker, A. "Data Bases, Expert Systems, and Prolog." in *Artificial Intelligence Applications for Business,* edited by W. Reitman. Norwood, NJ Ablex, 1984.

66. Weyer, Stephen A., and Borning, Alan H. "A Prototype Electronic Encyclopedia." *ACM Transactions on Office Information Systems* 3 (1985): 63–88.

67. Zaniolo, Carlo, Ait-Kaci, Hassan, Beech, David, Cammarata, Stephanie, and Maier, David. "Object Oriented Database Systems and Knowledge Systems." In *Expert Database Systems,* edited by Larry Kerschberg, pp. 49–65. Menlo Park, CA Benjamin/Cummings, 1986.

7

System Architectures for Prolog Execution*

Markian M. Gooley
Benjamin W. Wah

INTRODUCTION

Motivation

Expert systems are arguably the most successful and lucrative result of research in artificial intelligence. However, they generally are executed on conventional computers, not on machines designed to support the operations they frequently must perform. Worse yet, languages for writing expert systems, or *shells,* often have limited power [57] and are interpreted—i.e., executed by a program running on a computer—rather than compiled to the computer's actual instruction codes. As a result, expert systems tend to execute slowly and be limited by their shells [24]. Writing them in a general-purpose language improves their speed and versatility, but makes them harder to design, implement, and modify.

Why should those who study or implement expert systems take interest in Prolog? Prolog is no panacea, and it does not have some features built into it that a shell might have, such as the ability to handle uncertain information or generate explanations [24]. However,

1. Prolog has its own inference (backward-chaining), and search (depth-first) mechanisms [45], like a shell.
2. Unlike many shells, it also has the computational power of first-order logic [26].

* This work was supported in part by the National Aeronautics and Space Administration under grants NAG 1-613 and NCC 2-481.

3. Shells can readily be written in Prolog, though with some loss of speed. Such shells can use a different type of inference, handle uncertain information, provide explanations, and so forth [45].

4. A machine architecture (the *Warren abstract machine*) [54] already exists for Prolog and can be emulated in software or microcode or built as hardware; it is also the building block for Prolog multiprocessors [56]. Anyone designing a machine for expert systems will profit from familiarity with machines designed for Prolog.

Various authors have argued that Prolog should be used more widely for expert systems [5, 19, 45]. They cite some of the aforesaid arguments and suggest that expert systems written in Prolog require less code and execute more quickly than systems written in other languages. Most such Prolog expert systems, however, are still written where Prolog is popular (e.g., Japan), or in association with members of the logic programming community.

Prolog has been used to build expert systems for all the usual applications. An especially popular one is the design of circuits or computers: VLSI layouts [28], compacting microcode [39], and so forth. Other applications include diagnostic and therapeutic medicine [29], credit evaluation [3], and strategy for games, law [36, 59], and negotiation [30].

Overview

The intent of this chapter is to acquaint the reader with Prolog and Prolog machines, especially Warren's. First we introduce the language, beginning with simple examples and proceeding to more exact definitions. Then, again using examples, we describe Prolog's method of execution and some features that help suit it to expert systems. Next we describe the parts of the Warren abstract machine (WAM) [54], and show how it executes programs. We then consider parallel execution. After reviewing some of the parallel architectures proposed for expert system machines, we return to Prolog to look at the principal varieties of parallelism available and examples of the architectures which exploit them. Finally, we summarize our presentation and give our thoughts on machines for expert systems.

THE PROLOG LANGUAGE

As a supplement to this discussion, the reader may wish to consult an introductory text such as Clocksin and Mellish [7] or Sterling and Shapiro [45].

Tutorial Introduction

Facts.   A *fact* states a relationship between objects. An expert system implemented in Prolog has a knowledge base of facts. For example, here is one way to represent a family tree:

```
mother(jane, mrs_bennet).
mother(kitty, mrs_bennet).
mother(mary, mrs_bennet).
mother(lydia, mrs_bennet).
mother(elizabeth, mrs_bennet).

wife(mr_bennet, mrs_bennet).
wife(charles, jane).
wife(george, lydia).
wife(fitzwilliam, elizabeth).

girl(kitty).
girl(mary).
```

Thus, the `mother` of `jane` is `mrs_bennet`, the `wife` of `mr_bennet` is `mrs_bennet`, and so forth; `kitty` and `mary` are `girls`—unmarried females, actually.

Facts can hold a variety of information. For example, an expert system that helps prescribe drugs might include such facts as

```
interaction(penicillin, aspirin, 0.15).
prescribed_for(lomotil, diarrhea).
```

That is, "Penicillin and aspirin will interact with probability 0.15," and "Lomotil is prescribed for diarrhea."

Queries. We can query a database of facts to confirm what it contains. For the preceding family tree,

```
?- girl(mary).

yes ;

no
```

(The system's responses are in boldface.) The query matches a fact, and the Prolog system responds `yes`. If we type ; to test for another occurrence, Prolog checks the other facts of the relation `girl`, fails to find another match, and responds `no`.

Variables. So far we can test only whether a given fact is present in the system. To retrieve information from facts, we need *variables*. A variable occurring in a query can be *bound* to some object:

```
?- wife(Husband,Wife).

Husband = mr_bennet
Wife = mrs_bennet ;
```

```
Husband = charles
Wife = jane ;

Husband = george
Wife = lydia ;

Husband = fitzwilliam
Wife = elizabeth ;

no
```

Prolog looks at the facts for `wife` in the order that they are written, successively binding the variables `Husband` and `Wife` to husband-wife pairs. A similar query with only one variable gives the expected result:

```
?- wife(Husband,elizabeth).

Husband = fitzwilliam ;

no
```

Conjunctions.   Prolog allows conjunctive queries, which have answers if all of their components do. The conjunction is executed from left to right. For example, suppose that we want to know whether `mrs_bennet` has any married daughters. Then the following is the query (note that the ",", between its parts is a conjunction and is *not* the same as the commas within the tuples):

```
?- mother(D,mrs_bennet), wife(_,D).

D = jane ;

D = lydia ;

D = elizabeth ;

no
```

Prolog scans the facts for `mother` in order, binding `D` to `jane`. Then it scans the facts for `wife`, testing whether `jane` is a wife; she is. (Because we do not care who the husband is, we use "`_`", the *anonymous variable,* which matches anything and is never bound). When we ask for another answer with "`;`", Prolog seeks another husband-wife pair (it knows nothing of laws forbidding polygamy), fails to find one, and *backtracks* to `mother` to find another child of `mrs_bennet`. There it finds `lydia`, and so it again scans for facts for `wife`. `lydia` is also a wife. Again we force backtracking, and again Prolog scans the rest of `wife`, fails, backtracks to `mother` to find `elizabeth`, and proceeds to `wife` to find that she is a wife. We use "`;`", `wife` yields failure, so does `mother`, and Prolog returns `no`.

Rules. Prolog lets us define *rules* by which it can infer new relations from facts. We can base a rule on the query of the previous example:

```
married_daughter(Mother,Daughter):-
        mother(Daughter,Mother),
        wife(_,Daughter).
```

We can now use this rule instead of the compound query:

```
?- married_daughter(mrs_bennet,D).
```

Some relations require multiple rules, which give a *disjunction*. For instance, a parent is either a mother or married to a mother (assuming no illegitimacy):

```
parent(Child,Parent):- mother(Child,Parent).
parent(Child,Parent):-
        wife(Parent,Mother),
        mother(Child,Mother).
```

(Note that a variable is local to its rule: `Child` in the first rule has no relation to `Child` in the second.) Now consider the following query:

```
?- parent(jane,Parent).

Parent = mrs_bennet ;

Parent = mr_bennet ;

no
```

Prolog gets an answer from the first rule; then, when we use "`;`", it tries to get another answer, fails, and then uses the second rule, which yields another answer to "`;`" before failing.

Definitions

The foregoing should provide a "feel" for the rudiments of Prolog: information is stored as facts and retrieved using queries; variables and conjunction make useful queries possible; and rules define ways to infer further information. The examples also show something of Prolog's mechanism of execution.

Terms. We now proceed to define things more rigorously. The *term* is the basic unit of Prolog's syntax. A term is a *constant*, a *variable*, or a *compound term.* Constants are *numbers* or *atoms*, where an atom is an alphanumeric (including the character "_") string starting with a lowercase letter. Variables are alphanumeric strings starting with an uppercase letter or "_", with the solitary "_" reserved for the anonymous variable.

A compound term is an atom, called a *functor,* together with some number of *arguments* (its *arity*), which are also terms; e.g., the term `f(g,h(I,J),k)` has functor `f`, an arity of 3, and arguments `g`, `h(I,J)`, and `k`. Sometimes we consider an atom a compound term of arity 0. *Ground terms* contain no variables.

Clauses.   The facts, queries, and rules we have just seen are special cases of the Prolog *clause.* A clause has the form

$$\text{head:- goal\_1, goal\_2, ..., goal\_n.}$$

where the `head` and the `goals` are terms. The "`:-`" is a stylized arrow representing implication, because the clause is in fact a *Horn clause*, i.e., a conjunction of premises (goals) implying a single conclusion (head). The *logical* meaning of the clause is "The `head` holds *if* `goal_1` *and* `goal_2` *and* all the goals through `goal_n` hold." We can also consider the clause to have a *procedural* meaning, viz., "To do the task indicated by `head`, do `goal_1` *and* `goal_2` *and* all the goals through `goal_n`." [45] The goals form the *body* of the clause.

A fact, then, is a clause whose body is always true (hence omitted); e.g., `girl(mary).` is actually `girl(mary):-true.`, where `true` is a goal that always succeeds. Thus, `girl(mary).` means "`girl(mary)` holds if `true` holds," or "To prove `girl(mary)`, prove `true`." A query lacks a head. It has the form

$$\text{?- goal\_1, goal\_2, ..., goal\_n.}$$

but the "`?-`" is the same as a "`:-`"; i.e., we actually have

$$\text{false:- goal\_1, goal\_2, ..., goal\_n.}$$

In giving Prolog a query, we issue a challenge: "I say that this conjunction of goals implies falsity. Prove constructively that I'm wrong." A rule is simply the most general form of clause.

Predicates and programs.   A group of clauses whose heads have the same functor and arity is considered a *predicate*. A predicate is the disjunction of its clauses, as we saw in the example for `parent`; it is the Prolog version of a procedure. It can consist of facts, rules, or both. Often we refer to a predicate by its name and arity, i.e., *name/arity*, as in `parent/2`. A collection of predicates forms a *program.*

Prolog's Mechanism of Execution

We have already seen a couple of simple examples of Prolog execution. We now describe the general mechanism and give examples that are more complex.

Unification.   Suppose that we begin with a query with a single goal:

$$\text{?- q(a(X),Y).}$$

Prolog tries to match this with the heads of successive clauses of the predicate q/2:

```
q(b,X):- r(X), s(X).
q(a(X),b):- s(X).
q(a(b(c,d)),e).
```

Only if its head *unifies* with the calling goal will the rest of a clause be executed. Unification is an attempt to make two terms identical by instantiating variables; the set of instantiations is called the *most general unifier*. Thus, q(a(X),Y) does not unify with q(b,X), because no instantiation can make their first arguments the same (note again that the X in the first term and the X in the second term are distinct). However, q(a(X),Y) unifies with q(a(X),b): the distinct Xs are made equivalent, Y is set to b, and the second clause is executed. If backtracking reaches the third clause, goal and fact unify, with x = b(c,d) and Y = e.

Forward execution.   Forward execution of Prolog begins with a query. We can think of Prolog as maintaining a list of goals to execute [45]. It takes the leftmost goal of this list and tries to unify it with the head of a clause. If the unification succeeds, Prolog replaces the goal with the goals forming the body of the clause matched, keeping track of the instantiations involved. Then it repeats the process for the new leftmost goal. For instance,

```
?- q1, q2, q3.
```

becomes

```
r1, r2, r3, r4, q2, q3.
```

and then

```
s1, s2, r2, r3, r4, q2, q3.,
```

given appropriate clauses. (For brevity, we show no variables.) Eventually the leftmost goal matches a fact. Because facts have no bodies (strictly speaking, they have bodies with the trivial goal true), Prolog can delete the current goal and proceed to the next one. Hence, suppose that s1 and s2 match facts; then the list of goals becomes shorter:

```
<s1 matches...>
s2, r2, r3, r4, q2, q3.
<s2 matches...>
r2, r3, r4, q2, q3.
```

When the list of goals becomes empty, the original query is solved and Prolog returns the instantiations of variables appearing in it.

Backward execution.   If some goal cannot match any clause head, or if the user asks for another solution to a query, Prolog must backtrack. Returning to the preceding example, suppose that no clause matches `r2`; then Prolog backtracks to `s2` thus:

```
r2, r3, r4, q2, q3.
<backtracking...>
s2, r2, r3, r4, q2, q3.
```

Prolog undoes any instantiations done by `s2` and then tries to unify `s2` with the next untried clause of the predicate it calls. If it succeeds for some remaining clause, we might have the following:

```
t1, t2, t3, r2, r3, r4, q2, q3.
```

If not, Prolog backtracks to `s1`, undoing any instantiations done by `s1`, and tries the next clause of the predicate it calls. If it then succeeds, we might have the following:

```
s1, s2, r2, r3, r4, q2, q3.
```

```
u1, u2, s2, r2, r3, r4, q2, q3.
```

If not, we must backtrack to `r1`:

```
r1, r2, r3, r4, q2, q3.
```

If we end up backtracking to the original query and no alternatives remain to match its leftmost goal, the query fails.

Features of Prolog

Data structures and recursion.   Data structures are constructed from compound terms. We can represent a binary tree, for example, using a term $t(<Left>, <Right>)$, where $<Left>$ and $<Right>$ are either leaves or sub-terms representing subtrees. Thus, the tree shown in Figure 7–1 is represented in Prolog by

```
t(1, t(t(2, 3), t(t(4, t(5, 6)), 7)))
```

Prolog has a special functor, ".", for constructing *lists,* and a special atom, "[]", to represent the empty list. The list of the first five natural numbers is therefore `.(1,.(2,.(3,.(4,.(5,)))))`, but for convenience it is written `1,2,3,4,5`.

Handling such recursive data structures as trees and lists requires recursive predicates. This ubiquitous one appends two lists to create a third:

```
append([],L,L).
append([H|T],L,[H|T2]):- append(T,L,T2).
```

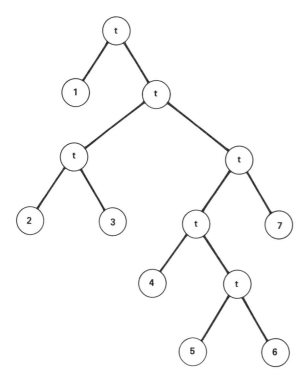

Figure 7–1 The term **t(1, t(tt2, 3), t(tt4, t(5, 6)), 7)))** as a tree.

Note the [H|T] in the second clause. This unifies with any nonempty list: H is set to the first element of the list and T to the remainder—the *car* and *cdr* of the list, for those who know Lisp.

Suppose that we call append/3 with lists as its first two arguments and a variable as its third. Then append's second clause matches, "decapitates" the first list and starts to build the third argument, and then calls itself with the *cdr* of the first argument. It repeats this until the first argument is " "; then the first clause matches and the second list is copied into the third argument. As the recursive calls finish, the chopped-off elements of the first list are attached to the third argument, creating what we want. For example, if we append a,b,c to 1,2,3, the successive calls and returns have the following pattern:

```
append([1,2,3],[a,b,c],Z)
        append([2,3],[a,b,c],Z)
                append([3],[a,b,c],Z)
                        append([],[a,b,c],Z)
                        append([],[a,b,c],[a,b,c])
                append([3],[a,b,c],[3,a,b,c])
        append([2,3],[a,b,c],[2,3,a,b,c])
append([1,2,3],[a,b,c],[1,2,3,a,b,c])
```

append/3 also shows that input and output arguments are sometimes inter-changeable in Prolog. Calling append/3 with two variables and a list gives, on back-tracking, all the combinations of lists that, when appended, would yield the original:

```
?- append(X,Y,[a,b,c]).

X = [a,b,c]
Y = [] ;

X = [a,b]
Y = [c] ;

X = [a]
Y = [b,c] ;

X = []
Y = [a,b,c] ;

no
```

The cut.   A call to a predicate might produce many answers, but we may need only one; several clauses may match a goal, but we might want only the results produced by the first. For interactive queries we may choose not to backtrack (we need not use ;), but this is not general enough.

Prolog provides a construct, the *cut* (written "!"), that satisfies these needs. "!" is written as a goal, although it is not in fact one [26]. When Prolog calls a predicate, matches a clause to the calling goal, and encounters a cut within a clause, the cut succeeds at once; however, if backtracking returns to the cut, the clause fails, no later clauses of the predicate are tried, and so the entire call fails. Consider the following predicate:

```
a(b,X):- !, c(X,Y), d(Y).
a(X,Y):- c(Y,X,Z), e(Z).
```

Calling **a/2** with certain arguments (e.g., two uninstantiated variables) ensures that only its first clause is tried: **a/2** will return whatever answer(s) **c/2** and **d/1** allow. Other cases match only the second clause. Without the cut, **a/2** would behave quite differently.

Negation.   Prolog is based on a subset of predicate logic; however, one feature of logic not included is the ability to represent negative information directly, i.e., to state that a relationship is false [7]. For instance, there is no negation operator "¬" to let us write

```
¬ girl(fitzwilliam).
```

```
¬ (mother(_,Woman), girl(Woman)).
```

or similar useful facts into our family tree example. Allowing negative facts or goals requires a complicated execution strategy that would make Prolog impractically slow [34]. Instead, Prolog assumes the *closed world assumption* [26]—that its data-base describes its "world" completely. In other words, it considers true anything that can be deduced from its database and it considers false anything that cannot. Querying the family tree, we obtain

```
?- wife(_,cynthia).

no

?- girl(cynthia).

no
```

That is, someone named Cynthia is probably female, but Prolog has no facts about cynthia and both queries fail. This is an example of *negation as failure* [34]: anything that cannot be proved is taken as untrue, just as if there were an explicit negative fact stating as much.

We can use negation as failure explicitly in goals, using the *built-in predicate* not (sometimes written "/+"). A built-in predicate is part of the Prolog system, often providing a function that cannot be described in Prolog itself; **not,** however, can be defined easily:

```
not(X):- X, !, fail.
not(X).
```

Note the goal X: Prolog lets instantiated variables be treated as goals. If X succeeds, the always-failing goal fail makes the clause fail, and the cut makes not(X) itself fail. If X fails, the second clause makes not(X) succeed.

Disjunction, if-then-else.   Prolog allows clauses to be written with explicit disjunctions. For example, the third of these has the same meaning as the first two combined:

```
a(X,Y):- b(X,Z), c(Y,Z).
a(X,Y):- d(X,Z), e(Z,Y).

a(X,Y):- b(X,Z), c(Y,Z); d(X,Z), e(Z,Y).
```

The disjunction ";" is not mere shorthand: the single clause-head saves a unifica-tion, and in some cases we can "factor out" calls common to several clauses.

Prolog's *if-then-else* statement combines the effects of the cut and the dis-junction, behaving as if defined by

```
(X -> Y ; Z):- X, !, Y.
(X -> Y ; Z):- Z.
```

The *else* is optional:

$$(X \rightarrow Y):- X, !, Y.$$

$(X \rightarrow Y ; Z)$ chooses Y if X succeeds and Z if it fails.

Dynamic predicates.   Prolog allows its database of clauses to be changed during execution. Facts or rules can be *asserted* and *retracted* using built-in predicates. `asserta/1` takes a fact or clause as an argument, makes it the first of its predicates, and succeeds; and `assertz/1` does the same, making it the last. (*a* is the first letter of the alphabet, *z* the last.) For example, `girl/1` has two facts:

```
?- girl (Girl).

Girl = kitty ;

Girl = mary ;

no
```

Now we add a new fact as its last and try it again:

```
?- assertz(girl(georgiana)), girl(Girl).

Girl = kitty ;

Girl = mary ;

Girl = georgiana ;

no
```

As the example shows, the assertion predicates do not succeed again on backtracking.

`retract/1` removes clauses from the database. It tries to unify its argument with the head of a clause of the appropriate predicate, just as with a predicate call. It removes the first clause with a head that matches. On backtracking, it tries to match and remove another clause, failing when no clauses match. It can delete an entire predicate, as seen in the following:

```
?- retract(girl(X)).

X = kitty ;

X = mary ;

X = georgiana ;
```

```
no
?- girl(X).

no
```

Input and output. Prolog has a collection of built-in predicates which perform input and output. They can open and close files, read or write single characters or Prolog terms, and so forth. Like the cut and the assertion and retraction predicates just described, these I/O predicates have *side-effects*: they perform actions unrelated to the logical meaning of a program [45]. A goal that prints a term, for instance, produces a visible result but does not affect the success of its clause.

read/1 reads Prolog terms and write/1 writes them; get/1 and put/1 do the same for characters. Note that read and put try to unify their arguments with their inputs, and fail when they cannot. see/1 and tell/1 open files for input or output, which are by default interactive; seen and told close them. Other I/O predicates, varying with the dialect of Prolog, exist as well. An example is:

```
double:- read(Term), write(Term), tab(4), write(Term), nl.

?- double.
|: knock.
knock    knock

yes
```

The system prompts for an input, which for read must be a Prolog term followed by a period (get is not so choosy). It writes the term, writes four spaces (tab/1 writes the number of spaces given by its argument), writes the term again, and then goes to a new line.

Metalogical features. Prolog also has built-in predicates that operate on terms and clauses, finding their properties, extracting their components, or building new terms from old. Those that test properties succeed if the property holds. var/1, for example, succeeds if its argument is a free variable:

```
?- var(X).

X = _0 ;

no
?- var(not_a_variable).

no
```

(The _0 is the variable's identifier or address, which depends on the implementation.)

Other built-in predicates build or decompose terms. `functor/3` returns the name and arity of a term, or, given a name and an arity, it builds a new term with new variables for arguments:

```
?- functor(a(b,c,d),F,N).

F = a
N = 3 ;

no
?- functor(X,a_const,5).

X = a_const(_6,_7,_8,_9,_10) ;

no
```

arg/3 extracts a given argument of a term, but fails if the "index" number is out of range:

```
?- arg(2,a(b,c(d,e),f),Comp).

Comp = c(d,e) ;

no
?- arg(5,a(b,c(d,e),f),Comp).

no
```

The predicate "=..", pronounced *univ* [7], translates between terms and lists; the functor of the term corresponds to the *car* of the list; the arguments, to the *cdr*.

```
?- a(b,c(d,e),f)  =.. List.

List = [a,b,c(d,e),f] ;

no
?- Term =.. [t,2,4,6,8].

Term = t(2,4,6,8) ;

no
```

`clause` **and interpreters.** The built-in predicate `clause/2` is especially useful for writing shells [45]. It allows a Prolog program to access its own clauses. Prolog tries to unify the first argument of `clause` with successive clauses of the appropriate predicate and, when it can, then tries to unify the second argument with the body of the clause. For instance, given the clauses

```
a(X,Y):- b(X), c(Y,Z), d(Z,X).
a(c,b):- b(X), e(X).
a(X,Y):- c(X,Y).
a(X,X).
```

this call behaves as follows:

```
?- clause(a(c,c),Body).

Body = b(c),c(c,_15),d(_15,c) ;

Body = c(c,c) ;

Body = true ;

no
```

Note that the second clause does not match and that the fact has the trivial goal **true** for a body.

An *interpreter* is a program that executes a language directly, perhaps translating it into an internal representation. It treats a program as a series of commands that change its state—rather like a high-level software analog of a computer. Many expert systems languages are still interpreted [24], and early implementations of Prolog [41] were all interpreters written in conventional languages such as Fortran or C. Prolog is now usually compiled, because that yields faster execution, typically five to ten times faster [9] for a given machine.

For certain applications, such as debugging, providing explanations, or experimenting with different strategies of executing a language, interpreters are still useful. They are easy to design and modify, and are often fast enough for interactive work [45]. clause lets us write a Prolog interpreter in Prolog itself:

```
solve(true).
solve((A,B)):- solve(A), solve(B).
solve(A):- clause(A,B), solve(B).
```

This looks trivial, but it can execute most programs that do not use built-in predicates. It is easily modified to handle full Prolog, act as a debugger, or support features needed for an expert system shell [45].

THE WARREN ABSTRACT MACHINE

Introduction

Most introductions to Prolog machines [23,27] describe in detail how a Prolog interpreter (written in a conventional language) works: how it handles forward execution, backtracking, control constructs, and the rest. Only then do they describe the *Warren abstract machine (WAM)* [54], on which most implementations of Prolog are based nowadays, and the progenitor of most parallel Prolog machines. We describe the WAM and its behavior directly, rather than explain things through an interpreter; the operation of the machine is no more difficult to understand on it own, and we spare the reader possible confusion between the two methods.

The WAM is an abstract machine with data areas, registers, and an instruction set tailored to execute Prolog. Warren devised its original version [53] to describe an intermediate language for his Prolog compiler. The compiler did two translations: from Prolog to the intermediate language, and then from the intermediate language to executable code for the DEC-10 computer. Later Warren altered the WAM [54] so that it could be implemented as a real machine. Many recent compilers [1,4,9] produce WAM code, called *byte-code* because of its terse instructions; this then runs on a WAM emulated in software or microcode, or built as hardware. Byte-code instructions range from simple to complex, from moving data to calling predicates.

Parts of the WAM

Figure 7–2 shows the data areas and registers of the WAM. Note that the contents of a register, say **Q**, are indicated by **(Q)**.

Data areas and their contents. For data, the WAM has five areas of memory. The *code area* contains the byte-code version of the program being executed; this does not change unless clauses are asserted or retracted. (We assume that programs are static: handling of dynamic predicates varies greatly among implementations, and we shall not discuss the details.) The *PDL* (*push-down list*) aids unification; normally it would be called a *stack*, but that word has another meaning in the WAM.

The other data areas are known as *stacks:* the (*local*) *stack*, the *heap* (*global stack*), and the *trail*. The heap contains compound terms (structures), the trail records how unifications bind variables, and the stack keeps track of the progress of execution.

A *symbol table*, not considered part of the WAM proper, contains symbols and arities for each functor (including alphanumeric constants) in the program, so that we can refer to each one by a pointer to its entry. New symbols that appear in data can be added to this table as a program runs (again, in ways varying among implementations).

Data and the heap. *Tags* let us tell variables, constants, structures, and lists apart readily. For a WAM emulated on a conventional machine, two or three bits of a 32-bit word should suffice; for a hardware WAM, longer tags might be more practical. For our examples [9], we assume a 32-bit word, with the two least significant bits forming the tag. (The machine addresses eight-bit bytes, and all data are 32-bit aligned words, so that the two least significant bits are superfluous for addressing.) An unbound (*free*) variable has tag *00* and contains its own address. A

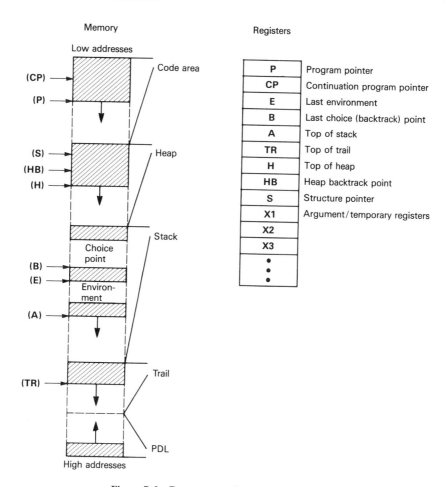

Figure 7–2   Data areas and registers of the WAM.

functor or constant has tag *01* and points to an entry in the symbol table. A number is a 30-bit integer with the tag *10;* it contains its own value. We can represent floating-point numbers (though of low precision) by using a third bit to distinguish between them and integers. A list has tag *11,* except for "[]", which is a constant.

When a program builds a data structure, it builds it atop the heap, with the WAM register **H** keeping track of where the top is. A structure with *n* arguments uses *n* + 1 contiguous words on the heap: the functor followed by its arguments. Figure 7–3 shows a complex structure on the heap. Free variables and structures appear as names, although in fact free variables point to themselves and constants and structures point to the symbol table. Note the terse representation of lists: for a pointer to a list, the *car* is the word pointed to, and the *cdr* is its successor.

One more point about data representation. We write of a variable or a struca(X,b(c,d(e,f),Y),[g,z,h])

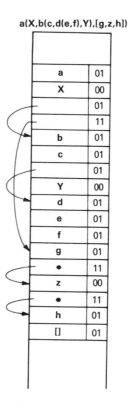

a	01
X	00
	01
	11
b	01
c	01
	01
Y	00
d	01
e	01
f	01
g	01
•	11
z	00
•	11
h	01
[]	01

Figure 7–3   A complex structure on the heap.

ture being "stored in" or "copied to" a certain location on the heap or stack or in a register. In many cases we mean that a pointer to it is put there, or possibly even a pointer to a pointer. Going down a chain of pointers to reach the actual variable cell or datum is known as *dereferencing* [27]. Figure 7–4 shows an example: a register **X1** points to a position on the stack which points to an unbound variable on the heap which points to itself. In dereferencing, the WAM "chases" the string of pointers until it finds the unbound variable, which it can then copy into **X1,** making it point to exactly the right location. (Dereference chains are very rarely [51] longer than this.) In describing the operation of the WAM, we shall sometimes mention that dereferencing occurs, but we shall not give details.

Execution and the stack.   Prolog's mechanism of execution requires that particular information be saved about the operations performed in reaching the current state—what one author [23] calls "the evolution of the locus of control." The stack does this by storing *environments* and *choice points.*

An environment [54] is pushed onto the stack when a calling goal tries a new clause of a predicate, provided that the clause is a rule with at least two goals. (In the section on registers and variables we show why rules of one goal and facts need

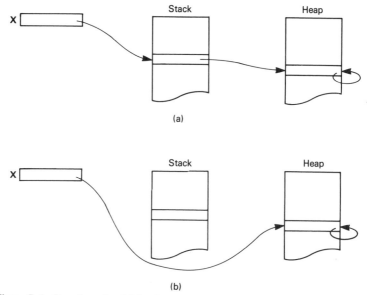

Figure 7–4   Dereferencing (a) Stack and heap before dereferencing. (b) Stack and heap after dereferencing.

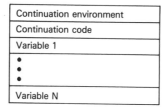

Figure 7–5   An environment.

no environment.) The environment contains a cell for each variable in the clause (again, there are exceptions), and a *continuation*. This is a pair of pointers, one to the code that should be executed after the calling goal succeeds (like a return address for a subroutine call), and the other to the environment already created for that code. Figure 7–5 shows the layout of an environment.

A choice point [54] is pushed onto the stack whenever the clause being tried is the first of a predicate that has more than one clause. It contains the current values of certain machine registers (**H, TR, B, CP, E,** and **X**) sufficient to restore the current state of computation, and a pointer to the next clause of the predicate. When a goal fails, the WAM restores its previous state from the most recent choice point and resumes execution with the next clause. Restoring the old state lets the recent information on the stack and structures on the heap be overwritten, but it doesn't undo instantiations made to extant variables. (That is the purpose of the trail.) Figure 7–6 shows the layout of a choice point.

Goal-argument M **XM**
•
•
•
Goal-argument 1 **X1**
Continuation environment **R**
Continuation code **CP**
Previous choice point **B**
Address of next clause
Trail pointer **TR**
Heap pointer **H**

Figure 7–6 A choice point, with corresponding registers.

Instantiations and the trail. Execution instantiates variables; thus, when backtracking discards the results of execution, some instantiations must be undone. When a goal fails, any new variables created by it are discarded automatically, but any variables that already existed and were free when it was called must be free again after it fails.

The problem is easy to solve: we record atop the trail the addresses of variable cells (on the stack or the heap) as they are bound. At every choice point we store the current value of **TR,** which points to the top of the trail. If the calling goal cannot be satisfied by the current clause, we clear every variable cell whose address appears on the trail later than the saved **TR,** and reset **TR** from the saved copy.

Registers and variables. The WAM has a set of registers which point into the data areas, and whose values are saved in choice points [54]. (See Figure 7–2.) **P,** the *program pointer,* points to the current instruction of the program. **CP,** the *continuation pointer,* holds the return address for the current predicate call—i.e., the location of the code to execute next (e.g., the next goal) if the current goal succeeds. **E** points to the *last environment,* letting us access the variables and continuation information stored in it. **B** points to the last choice point (point of *backtrack*), so that the WAM can restore its previous state and try any alternative clauses for the predicate being called. **A** points to the top of the stack, so that the WAM knows where to put new environments; **A** is not essential—the top of the stack is an offset from **E** or **B**—but it makes execution faster.

We have already seen **TR,** the top of the trail, and **H,** the top of the heap. **HB,** the *heap backtrack* point, holds the value of H at the time the last choice point (pointed to by **B**) was created. **S** points to existing structures on the heap, allowing access to their arguments. There is also a set of registers that hold both temporary variables of a clause and the arguments of a goal being called. Warren [54] calls these by different names when they are used for different purposes: **X** registers (**X1, X2,** and so on) for temporary variables, **A** registers (**A1, A2,** etc.) for arguments. We follow recent authors [16,27] and compilers and always call them **X** registers henceforth.

A *temporary variable* [54] occurs first in the head of a clause, in a structure, or in the last goal, but not in more than one goal of the body, counting the head as part of the first goal. Any condition in this seemingly peculiar set indicates that the variable exists elsewhere or will be needed only briefly, so that it will not have to be stored in an environment. A *permanent variable,* denoted **Y1, Y2,** and so forth, is any that is not temporary; it must be stored in an environment, where a cell is reserved for it, and the WAM addresses it by an offset from the pointer to its environment. Environments are arranged such that their variables' cells have the highest addresses. If the compiler puts variables in a suitable order, the top addresses of an environment can be *trimmed* away and used for the next stack item when the corresponding variables are no longer needed.

The WAM Instruction Set

WAM instructions fall into five classes: **get, put, unify, procedural,** and **indexing.** The entire set proposed by Warren is in Table 7–1, but we discuss each class separately, basing our descriptions on his [54]. Implementors [9,51] have extended the set, renamed some instructions, and so forth, but Warren's design remains the standard, and we use his names.

	Head	Body
Procedural	proceed	execute P call P, N deallocate
Get/put	get__variable Xn, Ai get__variable Yn, Ai get__value Xn, Ai get__value Yn, Ai get__constant constant, Ai get__nil Ai get__structure functor, Ai get__list Ai	put__variable Xn, Ai put__variable Yn, Ai put__unsafe__value Yn, Ai put__constant constant, Ai put__nil Ai put__structure functor, Ai put__list Ai
Unification	unify__void N unify__variable Xn unify__variable Yn unify__local__value Xn unify__local__value Yn unify__value Xn unify__value Yn unify__constant constant unify__nil	
Indexing	try__me__else label retry__me__else label trust__me__else fail switch__on__term var con lis str switch__on__constant N, table switch__on__structure N, table	try label retry label trust label

Table 7–1 WAM instructions.

get **instructions.**   A compiler generates a **get** instruction for each argument of a clause's head. They match a variable that is definitely uninstantiated (**get_variable**), a variable that might be instantiated (**get_value**), a constant (**get_constant**), a structure (**get_structure**), or a list (**get_nil, get_list**) to an argument (already copied to an **X** register with a **put** instruction) of a calling goal. A variable can be temporary (in an **X** register, so that the **get** moves it from one register to another) or permanent (in a slot **Y** of an environment). Note that the list instructions have only one argument: the functor or constant is known.

put **instructions.**   **Put** instructions load an argument of a goal into an **X** register, where a **get** can retrieve it. Each **put** is the analog of the **get** of similar name, except for **put_unsafe_value.** An *unsafe* variable does not first occur in the head or in a structure, and is therefore set by a **put_variable. put_unsafe_value** is used instead of **put_value** for the last goal in which an unsafe variable appears. Why?
     Suppose that the variable is uninstantiated. A cell for an uninstantiated variable points to itself, so that **put_value** copies a pointer to the variable into an **X** register. Now the portion of the environment containing the variable cells will be trimmed by the **execute** or **call** instruction executed presently. So unless the WAM instead reserves a cell on the heap for the variable and loads a pointer to it into the **X** register, that **X** will point to something else.

unify **instructions.**   A compiler generates a **unify** instruction for each argument of a structure (or list). A sequence of **unify**s is always preceded by a **get** or **put** of a structure or list. If the structure already exists, unification is between the argument of the instruction and the corresponding argument of the structure. The **S** register points to the structure, and is incremented for each successive argument. If the structure is being built, the **unify**s construct its new arguments atop the heap from their own arguments, updating the top-of-heap register **H.**
     unify_void N unifies some number **N** of anonymous (single-occurrence) variables, which require no variable cells. **unify_local_value** replaces **unify_value** if the variable has not been initialized to something on the heap (a *global* value).

Procedural instructions.   Procedural instructions handle the overheads of calling goals in the body of a clause and manage the stack space used by the environment. A fact compiles into **gets** (and possibly **unifys**), followed by **proceed,** which simply transfers control. A rule requires that space for an environment be **allocate**d on the stack. After that, the WAM must **get** the arguments of the head. For each goal, the arguments are **put** into the **A** registers, and the appropriate predicate is **called**. The second argument of **call** is the number of variables in the environment; initially there is a cell for each variable, but some can be discarded as the clause executes. The last goal of a clause needs nothing from the environment (recall the **put_unsafe_value** instruction that helps ensure this), so that the environment is **deallocate**d (removed) from the stack and the goal is called using **execute.**

Note that a rule with one goal needs no environment: **allocate** and **deallocate** are not used, and the goal is **executed.**

Indexing instructions. Naive implementations of Prolog [38,41] try to match a call with every clause of the appropriate predicate. Often this is a waste of time. Consider the following example:

```
a([],[]).
a([p(X,Y)|T],U):- ....
a([q(X,Y)|T],[r(Y,Z)|U]):- ....
```

Suppose that we call a/2 with a (nonempty) list as its first argument. Then trying the first clause is useless. Similarly, if the first argument is indeed the empty list, trying the other clauses is useless.

Indexing instructions are meant to keep the WAM from trying clauses that cannot match a call. They use the principal functor of the predicate-call's first argument (in register **X1**) as a *key* to decide which clauses to try. If **X1** dereferences to a variable, the WAM must try every clause. In order to handle this case, a **try_me_else** instruction precedes the code for the first clause, a **retry_me_else** that for intermediate clauses, and a **trust_me_else fail** that for the last clause. The operand is the address of the next clause; the **fail** of **trust_me_else** shows that no alternatives remain, and the call fails if this clause fails.

switch_on_term examines **X1.** Its four arguments are the addresses to branch to if the dereferenced **X1** is a variable, constant, list, or structure. The first is the address of the predicate's **try_me_else**; the others are addresses either of the code for a single matching clause or of that of a block of matching clauses. Such blocks have **try, retry,** and **trust** instructions before their initial, middle, and final clauses, respectively, analogous to the **try_me_else** instructions for the variable case. If diverse constants or structures appear in the first arguments of clauses, **switch_on_constant** and **switch_on_functor** look in hash tables to find the addresses of the code for each case.

Examples of Execution: append/3

The foregoing may seem cryptic, so in this section we present several examples to show that the operation of the WAM is actually quite straightforward. For each example, we give Prolog code, the corresponding WAM "assembly language," and descriptions of what happens in the WAM in response to various calls.

Earlier we presented append/3:

```
append([],L,L).
append([H|T],L,[H|T2]):- append(T,L,T2).
```

Compiled into WAM assembler, it looks like this:

```
procedure append/3
     switch_on_term _580,_578,_579,fail        /*var.,cont.,list,struct.*/
_580:                                          /*var.*/
     try_me_else _581,3                        /*create a choice point*/
_578:                                          /*const.*/
   get_value X2,X3
   get_nil X1
   proceed
_581:
   trust_me_else fail                          /*discard the choice point*/
_579:                                          /*list*/
   get_list X1
   unify_variable X4
   unify_variable X1
   get_list X3
   unify_value X4
   unify_value X3
   execute append/3
```

(This is output from a real compiler [51], slightly doctored to conform to the original WAM code.) The code demonstrates many things presented in the previous section. With a variable in the first argument, **switch_on_term** branches to the first label so that both clauses are tried; with a constant, it branches directly to the first clause; with a list, to the second; and with a structure, to failure, because neither clause head can match a call that has one in that position. The first clause is a fact, so that its empty body is "called" using **proceed**; the second has only one goal, so that no environment is **allocate**d (or, clearly, **deallocate**d); and the recursive call uses an **execute.**

    A deterministic call.   Let us follow the operation of the WAM as it executes the goal

$$\text{append}([a,b,c],[1,2,3],X).$$

Figure 7–7 shows the initial state of the registers and data areas. Note that the first three **X** registers contain the arguments of the call, in this case (pointers to) two lists on the heap and one variable of the current environment.

    Now the WAM calls append. The **switch_on_term** sees that **X1** is a list (by checking its tag) and branches to the label **_579,** the code for the second clause. All the **try** instructions are avoided, because no choice point needs to be created: append is deterministic in this mode, returning only one answer. **get_list** de-references the first argument, finds that it is a list, not a variable, and puts the WAM into *read mode*. This means that **S,** the register that points to structures, is set to the first argument of the list, and that subsequent **unify** instructions will try to match the existing list rather than build a new one.

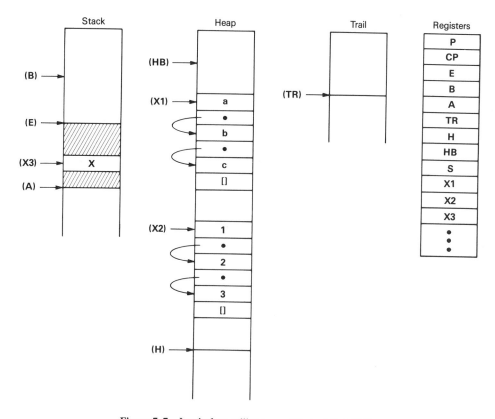

Figure 7–7   Just before calling **append([a,b,c],[1,2,3],X)**.

The first **unify_variable** copies **a**, the head of the list, into **X4** and increments **S** to point to the next argument, [b,c] (represented as .(b,.(c,[]))), the tail of the list. The next **unify_variable** then gets .(b,.(c,[])) into **X1**, which is also the first argument register for the next call. (The compiler is being clever here.) The second argument is passed unchanged to the call, so it is left alone.

The third argument, **X3**, is a variable; **get_list** therefore puts the WAM into *write mode*. Instead of addressing with **S** a list extant on the heap, the WAM copies **H** to **X3**, giving the copy a list tag. The **unify_value** then sets the head of the new list (atop the heap) to **a,** and the **unify_variable** makes the tail a free variable (untagged pointer to itself) and copies it to **X3** to prepare for the call. Now **X1** has the tail of the first list, **X2** the untouched second list, and **X3** the variable tail of the list being built, as shown in Figure 7–8. The WAM now makes the recursive call to **append,** using **execute** because there is no environment to maintain.

The recursive call proceeds much as the first one did. So does the next one. Finally the list is whittled down, and we call **append** with [] as its first argument. **switch_on_term** then branches to label **_578** and the code for the first clause. Next,

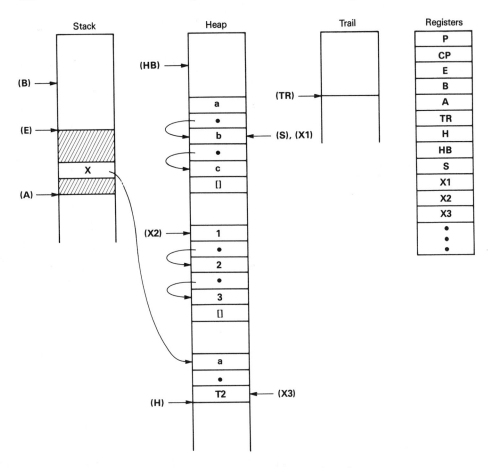

Figure 7–8   Just before the first recursive call.

get_value sets the variable atop the heap (pointed to by **X3**) to point to the list pointed to by **X2,** forming the "append" of the lists. Now the **get_nil** matches **X1,** and the **proceed** sets off a series of returns. At the end of these (see Figure 7–9) **X3** points to the new (slightly odd-looking) list atop the heap, and the call to **append** has finished.

A nondeterministic call.   Consider the call

```
?- append(X,Y,[a,b]).
```

which generates the three possible pairs of lists that, when appended, yield [a,b]. We assume that the **X** registers have been loaded with (pointers to) the two vari-

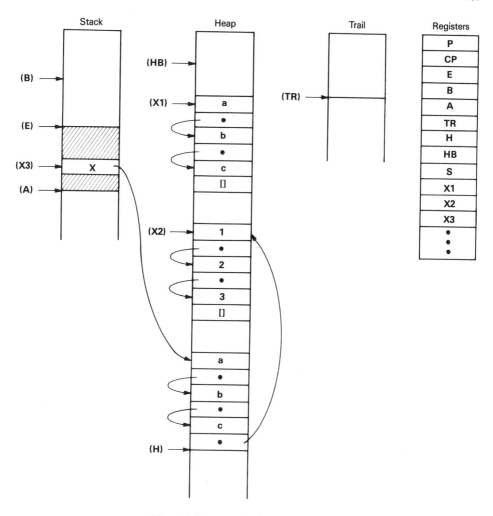

Figure 7–9   Just after the goal completes.

ables and the list, as shown in Figure 7–10. This time **switch_on_term** branches to
_580: the WAM will try both clauses. The **try_me_else** makes a choice point on the
stack, with three slots for the arguments and six more for the state of the machine,
viz., **E,** pointing to the current environment; **CP,** the current continuation; **B,** the
previous choice point; **L,** the next clause (the argument of the **try_me_else**); **TR,** the
top of the trail; and **H,** the top of the heap. The heap-backtrack pointer **HB** is set to
the current **H,** and **B** is set to the current top of the stack. That out of the way, the
get_value copies the list-pointer in **X3** to **X2,** the **get_nil** sets **X1** to [], and **proceed**
completes the call. We get X = [] and Y = [a, b], as shown in Figure 7–11.

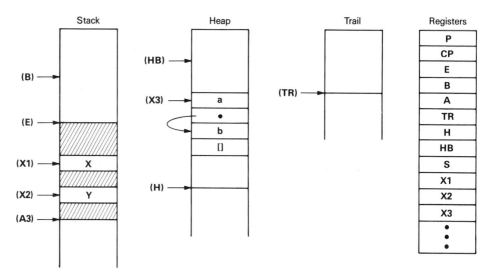

Figure 7–10   Just before calling **append(X,Y,[a,b])**.

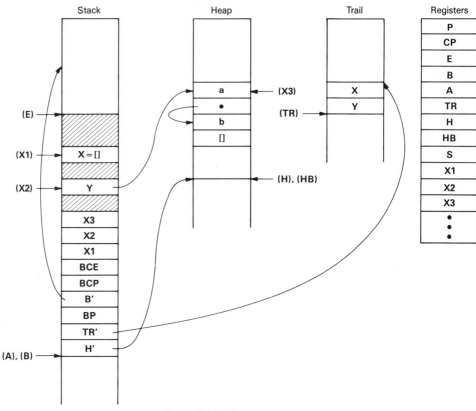

Figure 7–11   First answer.

Now suppose that we try the calling goal again. Then the WAM branches to the label **_581** of the next clause (retrieved from **L** in the choice point). There the **trust_me_else fail** resets registers **B** and **HB** with their values from the previous choice point and then discards the current choice point. This time the first **get_list** gets a variable and puts the WAM into write mode, building a new list atop the heap. Now the **unify_variable**s put (pointers to) the new (variable) head in **X4** and the new tail in **X1**. The second **get_list** gets the list [a,b], and the subsequent **unify** instructions make a the head of the new list and make **X3** point to [b] (Figure 7–12). The WAM then makes the recursive call.

switch_on_term branches to the **try_me_else**, which creates a choice point much as before. The **get**s point the second argument to [b] and complete the list on the heap with []. The **proceed** then completes the call, the previous call also completes, and append returns X = [a] and Y = [b] (see Figure 7–13).

If execution again backtracks to append, the WAM returns to the most recent choice point, where it gets the label **_581** of the second clause. Again the **trust_me_else fail** discards the choice point and retrieves the **B** and **HB** registers from the previous choice point. Everything happens much as it did the last time this clause was tried; before the recursive call, b is added to the list being built on the heap, and **X3** has [] (see Figure 7–14).

Again the **try_me_else** creates a choice point. The **get**s then set the second argument to [] and match the other [] on the heap. When all the calls complete, append returns X = [a,b] and Y = [] (see Figure 7–15).

No more answers are possible. Backtracking again restores the saved state from the choice point and then discards the choice point. The call fails on the **get_list X3** instruction, because X3 now points to a [].

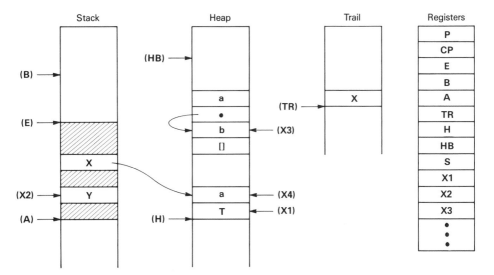

Figure 7–12   Just before the first recursive call.

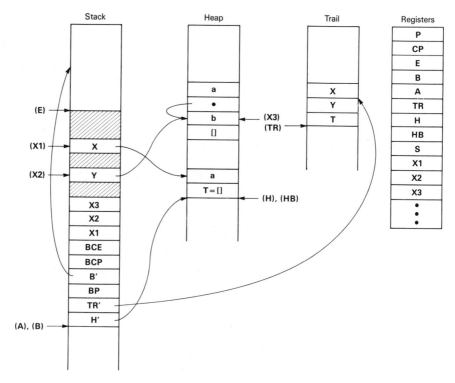

Figure 7-13   Second answer.

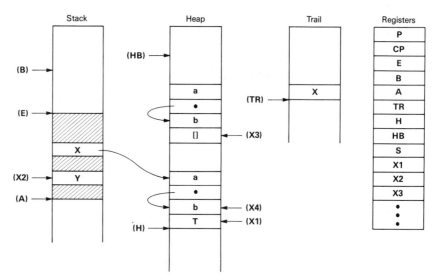

Figure 7-14   Just before the second recursive call.

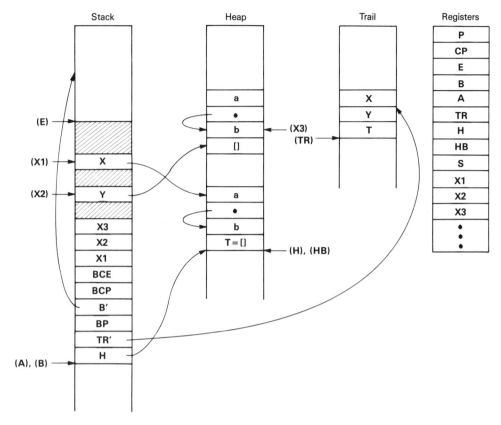

Figure 7–15   Third (final) answer.

Implementing the WAM

Essentially, there are three ways to implement a WAM: in software, microcode, and hardware. Each has its advantages: software is easy to modify and portable, microcode gives some of the speed of hardware but some of the flexibility of software, and hardware gives the best speed of all. On the other hand, software can be slow, microcode cryptic, and hardware inflexible and expensive.

Software.   A Prolog compiler can produce WAM instructions, or it can translate them to sequences of instructions native to the machine that it is compiling for. The first Prolog compiler [53], written by Warren for the DEC-10 and still held in high regard, did the latter, producing DEC-10 instructions from an early form of WAM code. Most academic and many commerical [1] compilers produce byte code and run it on a WAM emulator. The speed of such implementations depends on the emulator. Writing in a high-level language provides portability and easy maintenance at the expense of speed; assembly language and threaded code [1] are other possibilities.

Implementors who choose this method must live with the constraints of the underlying machine's architecture. Recall our examples, which are based on the public-domain SB-Prolog system [9] (a good implementation using a software WAM): on a machine with 32-bit words and addresses, we find that a tag larger than two bits costs us access to some of the virtual address space. There is no tidy way to handle floating-point numbers: a tag ruins their precision, accessing them with pointers is slow, using double precision creates a data item of another size. Managing tags is a constant nuisance if our target machine doesn't support them. Also, trying to use machine registers for **X** registers can be difficult; it is easier (but slower) to use memory instead [9].

Microcode.   There are several examples in the Prolog literature of WAMs implemented in the microcode of other machines [15,17]. Their execution speeds compare favorably to those of software emulators; however, the microcoder is at the mercy of the machine's architecture and microarchitecture. Much of the gain in performance seems to come from microcoded unification. Special-purpose micro-coded machines, with many registers and the ability to handle tags, should fare better than general-purpose machines [15]. With the rise of powerful microprocessors that are hardwired for speed, microcoded machines are less common now than a few years ago.

Hardware.   Many researchers have implemented the WAM in hardware [13,25,35,48]. In general, these machines have microcoded control, but of a WAM-style architecture. Typically they have large tags (e.g., a 40-bit word, eight bits of it tag), with some bits used to support "garbage collection." Memory management, dynamic predicates, tag checking, and the so-called garbage collection may all be supported in hardware. Some are stand-alone machines, reminiscent of Lisp machines; others are designed to be attached to a host computer.

PARALLEL MACHINES FOR PROLOG

Comparison: Parallel Machines for Expert Systems

Typically, machines designed to support expert systems do so by supporting production systems, assuming forward-chaining programs written in OPS5 or the like. All of them are parallel, and only one of them [42] consists of specialized processors analogous to the WAM. The others are collections of conventional processors, sometimes connected in a complex way, together with logic that is supposed to help production systems execute. The architecture proper is less important for these systems than the algorithms they run, notably parallel-match algorithms such as parallel Rete [31]. Early designs had about a thousand small processors, but now those with "tens" of processors [33], each one fairly powerful, are fashionable; most programs, however, lack the parallelism needed to exploit more than a few processors.

DADO [46,47] appears to be the earliest architecture meant expressly for expert systems. Up to several thousand processors, each with a small local memory and some circuitry for communication, are connected as a complete binary tree. A processor operates in SIMD (single instruction, multiple data) mode, executing instructions sent to all its descendents from some processor higher in the tree, or in MIMD (multiple instruction, multiple data) mode, executing instructions from its local memory. The rules of a production system can, for example, be distributed amongst the processors (ideally, each gets one rule), so that data to be matched against stored rules can be broadcast and the matching done in parallel.

DADO is really a general-purpose multiprocessor, as well- or ill-suited to executing production systems as a conventional computer. Diverse applications [47] have been proposed for DADO or run on the prototype machines—Prolog, Lisp, and image-processing software, for example. The largest prototype to date is the DADO2, with 1,023 eight-bit microprocessors.

Several recent machines are, essentially, modern versions of DADO: similar to general-purpose machines, with tens of closely coupled processors. The PSM architectures proposed by Gupta et al. [18] are typical: not more than 64 processors, each with a local memory and cache, with a shared global memory for the lot and a "hardware task scheduler." MANJI [32,33] is similar: a small number of powerful but ordinary microprocessors, this time with special multiport memories divided into pages and equipped with page tables. Each processor therefore has its own virtual memory which can be accessed by other processors at the same time.

Oshisanwo and Dasiewicz [37] propose a complicated model for parallel execution of production systems and then base an architecture on it. They use tens of identical processors, grouped into three very different modules that correspond to three parts of their model. One module is a DADO-style binary tree, another a collection of independent processors, and the third a collection of four-processor clusters.

PESA-1 [42] is the closest in spirit to the parallel Prolog machines we describe, in that its processors have a specialized instruction set, analogous to the WAM's. However, these processors are arranged into a pipeline, each stage being a row of processors sandwiched between two buses. Each bus serves as an input for one row and an output for the next, so that the pipeline forms a ring of alternating buses and processor-rows. Buses can be reconfigured to vary the number of stages or the number of processors in a stage, although it is not clear at what times this is done or how the machine's new configuration is decided on.

Prolog Machines

Parallel architectures for Prolog usually exploit *OR-parallelism, AND-parallelism,* or both. Usually they are collections of modified WAMs; experimental machines are often ordinary multiprocessors with each processor emulating a WAM. We describe first the different forms of parallelism (basing our classification on Conery's) and then some representative architectures and models of execution.

Forms of parallelism in Prolog.   OR-parallelism [8,55] is the parallel execution of the clauses that match a call to a predicate. Each clause provides some number of answers to the call, so that answers to a call are found in parallel. AND-parallelism [8] is the parallel execution of the goals in a clause. Each goal provides part of any solution to a clause, so that parts of a solution to a clause are found in parallel. Most other forms of parallelism are *low-level* [8], dealing with handling terms (as in parallel unification) or WAM instructions (as with a pipelined WAM), rather than larger objects such as goals or clauses.

Forms of OR-parallelism.   Conery [8] describes three types of OR-parallelism: *pure, OR-process,* and *search.* Pure OR-parallelism spawns a new process for every alternative clause; the process reports success (and the bindings it made) or failure, and then terminates. This tends to create a huge number of short-lived processes which do only simple computations and communicate a great deal, not a very practical design. The OR-parallelism used in recent machines (described in a later section) can be considered a restricted form of pure OR-parallelism. OR-processes resemble the objects of an object-oriented language: each is responsible for perhaps a few clauses or predicates of a program, and they communicate by passing messages. Search parallelism results from partitioning a program, distributing its clauses amongst processors. Typically this requires a program with many clauses per predicate, so that multiple processors work at matching a goal to one of these clauses.

Forms of AND-parallelism.   Stream parallelism treats a variable common to two goals as a channel of communication between them; for example, the first goal can build a list element by element, and the second can process each element of the list as it becomes available. This is a major source of parallelism in parallel languages related to Prolog, such as Concurrent Prolog [43], Parlog [6], and GHC [52]; users of these languages must specify it explicitly, annotating variables suitably. *AND-processors* try to solve goals of a clause simultaneously. In this case, variables shared between goals are a nuisance, because two goals running simultaneously may bind a variable inconsistently. We discuss two solutions to this shortly.

Other forms of parallelism.   Parallel unification [40] has already been considered; however, it seems that most unifications are trivial, that unification is too low-level to make communication practical between many processors, and that there is a theoretical limit on the speedup [14] (roughly logarithmic in the number of processors). Pipelining the WAM provides parallelism of a sort [49], but it does not appear to be effective [50]. Various combinations of OR- and AND-parallelism have been proposed [58].

Some parallel models and architectures for Prolog.   Early parallel architectures for Prolog resemble the general-purpose multiprocessors for production systems: the architecture is not as important as the algorithms that run on it. Most of the designs we present are more recent. As with the production-system machines and with multiprocessors in general, these have tens of processors rather than hundreds or thousands, and usually some form of shared global memory.

Conery's AND/OR-Process Model (AOPM). Conery [8] does not specify an architecture but assumes a set of processes that communicate by message-passing; a wide range of architectures can support this model of execution. Loosely speaking, his *AND/OR-Process Model* (AOPM) has two types of process. An *AND-process* manages a conjunction of goals, such as a compound query or the body of a clause, deciding which of its goals to evaluate next. It creates, for each selected goal, an OR-process that produces solutions for the goal. An *OR-process* will generally spawn descendent AND processes in turn, and so forth.

An OR-process finds all the clauses that match its goal. It creates an AND-process for each rule, keeping a list, but handles facts on its own. The OR-process sends its first answer (obtained by either means) to its parent AND-process and *gathers* any subsequent results. The parent might send a *redo* message, asking for another answer. If the OR-process has any, it returns one; if not, it sends redo messages to those of its descendent AND-processes that are still active. If all descendent ANDs are finished and the store of answers is exhausted, the OR-process responds to a redo with a *fail* message. When the parent AND fails (due to the failure of one of its ORs), it sends a *cancel* message to all its descendent ORs, which they in turn propagate to their ANDs. The message reaches the entire tree of processes, which terminates, starting from the leaves and progressing upwards.

AND-processes are more troublesome. When a variable occurs in more than one goal, the OR-processes for the goals might instantiate it to different values. Conery solves this by forbidding goals with a shared uninstantiated variable to run in parallel. One instance of a variable is selected (from a mixture of run-time and static information) as the *generator* of that variable's instantiation, with the others being *consumers*. Once the variable is instantiated, goals containing it can safely be executed in parallel.

Backtracking is difficult in the AOPM. As in the WAM or in any Prolog interpreter, we must undo bindings done by goals between the latest backtrack point and the point of failure; in the AOPM, the corresponding OR-processes will have to issue redo messages. Finding the latest backtrack point is complicated but practical.

The RAP Machine. DeGroot's *Restricted AND-parallelism* (RAP) [10,11] resembles the AOPM's AND-parallelism, but relies on compile-time rather than run-time analysis. RAP allows parallel execution only if a few simple run-time tests (e.g., of instantiation and independence of variables) can determine that it will not instantiate variables inconsistently. We lose instances of parallelism, but save run-time overhead. For example, if we have the clause

```
a(X,Y):- b(X), c(X,Y).
```

the compiler generates something equivalent to

```
a(X,Y):-
var(X)->
            b(X), c(X,Y)

        (b(x) & c(X,Y).
```

where the **&** represents parallel execution of goals. Thus, the parallel code runs only when it is safe to do so.

Hermenegildo [20–22] presents the *RAP machine,* a multiprocessor made of modified WAMs. He describes the extra capabilities a WAM needs to support AND-parallelism and then proposes extra hardware and an altered model of execution to provide them. A processor must be able to assign parallel work to other processors and keep track of the state of this work, yet retain the useful features of the original WAM. Hermenegildo shows that his design does these things and supports RAP. Figure 7–16 shows the data areas for one processor of the design and the structure of two new types of record.

Records for parallel calls, called *parcall frames,* now appear on the stack. Each processor also has a new *goal stack* onto which it pushes *goal frames* for goals that are ready to be executed in parallel. Each goal frame contains the information needed for remote execution, viz., a pointer to the predicate being called, a copy of the argument registers for the call, the predicate's arity, a pointer to its "parent" parcall frame (EPF), and its position within that parcall frame. When execution of a clause reaches a parallel call, a goal frame is pushed onto the goal stack for each of the goals, and processors (including the one executing the clause) can "steal" these frames and start to execute the goals.

The processor creates a parcall frame on the stack for each parallel call. Within this frame, each goal has a *slot* with three fields: the number of the processor that "stole" it for execution, a bit telling whether it still has alternatives, and a "ready" bit telling whether the goal's frame will actually be put on the goal stack (this is needed when execution backtracks into the parallel set: the retry should involve only goals with alternatives). The frame also holds the number of goals left to schedule, the number executing but not completed, a pointer to the first goal of the parallel call (the *Put Instruction Pointer,* used after backtracking to find parallel goals to be retried), a bit showing whether the parallel call has been backtracked into, the top of the goal stack when the parallel call began, a pointer to the previous parcall frame, and the previous parcall frame pointer (*CEPF*). PF is a new register that points to the last parcall frame—the one to try in case of backtracking.

Much of the information in the parcall frame supports backtracking. The scheme works in such manner that in a clause containing a parallel goal, goals can fail in three places: before the parallel goal, within it, and after it. In the first case, we backtrack as usual; in the second, the parallel goal fails and we backtrack to the previous goal; in the third, we backtrack as usual until we reenter the parallel goal. When we do, we consider only the goals that still have alternatives (recall that bit in

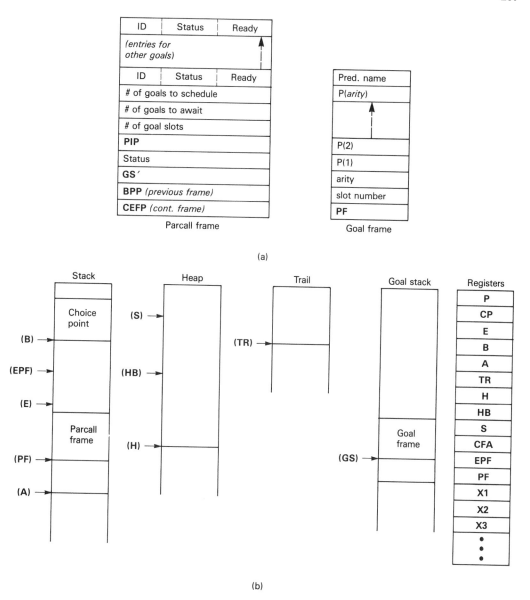

Figure 7–16 The RAP machine. (a) New data items. (b) Data areas and registers.

a parcall frame's slot). We backtrack among them in the usual way; when one succeeds, we lump those on its right into a smaller parallel goal and execute it (this is the use of the "ready" bits). Of course, if the goals all fail, we backtrack to the goal before the original parallel goal.

Recent OR-parallel Machines.   In the past few years various researchers have proposed several execution models for OR-parallelism, closely resembling each other and with corresponding architectures [55,56]. These models consider program execution as building an *OR-tree,* as shown in Figure 7–17. Note that each child of a node is the result of replacing the first goal with the body of a matching clause. If we traverse such a tree depth-first and from left to right, we get a series of lists of goals, resembling execution traces. This is just like serial Prolog execution.

Now suppose that we have a "pool" of *workers* [55]: modified WAMs or processes running on them. We begin by assigning a query (the root of the OR-tree) to one worker. It begins to work on the first clause that matches its first goal, i.e., the leftmost subtree. If other workers are idle, as of course they are initially, it assigns them the other subtrees, starting from the right. Each worker can do this with its own subtree, distributing subsubtrees of it to idle workers. If no other workers are idle, a worker simply executes its subtree by itself, just like an ordinary WAM, returning results to its parent. Then, when it can do no more, it becomes idle and waits for another task. Figure 7–18 gives the general idea: each number represents one of eight workers, and so the label of a node or tree tells which is working on it. Nodes **2** and **3** have been given the first available subtrees, **4** through **6** subsubtrees as they became available, and so forth.

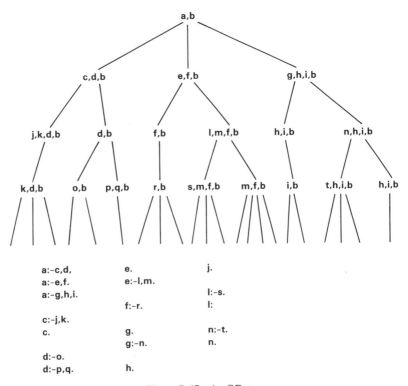

Figure 7–17   An OR-tree.

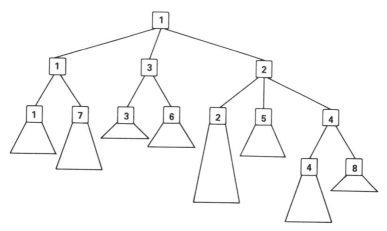

Figure 7–18 Dividing an OR-tree amongst workers.

The beauty of this scheme is that the available OR-parallelism, in theory, is always exactly right. We can give an idle worker its own subtree, or let a worker handle a large subtree on its own. If workers do not get tasks of roughly equal size, the ones that finish early can help the others. No worker is idle for long, and the workload seems to balance automatically. Compare this with the AOPM, which must restrain OR-parallel execution to prevent an exponential number of processes from being spawned, or with the RAP machine, which relies entirely on restricted AND-parallelism (perhaps too uncommon to be a mainstay [55]).

A major problem with implementing an OR-parallel machine is keeping track of the different bindings that different branches of execution make to the same variable [55]. Counting variations, about a dozen methods exist for doing this [56]. Most involve some sort of *binding array* or hash table for each worker or for each node of the OR-tree. For example, Warren's SRI model [55] gives each processor of a machine a local memory for storing a binding array.

Most of these machine models assume (or have been implemented on machines of) 16 to 32 processors, with very fast communication between them, e.g., with a shared global memory [12,44]. There are some exceptions, however [2]. The need to manage bindings quickly makes the tight coupling desirable. For instance, when a processor switches from one subtree to another, it needs to receive a set of bindings associated with the parent node of its new subtree. Whether these are readily available depends on the method for storing bindings; methods that save effort here require it elsewhere [56].

SUMMARY

Prolog is a reasonable alternative to other languages for implementing expert systems. It has more expressive power than conventional shells, yet shares many of their advantages, such as built-in inference and search mechanisms. As we have seen, it has a simple, fairly tidy syntax and an elegant mechansim of execution. Furthermore, an execution engine, the Warren abstract machine (WAM), already exists for Prolog: the language translates directly into instructions for the WAM. The WAM can be emulated in software or microcode, or built; in any case, it provides much faster execution than an interpreter.

Parallel machines designed expressly for expert systems usually support production systems. Most architectures are conventional multiprocessors with some hardware for communications or managing memory; only one appears to be based on processors analogous to the WAM. The software that performs the production-system operations in parallel is much more important than the architectures themselves. Parallel Prolog machines can be conventional multiprocessors, but more often they are collections of Warren engines. They can exploit any of several principal types of parallelism.

Implementors of expert systems should seriously consider Prolog, for both its capabilities and its speed of execution. Those who prefer to use expert system languages such as OPS5 should realize that these need a standard, serial abstract machine similar to the WAM; without the WAM, Prolog compilers and Prolog machines would be far more primitive than they are at present. The execution engine of the PESA-I processing elements [42] might be a step in the right direction, but someone needs to make a careful study of the serial execution of production systems.

REFERENCES

1. *ALS Prolog Technical Reference Manual,* Syracuse, New York: Applied Logic Systems, 1987.

2. Ali, K. A. M., "OR-Parallel Execution of Prolog on a Multi-Sequential Machine." *International Journal of Parallel Programming* 15 (1987): 189–214.

3. Ben-David, A., and Sterling, L. "A Prototype Expert System for Credit Evaluation." In *Artificial Intelligence in Economics and Management,* edited by L. F. Pau. pp. 121–128. Amsterdam: Elsevier, 1986.

4. Carlsson, M., and Widen, J. *SICStus Prolog User's Manual, SICS Research Report R88007.* Swedish Institute of Computer Science, February 1988.

5. Clark, K. L., and McCabe, F. G. "PROLOG: A Language for Implementing Expert Systems." In *Machine Intelligence 10,* edited by Y.-H. Pao. Chichester, England: Ellis Horwood, 1982.

6. Clark, K. L., and Gregory, S. "Notes on the Implementation of PARLOG." *Journal of Logic Programming* 2 (1985): 17–42.

7. Clocksin, W. F., and Mellish, C. S. *Programming in Prolog.* Berlin: Springer-Verlag, 1984.

8. Conery, J. S. *Parallel Execution of Logic Programs.* Boston: Kluwer Academic Publishers, 1987.

9. Debray, S. K. *The SB-Prolog System, Version 2.2.1: A User Manual.* Tucson, AZ, University of Arizona, 1987.

10. DeGroot, D. "Restricted AND-Parallelism." *International Conference on Fifth Generation Computer Systems.* Tokyo, 1984, pp. 471–478.

11. DeGroot, D. "Restricted AND-Parallelism and Side-Effects." *1987 Symposium on Logic Programming.* San Francisco, September 1987, pp. 80–89.

12. Disz, T., Lusk, E., and Overbeek, R. "Experiments with OR-parallel Logic Programs." *Fourth International Conference on Logic Programming.* Melbourne, 1987, pp. 576–600.

13. Dobry, T. P., Despain, A. M., and Patt, Y. N. "Performance Studies of a Prolog Machine Architecture." *Twelfth Annual International Symposium on Computer Architecture.* Boston, 1985, pp. 180–190.

14. Dwork, C., Kanellakis, P. C., and Mitchell, J. C. "On the Sequential Nature of Unification." *Journal of Logic Programming* 1 (1984): 35–50.

15. Fagin, B. S., Patt, Y. N., Srini, V., and Despain, A. M. "Compiling Prolog into Microcode: A Case Study Using the NCR/32-000." *MICRO 18 Proceedings.* Pacific Grove, CA, 1985, pp. 79–88.

16. Fagin, B. S., and Despain, A. M. "Performance Studies of a Parallel Prolog Architecture." *Fourteenth Annual International Symposium on Computer Architecture.* Pittsburgh, 1987, pp. 108–116.

17. Gee, J., Melvin, S. W., and Patt, Y. N. "Advantages of Implementing Prolog by Microprogramming a Host General Purpose Computer." *Fourth International Conference on Logic Programming.* Melbourne, 1987, pp. 1–20.

18. Gupta, A., et al. "Parallel Algorithms and Architectures for Rule-based Systems." *Thirteenth Annual International Symposium on Computer Architecture.* Tokyo, 1986, pp. 28–37.

19. Hammond, P. "Micro-PROLOG for Expert Systems." In *Micro-PROLOG: Programming in Logic,* edited by F. G. McCabe. Englewood Cliffs, New Jersey: Prentice-Hall, 1984.

20. Hermenegildo, M. V. "An Abstract Machine for Restricted AND-parallel Execution of Logic Programs." *Third International Conference on Logic Programming.* London, 1986, pp. 25–39.

21. Hermenegildo, M. V., and Nasr, R. I. "Efficient Management of Backtracking in AND-parallelism." *Third International Conference on Logic Programming.* London, 1986, pp. 40–54.

22. Hermenegildo, M. V. "Relating Goal Scheduling, Precedence, and Memory Management in AND-parallel Execution of Logic Programs." *Fourth International Conference on Logic Programming.* Melbourne, 1987, pp. 556–575.

23. Hogger, C. J. *Introduction to Logic Programming.* London: Academic Press, 1984.

24. Jackson, P. *Introduction to Expert Systems.* Workingham, England: Addison-Wesley, 1986.

25. Kaneda, Y., et al. "Sequential Prolog Machine PEK." *New Generation Computing* 4 (1986): 51–66.

26. Lloyd, J. W. *Foundations of Logic Programming.* Berlin: Springer-Verlag, 1984.

27. Maier, D., and Warren, D. S. *Computing with Logic.* Menlo Park, CA: Benjamin/Cummings, 1988.

28. Maruyama, F., et al. "Prolog-based Expert System for Logic Design." *International Conference on Fifth Generation Computer Systems.* Tokyo, 1984, pp. 563–571.

29. Matsumura, Y., et al. "Consultation System for Diagnosis of Headache and Facial Pain: RHINOS." In *Logic Programming '85: Proceedings of the Fourth Conference,* edited by E. Wada, pp. 287–298. Berlin: Springer-Verlag, 1985.

30. Matwin, S., et al. "Logic-based Tools for Negotiation Support." *1987 Symposium on Logic Programming.* San Francisco, September 1987, pp. 499–506.

31. Miranker, D. P., "Performance Estimates for the DADO Machine: A Comparison of TREAT and RETE." *International Conference on Fifth Generation Computer Systems.* Tokyo, 1984, pp. 449–457.

32. Miyazaki, J., et al. "MANJI: An Architecture for Production Systems." *Twentieth Annual Hawaii International Conference on System Sciences.* Honolulu, 1987.

33. Miyazaki, J., et al. "A Shared Memory Architecture for MANJI Production System Machine." In *Database Machines and Knowledge Base Machines.* edited by H. Tanaka, pp. 517–531. Boston: Kluwer Academic Publishers, 1988.

34. Naish, L. *Negation and Control in Prolog.* Berlin: Springer-Verlag, 1986.

35. Nakazaki, R., et al. "Design of a High-speed Prolog Machine." *Twelfth Annual International Symposium on Computer Architecture.* Boston, 1985, pp. 191–197.

36. Nitta, K., and Nagao, J. "KRIP: A Knowledge Representation System for Laws Related to Industrial Property." In *Logic Programming '85: Proceedings of the Fourth Conference,* edited by E. Wada, pp. 276–286. Berlin: Springer-Verlag, 1985.

37. Oshisanwo, A. O., and Dasiewicz, P. P. "A Parallel Model and Architecture for Production Systems." *International Conference on Parallel Processing.* St. Charles, IL, August 1987, pp. 147–153.

38. Pereira, F. C. N. *C-Prolog User's Manual.* Edinburgh: EdCAAd, 1983.

39. Poe, M. D. "Control of Heuristic Search in a PROLOG-based Microcode Synthesis Expert System." *International Conference on Fifth Generation Computer Systems.* Tokyo, 1984, pp. 589–595.

40. Robinson, J. "A Prolog Processor Based on a Pattern Matching Memory Device." *Third International Conference on Logic Programming.* London, 1986, pp. 172–179.

41. Sammut, R. A., and Sammut, C. A. "The Implementation of UNSW-Prolog." *Australian Computer Journal* 15 (1983): 58–64.

42. Schreiner, F., and Zimmerman, G. "PESA-I—A Parallel Architecture for Production Systems." *International Conference on Parallel Processing.* St. Charles, IL, August 1987, pp. 166–169.

43. Shapiro, E. Y. *A Subset of Concurrent Prolog and Its Interpreter, Technical Report TR-003.* Tokyo: Institute for New Generation Computer Technology, 1983.

44. Shen, K., and Warren, D. H. D. "A Simulation Study of the Argonne Model for Or-parallel Execution of Prolog." *1987 Symposium on Logic Programming.* San Francisco, September 1987, pp. 54–68.

45. Sterling, L., and Shapiro, E. Y. *The Art of Prolog.* Cambridge, MA: MIT Press, 1986.

46. Stolfo, S. J., Miranker, D. P., and Shaw, D. E. "Architecture and Applications of DADO: A Large Scale Parallel Computer for Artificial Intelligence." *Eighth International Joint Conference on Artificial Intelligence.* Karlsruhe, 1983, pp. 850–854.

47. Stolfo, S. J. "Initial Performance of the DADO2 Prototype." *Computer* 20 (1987): 75–83.

48. Taki, K., et al. "Hardware Design and Implementation of the Personal Sequential Inference Machine (PSI)." *International Conference on Fifth Generation Computer Systems*. Tokyo, 1984, pp. 398–409.

49. Tick, E. *An Overlapped Prolog Processor, Technical Note 308*. Menlo Park, CA: SRI International, 1983.

50. Tick, E., and Warren, D. H. D. "Towards a Pipelined Prolog Processor." *1984 Symposium on Logic Programming*. Atlantic City, February 1984, pp. 29–40.

51. Touati, H., and Despain, A. "An Empirical Study of the Warren Abstract Machine." *1987 Symposium on Logic Programming*. San Francisco, September 1987, pp. 114–124.

52. Ueda, K. "Guarded Horn Clauses." In *Logic Programming '85: Proceedings of the Fourth Conference,* edited by E. Wada, pp. 168–179. Berlin: Springer-Verlag, 1985.

53. Warren, D. H. D. *Applied Logic—Its Use and Implementation as a Programming Tool, Technical Note 290*. Menlo Park, CA: SRI International, 1983.

54. Warren, D. H. D. *An Abstract Prolog Instruction Set, Technical Note 309*. Menlo Park, CA: SRI International, 1983.

55. Warren, D. H. D. "The SRI Model for Or-parallel Execution of Prolog—Abstract Design and Implementation." *1987 Symposium on Logic Programming*. San Francisco, September 1987, pp. 92–102.

56. Warren, D. H. D. "Or-parallel Execution Models of Prolog." *1987 International Joint Conference on Theory and Practice of Software Development*. Pisa, Italy, March 1987, pp. 243–259.

57. Waterman, D. A., and Hayes-Roth, F. "An Investigation of Tools for Building Expert Systems." In *Building Expert Systems,* edited by D. B. Lenat, pp. 169–215. Reading, MA: Addison-Wesley, 1983.

58. Westphal, H., and Robert, P. "The PEPSys Model: Combining Backtracking, AND- and OR-parallelism." *1987 Symposium on Logic Programming*. San Francisco, September 1987, pp. 436–448.

59. Yoshino, H., et al. "Legal Expert System LES-2." In *Logic Programming '86: Proceedings of the Fifth Conference,* edited by E. Wada, pp. 34–45. Berlin: Springer-Verlag, 1986.

8

Building Blocks for Knowledge-based Systems Based on Generic Tasks: The Classification and Routine Design Examples

B. Chandrasekaran

NEED FOR TASK-SPECIFIC TOOLS

Expert system languages of the current generation—those that are based on rules, frames, or logic—do not distinguish between different types of knowledge-based reasoning. For example, one would expect that the task of designing a car would require significantly different reasoning strategies than the task of diagnosing a malfunction in a car. However, the expert system methodologies apply the same strategy (fire the rules whose conditions match, run the resolution engine on all propositions, etc.) to both design and diagnosis, as well as to any other task. Because of this, it has been argued that these methodologies are rather low level with respect to modeling the needed task-level behavior. In essence, these systems resemble an assembly language for writing expert systems. While this approach is obviously useful, clearly perspectives that more directly address the higher level issues of knowledge-based reasoning are needed for the next generation of AI development.

One example of a higher level approach is the *generic task* [9–11], whose aim is to identify building blocks of different types of reasoning such that each of the types is both generic and widely useful as components of complex reasoning tasks. To date, several such generic strategies have been identified which together account for a very large portion of current expert system capabilities. Each such strategy, or *task*, is characterized by:

1. The kinds of information required as input for the task and the information produced as a result of performing the task.

2. A way to represent and organize the knowledge that is needed to perform the generic task.

3. The process (algorithm, control, problem solving) that the task uses.

As each task and its associated structure is identified, languages are developed that encode both the problem-solving strategy and knowledge that is appropriate for solving problems of that type. These languages facilitate expert system development by giving the knowledge engineer access to tools which work at the level of the problem, not the level of the implementation language, as do rules or frames.

Below is a list of some of the generic tasks that we have found especially useful in building practical knowledge-based systems. As we shall see, a wide variety of diagnostic and routine design and planning problems come under this category.

1. *Hierarchical classification* is finding the categories in a classification hierarchy that apply to the situation being analyzed. The tool for classification is CSRL [6] (Conceptual Structures Representation Language). A significant portion of expert systems such as Mycin [26] and Prospector [16] can be viewed as classification systems.[1]

2. *Plan selection and refinement* is designing an object using hierarchical planning. DSPL [3, 4] (Design Specialists and Plans Language) is the tool for this generic task. The task performed by the expert systems Molgen [17] and R1 [22] can be viewed in this way. A variant of this task has been called *skeletal planning* in the literature.

3. *Knowledge-directed information passing* is determining the attribute of some datum based on the attributes of conceptually related data. The tool for this generic task is Idable (*intelligent data base language*). This task is often used in support of other tasks, such as classification or design, since all such tasks require access to a data base. A data base which uses domain-knowledge to transform data in whatever form the data are stored into a form needed for a certain task is what one might call an "intelligent" data base.

4. *Hypothesis matching* is matching hypotheses to a situation using a hierarchical representation of evidence abstractions. The general idea is that we have a set of data which potentially pertain to a concept. We then want to know how well the concept matches the data. For example, the concept may be a disease and the data may be patient data relevant to the disease, and we wish to know what the likelihood of the disease is. Hypothesis matching is a very common subtask in a number of reasoning tasks. The tool in our toolset for this task is Hyper (*Hyp*othesis match*er*).

5. *Hypothesis assembly* is constructing composite hypotheses in order to account for some set of data. Given a set of hypotheses, each explaining a subset of the data, the assembly task is to arrive at a composite hypothesis that explains all

---

[1] In fact, Clancey [15] has specifically analyzed MYCIN and shown it to be a kind of classification problem solving.

the data parsimoniously and as well as possible. Again, this task is a subtask in diagnostic reasoning as well as in theory formation in science. The task itself does not generate the initial hypotheses, which may come from some other problem-solving task, such as classification. Peirce [25] is the tool for the hypothesis assembly task; Internist [23] and Dendral [5] also perform this task in large measure, although not in the manner that Peirce proposes that it be done.

The following general points about the preceding generic knowledge-related are worth noting:

1. As mentioned, a number of well-known expert systems can be thought of as decomposable into one or more of the tasks appearing in the foregoing list. For example, R1 performs a simplified type of plan selection and refinement, while Mycin performs classification and data abstraction (one of the capabilities of knowledge-directed information passing) in its diagnostic part and plan selection in its therapy part. Note, however, that in all these instances the systems perform the tasks, but not necessarily in the manner that we propose they be performed. The claim is that once we understand the knowledge requirements and the inference strategies for each of the tasks, we can use methods that are more natural for the tasks.

2. We have mentioned that diagnosis uses one or more of the preceding generic tasks, e.g., classification and hypothesis assembly. Note, however, that we do not have a generic task called diagnosis in the list. The reason for this is that, while diagnosis is generic in the sense that it occurs in a number of domains and there are similarities in diagnostic methods that are domain-independent, it is still a compound task in the sense that a number of distinct types of knowledge and inferences are used in performing a diagnosis. Thus, the foregoing list of tasks can be used as natural building blocks for putting together a diagnostic problem solver. This illustrates an additional constraint on the notion of a generic task: the task needs to be coherent and simple in the sense that it ought to be characterizable by a simple type of knowledge and a family of inference types. This is what makes the term "building blocks" applicable to these items.

3. The list is not meant to be a complete list of generic tasks that are useful in knowledge-based problem solving. In fact, quite a large part of AI can be thought of as attempts to identify interesting problems, the kind of knowledge required for their solution, and the kinds of inferences useful in attaining that solution. Thus, in qualitative reasoning, the generic problem considered is one where, given the structure of a system, the system's behavior is to be derived in a qualitative way. The research program identifies the knowledge and inferences required for the task. In the appropriate context, each of these can then be thought of as possible generic tasks. Our goal at the Laboratory for Artificial Intelligence Research has been to produce a methodology and a tech-

nology that help in the analysis, design, construction, and debugging of practical knowledge systems, and thus we concentrated on the generic tasks that we felt would be most useful at this stage in the development of the technology. Research is also under way on generic tasks that would cover phenomena in deep models, from structure-to-behavior reasoning and functional reasoning.

In the rest of the chapter, we consider the use of a few of the tools involved, especially CSRL and DSPL, and indicate how they ease the task of building certain kinds of systems.

CLASSIFICATORY PROBLEM SOLVING AND CSRL[2]

Classification is a ubiquitous problem-solving activity in human reasoning. Hierarchical classification is a particular method of performing the classification task under certain conditions, namely, the availability of a classification hierarchy that organizes the classificatory hypotheses. For example, medical diagnosis uses disease hierarchies, and in many engineering domains malfunction hierarchies are quite common.

The generic task characterization of hierarchical classification is as follows:

Information required and results yielded. Hierarchical classification requires as input a data description of the problem to be solved. After processing, the task yields all the categories of the malfunction hierarchy that apply to the given data.

Knowledge and organization required. The classifier requires a preenumerated list of the categories that it will be using. Furthermore, these categories must be organized into a hierarchy in which the *children* (i.e., the subnodes) of a node represent subhypotheses of the *parent* (i.e., the superior node). Figure 8–1 illustrates a fragment of a tree from a hierarchical classification system for the diagnosis of fuel system malfunctions in a car engine. As the hierarchy is traversed from the top down, the categories (or in this particular case, hypotheses about the failure of the fuel system) become more specific. Thus, the children of the hypothesis "bad fuel problems" are the more specific hypotheses "low octane," "water in fuel," and "dirt in fuel."

Each node in the hierarchy is responsible for calculating the "degree of fit," or *confidence value,* of the hypotheses that the node represents. For example, the "bad fuel problems" node is responsible for determining whether there is a bad fuel problem and the degree of confidence it has in that decision. Each node can be thought of as an expert in determining whether the hypothesis it represents is true. For this reason, each node is termed a *specialist* in its small domain. To create each

---

[2] Much of the material in this section is from B. Chandrasekaran and William F. Punch III, "Hierarchical Classification: Its Usefulness for Diagnosis and Sensor Validation," an invited talk at the Second AIAA/NASA/USAF Symposium on Automation, Robotics and Advanced Computing for the National Space Program, March 9–11, 1987.

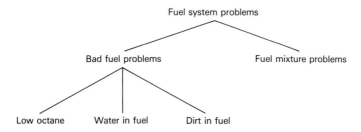

Figure 8–1 Fragment of fuel system classification tree.

specialist, knowledge must be provided to make the degree-of-confidence decision. The general idea is that each specialist specifies a list of *features* that are important in determining whether the hypothesis it represents is true and a list of *patterns* that map combinations of features to confidence values. In the fuel-system-problems specialist, such features might include gas mileage problems, poor performance, and difficulty in starting the engine, and one pattern might be that if all the features are present then the fuel-system-problems hypothesis is likely.

The Control Strategy of Hierarchical Classification

Given that the knowledge of the system is organized as a set of specialists in a hierarchy, how can the hierarchy be *efficiently* traversed? The process is accomplished primarily through a type of hypothesis refinement called *establish-refine*. Simply put, a specialist that *establishes* its hypothesis (i.e., gives the hypothesis a high confidence value) *refines* itself by activating its more detailed subspecialists, while a specialist that rules out or rejects its hypothesis (i.e., gives the hypothesis a low confidence value) does not send any messages to its subspecialists, thus avoiding that entire part of the hierarchy. The reason for this becomes obvious when one thinks again of how the specialists are organized. The subhypotheses of "fuel system problems," for example, are simply more detailed hypotheses. So if there is no evidence for "fuel system problems" (i.e., the hypothesis is ruled out), then there is no point in examining more detailed hypotheses about failures of the fuel system.

The establish-refine process continues until no more refinements can take place. This can occur either by having reached the tip level hypotheses of the hierarchy or by having ruled out mid-hierarchy hypotheses.

CSRL, a Language Tool for Hierarchical Classification Systems

CSRL (Conceptual Structure Representation Language) [6] is a language for writing hierarchical-classification expert systems. The current version of CSRL is really a mixture of both the hierarchical-classification problem solver and the hypothesis matcher. A new version of the hypothesis matcher alone is called Hyper, and more recently the problem solving involved has been generalized as a form of recognition [20]. In this section, we shall describe the older form of CSRL.

CSRL allows a knowledge engineer to do three things:

1. Create a hierarchy of malfunction hypotheses in a particular domain.
2. Encode the pattern-matching knowledge for each hypothesis into a specialist.
3. Control the process of establish-refine problem solving.

Encoding the Hierarchy of Malfunctions

In CSRL, a hierarchical classification system is implemented by individually defining a specialist for each malfunction hypothesis. The super- and subspecialists of a specialist are declared within the definition. Figure 8–2 is a skeletal outline of a specialist definition for the bad-fuel node from Figure 8–1. The DECLARE section specifies the relationship of this node to other specialists. The other sections of the specialist will be examined later.

```
(SPECIALIST BadFuel

    (DECLARE (SUPERSPECIALIST FuelSystem)

        (SUBSPECIALIST LowOctane WaterInFuel

        DirtInFuel))

    (KGS ...)

    (MESSAGES ...))
```

Figure 8–2   Skeletal specialist for BadFuel.

Designing a classification hierarchy is an important part of building a CSRL expert system, but the exact structure of the final system is a pragmatic decision rather than a search for the perfect hierarchy. The main criterion for evaluating a classification hierarchy is whether enough evidence is normally available to make confident decisions. To decompose a specialist into its subspecialists, the simplest method is to ask the domain expert what subhypotheses should be considered next. The subhypotheses should be subtypes of the specialist's hypothesis and will usually differ from one another based on a single attribute (e.g., location or cause).

Encoding Pattern-Matching Knowledge

The knowledge groups in the KGS section of the BadFuel specialist contain knowledge that matches the features of a specialist against the case data. Each knowledge group is used to determine a confidence value for some subset of features used by the specialist. As such, a knowledge group becomes an *evidential abstraction* of a particular set of features important to establishing the specialist. A knowledge group is implemented as a cluster of production rules that maps the values of a list of expressions (Boolean and arithmetic operations on data, values of other knowledge groups) to some conclusion on a discrete, symbolic scale.

```
(RELEVANT TABLE

  (MATCH

    (ASKYNU? "Is the car slow to respond")

    (ASKYNU? "Does the car start hard")

    (AND (ASKYNU? "Do you hear knocking or

            pinging sounds")

        (ASKYNU? "Does the problem occur while

            accelerating"))

  WITH (IF T ? ?

      THEN +3

      ELSEIF ? T ?

      THEN −3

      ELSEIF ? ? T

      THEN 3

      ELSE 1)))
```

Figure 8–3   Relevant knowledge group of BadFuel.

As an example, Figure 8–3 is the relevant knowledge group of the BadFuel specialist. The group determines whether the symptoms of the automobile are consistent with bad fuel problems. The expressions in the MATCH part query the user (who acts as the data base for this case) concerning whether the car is slow to respond, starts hard, has knocking or pinging sounds, or has the problem when accelerating. ASKYNU? is a LISP function which asks the user for a Y (yes), N (no), or U (unknown) answer and translates that answer into T (true), F (false), or U (unknown), the values of CSRL's three-valued logic. (Note that any LISP function may be used here.) The results of the MATCH expressions are then compared to a condition list in the WITH part of the knowledge group. For example, the first pattern, "T ? ?", in the figure tests whether the first match expression (ASKYNU? "Is the car slow to respond") is true (the ? in the pattern means "doesn't matter"). If so, then −3 becomes the value of the knowledge group.[3] Otherwise, subsequent patterns ("? T ?" or "? ? T") are evaluated. The value of the knowledge group will be 1 if no rule matches. This knowledge group encodes the following matching knowledge:

> If the car is slow to respond or if the car starts hard, then BadFuel is not relevant in this case. Otherwise, if there are knocking or pinging sounds and if the problem occurs while accelerating, then BadFuel is highly relevant. In all other cases, BadFuel is only mildly relevant.

[3] In this case, the values assigned are on a discrete scale from −3 to 3, −3 representing "ruled out" and 3 representing "confirmed."

Figure 8–4 is the summary knowledge group of BadFuel. Its MATCH expressions are the values of the relevant and gas knowledge groups (the latter queries the user about the temporal relationship between the onset of the problem and when gas was last bought). In this case, if the value of the relevant knowledge group is 3 and the value of the gas knowledge group is greater than or equal to 0, then the value of the summary knowledge group (and consequently the confidence value of BadFuel) is 3, indicating that a bad fuel problem is very likely.

```
(SUMMARY TABLE

  (MATCH RELEVANT gas

  WITH (IF 3 (GE 0)

      THEN 3

      ELSEIF 1 (GE 0)

      THEN 2

      ELSEIF ? (LT 0)

      THEN  – 3)))
```

Figure 8–4   Summary knowledge group of BadFuel.

This method of evidence combination allows the calculation of the confidence value to be hierarchically organized. That is, the results of any number of knowledge groups can be further abstracted by a knowledge group that can combine their values into a single confidence value.

Encoding Establish-Refine Strategy

The MESSAGES section of a specialist contains a list of message procedures which specify how the specialist will respond to different messages from its superspecialist. ESTABLISH and REFINE are predefined messages in CSRL; others may be created by the user. The ESTABLISH message procedure of a specialist determines the *confidence value* (i.e., the degree of fit) of the specialist's hypothesis. Figure 8–5 illustrates the ESTABLISH message procedure of the BadFuel specialist. "Relevant" and "summary" are names of knowledge groups of BadFuel (see previous section). "Self" is a keyword which refers to the name of the specialist. The procedure first tests the value of the relevant knowledge group. (If this knowledge group has not already been evaluated, it is automatically evaluated at this point.) If it is greater than or equal to 0, then BadFuel's confidence value is set to the value of the summary knowledge group; otherwise it is set to the value of the relevant knowl-

```
(ESTABLISH (IF (GE relevant 0)

  THEN (SETCONFIDENCE self summary)

  else (SETCONFIDENCE self relevant)))
```

Figure 8–5   ESTABLISH procedure of BadFuel.

edge group. A value of +2 or +3 indicates that the specialist is established. In this case, the procedure corresponds to the following strategy:

> First perform a preliminary check to make sure that BadFuel is a relevant hypothesis to hold. If it is not (i.e., if the value of the relevant knowledge group is less than 0), then set BadFuel's confidence value to the degree of relevance. Otherwise, perform more complicated reasoning (the summary knowledge group combines the values of other knowledge groups) to determine BadFuel's confidence value.

The REFINE message procedure determines which subspecialists should be invoked and which messages they are sent. Figure 8–6 shows a REFINE procedure which is a simplified version of the one that BadFuel uses. "Subspecialists" is a keyword which refers to the subspecialists of the current specialist. The procedure calls each subspecialist with an ESTABLISH message. If the subspecialist establishes itself (+? tests whether the confidence value is +2 or +3), then it is sent a REFINE message.

```
(REFINE (FOR specialist IN subspecialists

    DO (CALL specialist WITH ESTABLISH)

      (IF ( + ? specialist)

        THEN (CALL specialist

          WITH REFINE))))
```

Figure 8–6   Sample REFINE procedure.

Computational Advantages of Hierarchical Classification

The major advantage of a hierarchical classification system is the organization of both the hierarchy of malfunctions and the knowledge groups within a specialist. This organization allows an efficient examination of the knowledge of the system based on need.

Consider again the hierarchy of Figure 8–1. The problem solving begins by evaluating the specialist "fuel system problems." If that specialist is established, then the two subspecialists "bad fuel problems" and "fuel mixture problems" are invoked. If however, "bad fuel specialist" is not established, then none of its subspecialists will be invoked. Thus, if a specialist is ruled out (i.e., is not established), then none of the knowledge of its subspecialists need be run.

The same is true of the knowledge groups in the specialist: only that knowledge necessary to confirm or deny the knowledge group is run. If a row of the knowledge group is matched, then none of the subsequent rows are evaluated. Again, this results in running only the knowledge necessary for the problem at hand.

Compare this with other so-called hierarchical approaches to diagnosis. The *fault tree* is a sequence of causally related events that leads to an observable symptom in the system. Given an initial malfunction, all possible causal results of the event are traced out, terminating with the symptoms that would be observed by a human diagnostician. When applied to an entire system, the result is a network of events that represent all the causal relationships of the system's constituent parts. While useful in design tasks, application of fault trees to diagnosis has a couple of problems:

1. The combinatorial fan-out from an initial event can be very large, making the job of creating and traversing the network difficult. Compare this with the abstraction of hypotheses in hierarchical classification systems. Each node in the hierarchy represents a malfunction hypothesis that is listed in more detail through its subspecialists. If there are many subspecialists in the hierarchical decomposition of the domain, more levels of abstraction can be introduced to limit the fan-out. Such abstraction does not exist in fault tree representations.

2. Fault trees make no attempt to limit the number of nodes of the network that must be evaluated. Given a significant event, all possibilities are examined. By contrast, hierarchical classifiers make use of the abstraction of malfunction hypotheses to limit the number of nodes that must be examined based on the data of the case.

Practical Applications of Hierarchical Classification

A number of diagnostic systems have been built using the hierarchical classification approach provided by the CSRL tool. Let us consider some of these applications and their domains. In doing so, we note that Auto-Mech is strictly a pedagogical system, the nuclear power and chemical engineering plant systems are prototypes of larger systems needed for real-world applications, and Red, WELDEX, and ROMAD are being developed to be used in real-world situations.

Auto-Mech [30].   Auto-Mech is an expert system which diagnoses fuel problems in automobile engines. The purpose of the fuel system is to deliver a mixture of fuel and air to the air cylinders of the engine. It can be divided into major subsystems (fuel delivery, air intake, carburetor, and vacuum manifold) which correspond to initial hypotheses about fuel system faults.

Auto-Mech consists of 34 CSRL specialists in a hierarchy which varies from four to six levels deep. Before running, Auto-Mech collects some initial data from the user, including the major symptom that the user notices (such as stalling) and the situation in which this occurs (e.g., accelerating with a cold engine). Any additional questions are asked while Auto-Mech's specialists are running. The diagnosis continues until the user is satisfied that it is complete.

A major part of Auto-Mech's development was determining the assumptions that would be made about the design of the automobile engine and the data that the program would use. Different automobile engine designs have a significant effect on the hypotheses that are considered. An engine with a carburetor, for example, will have a different set of problems than an engine that uses fuel injection (the former can have a broken carburetor). The data were assumed to come from commonly available resources. The variety of computer analysis information that is available to mechanics today was not considered in order to simplify building Auto-Mech.

Red [28].   Red is an expert system whose domain is red blood cell antibody identification. An everyday problem that a blood bank contends with is the selection of units of blood for transfusion during major surgery. The primary difficulty is that antibodies in the patient's blood may attack the transfused blood, rendering the new blood useless as well as presenting additional danger to the patient. Thus, identifying the patient's antibodies and selecting blood which will not react with them is a critical task for nearly all red blood transfusions.

The Red expert system is composed of three major subsystems, one of which is implemented in CSRL. The non-CSRL subsystems are a data base which maintains and answers questions about reaction records (reactions of the patient's blood in selected blood samples under a variety of conditions) and an overview system, which assembles a composite hypothesis about the antibodies that would best explain the reaction record. (This assembly is itself a generic task called "abductive assembly," and a tool called PEIRCE can be used to build the assembly system.) CSRL is used to implement specialists corresponding to the common blood antibodies and to each antibody subtype (different ways that the antibody can react).

The major function of the Red specialists is to rule out antibodies and their subtypes whenever possible, thus simplifying the job of the overview subsystem, and to assign confidence values, informing the overview subsystem about which antibodies appear to be more plausibly operative. The specialists query the data base for information about the laboratory results and other patient information and also tell the data base to perform certain operations on reaction records.

Complex mechanical systems.   CSRL has been used in creating expert systems that diagnose faults in the domains of both nuclear power plants and chemical engineering.

The nuclear power industry must be very careful in the maintenance of operational power plants since mistakes can prove costly not only in terms of power plant damage but also in terms of radiation leakage and broad environmental damage. Nuclear power plants are therefore heavily monitored in many areas—so heavily, in fact, that it is difficult (if not impossible) for the operator to maintain an understanding of just what exactly is going on. The nuclear power plant expert system [19] is designed to take in large amounts of data and classify them into one of approximately 25 different failures. One advantage of the CSRL approach is that the operator can be informed about the problem at a high level if no specific failure can be discovered.

The problems of the chemical engineering plant are similar to those of the nuclear power plant, but there are a number of differences. While safety is of course of concern, there is also the problem of product quality in a chemical engineering plant. If a malfunction occurs that produces an unusable product, the operation must be brought quickly back into line or large amounts of material will be wasted. The chemical engineering expert system [27] diagnoses a typical reactor that produces a solid product as a result of the reaction of a liquid product with oxygen. It consists of approximately 30 specialists that represent hypotheses about failures of the various physical parts of the plant. In addition to using data that monitor the state of the reactor, these specialists also use data about product quality to make the confidence value decision.

Other real-world uses of CSRL. CSRL is being used to develop two commercial systems by the Knowledge Based Systems group at the Battelle Columbus Institute. WELDEX and ROMAD are diagnostic systems for detecting welding defects and evaluating machinery, respectively. A brief description of WELDEX follows.

Welding industry standards and regulations require careful inspection of every weld and a very high level of quality control. Thus, industries which rely on welding technology, such as the gas pipeline industry, usually employ radiographic inspection, a tedious, time-consuming, and expensive operation. The problem these industries face can be decomposed into two tasks: visual processing of the radiograph to extract relevant features of the weld, and mapping these visual features to the welding defects which give rise to them. WELDEX is intended to perform the second of these. The current prototype consists of 25 CSRL specialists that are organized around different regions of the weld, taking advantage of the fact that each class of defects tends to occur in a particular region. The knowledge groups in these specialists concentrate on the optical contrast, shape, size, and location of the radiographic features. A customer version of WELDEX is currently being developed. Future work will likely involve developing a visual processing system whose output would be processed by WELDEX, thus automating both components of the radiographic inspection task.

ROUTINE DESIGN AND DSPL[4]

Design is in general complex and, from the viewpoint of AI, a relatively poorly understood activity. However, there is a core process in design that has the following characteristics. (1) Design knowledge regarding the problem is available such that the problem can be decomposed into a number of smaller design problems, each of which might in turn be further decomposable. (2) Additionally, for each such problem, there are known methods called abstract *design plans* that result in a successful design. Whenever a design problem can be solved with such decompositions and design plans, and whenever the design plans themselves are straightforward, i.e., without hidden problem solving in their primitive operations, the

---

[4] Parts of this section are taken from a number of papers coauthored with D. C. Brown.

situation is called *routine design.* Although routine, the task is not simple and is still a problem-solving activity. Especially when some of the design plans fail, alternative plans need to be chosen, and decisions about how far to back up the design and what sort of changes are to be made to it must be made at run time. Enough design activity in industry falls in this class to warrant serious research into the problem.

DSPL is a language designed by D. C. Brown [3] which captures the problem-decomposition knowledge in the form of a hierarchy of *design specialists* and the planning knowledge of each specialist in the form of *design plans.* The specialists also have a certain amount of compiled *failure-handling knowledge,* i.e., knowledge that helps them recover when any of the chosen plans fails to accomplish its mission.

The approach taken is to consider design knowledge to be in the form of actively cooperative design specialists. These specialists are organized in a hierarchy that reflects the human designer's conceptual organization of the design activity. The specialists use their own local design knowledge, but can also use the specialists directly below them in the hierarchy. Such use is controlled by plans embedded in every specialist. Each specialist is responsible for some portion of the design, its plans representing alternative methods for designing that portion. Communication among specialists is in the form of messages that flow up and down the hierarchy between the specialists and between their local agents (i.e., local design knowledge). Messages flowing up may indicate either failure or success.

The domain chosen for the application of DSPL was that of designing an air cylinder that was used by a local company in many pieces of equipment but which needed to be redesigned each time due to changing requirements, such as the air pressure and the length of the stroke of the cylinder. A system called AIR-CYL [4] was written that does the design given a set of requirements.

DSPL: The Design Specialists and Plans Language

The air cylinder (AC) shown in Figure 8–7 has about 15 parts, almost all of which are manufactured by the company according to their own particular designs, since their requirements are such that their components cannot be purchased. The AC is thus redesigned and changed slightly for applications with markedly different requirements. This characteristic lends the device readily to routine design. In the AC's operation, compressed air forces a piston back into a tube against a spring. Movement is limited by a bumper. The spring returns the piston, together with its attached "load," to its original position when the air pressure drops.

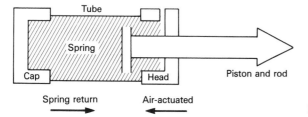

Figure 8–7 Air cylinder.

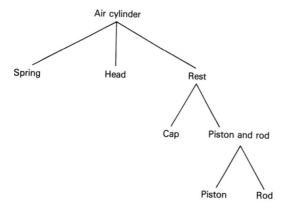

Figure 8–8   Specialist hierarchy for designing an air cylinder.

The corresponding design specialist hierarchy is given in Figure 8–8. The expert system for the design of air cylinders is organized as a hierarchy of such specialists.

DSPL provides a way of writing declarations for specialists, plans, tasks, steps, constraints, failure handlers, redesigners, sponsors, and selectors that allow the user to specify the knowledge contained in them. In the following section we address each of these declarations in turn.

To build a design expert system (DES) in DSPL, the user declares all the agents (i.e., active design knowledge) required and then allows the underlying system to link them together after some checking. Once formed, the DES can be invoked by requesting a design from the topmost specialist. The design then proceeds according to the specialist's plans. After a successful termination, the design data base contains the completed design. If a failure occurs, reasons are given. The DSPL system provides the underlying problem-solving control.

Design Agents

Specialists.   A specialist is a design agent that will attempt to design a section of the component. The specialists chosen, their responsibilities, and their hierarchical organization will reflect the mechanical designer's underlying conceptual structure of the problem domain. Exactly what each specialist's responsibilities are depends on where in the hierarchy it is placed. Higher specialists have more general responsibilities. Thus, the topmost specialist is responsible for the whole design. A specialist lower down in the hierarchy makes more detailed decisions. Each specialist has the ability to make design decisions about the part, parts, or function in which it specializes. Those decisions are made in the context of previous design decisions made by other specialists. A specialist can do its piece of design by itself, or it can utilize the services of other specialists below it in the hierarchy. This cooperative design activity of the specialists is called *design refinement*.

Every specialist also has some local design knowledge, expressed in the form of constraints. These are used to decide on the suitability of incoming requirements and data and on the ultimate success of the specialist itself (i.e., the constraints capture those major things that must be true of the specialist's design before it can be considered successfully completed). Other constraints, embedded in the specialist's plans, are used to check the correctness of intermediate design decisions. Still other constraints are present in the design data base as general consistency checks. A typical specialist is shown in Figure 8–9.

```
(SPECIALIST

    (NAME     Head)

    (USED-BY AirCylinder)

    (USES     None)

    (DESIGN-PLANS      HeadDP1)

    (DESIGN-PLAN-SELECTOR  Headdpselector)

    (ROUGH-DESIGN-PLANS   HeadRDP1)

    (INITIAL-CONSTRAINTS    None)

    (FINAL-CONSTRAINTS    None)
```

Figure 8–9   Specialist Head.

Selectors are used to select from amongst the specialist's plans. If no selector is specified a default selector is used which selects plans in the order of their declaration. Note that in the declaration of the selector, as with other declarations, the order of the individual parts of the declaration may vary according to the user's wishes.

Plans.   Each specialist has a collection of plans that may be selected depending on the situation, and it will follow the plan in order to achieve that part of the design for which it is responsible. A plan consists of a sequence of calls to specialists or tasks (see next), possibly with interspersed constraints. It represents one method for designing the section of the component represented by the specialist. The specialists below the plan will refine the design independently, tasks produce further values, and constraints will check on the integrity of the decisions made, while the whole plan gives the specific sequence in which the agents may be invoked. Typically, as one goes down in the hierarchy, the plans tend to become fewer in number and more straightforward. An example of this is shown in Figure 8–10.

The type of a plan can be "Design" or "RoughDesign," depending on which phase of the design the knowledge applies to. The SPONSOR's job is to give an opinion to a selector about how suitable the plan is given the current state of the design. The BODY contains the details of the plan and consists of an ordered list of plan items. In the example presented, the plan consists entirely of tasks, with the exception of a constraint test and the last item, which is a function provided by DSPL to print out the attributes and values of some part of the design.

```
(PLAN

    (NAME    HEADDP1)

    (TYPE    Design)

    (USED-BY Head)

    (SPONSOR HeadDP1Sponsor)

    (BODY HeadTubeSeat)

        MountingHoles

        Bearings

        SealAndWiper

        AirCavity

        AirInlet

        (CHECK-CONSTRAINT Air)

        TieRodHoles

    (REPORT-ON Head)
```

Figure 8–10   Plan HeadDP1.

Steps, tasks, and constraints.   A step may be considered a design agent that can make one design decision given the current state of the design and taking into account any constraints. For example, one step would decide on the material for some subcomponent, while another would decide on its thickness.

A typical step in AIR-CYL is given in Figure 8–11. The step is USED-BY the AirCavity task. The ATTRIBUTE-NAME is the attribute for which the step is to design a value—that is, the internal diameter of the air cavity in the head of the air cylinder. If a failure occurs, the REDESIGNER will attempt to recover from it by altering the value of the attribute just selected. The declaration REDESIGN NOT-POSSIBLE is also allowed. If the step itself fails, the FAILURE-SUGGESTIONS get passed up to the controlling task in a failure message. The suggestions refer to attributes that might be the cause of the failure. Each item in the suggestion list is evaluated at failure time. Conditional suggestions such as (IF (. x y) THEN (SUGGEST ...)) are allowed. However, if the suggestion includes an expression, as in (DECREASE xyz BY (+pqr 0.56)), then the SUGGEST function will arrange for the value to be computed. The actions DECREASE, INCREASE, and CHANGE refer to attributes, such as RodDiameter. In the current system, all attribute names must be unique.

The BODY of the step is divided into KNOWN and DECISION sections. The keywords KNOWNS and DECISIONS will work just as well, and, in general, singular or plural keywords may be used as required. The KNOWN section obtains the values from the design data base by doing KB-FETCH, which uses the component and attribute names. The single quote (') is used to indicate that the name given is to be used directly without evaluation, as opposed to the use of a variable (e.g., HeadMaterial), which should be evaluated prior to use (e.g., giving the value "Aluminum").

```
(STEP

    (NAME        AirCavityID)

    (USED-BY        AirCavity)

    (ATTRIBUTE-NAME HeadAirCavityID)

    (REDESIGNER      AirCavityIDRedesigner)

    (FAILURE-SUGGESTIONS)

        (SUGGEST (DECREASE RodDiameter))

        (SUGGEST (DECREASE HeadBearingThickness))

        (SUGGEST (CHANGE HeadMaterial

            TO DECREASE MinThickness))


(COMMENT "Find air cavity internal diam")

(BODY

    (KNOWN

    BearingThickness

        (KB-FETCH      'Head 'HeadBearingThickness)

    RodDiameter

        (KB-FETCH      'Rod 'RodDiameter)

    HeadMaterial

        (KB-FETCH      'Head 'HeadMaterial)

    MiniThickness

        (KB-FETCH      HeadMaterial 'MinThickness)


(DECISIONS

MaxRodRadius (VALUE+ (HALF RodDiameter))

MaxBearingThickness

        (VALUE+ BearingThickness)

AirCavityRadius

        (+ MinThickness

            (+ MaxRodRadius

                MaxBearingThickness))

AirCavityID      (DOUBLE AirCavityRadius)

REPLY (TEST-CONSTRAINT ACID)

REPLY (KB-STORE

    'Head 'HeadAirCavityID AirCavityID)
```

Figure 8–11 Step AirCavityID.

231

The DECISIONS section contains the design knowledge. It consists of variable-action pairs, where the action is evaluated and its value is assigned to the variable. The variable may then be used in subsequent actions in the step. The variables set in the KNOWNS section may also be used. Arithmetic expressions use prefix operators. The function VALUE+ returns the value plus the positive tolerance of the value and, consequently, provides the largest magnitude for that value. Many other functions are available.

There are two distinguished variable names: REPLY and COMMENT. COMMENT acts as a dummy assignment and expects a string as the action. This is just a way of inserting a comment into the body of the step. REPLY is used when there is no value produced by the action, and a message showing success or failure is produced instead. TEST-CONSTRAINT and KB-STORE are two examples of the action of REPLY. TEST-CONSTRAINT while KB-STORE puts the value calculated by the step into the design data base. It produces a failure message if a constraint in the design data base fails. Any failure will stop the execution of the body and cause the DECISION section to fail.

A task is a design agent which is expressed as a sequence of steps, possibly with interspersed constraints. It is responsible for handling the design of one logically, structurally, or functionally coherent section of the component—for example, a seat for a seal, or a hole for a bolt.

A constraint is an agent that will test for a particular relationship between two or more attributes at some particular stage of the design. Constraints can occur at almost any place in the hierarchy. For example, a constraint might check that a hole for a bolt is not too small to be machinable given the material being used.

Other Features

The main purpose of this exposition is not to give a complete description of DSPL, but to give a feel for the task-specific nature of the tool. Accordingly, we briefly describe a few other essential features of the language.

A *failure-handling and redesign* capability is an important requirement for anything more complicated than relatively simple design problems. DSPL does not have failure analysis capabilities, but it can accept explicit knowledge about how to handle different kinds of failures during design. All design agents detect their own failure, are able to determine what went wrong (at least superficially), attempt to see if they can fix the problem locally, do so if they can, and report the failure only if all attempts to remedy it fail. Agents which have some control over other agents can use those agents in their attempts to correct the detected problem.

Each kind of agent has a different kind of reason for failing. For example, a step finds that a decision violates some constraint, a task discovers that a step's failure can't be mended locally, a plan fails if it is discovered that it is not applicable to the situation to which it is being applied, and a specialist fails if all of its plans fail.

For every kind of failure, a message giving details is generated and passed back to the calling agent. Wherever possible, the message includes suggestions about what might be done to alleviate the problem. As there are usually many kinds of problems that can occur, an agent will first look at the message to decide what went on below. This examination is done by the failure handler associated with the agent. Much of the failure analysis is provided by the system, but in some cases (for example, constraint failures), the user (that is, the person using the plan language to write a design system) has to supply some details. For some conditions immediate failure can be specified, while for others a redesign might be attempted.

Knowledge about how to recover from failure can be coded as a *redesigner*. Since there appears to be a difference between the "most reasonable choice" knowledge encoded in a step and the "most reasonable adjustment" knowledge encoded in a redesigner, DSPL provides a number of constructs for representing failure-handling knowledge of both types.

A *sponsor* is associated with a plan and is responsible for estimating the suitability of the plan for a particular design situation. A *selector* takes the output of the sponsor and decides whether or not to use the plan if it has been recommended as suitable. The sponsor is expected to provide a suitability value for the plan, and if it cannot, a "use of plan language" failure will occur.

The *selector* takes as input the names of the plans being considered and their suitabilities for use in the design situation as decided by their sponsors. It then picks a plan for the specialist to execute.

Use and Extensions of DSPL

DSPL is used chiefly for routine-design problem solving. It has been used for the construction of MPA, a system for routine logistics planning [13], and in the construction of a design system in the domain of chemical engineering [24]. More work needs to be done to test its applicability to other design problems and other domains. Extensions must be made to the theory in order to handle design activities which are not of the type where both problem solving and knowledge are known in advance. The identification of some of these types of design knowledge and their use would be a substantial contribution toward understanding routine design activity.

THE GENERIC TASK TOOLSET

Thus far, we have outlined the generic task theory and described two generic task tools: CSRL and DSPL. Tools for analyzing and coding other generic tasks also exist in varying degrees of completeness. These tools are currently available for the Interlisp/Loops environment in the Xerox 1100 series of Lisp machines. CSRL and DSPL are also available in versions that are compatible with the KEE development system of Intellicorp. CSRL is available as a supported product from Battelle

Memorial Laboratories, Artificial Intelligence Group, in Columbus, Ohio, including versions in Commonlisp. Currently, a project is under way at Battelle's Laboratory for Artificial Intelligence Research for the entire toolset to be made available in Commonlisp.

The integrated generic task toolset is extensible in the sense that more generic tools can be added as they are invented and additional problem solvers can be invoked as needed. The tools are intended to take advantage of the following features of the generic tasks [7]:

- *Multiformity.* The more traditional architectures for the construction of knowledge-based systems emphasize the advantages of uniformity of representation and inference. However, we argued earlier that in spite of the advantage of simplicity, uniformity results in a level-of-abstraction problem: a uniform representation cannot capture important distinctions between different kinds of problems, and a uniform inference engine does not provide different control structures for different kinds of problems.

  The generic task approach makes use of multiformity. Each generic task provides a different way to organize and use knowledge. The knowledge engineer can then choose which generic task is best for performing a particular function, or he or she can use different generic tasks for performing the same function. Different problems can use different generic tasks and different combinations of generic tasks.

- *Modularity.* A knowledge-based system can be designed by functionally decomposing its intended problem-solving task into several cooperating generic tasks, as illustrated in the earlier discussion on diagnosis. Each generic task provides a way to decompose a particular function into its conceptual parts, e.g., the categories for hierarchical classification, and allows domain knowledge of other forms to be inserted into a generic task, e.g., evidence-combination knowledge in hierarchical classification [29]. Each generic task localizes the knowledge that is used to satisfy local goals.

- *Knowledge acquisition.* Each generic task is associated with its own knowledge acquisition strategy for building an efficient problem solver [8]. For example, in hierarchical classification the knowledge engineer needs to find out which specific categories should be contained in the classification hierarchy and which general categories provide the most leverage for the establish-refine strategy.

- *Explanation.* Explanation relates to problem solving in expert systems in two important ways: explaining how the data match local goals and how the control strategy operates [12]. Also, the control strategy of each generic task is specific enough for generating explanations of why the problem solver chose to evaluate or not to evaluate a piece of knowledge. It is able to do this because of the higher level of abstraction in which control is specified for generic tasks.

- *Exploiting the interaction between knowledge and inference.* Rather than trying to separate knowledge from its use, each generic task specifically integrates a particular way of representing knowledge with a particular way of using that knowledge. In this manner, the knowledge engineer may focus attention on representing and organizing knowledge for problem solving.
- *Tractability.* Under reasonable assumptions, each generic task generally provides tractable problem solving [1, 18]. (One major exception is abductive assembly, which can become intractable under certain conditions, making it hard for humans and machines to perform the task.) The main reasons why the generic tasks are tractable are that a problem can be decomposed into small, efficient units, and knowledge can be organized to take care of combinatorial interactions in advance.

It should be noted that these advantages are attained at the cost of generality: each generic task is purposely constrained to perform a limited type of problem solving and requires the availability of appropriate domain knowledge.

CONCLUDING REMARKS

In the late 1970s, when we embarked on research into identifying generic tasks and the forms of knowledge and control required to perform them, the dominant paradigms in knowledge-based systems were the rule and frame types of architectures. While our work on use-specific architectures was evolving, dissatisfaction at the limited vocabulary of tasks that these architectures were offering was growing at other research centers. Clancey [14] in particular noted the need for specifying the information processing involved by using a vocabulary of higher level tasks. Task-level architectures have been gathering momentum lately: McDermott and co-workers [21] have built SALT, a shell for a class of design problems in which critiquing proposed designs by checking for violations of constraints is applicable. Clancey [15] has proposed a shell called Heracles which incorporates a strategy for diagnosis that he calls *heuristic classification*. Bennett [2] has devised COAST, a shell for the design of problem-solving systems dealing with configurations. All these approaches share the basic thesis of our own work, viz., the need for task-specific analyses and architectural support for the task.

However, there are important differences between these approaches as well. One class of approaches consider particular high-level problems and propose architectures that support specific behavioral strategies for them. For example, Clancey's heuristic classification is a behavioral strategy for diagnosis, and the SALT system similarly uses propose-and-revise as a strategy for a class of design problems. In contrast, the generic tasks in this paper are presented as building blocks out of which more complex problem-solvers or architectures for them can be fabricated. For example, we described in this paper how the generic tasks can be used to build diagnostic problem solvers. It is only a short step away to use the generic tasks to build a high-level diagnostic architecture (i.e., a diagnostic shell). As long as the strategy captures the knowledge and inference in the domain, the diagnostic system builder using such a higher level architecture need not concern himself with the generic task level explicitly; the architecture will directly guide him in decomposing the diagnostic problem into constituent generic tasks and integrate them appropriately for the diagnostic problem at hand.

There exists tasks and strategies for them that may not correspond to human problem solving expertise because they are intensive in the sort of calculations for which human problem solving is inappropriate. For example, human experts are not particularly good at general constraint-satisfaction problems of some complexity. Nevertheless, architectures can be devised which directly support such computation-intensive tasks. Bennet's COAST system is an example of such an architecture.

Once we identify task-level architectures as the issue of highest priority, a number of questions immediately arise. What is the criterion by which a task not only is deemed to be generic but is appropriate for modularization as an architecture? What about an architecture for the generic task of "investment decisions"? Diagnosis? Diagnosis of process control systems? Is uncertainty management a task for which it will be useful to have an architecture? Are we going to proliferate different architectures for different tasks? What are the relationships between these architectures? Which, if any, of the architectures can be built out of other architectures? I do not propose to answer all these questions here, but they seem to be the appropriate kinds of questions to ask when one moves away from the comfort of universal architectures and begins to work with different architectures for different problems.

At this stage in the development of these new ideas, the empirical investigation of different proposals from the viewpoint of usefulness, tractability, and decomposability is the best strategy. Practically speaking, any architecture that has a useful function and for which one can identify knowledge primitives and an inference method ought to be considered a valid candidate for experimentation. As the tools evolve, one may find that some of the architectures are further decomposable into equally useful, but more primitive, architectures, or that some of them do not represent particularly useful functionalities, and so on.

The generic tasks discussed in this chapter were specifically chosen to be useful as tools for building diagnosis, planning, and design systems with compiled expertise. For capturing intelligent problem solving in general, we will undoubtedly require many more elementary strategies and ways of integrating them. For example, the problem-solving activities in qualitative reasoning and device understanding—e.g., qualitative simulation, consolidation, and functional representation—all have well-defined information-processing functions, specific knowledge representation primitives, and inference methods. Thus, candidates for generic information-processing modules in the sense discussed here are indeed many. The work involved in this paper should be viewed as the beginning of a new kind of technology for building knowledge systems.

ACKNOWLEDGMENTS

I am indebted to my colleagues with whom I have written a number of papers over the years on the generic task approach. I have used excerpts from some of these papers in this chapter. In particular, I have availed myself of the papers by the author and W. Punch, the author and D. C. Brown, and the author, T. C. Bylander, and John Josephson. I acknowledge the assistance of Richard Fox and Vibhu Mittal in the preparation of this chapter, and I also gratefully acknowledge the support of the Defense Advanced Research Projects Agency, RADC Contract F30602-85-C-0010, and the Air Force Office of Scientific Research, grant 87-0090.

REFERENCES

1. Allemang, D., Tanner, M. C., Bylander, T. C., and Josephson, J. R. "On the Computational Complexity of Hypothesis Assembly." *Proceedings of the Tenth International Joint Conference on Artificial Intelligence.* Milan, Italy, August 1987, pp. 1112–1117.

2. Bennet, J. "COAST: A Task-specific Tool for Reasoning about Configurations Organization." *Proceedings of American Association of Artificial Intelligence Workshop on High-Level Tools.* Shawnee Park, Ohio, 1986.

3. Brown, D. C. *Expert Systems for Design Problem-solving Using Design Refinement with Plan Selection and Redesign.* Ph.D. dissertation, The Ohio State University, 1984.

4. Brown, D. C., and Chandrasekaran, B. "Knowledge and Control for a Mechanical Design Expert System." *IEEE Computer* 19 (1986): 92–101.

5. Buchanan, B., Sutherland, G., and Feigenbaum, E. A. *Heuristic DENDRAL: A Program for Generating Explanatory Hypotheses in Organic Chemistry.* New York: American Elsevier, 1969.

6. Bylander, T. C., and Mittal, S. "CSRL: A Language for Classificatory Problem Solving and Uncertainty Handling." *AI Magazine* 7 (1986): 66–76.

7. Bylander, T. C., "The Generic Task Toolset." *Proceedings of the Second International Conference on Human-Computer Interaction.* Honolulu, August 1987.

8. Bylander, T., and Chandrasekaran, B. "Generic Tasks for Knowledge-based Reasoning: The "Right" Level of Abstraction for Knowledge Acquisition." *International Journal of Man-Machine Studies* 26 (1987): 231–243.

9. Chandrasekaran, B. "Towards a Taxonomy of Problem-solving Types." *AI Magazine* 4 (1983): 9–17.

10. Chandrasekaran, B. "Generic Tasks in Knowledge-based Reasoning: High-level Building Blocks for Expert System Design." *IEEE Expert* 1 (1986): 23–30.

11. Chandrasekaran, B. "Towards a Functional Architecture for Intelligence Based on

Generic Information Processing Tasks. *Proceedings of the Tenth International Joint Conference on Artificial Intelligence.* Milan, Italy, August 1987, pp. 1183–1192.

12. Chandrasekaran, B., Tanner, M. C., and Josephson, J. R. "Explanation: The Role of Control Strategies and Deep Models." In *Expert Systems: The User Interface,* edited by J. Hendler, pp. 219–248. Norwood, NJ: Ablex, 1987.

13. Chandrasekaran, B., Josephson, J. R., Keuneke, A., and Herman, D. "An Approach to Routine Planning." *International Journal of Man-Machine Studies,* forthcoming.

14. Clancey, W. J. "NEOMYCIN: Reconfiguring a Rule-based Expert System for Application to Teaching." *Proceedings of the Seventh International Joint Conference on Artificial Intelligence.* Vancouver, Canada, 1981, pp. 829–836.

15. Clancey, W. J. "Heuristic Classification." *Artificial Intelligence* 27 (1985): 289–350.

16. Duda, R. O., Gaschnig, J. G., and Hart, P. E. "Model Design in the Prospector Consultant System for Mineral Exploration." In *Expert Systems in the Microelectronic Age,* edited by D. Michie, pp. 153–167. Edinburgh: Edinburgh University Press, 1980.

17. Friedland, P. *Knowledge-based Experiment Design in Molecular Genetics.* Ph.D. dissertation, Stanford University, 1979.

18. Goel, A., Soundararajan, N., and Chandrasekaran, B. "Complexity in Classificatory Reasoning." *Proceedings of the National Conference of the American Association for Artificial Intelligence,* Seattle, July 13–18, 1987, pp. 421–425.

19. Hashemi, S., Hajek, B. K., Miller, D. W., Chandrasekaran, B., and Josephson, J. R. "Expert Systems Application to Plant Diagnosis and Sensor Data Validation." *Proceedings of the Sixth Power Plant Dynamics, Control and Testing Symposium,* Knoxville, April 1986.

20. Josephson, J. R., Smetters, D., Welch, A. K., Fox, R., Flores, G., and Lyndes, D. *Generic Task Toolset Draco Release—Beta Test Including RA.* Technical report, Computer & Information Science Department, Laboratory for Artificial Intelligence Research, The Ohio State University, Columbus, OH, February 1988.

21. Marcus, S., and McDermott, J. *SALT: A Knowledge Acquisition Tool for Propose-and-revise Systems.* Technical report, Department of Computer Science, Carnegie-Mellon University, Pittsburgh, PA, 1987.

22. McDermott, J. "R1: A Rule-based Configurer of Computer Systems." *Artificial Intelligence* 19 (1982): 39–88.

23. Miller, R. A., Pople, H. E., and Meyers, J. D. "Internist-1, an Experimental Computer-based Diagnostic Consultant for General Internal Medicine." In *Readings in Medical Artificial Intelligence,* edited by E. H. Shortliffe and W. J. Clancey, pp. 190–209. Reading, MA: Addison-Wesley, 1984. First published in *New England Journal of Medicine* 307 (1982): 468–476.

24. Myers, D. R., Davis, J. F., and Herman, D. "A Task Oriented Approach to Knowledge-based Systems for Process Engineering Design." *Computers and Chemical Engineering* 12 (1988): 959–971. Special issue on AI in chemical engineering research and development, August 1988.

25. Punch, W. F., III, Tanner, M. C., and Josephson, J. R. "Design Consideration for PEIRCE, a High Level Language for Hypothesis Assembly." *Expert Systems in Government Symposium,* Washington, October 1986, pp. 279–281.

26. Shortliffe, E. H. *Computer-based Medical Consultations: MYCIN.* New York: Elsevier/ North-Holland, 1976.

27. Shum, S. K., Davis, J. F., Punch, W. F., III, and Chandrasekaran, B. "An Expert System Approach for Malfunction Diagnosis in Chemical Plants." *Computers and Chemical Engineering* 12 (1988): 27–36.

28. Smith, J. W., Svirbely, J. R., Evans, C. A., Strohm, P., Josephson, J. R., and Tanner, M. "Red: A Red-cell Antibody Identification Expert Module." *Journal of Medical Systems* 9 (1985): 121–138.

29. Sticklen, J. *MDX2: An Integrated Medical Diagnostic System.* Ph.D. dissertation, The Ohio State University, 1987.

30. Tanner, M. C., and Bylander, T. C. "Application of the CSRL Language to the Design of Expert Diagnosis Systems: The Auto-Mech Experience." In *Artificial Intelligence in Maintenance,* edited by J. J. Richardson. Park Ridge, NJ: Noyes Publications, 1985.

9

Managing Uncertainty in Expert Systems: Rationale, Theory, and Techniques

Henry Hamburger
Lashon B. Booker

ASPECTS OF UNCERTAINTY

As humans, we live in a world that often requires decisions and actions in the face of uncertainties and imprecisions. If an expert system is to help with those decisions, it must represent and manipulate those uncertainties and imprecisions. This chapter treats imperfect information in three sections. The first is a qualitative overview of where, how, and why uncertainty and imprecision arise in expert systems. In the second section, we introduce some important formalisms and give an indication of their strengths and weaknesses. The final section shows how one very promising approach has been applied in a particular domain.

An expert system uses knowledge of its subject matter as well as specific information about the particular situation it is currently handling. Both of these, the knowledge and the information, may be imperfect in a variety of ways, and expert systems must deal with whatever imperfections occur. To ignore even partial ignorance may give the user a false and dangerous sense of security; to be stymied by it may result in unnecessary paralysis. Like a human expert, a system should be able to make progress, perhaps even to reach decisions, in cases where a lack of full knowledge is relatively unimportant. In other cases, an appropriate behavior may be to give a tentative conclusion, accompanied by some kind of uncertainty assessment.

Kinds of Imperfect Knowledge and Information

Imperfections in knowledge take a variety of forms. Aside from a piece of information being missing altogether, a less extreme possibility is that the information is likely rather than absolutely certain, or that it is vague or imprecise. To begin with likelihood, one may know how likely or probable some proposition is, without knowing whether the proposition is true or false. This epistemological condition is often formally expressed by the mathematics of probability. In the context of expert systems, one often knows that some things are more likely than others; for example, some diseases are rare, others are common, and this is true as well of mineral deposits, circuit faults, etc. Such information can be used to assign an initial numerical value to each hypothesis. In a probabilistic treatment, this number is the so-called prior probability. In addition to propositions, an expert system may have rules that connect the various propositions. A rule may connect a hypothesis with evidence that favors that hypothesis when it occurs. If the evidence then actually occurs, the rule fires and a numerical value associated with the rule may combine with previously determined numbers to produce an updated value, which in a probabilistic treatment would be a posterior probability. One might hope this would be done in a manner conforming strictly to mathematically justifiable laws, a point to which we shall return.

One important justification for the use of the numerical values associated with rules arises in what is sometimes called abductive reasoning, the seeking of a plausible explanation for a set of observations. Consider the general problem of performing a diagnosis, be it of human diseases, plant diseases, or equipment faults. Suppose we know that defect #1 (which in the medical case would be the presence of a disease-inducing organism) gives rise to symptom #7 and that defect #2 also gives rise to symptom #7. Then when symptom #7 is observed, and we seek an explanation of its occurrence, we can reasonably look to either of the defects, but neither of them is necessarily involved, since the other could be responsible. Therefore, we seem to need a rule that responds to the observation of symptom #7 by increasing, for each of the defects, the value of a parameter that represents the likelihood of that defect's involvement in the symptom. However, neither defect should be made certain, even when the symptom is certainly observed. Just what the likelihood parameter is and how it behaves we leave open for now. Probability is one candidate, but there are others, as will be seen later.

Another kind of middle-ground situation, different from likelihood, arises from vague attributes, like "rainy," "old," "reliable," and other notions expressible by adjectives that can comfortably be modified by the likes of "very" and "moderately." In terms of elementary logic, vagueness concerns predicates, whereas probability is associated with propositions. Suppose an expert system for job counseling has a rule that demotes rainy cities if a client plays tennis, and so it needs to know if New York is rainy. Well, New York is moderately rainy—rainier than some cities, drier than others—but this is not a matter of probability. Indeed, the information here need not even be imperfect, since we may be perfectly informed about the (long-term, average annual) rainfall in all cities. More to the point is the imperfect match between fact and rule, with the antecedent of the rule calling for a rainy city and the fact supplying only a somewhat rainy city.

Imprecision is yet another matter, different from both vagueness and likelihood. For one thing, imprecise equipment can give an imprecise estimate of the value of a parameter. Or, an inference from low-resolution information may be imprecise. For example, our knowledge of how rainy New York is may be imprecise because it consists only of what we deduce from the fact that all northeastern U.S. coastal cities have at least 25 inches of rainfall. There is thus a clear distinction between imprecision of knowledge and vagueness of language.

Since it is predicates that are vague but propositions that have probabilities, it should not be surprising that the two can occur together. Indeed, likelihood, vagueness, and imprecision can occur in all conceivable combinations. We next give an example for each of the three pairs of them and, in the next paragraph, an example with all three. In the example about rain on the northeast coast, one could conclude that New York is at least moderately rainy but possibly more so, a statement that reflects imprecise knowledge with respect to a vague predicate. Vagueness and probabilistic notions can both be relevant in the case of a company that randomly assigns new employees among its facilities in several cities which are rainy to various degrees. Finally, probability itself can be an imprecise parameter: to know that a coin is somewhat weighted to favor heads is to know that the probability of heads is between ½ and 1.

Fuzzy set theory is a formalism for reasoning about vagueness and imprecision, and fuzzy formalisms have even been extended to incorporate probability [34, 35]. Since many useful rules of thumb can be expressed in ordinary language using words that correspond to fuzzy and probabilistic notions, fuzzyists believe it is essential for expert systems to have a formalism rich enough to embrace both notions. An example [35] that brings together all three imperfections is, "If a car is old, then it probably is unreliable." Here age and (un)reliability are vague predicates, and "probably" expresses an imprecise probability. The rule does not guarantee that even an exceedingly old car is unreliable, nor does it tell us precisely how unreliable such a car might be. Still, it does seem to express some knowledge that could be useful to a person or a system charged with figuring out good transportation advice.

Yet another kind of limitation on knowledge can arise from ordinary assertions of class attributes like "Birds fly" or "Birds lay eggs." For these examples, one may envision a knowledge engineer eliciting from an expert on ornithology the requisite knowledge for aviary or zoo design. First note that it is unworkable to interpret the statements as certain by accepting simple translations to predicate calculus like "For every x, if x is a bird then x flies." For "If . . . 'Birds fly' really means 'Most birds fly,' then birds don't fly in the spring. In nesting season, baby birds outnumber adults. Baby birds don't fly" [18]. In other words, one seemingly natural probabilistic formulation of the statement fails. The fuzzy set approach allows us to talk about partial membership in a set, but puts us in the uncomfortable stance of claiming (on the usual interpretation of fuzzy sets) that a baby bird is not fully a bird. The second of the statements in question seems to raise even more severe problems than the first: "'Birds lay eggs' . . . is out-and-out false year round of at least half the population (none of the males do)" [18]. Again, probability seems not to be the right concept, since a randomly chosen bird is more likely not to egg-layer than to be one. Yet imprecision seems inappropriate too, since each individual either is or is not an egg-layer.

A reasonable reaction to these observations is to refine the rules. As for birds flying, we might be content to say that adult birds fly, we might perhaps have two rules, one saying that birds (generally speaking) fly and the other that baby birds don't, with the latter, being more specific, taking precedence. We humans, of course, carry around the more powerful piece of knowledge that the young of many species develop many of the species characteristics only gradually, and that this is more likely to be more strongly the case for relatively complex species. Allowing that knowledge to apply to "Birds fly" would forestall our having to maintain that even baby birds fly.

Our knowledge of egg-laying is also broadly applicable—to wit, mode of reproduction is a characteristic of species. Thus, someone who says "Birds lay eggs" can easily be talking about species rather than individual organisms. This understood, one may then interpret "Birds lay eggs" probabilistically: given a species of bird, it is much more likely than not to reproduce via laying eggs. Another powerful piece of widely shared knowledge helps us to confirm what a very reasonable kind of assertion it is that birds lay eggs: we know that a reproductive mode often happens to be shared by related species, such as the various kinds of birds. These considerations are not at all undermined by the fact that the laying of eggs is typically the province of mature females, who may constitute a minority.

Decisions and Information

As noted at the outset of this chapter, the world demands decisions and actions. Not to make an active decision is implicitly to choose the action of doing nothing. How, then, might a person or an expert system go about reaching decisions under uncertainty? When the uncertainty is probabilistic, one approach is to assign a numerical utility to each possible outcome and make choices that maximize expected utility. This utility-theoretic approach may be regarded as either prescriptive of what one should do or descriptive of what people in fact do. The theory succeeds descriptively to the extent that for each individual it is possible to find an assignment of that person's utilities and probabilities that is consistent across many (in principle, all) decision situations. Practical techniques include pinning down a person's utilities by presenting situations involving simple probabilistic events like a coin toss and, conversely, pinning down probabilities by using decision situations with simple outcomes like small monetary rewards. Besides testing the validity of the theory, these techniques could, if one accepts the theory, serve as a kind of knowledge acquisition scheme for eliciting knowledge about relevant utilities and probabilities.

Surprisingly, a theory of utility maximization does not appear to give an adequate account of all human decision making. Systematic violations of the theory can be induced by taking a strikingly simple situation and manipulating the frame of reference in which it is viewed so as to highlight a favorable or adverse aspect. For example, one can present a decision problem concerning alternative immunization programs in terms of people saved and then present the equivalent problem in terms of how many will die [32]. In experiments of this sort, half or more of those queried in each of several problems gave inconsistent responses from one frame of reference to another. These results need not, and perhaps should not, keep us from taking utility maximization as prescriptive for expert systems, but they certainly suggest scrutiny of how utilities are to be derived in the first place from people's choices. Subject to this cautionary note, we now provisionally accept the theory of utility maximization, to see how it can be used.

Even in a situation without precise probabilities, utility maximization may offer a recommendation. Thus, the following brief treatment will help fix ideas about relationships among probability, precision, and decision. Suppose you are a maximizer of expected utility and also happen to be consciously aware of your utility values and probabilistic computations. Consider a choice between two acts, one leading with certainty to outcome A and the other yielding, in effect, a lottery: either result B, with (precise) probability p, or result C, with probability $1 - p$. Let each of A, B, and C also stand for its own utility, and assume that $B > A > C$. Then for one particular value of p, specifically, for $p = (A - C)/(B - C)$, you will be indifferent between your options and can choose either. For smaller p you take A, and for larger p the probabilistic package.

Knowing the precise value of p has thus led to an easy decision. It is sometimes also possible to maximize utility with an imprecise p. In the preceding example, if you can just somehow narrow down the value of p to some interval, and if that interval lies entirely to one side or the other of $(A - C)/(B - C)$, then you have just as easy a decision as before. But suppose you narrow down your probability estimate to an interval only to find that your indifference point $(A - C)/(B - C)$ lies inside that interval. Now it is no longer clear which choice yields the maximum expected utility. One way out in this case is to assume some particular density function over the probabilities in the interval—perhaps a uniform function. But to use such a metaprobabilistic technique is really equivalent to asserting that you know the exact probability, which will just be the mean probability according to the density function. Other approaches include picking an option whose worst (not average) associated result is as good or better than that of any other option. In general, it is not possible to meet simultaneously all the decision-making criteria that one might reasonably desire [23].

In a situation like this one, with imprecise probabilities impeding a decision, it may be fruitful to pursue a technique called *extending the conversation* (see [12], which credits Tribus). To fix ideas, suppose that in outcome B you get two dollars, in A you get one dollar, and in C you get nothing. For simplicity, we assume that utility is a linear function of dollars. In that case, maximizing the expected value of dollars is equivalent to maximizing the expected value of utility, and we can write $(A - C)/(B - C) = 0.5$. Now suppose that you have narrowed down the probability p to the range [0.2, 0.6] and that p is based on the outcome of an event D. We extend the conversation by asking you about D and discover that you believe that D depends upon some other event E. Moreover, you turn out to be comfortable supplying point values for the conditional probabilities $P(D|E)$ and $P(D|\overline{E})$, that is, the probability of D on the conditions, respectively, that E certainly occurs and that E certainly fails to occur. In particular, you give $P(D|E) = 0.6$ and $P(D|\overline{E}) = 0.2$. At this point, we question you about E. If you can give a point probability for E, then we can compute one for D as well, to wit, $P(D) = P(E)P(D|E) + P(\overline{E})P(D|\overline{E})$, and we are back to the case of precise probability.

Extending the conversation here has thus made two additional computations possible. First, we can determine just how much knowing the actual outcome of E in a particular scenario should be worth to you, in case such information is available at some cost. The choice to "buy" information is a common one. For a doctor, running a lab test is a purchase of information, with the costs coming in the form of not only direct dollar amounts charged by the lab but also the doctor's time to interpret the report and the possible deterioration of the patient's condition in the intervening time period. More severe costs in patient condition may attach to exploratory surgery. Utilities must now be associated with complex outcomes combining final outcomes and the intermediate effects of the metaphorical purchase of information.

The second computational possibility opened up by extending the conversation is not mentioned in [12], but follows from the straightforward use of convex sets of probability functions [16]. Suppose that E itself has an imprecise probability, one that can only be narrowed to an interval. Then, although this knowledge does not restrict the probability of D to a point, it does indirectly narrow its range via the conditional probabilities. Thus, if E is in $[0, 0.5]$, D must be in $[0.2, 0.4]$ so $(A - C)/(B - C) = 0.5$ is outside the relevant interval and a decision can again be made. Indeed, even if the conditional probabilities relating D and E were expanded from point values to small intervals surrounding those points, this same result would hold. So extending the conversation can be useful even in the absence of point probabilities.

A Note on Human Expertise

Many expert systems mimic the reasoning of human experts. Is this a good strategy for approaching the handling of uncertainty? Two reasons for mimicry in expert systems are the facilitation of explanation (humans can understand human-like arguments) and the so-called existence proof (there must be some way to do it like humans because humans do it like humans). One could apply these arguments to uncertainty handling. The very idea of incorporating uncertainty in medical expert systems seems to have arisen in response to experts (doctors) hedging their statements about diagnosis during the knowledge acquisition process for Mycin [5]. Beyond such spontaneous linguistic expressions of uncertainty, an expert may even be willing to supply numerical ratings. However, it does not seem to be the case that experts consciously carry out numerical calculations, a huge number of which would be needed for making inferences in a high-performance expert system. Of course, people may do something with apparent ease only because they are "wired" for it (e.g., walking and seeing), not because it is computationally easy. Perhaps human uncertainty computation is complex, distributed, and unconscious. It is also relevant that although probability is commonly treated quantitatively, it (like physics) can be approached from a qualitative viewpoint [15], a tack that might well contribute to modeling the cognition of uncertainty. Current research on the handling of uncertainty in expert systems has been moving toward mathematically justified interpretable formalisms, with attention also to computational efficiency. We turn to selected portions of that research next.

METHODS OF REPRESENTATION AND COMBINATION

Probability

Of the mathematical techniques dealing with imperfect information, probability has the oldest pedigree and seems the best place to start. Probability, however, can be understood and formalized in a surprising variety of ways [10], so it is wise to be explicit about what one means by it. In particular, one may wonder, "Where do the numbers come from?" From an expert, presumably, although one might also think of basing them on systematically recorded observations of relevant real events. The latter approach assumes a large number of observations per number obtained, and we shall point out subsequently that many numbers are needed. Moreover, the observations should occur in an unvarying environment, a condition violated in many domains by rapidly changing technologies (and, in the case of medicine, changing microorganisms). By turning to an expert, one conceals but does not resolve the problem. The following definition sidesteps the issue by not asking where the numbers come from:

> A *probability measure P* is a mapping from a set of propositions to numbers in the interval [0,1]. The set of propositions is to be closed under the usual logical operations and have distinct elements that map to 1 and to 0. Also, if $P(p \text{ and } q) = 0$, then $P(p \text{ or } q) = P(p) + P(q)$.

From this formulation some familiar results follow, notably that if p entails q then $P(p) \leq P(q)$ and that $P(p) + P(\bar{p}) = 1$. By definition, $P(p \text{ and } q)$ is called the *joint probability of p and q,* and the *conditional probability of q given p,* denoted $P(q|p)$, is $P(p \text{ and } q)/P(p)$. The proposition q is said to be *independent* of p if conditioning it with respect to p has no effect, that is, if $P(q|p) = P(q)$. Multiplying the latter equation by $P(p)$ and using the definition of conditional probability gives the product formula for independence, $P(p \text{ and } q) = P(p)P(q)$, which reflects the symmetry of the idea of independence.

With no assumptions about independence, a computational situation can quickly lose precision. For example, consider two events, each with the precise probability 0.5. Without further information, all one can say about their joint probability is that it is somewhere between 0 and 0.5. It is 0 if in fact exactly one of them always occurs, and it is 0.5 if in fact either both must occur or neither. Now consider the disjunction of two such joint events, again with no information or assumptions about dependence or independence. This disjunction can have any probability in the entire allowed range [0,1]. So by being agnostic about the direction and degree of any possible dependence, we quickly descend from precision to ignorance. By contrast, with independence assumed, a single probability is found, 0.25 for each conjunction and $1 - (1 - 0.25)^2 \approx 0.44$ for the final result. Assumptions about independence are tempting for other reasons too, but clearly, they must not be used unless warranted.

A computational approach to the independence issue appears in [22]. This system permits a user to specify independence in some places and positive or negative dependence in others. In the foregoing example, suppose that the first two conjuncts are known to be positively correlated to some unknown extent. Then their joint probability is in [0.25, 0.5]. Also, suppose that the second two conjuncts are negatively correlated, again to an unknown extent. Then for this pair the joint probability is in [0, 0.25]. Now if the two resulting (joint) events are known to be independent, the probability of this disjunction is constrained to the interval [0.25, 0.625]. If our assumptions have been valid, so that this result reflects what we really do know about the dependencies, it will be both more reliable than the single value and more useful than the uniformative range [0, 1].

Bayes' Rule and Quasi-Bayesian Updating

With conditional probability defined, it is a short step to the simplest formulation of Bayes' rule, which, in this and more complex forms, has seen much discussion and use in expert systems. Bayes' rule is given by

$$P(H|E) = \frac{P(E|H)P(H)}{P(E)} \qquad (9\text{--}1)$$

An early influential paper [9] begins, for simplicity, with this relationship between a single hypothesis H and a single piece of possible evidence for it, E. Each is uncertain, and each is viewed as a node in a large network in which the evidential relationship between them is an arc. A single node can and typically does play the role of both hypothesis and evidence. In general, a hypothesis may be supported by any number of pieces of evidence.

A variant of Eq. 9–1 is formed is replacing H with $\bar{H}$, the nonoccurrence of H. Dividing the formula that results from such a replacement into Eq. 9–1 yields

$$O(H|E) = \lambda O(H) \qquad (9\text{--}2)$$

where, by definition,

$$\lambda = \frac{P(E|H)}{P(E|\bar{H})} \qquad (9\text{--}3)$$

and the symbol O stands for "odds." The usual sense of "odds" is that if something has probability x, the odds on it are x to $1 - x$. Interpreting "to" as division yields $O(H) = P(H)/[1 - P(H)]$. Correspondingly, for conditioning with respect to E, $O(H|E) = P(H|E)/[1 - P(H|E)]$. Probability and odds carry the same information about an event, and each can be recovered from the other. Equation 9–2 gives the posterior odds on H conditioned on E, given the prior odds on H and λ, so it may be viewed as an updating formula for the odds on H when E is observed to be certainly true. Replacing E by its negation $\overline{E}$ throughout yields a corresponding formula for updating in response to $\overline{E}$, the observation that E is certainly false, to wit,

$$O(H|\overline{E}) = \overline{\lambda} O(H) \qquad (9\text{--}4)$$

where $\overline{\lambda}$ is found by inserting $\overline{E}$ in place of E in Eq. 9–3.

Both Bayes' rule and the updating rules derived from it can be made more general by taking into account the important possibility of multiple pieces of evidence acting on a single hypothesis. Moreover, real expert systems require consideration of not just one hypothesis H and its negation, but a set of hypotheses. Thus, one needs generalized updating of the odds for hypothesis H_i on the basis of information about relevant items E_{ij} of evidence. An early approximate approach [9] makes use of λ'_{ij}s, where the prime indicates interpolation between the corresponding generalized λ and $\overline{\lambda}$. The resulting more general formulas give rise to some dilemmas with respect to their justifiable use in practical situations. We briefly touch on these now, and later discuss recent work, notably [20], that derives theoretically sound general formulas.

On one view, the gist of the problem is a tradeoff: the potentially large number of conditional probabilities versus certain simplifying assumptions for reducing that number. Even a moderate-sized application may have a huge number of conditional probabilities associated with it, since in general the number of conditionals can rise exponentially with the number of propositions in the system. The large numbers potentially pose a critical knowledge acquisition problem, since no expert will be able to supply thousands, much less billions, of reliable probabilities. This observation is not a criticism of probability theory; indeed, one may credit probability theory with making plain the potential complexity of the relationships. Paring the requisite knowledge down to manageable proportions demands simplifying assumptions, together with justification for their use in a particular application.

One popular assumption, sometimes hard to justify but needed just to use Bayes' rule at all, is the existence of an exhaustive and mutually exclusive set of hypotheses. In the medical arena, this would entail either disallowing multiple diseases or else regarding each possible combination of diseases as a hypothesis, thereby exponentially increasing the number of hypotheses. Next, one may assume that given a particular hypothesis, the various pieces of evidence for it are conditionally independent. This assumption is expressed in the formula

$$P(E_{i1} \text{ and } E_{i2} \text{ and } \cdots \text{ and } E_{im}|H_i) = \prod_{j=1}^{m} P(E_{ij}|H_i) \qquad (9\text{--}5)$$

which is analogous to the formula given earlier for ordinary (unconditional) independence, that is, $P(p \text{ and } q) = P(p)P(q)$. Notice that both formulas express the probability of a joint event as a product of probabilities of individual events.

Where justified, the conditional-independence assumption embodied in Eq. 9–5 yields a tremendous reduction in the number of probabilities to specify. It also permits the generalized λ-updating approach alluded to before. One kind of violation of Eq. 9–5 occurs when an item of evidence is indirectly connected to the same hypothesis by two paths of evidence-hypothesis links, a problem that has been addressed in [19] and [7].

A numerical example will show that conditional independence can make sense even for pieces of evidence with a superficial tendency to occur together. Suppose we observe symptoms S_1 and S_2 each in 10% of a population. If they were independent their joint probability would be 0.01, but in fact we observe it to be 0.05. So S_1 and S_2 tend to occur together in the population at large. Yet these symptoms may still be conditionally independent. For they might occur only in people with disease D, who constitute 20% of the population. For each diseased person, nature flips two true coins independently to determine the presence or absence of symptoms S_1 and S_2. The situation then gives rise to the preceding observations, yet with the promised conditional independence; formally, we have $P(S_1 \text{ and } S_2|D) = P(S_1|D)P(S_2|D)$.

Certainty Factors

Like conditional probabilities, certainty factors deal with the idea that belief in one particular proposition may lend support to belief in some other one. Certainty factors apply not to individual propositions, but to the link between propositions, and so play a role in the updating process as new information comes into a system. A key difference between certainty factors and conditional probabilities is that with certainty factors there is an attempt to keep separate the positive and the negative evidence for a proposition. Some have said that such separation conforms well to human expert reasoning. There are also technical reasons for the separation, such as wanting conclusions not to be based on the order in which information is received, a point to which we shall return.

Certainty factors deserve attention because of their widespread use and because they provide some interesting lessons about the expression of uncertainty in expert systems. Initially, the technique was promoted on the basis that it was easy to use and was associated with a successful system, Mycin [29]. There was, however, some uneasiness about how formally justifiable the computation really was. One reaction was to pursue certain practical investigations, including both sensitivity analysis within a domain and the use of the technique in new domains, in the hope that the technique would prove worthy. Alternatively, one can pursue a theoretical strategy, attempting to understand the formalism itself better and to revise it into a sounder form. A particularly successful undertaking of the latter kind is [11], in which the theory of certainty factors is revised, generalized, and put into a formal relation to probability theory without sacrificing the initial intuition concerning its ease of use. In this work, moreover, the notion of insensitivity to the order of arrival of evidence is elevated to the status of an axiom, as are several other desiderata, all of which are then obeyed by the resulting formalism.

The original intuitive impetus for the certainty factor idea was that the kinds of numbers it demands might be relatively easy for an expert to supply. What the technique requires a numerical estimate for is, roughly speaking, the strength of the evidential link from a piece of evidence E to a hypothesis H. If observing E tends to support one's belief that H holds, we can write

$$CF(H, E) = \frac{P(H|E) - P(H)}{1 - P(H)} \qquad \text{if } P(H|E) > P(H) \qquad (9\text{--}6a)$$

The idea here is that the denominator is the amount by which it is conceivable to increase the probability of H from its *a priori* value (up to no more than 1), and so the entire fraction is the proportion of that (potential) amount by which the occurrence of E actually does change the probability of H. This definition is then extended by furnishing the equation

$$CF(H, E) = \frac{P(H|E) - P(H)}{P(H)} \qquad \text{if } P(H|E) < P(H) \qquad (9\text{--}6b)$$

to deal with evidence in the opposite direction. Here the question is, What proportion of the potential distance down to zero is actually covered by the difference between the posterior and prior probabilities? Actually, as indicated earlier, the positive and negative pieces of evidence are accumulated separately and then combined by a formula that is intuitively reasonable but rather ad hoc.

Shortliffe, the original developer of Mycin, believed that certainty factors were easier for an expert to specify than prior and posterior probabilities. One of his key arguments can be put in the form of the statement [5], "I don't know what the probability is that all ravens are black, but I *do* know that every time you show me an additional black raven my belief is increased by x that all ravens are black." Although Eqs. 9–6a and b may look plausible, they have a highly undesirable property if used to update conditional probabilities as evidence arrives. Specifically, if two pieces of evidence bear on a hypothesis, one supporting it and the other tending to disconfirm it, the order in which the two updates takes place affects the outcome of the computation. For example, with a prior probability of $\frac{1}{2}$, applying certainty factors $\frac{1}{2}$ and $-\frac{1}{2}$ yields successive posterior probabilities of .75 (halfway from the prior probability to 1) and finally .375 (halfway from .75 to 0). Applying the same two certainty factors in the opposite order yields, by a similar computation, .625. One can avoid this sort of difficulty by not introducing the probabilistic interpretation implicit in Eqs. 9–6. Instead, working with certainty factors directly, one can conclude that a particular hypothesis has a lot of support in the current situation. The technique, however, leaves unanswered the question of how to combine this information with how rarely that hypothesis holds in general. In short, you can suppress prior probabilities, but not the problem they are designed to solve.

Theory of Belief Functions

Uncertainty begets uncertainty: we start with uncertain propositions, and, having turned to a probabilistic representation, we then question the accuracy of the numerical probabilities, since, after all, they are typically based on avowed guesses by our experts. To reflect this kind of uncertainty, one can abandon the idea of single-valued probabilities. There are at least three means of replacing such probabilities: probability intervals, convex sets of probability functions, and belief functions. Earlier, we touched on the first of these, that of replacing each probability by two numbers that specify an interval of possible values, and showed how one might be able to do actual computation with such intervals. The second and third approaches warrant more attention.

The idea of a convex set of probability functions is more general than that of probability intervals, as the following examples should make reasonably clear. First, suppose the probability of some proposition p lies within the interval $[0.1, 0.4]$. To represent this situation by a set of probability functions, posit, for every α in $[0,1]$, a probability function P_α such that $P_\alpha(p) = 0.1 + 0.3\alpha$ and $P_\alpha(\bar{p}) = 0.6 + 0.3(1 - \alpha)$. This set of probability functions is convex since taking a linear combination of any two of its elements yields a probability function among the P_α. It is not hard to show that even for more complex situations, probability intervals can be supplanted by sets of probability functions in a manner that generalizes what is done in this example [16].

To see the greater power of these convex sets in comparison to intervals, consider two examples, each with the three outcomes A, B, and C. In one case, $P(A)$ is constrained to be less than $\frac{1}{2}$; in the other case, there is a constraint that $P(A) \leq P(B)$. In terms of interval constraints on the individual outcomes the second case yields numerical results identical to the first, yet we sense that the two cases are indeed different, and in a manner that a convex set of probability functions permits us to express; viz., $P(A) = 0.5\alpha$, $P(B) = 0.5\alpha + (1 - \alpha)\beta$, and $P(C) = (1 - \alpha)(1 - \beta)$, where each of α and β is in $[0,1]$.

Still another approach to loosening up the conceptualization that is (apparently) imposed by probabilities, and one that has received widespread attention, is the theory of belief functions. Consider the set of answers to some question or the set of possible states of some world. Where probability would posit a random element of such a set, here one posits instead a random subset. In other words, there is a probability mass function m which assigns mass not only to the basic, disjoint states of the world but also to combinations of such states. According to this theory, no mass can be negative and the sum of all masses respecting a given situation must be 1. A full mathematical treatment of this idea given in [26], where it is handled in concert with Dempster's rule for combining evidence, is discussed in the next section.

The belief function *Bel,* which gives the theory its name, is associated with the mass function and determined by it. Specifically, the value of the belief function for any set is the sum of the masses of all its (nonempty) subsets. For example, for states

A, B, and possibly some others, we have $Bel(\{A,B\}) = m(A) + m(B) + m(\{A,B\})$. (For simplicity, we shall henceforth leave out the braces for sets when they are immediately enclosed in parentheses, writing, e.g., $Bel(A,B)$ for $Bel(\{A,B\})$.) The idea behind belief functions is that your belief in the realization of the set of states $\{A,B\}$ is affected by your evidence supporting each state separately together with evidence that somehow supports them collectively. This arrangement has the desirable consequence that if S_1 is a subset of S_2, so that the occurrence of S_1 entails that of S_2, then $Bel(S_1) \leq Bel(S_2)$. Also defined is the plausibility function Pl. To get the plausibility of some set, you throw in the masses of all sets not disjoint from the one under consideration. This means that for any disjunction S of states, $Pl(S) = 1 - Bel(comp(S))$, where $comp$ is the set complement with respect to the set of states. If there are three states, A, B, and C, then $Pl(A,B) = 1 - M(C)$.

Since the belief function seems conceptually more central than the masses, one might hope to be able to specify its values directly. Indeed, one can recover a unique nonnegative mass function from a given belief function, provided that certain inequalities hold among the belief values. For example [26],

$$
\begin{aligned}
Bel(A,B,C) &= m(A) + m(B) + m(C) + m(A,B) + m(A,C) + m(B,C) \\
&\quad + m(A,B,C) \\
&\geq [m(A) + m(B) + m(A,B)] \\
&\quad + [m(B) + m(C) + m(B,C)] - m(B) \\
&= Bel(A,B) + Bel(B,C) - Bel(B) \qquad (9\text{-}7)
\end{aligned}
$$

The number of masses to be assigned can be very large, even in a relatively simple situation. In a world of two propositions, A and B, there are four ($= 2^2$) states: AB, $A\overline{B}$, $\overline{A}B$, and $\overline{A}\,\overline{B}$. Before determining how many masses this necessitates, note for comparison that to specify a (single) probability function four numbers suffice, one for each state (one is dependent on the other three). All marginal and conditional probabilities would then follow. When it comes to a mass distribution, one assigns mass not only to these four states but also to the various nonempty disjunctions of them. In theory, an n-proposition world requires the specification of $2^{2^n} - 1$ mass numbers (all but one independent), which is in the billions even for so small a value of n as 5. In practice, however, many of these numbers would presumably be zero. Moreover, the method may be cognitively comfortable in some cases: if you have no idea about any of the probabilities, you can assign all the mass to the disjunction of all the states. As another example, in a world of two propositions A and B, if you are confident about some value for the likelihood of proposition A, but have no idea about the likelihood of proposition B, you can assign a suitable mass to the set of states $\{AB, A\overline{B}\}$ and all the remaining mass to $\{\overline{A}B, \overline{A}\,\overline{B}\}$.

The belief and plausibility functions bear a resemblance to lower and upper bounds, respectively, on probability. This resemblance (which is *not* an equivalence) makes possible a comparison of the belief function approach with that of probability intervals and also with the notion of a convex set of probability functions. To represent the very simple example of a proposition whose probability of being true lies within the interval $[0.1, 0.4]$, one can assign masses $m(A) = 0.1$,

$m(B) = 0.6$, and $m(A,B) = 0.3$. If one then accepts the lower and upper bounds interpretation of *Bel* and *Pl*, it is fairly straightforward to show that for any mass function there corresponds a convex set of probability functions that imputes the same probability bounds, and that the converse does not hold [16]. This result points up a limitation on the respresentational power of mass functions but need not, by itself, be regarded as damaging. A relatively constrained representation can be desirable if the constraint reflects some reality about human cognition, say, by eliminating bizarre possibilities. Unfortunately for such an argument, no great contortions are needed to come up with an example for which it is impossible to construct a permissible mass function. Black [2] provides a particularly simple example of such a violation.

In the example, two coins, each having a probability in [0.5,1] of turning up heads (H), are flipped independently, and it is assumed that values of the belief function *Bel* are determined by lower bounds on corresponding probabilities. Let A, B, C, and D be the four basic disjoint events *HH, HT, TH,* and *TT*. Since $P(A) \geq 0.25$ (and since there is no greater lower bound), we assign $Bel(A) = 0.25$. Next, $P(A \ or \ B) = P(H\_) \geq 0.5$, where "_" stands for ignorance about H vs. T, so $Bel(A,B) = 0.5$. Denoting the two probabilities of heads u and v (each $\geq \frac{1}{2}$), we also have $P(A \ or \ D) = uv + (1-u)(1-v) = \frac{1}{2} + 2(u - \frac{1}{2})(v - \frac{1}{2}) \geq \frac{1}{2}$. Thus, we take $Bel(A,D) = \frac{1}{2}$. Also, $P(A \ or \ B \ or \ D) = 1 - v(1-u) \geq \frac{1}{2}$, so we take $Bel(A,B,D) = \frac{1}{2}$. The existence of a positive mass function requires the general constraint on *Bel* derived earlier in Eq. 9–7. Invoking the inequality contained therein, with D in place of C, we find that it is violated by the numerical results just obtained. Consequently, using these and other similarly obtained *Bel* values to uncover the requisite mass distribution m leads to negative values for at least one of the masses.

Combining and Propagating Uncertain Evidence

One strategy for reasoning under various forms of uncertainty is to start with formulas of propositional logic and try to generalize them to allow for values in the range [0,1], rather than allowing simply the endpoints 1 for truth and 0 for falsehood that are meaningful in a world of certainty. Bonissone points out that "the generalizations of conjunctions and disjunctions play a vital role in the management of uncertainty in expert systems: they are used in evaluating the satisfaction of premises, in propagating uncertainty through rule chaining, and in consolidating the same conclusion derived from different rules" [3]. He draws together from the literature several families of so-called T-norms, which are generalizations of conjunction.

Three of these T-norms make interesting examples because they bear interesting relationships to rules of probability. One is $T_2(a,b) = ab$, which corresponds to joint probability under independence. Another, $T_3(a,b) = min(a,b)$, is (in addition to turning up in the intersection formula for fuzzy sets) the joint probability of two propositions whose occurrence is maximally positively correlated, so that one entails the other. The opposite case, that of maximal negative correlation, is reflected by $T_1(a,b) = max(0, a + b - 1)$. To see this, note that two events whose probabilities sum to 1 or less need never occur together; the expression $a + b - 1$, the extent to which the sum of the two probabilities exceeds 1, puts a minimum on how often the events must occur together.

The T-norms generalize conjunctions in that each is a function T from $[0,1] \times [0,1]$ to $[0,1]$ that is associative, commutative, and monotonic, and that obeys certain boundary constraints to be given shortly. Drawing a variety of functions together under one formal specification like this permits comparisons which can yield considerable insight and has the mathematical advantage of allowing results to be proved about all of them at once. Associativity and commutativity are familiar properties of conjunction, and their generalization from Boolean to real values requires no comment. Note that monotonicity holds for ordinary conjunction, since increasing either of its arguments (from 0 to 1) cannot decrease the value of a conjunction. The boundary constraints regarding T-norms are $T(0,0) = 0$ and $T(a,1) = a$. In a manner similar to that for conjunction, generalizations of disjunction and negation can be introduced in such a way that the three are related by generalizations of De Morgan's laws. Disjunction is of particular interest since it can be used to express implication; in other words, $p \rightarrow q$ is equivalent to $\bar{p}$ or q. This suggests one method of propagating uncertainty across a rule, viz., by an uncertainty-based generalization of *modus ponens*, the rule of logic that permits concluding proposition q whenever p and $p \rightarrow q$ are true. We shall return to this idea shortly.

Indeed, not only *modus ponens*, but other deductive rules as well, have interesting analogies under uncertainty. We next show how Prade [21] deals with analogies to *modus ponens* and later extend resolution similarly, following Chatalic [7]. According to *modus ponens*, if we know that p is true and we know that $p \rightarrow q$, we are entitled to deduce q. Although $p \rightarrow q$ ($= \bar{p}$ or q) is just another proposition like p, it can be regarded as a rule in a system of certainties. Prade presents a variety of uncertain analogies to *modus ponens*. One possibility involves bounds on probabilities of propositions and is given by

$$\frac{P(p \text{ or } q) \geq a \quad \text{and} \quad P(p) \geq b}{P(q) \geq max(0, a + b - 1)} \tag{9–8}$$

To get this result, we take the conjunction of p and $p \rightarrow q$, using the T-norm T_1, which gives an appropriate lower bound since, as noted earlier, it expresses the case of a maximally negative correlation.

Equation 9–8 combines two pieces of information. The combining of evidence expressed in the form of belief functions can be achieved by a technique known as *Dempster's rule*. This idea has been the focus of much attention in the last few years. Suppose you have two independent belief functions Bel_1 and Bel_2 which, let us say for simplicity, are defined over the same set of states. Then Dempster's rule permits you to calculate a new belief function Bel that summarizes the evidence reflected in the original two. There are several equivalent ways to express the rule, of which perhaps the most elegant involves defining a commonality function [27] which equals, for any set, the sum of the masses of all its supersets (including itself). The resulting combined commonality function is proportional simply to the product of the two given commonality functions. It is meaningful to state Dempster's rule, which is actually for the combining of belief functions, as if it combined commonality functions because the same information is contained in the commonality function as in the belief or plausibility or mass function; indeed, any of them can be recovered from any of the others.

This last observation suggests that it is equally acceptable to state Dempster's rule in terms of mass functions. In fact, we now do just that, since mass functions make it easier to comprehend what the rule does. Given mass functions m_1 and m_2 over the nonempty subsets of some set Θ of possible states, we wish to combine them by Dempster's rule into a resultant mass function m. We view the computation as having two steps: first, form m', an unnormalized version of m, and then normalize it to form m, so that the values of m over all nonempty subsets of Θ sum to 1. To calculate m', consider all the ordered pairs (S_i, S_j) of sets of states. Each such pair contributes $m_1(S_i)m_2(S_j)$ to the mass of the set $S_i \cap S_j$, provided the latter is nonempty. For each subset, the sum of the contributions to it are added to get the value m' assigns it. When $S_i \cap S_j$ is empty, the product of the masses is discarded, that is, not contributed to any subset. Such cases are taken to indicate conflicts between the independent sources of information that gave rise to the two mass functions. Without such conflicts, the normalization step would be unnecessary.

For example, for states A and $\overline{A}$, suppose that the mass function m_1 is in accord with our earlier example, with $m_1(A) = 0.1$, $m_1(\overline{A}) = 0.6$, and $m_1(A \text{ or } \overline{A}) = 0.3$. It is then of interest to consider certain special cases for m_2: complete certainty, complete uncertainty, a mass function opposite to m_1, and one identical to it. In such straightforward cases, one may have pretheoretic intuitions and expect any combinatory rule to obey them. For example, we may expect perfect certainty to rule and utter uncertainty (all mass assigned to Θ) to yield. Also, symmetry arguments should apply to opposite sources. Finally, one might expect compatible evidence from independent sources to lead to a resultant belief with more support than either source belief shows separately.

To test our pretheoretic intuitions, first take certainty, letting $m_2(A) = 1$. Then $m'(A) = 0.1 + 0.3 = 0.4$, with contributions from $A \cap A = A$ and from $A \cap \{A, \overline{A}\} = A$. The remaining mass product corresponds to the empty intersection, $A \cap \overline{A}$. Since m' is nonzero only at A, normalization yields a resultant mass function that also is nonzero only at A, with $m(A) = 1$. Thus, as expected, the certainty represented by m_2 forces certainty in the resultant. The case of utter uncertainty is $m_2(A, \overline{A}) = 1$. The reader can ascertain that the resulting mass is just m_1 itself, as expected again. For m_2 opposite to m_1, that is, with the values for A and for $\overline{A}$ interchanged, the computation is more complex. However, it is analogous to that spelled out next for identical m_1 and m_2; so we give the result here, which is symmetric, as anticipated: $m(A) = m(\overline{A}) = \frac{3}{7}$ and $m(A, \overline{A}) = \frac{1}{7}$.

To compute m when m_2 is identical to m_1, first note that there are nine ($= 3 \times 3$) intersections of ordered pairs of sets. Three of these intersections contribute mass to A, three to $\overline{A}$, and one to $\{A,\overline{A}\}$. The remaining two intersections, $A \cap \overline{A}$ and $\overline{A} \cap A$, are empty. The unnormalized mass of A, that is, $m'(A)$, comes from $A \cap A$, $A \cap \{A,\overline{A}\}$, and its reverse and has the value $(.1)(.1) + (.1)(.3) + (.3)(.1) = .07$. Similarly, $m'(\overline{A}) = .36 + .18 + .18 = .72$, and $m'(A,\overline{A}) = .09$. Normalizing yields $m(A) \approx .08$, $m(\overline{A}) \approx .82$, and $m(A,\overline{A}) \approx .10$.

In some ways, the result of this example is intuitively appealing. First, it seems reasonable that two sources for which there is independent consistent evidence would combine to yield decreased uncertainty, signified by a resultant belief that accords less mass (approximately .1 rather than .3) to the noncommittal set $\{A,\overline{A}\}$. Next, each source independently reflects evidence supporting a relatively high belief in $\overline{A}$, and this independent agreement yields an even higher degree of belief in $\overline{A}$, approximately .82 versus .6, than either source justifies alone. Notice, however, that this result would not survive if $\overline{A}$ were divided into many states, each with individual support. To see this most simply, divide $\overline{A}$ into six states, each individually assigned a mass of .1. By symmetry, it is clear that these are now affected no differently than A by the aggregation under Dempster's rule of several independent agreeing sources. The point is that the behavior of the combination rule is strongly affected by the choice of the so-called frame of discernment.

Another way in which Dempster's rule for combining evidence appears to yield results of dubious plausibility arises from its approach to conflicting evidence. Recall that the rule simply discards mass products that correspond to empty intersections, in effect distribution itself via normalization to the nonempty intersections. One consequence is a kind of dark-horse phenomenon in which, with states A, B, and C, one source assigns $m_1(A) = 0$ and $m_1(B) \ll m_1(C)$ and the other assigns $m_2(C) = 0$ and $m_2(B) \ll m_2(A)$. (The symbol "$\ll$" means "is much less than.") Neither function assigns any mass to sets with more than one element. It is then straightforward to show that the result is certainty for B despite its having little support from either source. One might argue for this result by taking it to indicate that if two credible sources each absolutely discredit a different option, then only some other option, in this case B, can be right. Or we might question the reliability of one or another of the sources, but the method takes no explicit account of such a possibility.

An interesting computational system incorporating and adding to the various ideas already introduced is found in [7]. Like Prospector and many other expert systems that have followed it, this work begins with uncertain if-then rules. Here, however, the rules are taken to be analogous to undirected logical forms, so that an uncertain version of IF A_1 and A_2 and $\cdots$ THEN B becomes an uncertain version of the equivalent formula of propositional logic, $\overline{A}_1$ or $\overline{A}_2 \ldots$ or B, much as in preparation for resolution theorem proving. The nondirectional treatment in this work means that in effect all rules are satisfied simultaneously. Uncertain rules in this form have their effect combined in a manner that reflects Dempster's rule, as may be seen from the particularly simple case of *modus ponens*, which can be regarded as the combination of two implications, of which one, $p \rightarrow q$, has an antecedent with a single conjunct and the other, p, has a null antecedent. Combining these two by

Dempster's rule will bring out some important aspects of the approach taken in this chapter.

The first thing to notice is that $p \rightarrow q$ is shorthand for a set of three states, $\{pq, \overline{p}q, \overline{pq}\}$. Next, although p seems to belong to a set of just two states, viz., itself and $\overline{p}$, we must extend it in this context to take q into account. To do this, regard p as the set of states, $\{pq, p\overline{q}\}$. According to the way this method is laid out, each of the formulas p and $p \rightarrow q$ has initially been assigned a belief value and a plausibility value. By a kind of nonpresumptuousness principle, mass is assigned to the largest set of states consistent with these belief and plausibility values.

Formally, we start with $Bel(p) = \alpha$ and $Pl(p) = 1 - \beta$, where $\beta > \alpha$, and similarly, $Bel(p \rightarrow q) = \gamma$ and $Pl(p \rightarrow q) = 1 - \delta$, where $\delta > \gamma$. The last of these equations means that the mass $1 - \delta$ is assigned to the singleton set $\{p\overline{q}\}$, which is logically equivalent to $\overline{p \rightarrow q}$. An example of one of the nine $(= 3 \times 3)$ products of masses contributed to an intersection of sets is $\alpha\gamma$ contributed to $\{pq, p\overline{q}\} \cap \{pq, \overline{p}q, \overline{pq}\} = \{pq\}$. This is the only contribution to any (proper or improper) subset of $\{pq, \overline{p}q\}$. Ignoring conflict, and hence normalization, one would obtain, from the foregoing, $Bel(q) = \alpha\gamma$. To compute $Pl(q)$, we look for intersections that do not overlap q and subtract the corresponding contributed masses from 1. Such intersections would have to be subsets of $\{p\overline{q}, \overline{pq}\}$. There are two suitable intersections, each yielding the singleton set $\{p\overline{q}\}$. One is the intersection of $\{p\overline{q}\}$ with the universal set, yielding a mass product of $(1 - \delta)(\beta - \alpha)$, and the other is the intersection of $\{p\overline{q}\}$ with $\{pq, p\overline{q}\}$, with a mass product of $(1 - \delta)(\alpha)$. Subtracting the sum of these two contributions from 1 and again ignoring normalization gives $Pl(q) = 1 - \beta(1 - \delta)$. This is formula III in [7].

In general, rules can have more than one antecedent. Moreover, each antecedent is allowed to range over a finite number of values rather than, as in the foregoing, just the two values of affirmation and negation. Beyond these steps toward generality, there is the formation of a network, to guide computation, as follows. For each rule in disjunctive form, there is a rule node and a node for each of its disjoined propositions (including the one that was initially the conclusion of the rule; a disjunct does not appear twice in the network even if it appears in more than one rule). Two propositions in the network may be connected by more than one path, so that there are dependencies. For these to receive appropriate treatment, rules and/or propositions collapse into corresponding compound versions. In a similar spirit, Yager [34] combines techniques even further, incorporating fuzziness and probabilistic considerations.

Belief Networks

A fundamental assumption made by most computational approaches to uncertainty in rule-based systems is that uncertain inferences can be modularized just like logical inferences. An uncertain rule of the form "*A* implies *B* with strength *S*" is *modular* in the sense that it is used to update belief in *B* no matter how our belief in *A* was derived, and no matter what else is in the knowledge base [20]. This point of view has recently been questioned, however, as the implications of the modularity assumption have become more clearly understood [13], [14], [20]. The problem is that uncertain reasoning often must handle dependencies among hypotheses that are inherently *not* modular, and accounting for these dependencies requires several capabilities such as retracting conclusions or mixing together forward and backward inferences, which can be difficult to implement using rules.

The following example by Henrion [14] illustrates how these complications can arise in very simple reasoning tasks:

> Suppose you find yourself sneezing unexpectedly in the house of an acquaintance. It might either be due to an incipient cold or your allergy to cats. You then observe animal paw marks, which increases your judged probability of a cat in the vicinity (diagnostic inference), which, in turn, increases the probability that you are having an allergic reaction (predictive inference). This also explains away the sneezing, and so decreases the probability you are getting a cold. [p. 325]

Several dependencies among the propositions in this example pose a potential problem for rule-based computations. First, note that the immediate conclusion one might make after a sneeze is that a cold is likely, perhaps because you know that it is flu season. However, upon obtaining evidence suggesting an allergic reaction, any determination about a cold based on the sneeze has to be retracted because the allergy "explains away" the sneezing episode. This nonmonotonic behavior is difficult to model using rules like "If you sneeze, then it is likely you are catching a cold," which say nothing about the background assumptions that make such an inference legitimate. There is no information in the rule indicating what the exceptions are. A more fundamental difficulty, though, is that the interaction between the cold and allergy hypotheses is a dynamic one. Until there is a sneeze, belief about a cold is independent of belief about an allergic reaction. It is only when the sneeze occurs that they become correlated. Another kind of dynamic interaction takes place between the belief about the allergic reaction and the belief about the paw marks. As long as you are not sure about the presence of a cat, observations about paw marks affect the belief in an allergic reaction. Once a cat is observed, however, the paw marks have no impact on the deliberations about an allergy. Thus, your belief in an allergic reaction would not change even if, for example, you were told that the paw marks you observed were made by a plastic toy. The presence of a cat is the most directly relevant piece of knowledge.

Handling these interactions with rules can be done by carefully enumerating all of the relevant exceptions to each rule and monitoring forward (diagnostic) and backward (predictive) inferences between two hypotheses to avoid circular reasoning. This is usually very awkward, however, because the rules become complex and the basic relationships among the hypotheses are obscured. An alternative approach to the problem is to abandon the modularity of rule-based updating and represent the relationships among propositions explicitly. This type of representation is available in computational schemes that use *belief networks* [19]. A belief network is a graphical representation of the dependencies among propositions. Each node in a belief network designates an uncertain variable. Variables are uncertain in the sense that they each have a set of distinctive, exhaustive possibilities or values, and only one of those values can be correct. The current knowledge or opinion about which value is correct is represented by a *belief distribution* at each node that characterizes the belief for every value. The links between nodes in a belief network represent direct dependencies between propositions. Attached to each link is a transition function that specifies how the belief distribution of one node influences the belief distribution of the other. When there is no link connecting two nodes, the belief distributions of those nodes do not directly influence each other.

There are two big advantages to the belief network representation. First, it provides a qualitative model of the inherent structure of a problem in uncertain reasoning. Returning to Henrion's example, we can describe the sneezing problem using the network of relations shown in Figure 9–1. The links in this network designate causal dependencies between variables, with the arrows indicating the direction of causality. The knowledge that an allergic reaction can "explain away" the sneeze and make a cold less credible is represented by the topology of the network. This is a built-in feature of the way all cause-and-effect relationships are interpreted. The many exceptions and implicit relations that must be listed explicitly in a rule-based approach are thereby efficiently summarized by the paths

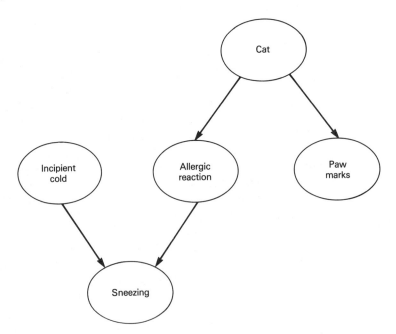

Figure 9–1 Brief network for Henrion's sneeze example.

between nodes in a belief network. The second advantage of belief networks is that they can be used as inference engines. The information needed to update the belief distribution at a node is available locally from that node's neighbors. This makes it possible to use distributed, message-passing computations to propagate the effects of changes in belief. Because this kind of computation only requires interactions among semantically related variables, each step in the process has a meaningful interpretation.

Belief network schemes have been devised for Bayesian computations and for belief functions. Probabilistic methods like *Bayesian networks* [19] and *influence diagrams* [25] quantify links with conditional probabilities and use probability distributions to characterize beliefs about uncertain variables. Similar techniques are available using belief functions as the representation of belief in networks called *galleries* [17] and *qualitative Markov networks* [28]. The work by Pearl [19] is especially noteworthy because it was the first practical method to use qualitative, knowledge-based constructs in a Bayesian computation while maintaining strict compliance with probability theory. Accordingly, we conclude this section with a brief discussion of Pearl's algorithm for updating Bayesian networks.

Bayesian networks represent causal relationships among a set of multivalued variables. The directionality of the links is from causes to manifestations, each link emanating from a parent node in the graph. The strength of each causal dependence is quantified using a matrix of probabilities conditioned on the states of the parent nodes. Pearl's belief-updating scheme keeps track of two sources of support for belief at each node: the diagnostic support derived from evidence gathered by descendants of the node and the causal support derived from evidence gathered by parents of the node. Diagnostic support provides the kind of information summarized in a likelihood ratio for binary variables. Causal support is the analogue of a prior probability, summarizing the background knowledge lending support to a belief. These two kinds of evidential support are combined to compute the belief at a node with a computation that generalizes the odds/likelihood version of Bayes' rule. Each source of support is summarized by a separate local parameter, which makes it possible to perform diagnostic and causal inferences at the same time. These two local parameters, together with the matrix of numbers quantifying the relationship between the node and its parents, are all that is required to update beliefs. Incoming evidence is treated as a new source of diagnostic support for a node. It serves as an activation signal, causing belief at that node to be recomputed and support for neighboring nodes to be revised. The revised support is transmitted to the neighboring nodes, thereby propagating the impact of the evidence. Propagation continues until the network reaches equilibrium. The overall computation assigns a belief to each node that is consistent with probability theory.

Pearl's distributed approach to Bayesian reasoning has been influential in refuting many of the common objections to using the probability calculus in knowledge-based systems. Henrion [14] and Spiegelhalter [30] provide extensive discussions of the many reasons behind the resurgence of interest in probability. The following reasons are most directly related to Bayesian networks:

- The need for exhaustive data about joint statistics can be avoided by using the qualitative structure of the problem. Specifically, the topology of a Bayesian network is a qualitative representation of the dependencies and conditional dependencies constraining a set of variables. This structure reduces the task of specifying the complete joint distribution over all variables to the much simpler task of making local quantitative judgments for small clusters of variables. Even though these probability assessments are made locally, their combined effect is guaranteed to be consistent.

- A single-number representation does not convey the precision of the available knowledge, nor does it indicate the relative amounts of evidence for and against a given belief. In Pearl's scheme, however, the distinction between sources of belief and sources of disbelief is maintained by using likelihood ratios to represent diagnostic support. Likelihood ratios make it possible to clearly specify the level of commitment that a piece of evidence has. For example, the same piece of data might confirm some values of a variable, disconfirm others, and be completely neutral regarding all the rest. Moreover, the graph structure contains all the information needed to trace the sources of support for a belief and compute a standard deviation that represents the precision of that belief [30].

- The problems arising from the kind of unrealistic independence assumptions made in quasi-Bayesian schemes can be eliminated by generalizing the notion of propositions to include multivalued variables. This change makes the conditional independence assumptions required for a coherent probabilistic approach intuitive and reasonable.

While the debate about which techniques best suit the needs of expert systems is far from over, Pearl's work has helped to make probability theory a leading contender.

CASE STUDY: UNCERTAINTY IN SHIP CLASSIFICATION PROBLEMS

There has not been a great deal of work comparing the performance of various techniques for uncertain reasoning in different circumstances. The comparisons that have been made, however, indicate that no scheme is ideal for all situations. Indeed, it is not hard to construct examples in which many widely used techniques produce conclusions that are undesirable, sometimes even worse than random guessing [33]. Accordingly, it is premature to draw conclusions about the exact circumstances in which a given technique is reliable. Nevertheless, it is clear that the choice of which method to use in a particular application should not be made arbitrarily. This section describes a problem in ship classification and discusses the way uncertain inferences relating thereto are structured and computed. It is an example of the kind of considerations that guide such choices in a real-life application.

Classifying Ship Images

Classification problem solving is a ubiquitous activity in knowledge-based systems [8]. Ongoing research at the Navy Center for Applied Research in AI (NCARAI) is concerned with some ship classification problems that are especially difficult and challenging [4]. Having ship images classified correctly is obviously important to the Navy, which has invested heavily in training personnel to analyze and interpret images under operational conditions. The task is difficult regardless of what kind of sensor information is used—visual, infrared, radar, or sonar—because sharp feature details are not readily available. Images are most often obtained during a brief observation interval from distances that make high resolution difficult to achieve. Also, the viewing angle is usually a matter of opportunity rather than choice, and the observer must make do with the prevailing visibility, weather, and lighting conditions at sea. Still another factor degrading image quality is the fact that sensor platforms are often buffeted by turbulence in the air or the ocean. These difficulties are of course exacerbated when the classification must be done in real time using meager computing facilities. The quality of images produced in this way is likely to be lower than that attainable using sophisticated enhancement techniques that require powerful computing resources. All of this is in addition to the complexity faced when distinguishing among hundreds of classes of vessels, some of which differ only in fine feature details.

Any complete solution to these classification problems must account for data at several levels of granularity, ranging from raw sensor returns to partially reliable intelligence reports about ship identification. Several methodologies are available for transforming these data into evidence that is useful for classification: signal-processing, pattern recognition and feature extraction algorithms, and knowledge-based approaches to feature interpretation. The goal of classification problem solving is to achieve a coherent analysis of sensor returns by selectively applying the methodologies to the data and then choosing the most plausible solution.

Orchestrating this entire process is a complex job. The research at NCARAI has focused on managing the uncertainty associated with feature data and other evidence, to help assure that plausible inferences are made about the implications of that evidence. Uncertainty has many potential sources in ship classification problems: sensors are rarely completely accurate or reliable; observations and feature extraction techniques can be flawed; there may be no strong correlations between manifestations and causes; some of the evidence may be contradictory; and so on. Confidence in the reliability of machine-drawn inferences is a critically important issue for the Navy. It is therefore crucial that a knowledge-based approach to this problem manage uncertainty with representations and techniques based on sound theory and clear semantics.

Characteristics of the Problem Domain

In order to evaluate which methods for managing uncertainty are appropriate for ship classification, we must first understand the kind of knowledge available to solve these problems. The following general characterizations of ship classification provide the necessary constraints:

Unstructured environments.   There is often little control over or information about the conditions under which a sensor is used. Parameters like aspect angle, scale, scattering properties, and so forth may be unknown. This makes it difficult to accurately predict how a hypothesized object should appear in the sensor returns. If its ability to predict is weak, a classification problem solver cannot make good judgments about what evidence will be available or when it will become available. Problem-solving strategies must therefore be flexible and opportunistic. Work on a hypothesis must be suspended if the evidence needed to definitively establish or reject it is not available, or if evidence arrives that makes some other hypothesis more attractive. Uncertainty management schemes that insist on rigid strategies for establishing and refining hypotheses (e.g., [6]) are not well suited to handle this situation.

Inherent ambiguities.   For many sensors, there is no one-to-one mapping between manifestations in the sensor domain and features in the object domain. Consequently, patterns of features extracted from the sensor returns might have more than one plausible cause in the object domain. Maintaining consistent beliefs for several explanations of a given manifestation requires careful attention to the way alternative causes interact. As noted earlier in the discussion of belief networks, most rule-based formalisms for uncertain inference either handle this problem awkwardly or cannot handle it at all.

Empirical data.   Problems in the Navy domain often come with large amounts of data concerning the structure of ships, how many ships there are, where they are most frequently found, etc. These data can be used to compute statistical expectations about which manifestations of features and feature combinations will be observed when a ship is sensed and which ships are *a priori* more likely to be encountered. The uncertain inference technique chosen for this problem should be capable of using such data in some well-understood way. In particular, methods that have no provision for using prior information are to be avoided because they can generate conclusions that are badly mistaken [14].

Limited resources.   Whenever ship classification is done under operational conditions, resource limitations become a problem. Time and computing capacity may preclude expensive inferences or any information gathering not absolutely necessary to make a decision. Under these circumstances, model-driven (or causal) reasoning is crucial for pruning away implausible hypotheses. The inference technique must consequently handle diagnostic and predictive inferences in combination. Moreover, some reasonable theory must be available for converting the beliefs computed by the inference method into cost-effective decisions.

These considerations suggest the need for explicitly representing the dependencies among hypotheses and asynchronously updating each relevant hypothesis as new evidence becomes available. Reasoning techniques that use beliefs networks are well suited for such a job. Because probability theory is still the only inference calculus that has both a clear approach to decision making under uncertainty and well-established methods for using empirical data [14], Bayesian networks are a good choice for the ship classification problem.

A Small Example

The implementation issues can be brought more clearly into focus by considering the following small example taken from a real Navy problem. Because of the meager computational facilities available on most military platforms, sensor operators are usually used as a primary pattern recognition resource in the classification process. The operator begins the process by registering the location of certain gross ship components in the image. Simple computational tools are then used to estimate various physical dimensions of the ship and crudely match these measurements with entries in a data base of ship structural descriptions. Those ships that are plausible matches are rank-ordered, if possible, and then displayed to the operator. At this point the operator is on his or her own and must look for small feature differences to resolve ambiguities. This usually requires the use of "classification keys" for discriminating one kind of ship from another.

The crucial phase of the classification process is the use of these classification keys. The keys are used to refine classificatory hypotheses in the following series of steps that is standard for all image data, regardless of the sensor in question:

- Establish a coarse-grained functional classification for the ship image, for example, military combatant versus commercial vessel.
- Establish the *Naval Class* of the ship image, which identifies it as belonging to a group of ships built to the same design and known collectively by the lead ship's name.
- Determine the name or hull number of the ship.

The operator is required to make several judgments about the quality of information in the image, which keys to use, and when to use them. This requires considerable expertise when difficult discriminations must be made. The information needed to achieve each step is not always available or easy to obtain, and the best sequence of classification keys to use is not always obvious.

Many different features provide useful evidence for refining hypotheses about a ship's image: the shape of the stern, curvature of the sides, location of weapons, configuration of the superstructure, etc. In order to simplify the explanation of the reasoning task, we only give details here about how the shape of the stern implies Naval Class. The knowledge for this problem was provided by an expert image analyst, who described ten Naval Classes that have similar imagery and are often difficult to distinguish from one another. These descriptions are given in Table 9–1, which describes the stern shape for each of the ten classes. The descriptions include a subjectively determined weight for each feature attribute and Naval Class combination. This number indicates an expectation about whether that attribute will be manifested in the imagery. The weights are given on a scale of 0 to 10, with 0 meaning the attribute should never be detected and 10 meaning it should always be detected. Two structures with the same weight for a given attribute cannot be distinguished on that basis alone. Thus, the sterns of the Sverdlov and Forrest Sherman are square to the same extent.

Table 9–1   Ship stern descriptions.

Shape attribute	Stern type				
	Type 1	Type 2	Type 3	Type 4	Type 5
	Virginia	Belknap Leahy	Sverdlov	Bainbridge California Coontz Long Beach Truxtun	Forrest Sherman
Square	10	0	1	0	1
Round	0	10	0	5	2
Tapered	0	0	10	0	0

The knowledge given in the table can be organized into a simple hierarchy of hypotheses having four levels: Naval Class, major structural components, features, and observations. At the top of the hierarchy is the hypothesis about the true Naval Class of the ship in the image. This hypothesis is an uncertain variable having ten distinct possible values.[1] Note that the belief distribution computed for this variable does not represent a classification or decision: it is simply a summary of the rational weighing of all the available evidence that can be used later in some clearly defined decision procedures [30]. Presumably, Naval Class cannot be directly determined, so at the next level are hypotheses about the gross structural components of the ship—the stern, deck, superstructural blocks, etc. The table indicates that there are five types of stern, so the stern hypothesis is a variable having five possible values. Sometimes evidence is available that directly bears on knowledge at this level. For

---

[1] For a simplification, we assume that no other Naval Classes are possible. This assumption can be relaxed by including the class "other" as a possible value to represent ignorance and revising our quantitative judgments accordingly.

instance, the stern of the Sverdlov class is very distinctive and can often be recognized immediately. In most cases, though, stern type has to be determined from the shape attributes in the next level of the hierarchy. For the stern components of this set of ships, there are two ways for a stern to be square, three ways to be round, and one way to be tapered. An example of the kind of evidence relevant here is some information about the degree of curvature of the stern. In practice, it is often difficult even to obtain evidence at this level. A poor-quality image or a nonexpert observer might only be able to provide evidence that the stern in the image is somewhat rounded, period. Thus, the lowest level in the hierarchy includes hypotheses representing these very simple assertions.

The Bayesian network representation for the ship classification problem is organized to model the four-level knowledge hierarchy just described. Figure 9–2 shows the portion of the overall network that is concerned with how the shape of the stern influences the Naval Class hypothesis. Each ellipse designates a variable, with the set of possible values shown in parentheses. The bottom nodes correspond to

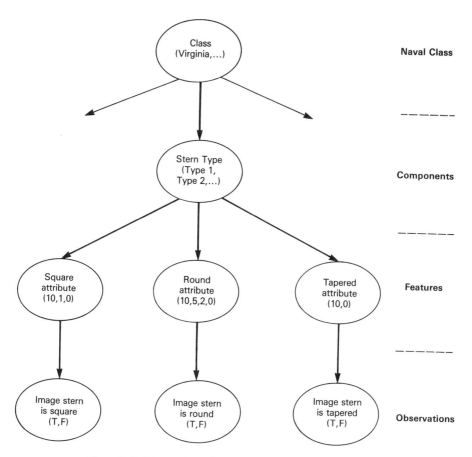

Figure 9–2 Excerpt from the ship classification Bayesian network.

the three simplest kinds of observations about the shape of the stern in the image. Each of these observations is a manifestation of the shape attributes of the ship being imaged. Since the weights given in Table 9–1 designate expectations about what will appear in the imagery, we can use them to quantify the links between observations and their immediate cause at the next level in the hierarchy. For example, the relationship between the square attribute and observable squareness in the image is given by the following conditional probabilities:

Prob(squareness is detectable | stern with square attribute of 10) = 1.0
Prob(squareness is detectable | stern with square attribute of 1) = 0.1
Prob(squareness is detectable | stern with square attribute of 0) = 0

A more realistic model would modify these quantitative assessments to account for any uncertainty in the imaging process [1] and lack of precision in assessing the original weights [31]. At the third level in the hierarchy, belief is computed about the overall stern shape. The influence of this hypothesis on shape attributes is quantified using simple counting arguments: we count the number of Naval Classes with a given stern type that have a particular shape attribute and divide by the number of classes having that stern type. For example, the influence of the stern type variable on the square attribute variable is determined by the following probabilities:

Prob(stern with square attribute of 10 | stern is Type 1) = 1.0
Prob(stern with square attribute of 1 | stern is Type 3) = 1.0
Prob(stern with square attribute of 1 | stern is Type 5) = 1.0
Prob(stern with square attribute of 0 | stern is Type 2) = 1.0
Prob(stern with square attribute of 0 | stern is Type 4) = 1.0

The probabilities are straightforward in this case because the stern type definitions were based strictly on combinations of shape attribute values, and every stern in a given type has the same value for each shape attribute. Similar counting arguments are used to quantify the relationship between Naval Class and stern type. The quantification of the network is completed by assessing prior probabilities for the Naval Class variable.

A complete version of the ship classification network has been extensively tested on 119 ship images. Experts in the Navy have reviewed the belief distributions computed for the test images and found them comparable to what a knowledgeable human analyst would infer from the evidence. (See [4] for more details about the complete system and its performance.)

CONCLUSION

Reasoning involving uncertainty is now recognized as a pivotal factor in the success and credibility of expert systems in complex problem domains. Consequently, the last few years have witnessed a dramatic increase in research in this area. Techniques for this kind of reasoning have been devised that have solid theoretical justifications [19, 28], and tools are being developed to make these techniques available to knowledge engineers [17, 25, 4]. Much work remains to be done, however. Every technique has strengths and weaknesses for practical applications that have not yet been thoroughly analyzed. Experience with implementations involving large scale, real-world problems is needed before we can understand how useful these methods are for those who develop and use expert systems. Nevertheless, the work done so far makes it clear that reasoning involving uncertainty is an inherently complex task that influences every aspect of expert system design and performance.

In particular, it is important to keep in mind that an expert system cannot make plausible inferences simply by computing measures of belief. Computations of belief require information, and there are usually costs associated with acquiring that information. Any system that does not intelligently use these costs to constrain its inferences will lack credibility in a real-world application. Moreover, a measure of belief does not by itself constitute a decision or license to act; it is only a summary of the rational weighing of all the available evidence, and it must be used as input to some well-defined decision procedure. Unless the decision procedure adequately accounts for beliefs, preferences as to outcomes, and costs of actions—all within the context of the prevailing problem-solving strategy—the system's reasoning will not be accepted as very plausible or sensible. A calculus of belief is therefore the foundation of any solution to problems in reasoning involving uncertainty, but it is by no means the only requirement.

Does it matter which technique is chosen for a given application? After all, successful expert systems have been developed using methods for reasoning involving uncertainty that were admittedly ad hoc or poorly understood. As sensitivity analyses and empirical tests of these methods are conducted to probe their robustness, practitioners are becoming aware that their successful use cannot be taken for granted (see, e.g., [5]). Indeed, it is not hard to construct examples in which many widely used techniques produce conclusions that are undesirable, sometimes even worse than random guessing [33]. Thus, it is not easy to draw conclusions about the exact circumstances in which a given technique is reliable. Nevertheless, it is clear that the choice of which method to use in a particular application should not be made arbitrarily.

REFERENCES

1. Binford, T., Levitt, T., and Mann, W. "Bayesian Inference in Model-based Machine Vision." *Proceedings of the Third Workshop on Uncertainty in Artificial Intelligence.* Seattle, 1987, pp. 86–92.
2. Black, P. K. "Is Shafer General Bayes?" *Proceedings of the Third Workshop on Uncertainty in Artificial Intelligence.* Seattle, 1987, pp. 2–9.
3. Bonissone, P. P., and Decker, K. S. "Selecting Uncertainty Calculi and Granularity: An Experiment in Trading Off Precision and Complexity." In *Uncertainty in Artificial Intelligence,* edited by L. N. Kanal and J. Lemmer, pp. 217–247. Amsterdam: North-Holland, 1986.

4. Booker, L. "Plausible Reasoning in Classification Problem Solving." In *Image Understanding in Unstructured Environments,* edited by S. Chen, World Scientific Publishing Co., 1988.

5. Buchanan, B. G., and Shortliffe, E. H. *Rule-based Expert Systems*. Reading, MA: Addison-Wesley, 1984.

6. Bylander T., and Mittal, S. "CSRL: A Language for Classificatory Problem Solving and Uncertainty Handling." *AI Magazine* 7 (1986):66–77.

7. Chatalic, P., Dubois, D., and Prade, H. "An Approach to Approximate Reasoning Based on the Dempster Rule of Combination." *International Journal of Expert Systems Research and Applications* 1 (1987):67–85.

8. Clancey, W. "Classification Problem Solving." *Proceedings of the Fourth National Conference on Artificial Intelligence.* Austin, University of Texas, 1984, pp. 49–55.

9. Duda, R. O., Hart, P. E., and Nilsson, N. J. "Subjective Bayesian Methods for Rule-based Inference Systems." *SRI International Technical Note 124.* Palo Alto: CA, 1976.

10. Fine, T. L. *Theories of Probability: An Examination of Foundations.* New York: Academic Press, 1973.

11. Heckerman, D. "Probabilistic Interpretations for Mycin's Certainty Factors." In *Uncertainty in Artificial Intelligence,* edited by L. N. Kanal and J. Lemmer, pp. 67–96. Amsterdam: North-Holland, 1986.

12. Heckerman, D., and Jimison, H. "A perspective on Confidence and Its Use in Focusing Attention During Knowledge Acquisition." *Proceedings of the Third Workshop on Uncertainty in Artificial Intelligence.* Seattle, 1987, pp. 123–131.

13. Heckerman, D., and Horvitz, E. "On the Expressiveness of Rule-based Systems for Reasoning with Uncertainty." *Proceedings of the Sixth National Conference on Artificial Intelligence.* Seattle, 1987, pp. 121–126.

14. Henrion, M. "Should We Use Probability in Uncertain Inference Systems?" *Proceedings of the Eighth Annual Conference of the Cognitive Science Society.* Amherst, MA, 1986, pp. 320–330.

15. Krantz, D. H., Luce, R. D., Suppes, P., and Tversky, A. *Foundations of Measurement.* New York: Academic Press, 1971.

16. Kyburg, H. E. "Bayesian and Non-Bayesian Evidential Updating." *Artificial Intelligence* 31 (1987): 271–293.

17. Lowrance, J., Garvey, T., and Strat, T. "A Framework for Evidential-reasoning systems." *Proceedings of the Fifth National Conference on Artificial Intelligence.* Philadelphia, 1986, pp. 896–903.

18. Nutter, J. T. "Uncertainty and Probability." *Proceedings of the Tenth International Joint Conference on Artificial Intelligence.* 1987, pp. 373–379.

19. Pearl, J. "Fusion, Propagation and Structuring in Belief Networks." *Artificial Intelligence* 29 (1986): 241–288.

20. Pearl, J. "Evidential Reasoning under Uncertainty." *Technical report R-107, UCLA Cognitive Systems Laboratory.* Los Angeles: CA, 1988.

21. Prade, H. "A Computational Approach to Approximate and Plausible Reasoning with Applications to Expert Systems." *IEEE Transactions on Pattern Analysis and Machine Intelligence* 7 (1985): 260–283.

22. Quinlan, J. R. "Inferno: A Cautious Approach to Uncertain Inference." *Computer Journal* 26 (1983): 255–269.

23. Savage, L. J. *The Foundations of Statistics.* New York: John Wiley and Sons, 1954.

24. Shachter, R. "Evaluating Influence Diagrams." *Operations Research* 36 (1986): 871–882.

25. Shachter, R. "DAVID: Influence Diagram Processing System for the Macintosh." In *Uncertainty in Artificial Intelligence 2,* edited by J. Lemmer and L. Kanal, pp 191–196. Amsterdam: North-Holland, 1988.

26. Shafer, G. *A Mathematical Theory of Evidence.* Princeton, NJ: Princeton University Press, 1976.

27. Shafer, G., and Logan, R. "Implementing Dempster's Rule for Hierarchical Evidence." *Artificial Intelligence* 33 (1987): 271–298.

28. Shenoy, P., and Shafer, G. "Propagating Belief Functions with Local Computations." *IEEE Expert* (Fall 1986), pp. 43–51.

29. Shortliffe, E. H. *Computer-based Medical Consultations: MYCIN.* New York: American Elsevier, 1976.

30. Spiegelhalter, D. "A Statistical View of Uncertainty in Expert Systems." In *Artificial Intelligence and Statistics,* edited by W. Gale, pp. 17–55. Reading, MA: Addison-Wesley, 1986.

31. Spiegelhalter, D. "Probabilistic Reasoning in Predictive Expert Systems." In *Uncertainty in Artificial Intelligence,* edited by L. N. Kanal and J. Lemmer, pp. 47–67. Amsterdam: North-Holland, 1986.

32. Tversky, A., and Kahneman, D. "Rational Choice and the Framing of Decisions." *Technical Report, Office of Naval Research Contract Number N00014-84-K-0615.* 1986.

33. Wise, B., and Henrion, M. "Comparing Uncertain Inference Systems to Probability" In *Uncertainty in Artificial Intelligence,* edited by L. N. Kanal and J. Lemmer, pp. 69–83. Amsterdam: North-Holland, 1986.

34. Yager, R. "Toward a General Theory of Reasoning with Uncertainty; part II: Probability." *International Journal of Man-Machine Studies* 25 (1986): 613–631.

35. Zadeh, L. A. "The Role of Fuzzy Logic in the Management of Uncertainty in Expert Systems." In *Approximate Reasoning in Expert Systems,* edited by M. M. Gupta, A. Kandel, W. Bandler, and J. B. Kiszka, pp. 3–31. Amsterdam: North-Holland, 1985.

10

Knowledge Representation Methodologies for Expert Systems Development

Connie Loggia Ramsey
Alan C. Schultz

INTRODUCTION

Why have knowledge representations? Human knowledge is ill-structured and often contradictory, and can change over time. Furthermore, exactly how do humans represent knowledge? Clearly, if we are to write programs which must reason about knowledge, we need some method for storing that knowledge in a form that is readily usable by a computer. The key constraints for a machine representation are that it must be efficient in time and space, it must be understandable to humans, and it must support reasoning; that is, just representing knowledge is not enough—there must be a way to use it.

Most of the representational schemes currently used for expert systems were developed in the mid-1960s to mid-1970s as a result of a debate over the merits of procedural knowledge versus declarative knowledge. During this time the focus for a large part of the artificial intelligence (AI) community was on knowledge representation.

This chapter will explore various knowledge representation schemes and show some examples of these schemes as used in current state-of-the-art systems. We begin with an examination of some features that we can use in comparing these representation schemes. Consider these features while reading about each scheme.

Features to Consider when Choosing a Knowledge Representation Formalism

Ease of representation for particular domains. In general, a knowledge representation scheme must be able to express such things as objects, events, relationships, concepts, goals, and even metaknowledge such as motivation. Sometimes spatial and temporal considerations must be taken into account, a characteristic referred to as the *expressibility* of the representation. A major influence in deciding on a particular representation scheme is the domain of the expert system: the knowledge representation must be able to describe every needed aspect of the domain in a concise way. Also, the preexisting format of the application knowledge should be considered: it is much easier to keep the knowledge in the same or a similar format than to encode it in a completely different format. Finally, the intended use of the expert system must also be given consideration when choosing a knowledge representation scheme.

Efficiency of space and time.   The representation not only needs to allow for expressibility, but it must also be efficient in terms of the amount of space required to encode the knowledge. The goal is to have a concise formulation of the knowledge without having superfluous information. Equally important is efficiency of time. The amount of time required to manipulate the knowledge is a matter of the reasoning involved, but the representation should strive to minimize the processing time taken.

Ease of human understanding.   One of the earliest arguments for using declarative representation was for understandability. The issues are wide ranging. One factor is the ability of a human expert, who may not be a computer scientist, to be able to read the knowledge base in order to evaluate the correctness or completeness of the information. Another consideration is knowledge acquisition: the human expert or knowledge engineer should be able to encode new information easily using the chosen knowledge representation scheme. Yet another issue is the ability to modify and maintain the knowledge base: some representation schemes allow for easier maintainability of the expert information in the knowledge base than do others. A related concern is the ability to modularize the code.

Relationship between knowledge base and inference engine.   The choices of a knowledge representation scheme and an inference engine often depend on each other. In some cases, the type of inferences needed may constrain the choices of knowledge representation. If a particular inference engine is needed for the expert task, then a representation must be chosen to match the engine; that is, the data structure must be usable by the inference engine. (Recall the earlier discussion of efficiency.)

Uncertainty.   Knowledge about real-world problems is often uncertain. Accordingly, the knowledge representation formalism chosen must be able to handle reasoning with uncertainty if the problem domain has a great deal of uncertainty associated with it.

FORMALISMS FOR KNOWLEDGE REPRESENTATION

Rule-based Representation

Rule-based systems (also called production systems) are comprised of rules, working memory, and a rule interpreter. The domain knowledge in a rule-based system is represented as a set of rules. In their simplest form, rules are condition-action pairs specifying that *if* some *condition* is true, *then* some *action* is performed. Working memory is used to store facts or assertions created by the rules. The rule interpreter applies (fires) a rule when its condition is satisfied by elements in working memory and carries out the action, which is usually to change working memory. The rules might be considered long-term memory, and the working memory short-term memory. We refer to the conditional part (also called the antecedent) of the rule as the left-hand side (LHS) and the action part (also called the consequent) as the right-hand side (RHS).

Here is a small part of a simple rule base that will help a home owner pay the bills:

```
R0: IF mortgage is due

    AND checking account has enough money to pay mortgage

   THEN pay mortgage

    AND reduce checking balance by amount of mortgage


R1: IF mortgage is due

    AND not enough money in checking account

    AND enough money in savings account

   THEN transfer money from savings to checking

    AND update amounts in savings and checking accounts

    AND pay mortgage


R2: IF mortgage is due

    AND not enough money in savings and checking

   THEN apply for loan with bank
```

```
R3: IF electric bill is due

    AND enough money in checking

   THEN pay electric bill

    AND reduce amount in checking by amount of electric bill


R4: IF no bills are currently due

    AND checking account has excess of money

   THEN transfer money from checking account to savings account
```

As we can see from this example, the LHS and RHS may have more than one clause. Typically, when the LHS has more than one clause (or predicate), the clauses are treated as a conjunction, i.e., all the clauses must be true (match elements from working memory) for the rule to be applied. Often the negation of a clause is allowed, which indicates that the clause should not match an element in working memory. When the RHS has more than one action, all the actions are performed.

Variations. In its simplest form, a rule is just a list of literals that must exactly match an element in working memory. More often, the pattern in the LHS allows some parts of the element to be ignored so that only the explicitly mentioned parts need to match. However, most systems allow a richer representation. We next explore the many variations that exist in different rule-based systems.

While we used natural language in the example of the bill-paying rule base, we must, by design, restrict our rule-based representation to a limited, machine-processable representation. In general, we can think of a clause of our LHS as being a list that contains the name of an object followed by pairs of attributes and values associated with that object. Although this is not a standard, it is a natural representation for objects in working memory and can be simulated with almost all rule-based systems. To develop the ideas that follow, we shall use a representation similar to OPS5, a well-known rule-based system [5]. According to this representation, rule R0 might look as follows:

```
R0: IF (bill ∧name mortgage ∧status due ∧amount 500)

    AND (account ∧name checking ∧balance 500)

   THEN (assert (pay ∧item mortgage))

    AND (remove (bill ∧name mortgage ∧status due ∧amount 500))
```

```
AND (remove (account ∧name checking ∧balance 500))

AND (assert (account ∧name checking ∧balance 0))
```

And working memory might have the following contents:

```
WM: (bill ∧name mortgage ∧status due ∧amount 500)

     (account ∧name checking ∧balance 500)
```

In this representation of the rule, *bill* is an object, and *name, status,* and *amount* are attributes that are followed by their values; note that attributes are preceded by the caret symbol. The primitives *remove* and *assert* are respectively used to remove items from and add items to working memory. While these primitives are usually part of most rule-based expert systems, some systems only allow you to add to working memory, replacing older elements with more recent elements. (This concept will be discussed later.) The preceding example of R0 is actually very trivial, for a couple of reasons: a rule would have to be created for each dollar amount and for all types of bills. We next consider mechanisms that give us greater flexibility.

Variables. In the foregoing example, we had to list each type of bill in the rule base; but it might be impossible to enumerate all situations in a given rule base. Accordingly, in order to introduce generality, most rule-based systems allow variable bindings in the terms. When unbound, the variables are allowed to match any value for an attribute, but once bound, they can only match the constant to which they were initially bound. This is called instantiating a rule. Let us rewrite our example using variables to introduce generality; words surrounded by angle brackets denote the variables.

```
R0: IF (bill ∧name <BILL> ∧status due ∧amount <AMOUNT>)

    AND (account ∧name checking ∧balance <AMOUNT>)

  THEN (assert (pay ∧item <BILL>))

    AND (remove (bill ∧name <BILL> ∧status due ∧amount
        <AMOUNT>))

    AND (remove (account ∧name checking ∧balance <AMOUNT>))

    AND (assert (account ∧name checking ∧balance 0))
```

Thus, if the item

```
WM: (bill ∧name electric ∧status due ∧amount 100)
```

were in working memory, then the first clause of our rule would be instantiated with *<BILL>* bound to *electric* and *<AMOUNT>* bound to *100*. These bindings must then stay consistent throughout the rest of the rule. If the rule cannot be satisfied completely with one set of bindings, all others are tried.

Note that variables are useful for more than just generality: they also allow certain arithmetic and relational operations to be carried out more easily.

Arithmetic Operations, Ranges, and Relational Operations. We still have one major problem with the bill-paying rule: the rule only covers the case where we have exactly the right amount to pay the bill. To allow for the case where we have more than enough money to pay the bill, we must have relational, arithmetic, and alternative (disjunctive) operations in addition to variables. We shall use curly brackets to surround conjunctive combinations of relational operations, and have arithmetic expressions placed simply in parentheses on the RHS. We then get the following version of the bill-paying rule:

```
RO: IF (bill ∧name <BILL> ∧status due ∧amount <AMOUNT>)

    AND (account ∧name checking ∧balance
        {<BALANCE> >= <AMOUNT>})

   THEN (assert (pay ∧item <BILL>))

    AND (remove (bill ∧name <BILL> ∧status due ∧amount
        <AMOUNT>))

    AND (remove (account ∧name checking ∧balance <AMOUNT>))

    AND (assert (account ∧name checking ∧balance
        (<BALANCE> - <AMOUNT>)))
```

Here, we see that the balance of the checking account must be greater than or equal to the amount of the bill, and when we assert the new account information we can simply give the difference. In order to specify a range, we would simply use two tests in the curly brackets to delimit the lower and upper bounds of the range.

Some systems have the ability to select from among alternatives in the LHS (disjunction). In our system, we shall show alternatives as a list that is surrounded by square brackets and that may replace simple attribute values as follows:

```
RO: IF (bill ∧name <BILL> ∧status [due over_due] ∧amount
    <AMOUNT>)

    AND (account ∧name checking ∧balance
        {<BALANCE> >= <AMOUNT>})

   THEN (assert (pay ∧item <BILL>))
```

```
AND (remove (bill ∧name <BILL> ∧status due ∧amount
     <AMOUNT>))

AND (remove (account ∧name checking ∧balance <AMOUNT>))

AND (assert (account ∧name checking ∧balance
     (<BALANCE>-<AMOUNT>))))
```

With the elements

```
WM: (bill ∧name mortgage ∧status due ∧amount 700)

    (bill ∧name electric ∧status over_due ∧amount 200)

    (bill ∧name water ∧status not_due ∧amount 50)

    (account ∧name checking ∧balance 900)
```

in working memory, either of the first two elements can be instantiated for the first clause. However, the third element cannot become instantiated in such manner.

Certainty Factors. *Certainty factors* are a way to indicate that facts might not be known with 100% confidence. An example of an early system that used certainty factors is Mycin [6]. Certainty factors allow for the representation of inexact or incomplete knowledge and may be used at the level of a datum or at the level of rules. In the first case, they represent the certainty with which facts are believed. In the second case, they indicate that the rule is not completely reliable or might be true only some of the time. In the latter case, some mechanism must be built in that allows these rule-level certainty factors to influence the firing of the rules.

In general, methods for manipulating certainty factors are more informal than probabilistic calculations.

Side Effects. Almost all rule-based systems allow actions to do more than only affect working memory. For example, most allow printing of data on the screen, reading and writing data to and from files, etc. A few systems allow the RHS to call user-written routines in a procedural language. This ability expands the capability that a rule-based system has with respect to the selection of actions. In some cases, the LHS is also allowed to call a user-defined function, in which case the function usually returns a true or a false value.

Conflict Resolution and How It Affects Representation. Conflict resolution is the mechanism by which the system decides which of several possible rules should be fired at any given time. If more than one rule can be instantiated and matched, the system must decide which to actually fire. Although this is not usually considered a representation issue, the type of conflict resolution will affect the representation used for the problem.

There are three common resolution schemes: *recency, specificity,* and *refrac-*

tion. Each of these may be used alone or in combination to decide on which rule will be selected. Recency gives the elements in working memory a time tag, and instantiations are ordered according to the recency of the working memory elements that take part in the instantiation. Specificity indicates that more specific, and therefore harder to satisfy, rules should fire before more general rules. Refraction refers to the fact that an instantiation of a rule cannot fire twice on the same data from working memory.

If recency is emphasized (particulary for the first clause), then the first clause is usually a goal (or subgoal) to be matched. For example, consider the rules

```
IF goal is to put block A on block B

AND block B has other blocks on it

Then assert subgoal to remove blocks from B

IF subgoal is to uncover block B

THEN move robot arm...
```

This scheme allows a goal-oriented control regime. The rules in a system like this would have goals in the first clause and actions that asserted new goals. The most recently created goals would be worked on first, and as goals were solved, the system would eventually return to satisfy the initial goal.

Specificity allows the system to handle exceptions to general rules. In a system where specificity is emphasized, rules would capture general properties of the knowledge and exceptions would be refinements of the more general rules. Specificity would guarantee that the exceptions were properly handled.

With refraction, we avoid the same rule repeatedly firing, particularly in systems that do not allow deletion of previous working memory elements. However, if new elements are created (or existing ones modified), then the rule might fire again. On the other hand, if it is desired that a rule be able to fire more than once for the same data, then the element in question must be reasserted if refraction is being used.

Advantages and disadvantages.   Often, the applicability of a representation hinges on the domain to which it is applied. Rule-based systems are appropriate when the knowledge to be represented can be expressed as chunks of separate information and when the chunks of knowledge have some independence. Domains to which rule-based systems have been successfully applied include design, diagnosis, interpretation, monitoring, and planning.

One characteristic of rule-based systems that is both an advantage and disadvantage is *expressibility*. On the one hand, the syntax of rule-based systems allows for easy expression of pattern-action statements, while on the other, rule-based systems do not allow for any natural representation of highly structured information. Also, the limitations of the Boolean operators allowed in the system may force an unnatural set of rules.

Two often-praised attributes of rule-based systems are *modularity* and *modifiability*. Since each rule captures a single piece of knowledge that is supposed to be nearly independent, rule-based systems are claimed to be modular, and the addition of rules is held to introduce very few side effects. This, however, is not always true, and it depends on the nature of the rules. For example, if a set of rules depends on the assertion of a goal being stored in working memory, and the rule that asserts the goal is either removed or altered, all of the rules that trigger on that goal might be affected. Some solutions to this problem have been addressed by research that tries to cluster related rules [13]. Where rules are independent, new rules may be added to the rule base without any change to existing rules.

Understandability is another attribute of rule-based systems. Because each rule is the embodiment of a chunk of knowledge, it is relatively easy for a domain expert to read the rule base and see the knowledge in the system. However, as before, in a very large system, unless related rules are grouped together, it might be hard to get the "whole picture."

Semantic Networks

A semantic network is a graph consisting of nodes and links. Each node represents one or more data items such as objects, concepts, events, or hypotheses, while each link between two nodes represents a binary relationship between those nodes. Pictorially, the nodes are generally represented as circles or squares, and the links can be directed arcs. The nodes may be labeled to distinguish among different kinds of nodes, and the same is true for the links. Figure 10–1 shows a simple network that depicts the fact that there is a red ball.

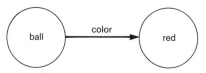

Figure 10–1 Network representing the fact that there is a red ball.

Historically, semantic networks have been used for a variety of purposes, and there have been many types of inference methods developed. The inference mechanism used in conjunction with a given semantic network depends on what type of information is represented in the nodes and what task the expert system is to perform.

Semantic networks are often used to describe hierarchical information (see Figure 10–2). Nodes can represent classes or instances of objects, and links can define relationships between, and characteristics of, the classes or instances. The relationships can show class-subclass information which defines the hierarchy. Also, a distinction can be made between a class and an instance of the class. For example, in the network in the figure, *pekingese, shih tzu, dog,* and *mammal* represent classes, while *Tanya* and *Suki* are particular instances of these classes. The link between *dog* and *mammal* is an AKO (A Kind Of) link to show that *dog* is a subclass of *mammal*. The link between *Tanya* and *pekingese* is an ISA link to show that *Tanya* is an instance of *pekingese*. Note that the AKO and ISA relationships are equivalent to the set-theoretic notions of subsets and set membership, respectively. Unfortunately, the labels AKO and ISA are not universally accepted; for example, some researchers use ISA for AKO and INSTANCE-OF for ISA, and some networks do not distinguish at all between these categories and may label all of the links ISA.

Other links can define *attributes* of the classes or instances. Thus, the link *body-covering* defines an attribute of *mammal* and the value of this attribute is *hair*. These attribute links are basically equivalent to *slots* in a frame: the slot name is given as the label of the link, and the value is then the node on the other side of the link. Frame-based systems can often be thought of as semantic networks: a frame can be thought of as a class node, and the slots which represent attributes of, or relationships between, frames can be viewed as implicit links. On the other hand, the nodes of semantic networks can represent frames. Then we can easily use the idea of predefined slots for nodes where certain attributes are *expected*, and we can

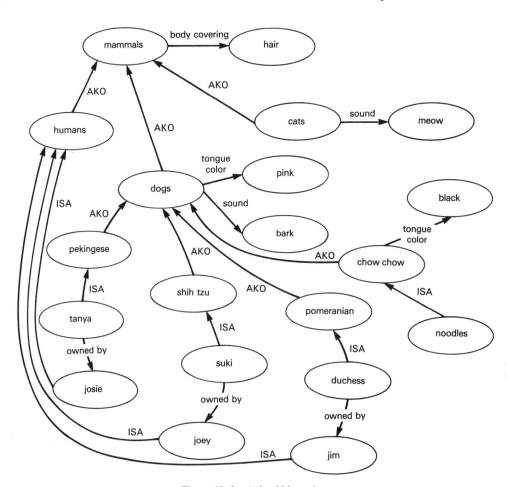

Figure 10–2   Animal hierarchy.

further use *default* values for some of these slots. Frames are discussed later in the chapter.

Using the AKO and ISA relationships between nodes, we can apply the semantics of value inheritance. For example, as shown in Figure 10–2, *tongue-color* is an attribute of *dog* and the value of this attribute is *pink*. Now, if we want to know the color of Tanya's tongue, then we can check the *Tanya* node to see if there is a *tongue-color* attribute. There is not, so we move up the ISA link to the *pekingese* node and we see that *pekingese* does not have this attribute directly attached either. So again we move up the AKO link to the *dog* node and we see that *dog* has a *tongue-color* link to the node *pink*. So we inherit the value *pink,* and we know that Tanya has a pink tongue. Of course, we could always override this information by attaching the attribute to the more specific subclass, as we have done with the node *chow chow* to indicate that these dogs have black tongues. This works because we always start out at the most specific node to find out information before moving up the link to the more general node.

In the same sense, we can use a tree to represent a classification hierarchy or discrimination net. The root node is the most general class or set, representing everything in the hierarchy. The successors represent more and more specialized subclasses. One methodology called *establish/refine* has been developed by Chandrasekaran [8, 11] for reasoning with this type of classification hierarchy. A node may be *established* by checking it against the information from the particular case being classified. Once it is established, the subclasses of the node are considered (the *refinement*) to see if one of them can be established. If a node is rejected, then all its subclasses are also rejected. As an example, if we want to classify a certain animal that has hair, barks, and has a black tongue, we would first try to establish that this is indeed a mammal. We can establish this because mammals have hair. Now we refine this by checking the information for this case against the attributes of the subclasses of *mammal.* Now we can establish *dog* because the animal barks. Again, we can refine and establish *chow chow* because of the animal's black tongue. This is, of course, a very simplistic example, but the ideas can be extended to more complex hierarchies (see [27]).

In Figure 10–2, the semantic network is basically just a collection of binary predicates such as the following:

ISA (Tanya, pekingese)

AKO (pekingese, dog)

AKO (dog, mammal)

Body-covering (mammal, hair)

Often, we need predicates of higher degrees to represent situations or events. Such predicates can be represented by providing a central node which has binary relationships with all of the other pieces of information pertaining to the situation or event [26]. An example is presented in Figure 10–3, where we represent the fact that Tom bought Anne's house for $200,000. Again, we can have predefined slots for the situation or event node as we might have in a frame. A *buying-event* would typically have a *buyer,* a *seller,* an *object,* and a *cost* associated with it; default values can be provided as well. Notice that the representational power of semantic networks is similar to that of the predicate calculus. However, semantic networks provide additional information by indicating the distance between nodes. The more related the nodes are, the closer together they are in the network; this is an advantage because search algorithms used in conjunction with semantic networks can be much more efficient.

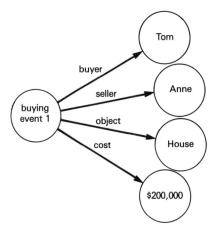

Figure 10–3 Predicates of higher degrees.

Another feature which may be added to semantic networks is the attachment of *procedures* to nodes. (This is often used in frame-based systems.) An algorithmic procedure may be invoked if one needs to find out something about a particular node. An advantage to using procedures rather than storing the information is that a potentially long calculation is performed only if needed. In addition, some of the necessary component information may change dynamically, so this flexibility would be very desirable.

When Quillian [21] first proposed semantic networks, he developed a type of inference which involves the activation of nodes, in which a search emanates from each of the nodes under consideration until the intersection of all of them is found. However, this is often not an efficient search, particularly for negative responses, because the search may have to spread out as far as it can go before it is certain that the indicated relationship does not exist.

A popular inference method for reasoning with semantic networks involves matching. For instance, if we have the semantic network of Figure 10–2, and we want to know what Jim owns, we would match *Jim* against the node labeled *Jim* and we would get the answer by retrieving the value of the node on the other side of the *owned-by* link. Then we would know that Jim owns *Duchess*. Now suppose we want to know whether Joey owns a dog. Here we cannot match directly; the matcher must *deduce* this fact by using the ISA and AKO relationships. Since Joey owns *Suki* and Suki is a *shih tzu,* which is a kind of *dog,* we can deduce that Joey owns a dog.

There are many variations of semantic networks. One such variation involves *partitioning* the network into spaces for organizational reasons [12]. The partitioning allows for the handling of logical quantification and connectives. Nodes and links can belong to one or more spaces, and operations can be performed on these spaces. PROSPECTOR [10] is an expert system which used partitioned networks to encode information.

Another interesting use of semantic network organization is for expert systems which handle uncertain reasoning. The Navy's Bayesian Reasoning Tool (BaRT) is a system where the underlying structure is a semantic network. Here, the nodes represent hypotheses and the links represent a direct casual dependence between two hypotheses. The inference engine uses Bayesian reasoning to perform belief maintenance.

Advantages and disadvantages. A major advantage of using semantic networks is that related facts are located next to each other with direct links between them, so searching for information is generally straightforward. One simply follows the appropriate links, and this is often only one step in the search path. Semantic networks provide clear descriptions of knowledge because they give a picture of the structure of the information. The method also provides a convenient way of dealing with hierarchies, because the links provide a natural connection between classes and subclasses.

A drawback to semantic networks is that there are no formal ways of dealing with them; rather, the meaning of a semantic network depends on the reasoning procedures associated with it. Also, the structure of a real problem can get very complex, so a search may become inefficient.

Frames

Frames, originally developed by Minsky [15], are a straightforward way to represent descriptive information. Each frame contains information about one particular object, concept, or event and typically has *slots* which contain values. Often, a frame will describe a *stereotyped* class of objects, concepts, or events which has a set of expected slots. The *prototype* frame for a class will contain the list of slots applicable to the class and can also contain default values or valid ranges of values for these slots. An *instance* frame for that class will then contain the detailed information for that particular instance. For example, we might choose to represent the object *book* as a frame. The prototype frame for this class of objects might then look like the following:

BOOK FRAME

IS-PART-OF: library
Subject:
Author:
Title:
Binding: Default = Hardcover
Pages: an integer

Now we can create an instance of this frame for a copy of a specific book:

BOOK-1 FRAME

ISA: book
Subject: Computer Science
Author: Donald E. Knuth
Title: Fundamental Algorithms
Binding: Hardcover
Pages: 634

Note that the slots of the instance were inherited from the prototype frame for *book*. In addition, the *default value* for *binding* was inherited, making the frame easier to instantiate. Of course, we could always override this information for, say, an instance of a paperback book by simply replacing the value of *binding* with *paperback*. We also indicated a *valid type* for the values of the slot *pages;* if we had put anything other than an integer number in that slot, we likely would have been notified of an error. We could also indicate *ranges* for the values similarly.

Notice that frames provide a method of clustering all relevant information concerning the object at hand. This allows immediate access to information about the object, which cuts down on search time. Since the slots are predefined in the prototype frame for the particular instance of the object, there is a certain amount of *expectation* associated with finding information: we know we can go to any instance and request the value of a certain slot because we *expect* it to be there.

Like semantic networks, frames are often used to represent hierarchical information. We can use ISA and AKO slots for frames in the same way that we used ISA and AKO links in semantic networks. The ISA slot defines an *instance* of a class (the class is defined by the prototype frame), and the AKO slot defines the class-subclass relationship between frames. This allows inheritance of values from general classes to more specific subclasses or from classes to instances. A small example that represents a hierarchy about dogs is the following:

DOG FRAME

AKO: Mammal
Sound: Bark
Tongue-Color: Pink

PEKINGESE FRAME

AKO: Dog
Size: Small
Color:
Owned-by:

TANYA FRAME

ISA: Pekingese
Size: Small
Color: Tan
Owned-by: Josie

Now, through *matching, expectation,* and *inheritance of values,* we can find information. For instance, if we want to know Tanya's color, we simply *match* against the frame *Tanya* and retrieve the value for the slot *color* to find out that she is *tan.* If we now want to know the color of Tanya's tongue, we can check the *Tanya* frame first (to make sure that the more general trait of pink tongue-color for all dogs has not been overridden for this specific instance) and then, since there is no slot for *tongue-color,* we can follow the ISA/AKO slots to the *pekingese* frame, and then again to the *dog* frame. Now we can inherit *pink* as the color of Tanya's tongue. We can also *deduce* facts through certain links. For instance, we can deduce that *Tanya* is a *dog* because we know that *Tanya* is a *pekingese* and *pekingese* is a kind of *dog.*

Notice that the information contained in this example is very similar to the information in Figure 10–2. Indeed, frames and semantic networks are often equivalent representations. In the example, the *links* are implied through certain slots, such as the AKO slots which *connect* the frames.

Another type of reasoning can be performed in conjunction with *procedures* that are attached to slots. Here, instead of storing a value in a slot, a program or algorithm is provided which can calculate the value if and when it is needed. A complicated calculation can be avoided if it is not needed. Also, this is a good technique to use when some of the information needed to perform the calculation might be replaced dynamically. The result of the calculation can be stored once it is computed, or, if it becomes obsolete too quickly, it can simply be provided to the user.

For example, suppose we had an expert system which provides real estate advice. While using the system, we might need to check whether Tom could afford to buy a certain house. We might know the price of the house, the current interest rate for mortgages, Tom's salary, and Tom's savings. (If one of these values is missing, the expert system could detect the empty slot and ask the user to provide this information.) Then we might have an algorithm which approximates down payment, closing costs, and mortgage payments given the price of the house, and made a determination on whether Tom could afford to buy the house. Such a system is given by the following:

TOM FRAME

ISA: Person
Salary: $60,000
Savings: $45,000
May-buy: House-1
Bank: Bank-1
Afford: Calculation-1

HOUSE-1 FRAME

Levels: 3
Bedrooms: 4
Cost: $180,000

BANK-1 FRAME

Interest-Rate: 10%
Points: 2

CALCULATION-1 PROCEDURE

House-cost = cost of current house
Down-payment = 0.1 * House-cost
Closing-costs = .07 * House-cost
Points-cost = Points from current bank * .01 * House-cost
If (((Salary of person * 3) *is greater than or equal to* House-cost)
and
((Down-payment + Closing-costs + Points-cost) *is less than or equal to* Savings
of person))
Then return TRUE
Else return FALSE

Clearly, the flexibility of this kind of system is highly desirable. Note that we can also have *triggers* which transfer control of the expert system when necessary. For instance, we might have a trigger connected to the *may-buy* slot which transfers control to the *afford* slot if a different house is chosen as the value of the slot.

Frame systems such as the one described share many important features with object-oriented programming techniques. Both can contain definitions of classes and instances of those classes. Also, procedures attached to slots are similar to the *methods* of object-oriented programming.

Another method of inference which can be used with frames to perform diagnostic reasoning is called "frame-based abduction." This method is typically based on hypothesize-and-test cycles which model human reasoning. Given one or more initial problem features (which would be listed in the slots of the frames), the expert system generates a set of potential hypotheses or "causes" which can explain the problem features. These hypotheses are then tested by the use of various procedures which measure their ability to account for the known features, and the generation of new questions which will help to discriminate among the most likely hypotheses. The cycle is then repeated with the additional information acquired. Reasoning from observed facts to the "best explanation" is sometimes referred to as *abduction* [23].

Some studies have concluded that diagnostic reasoning is a sequential hypothesize-and-test process, so it is not surprising that many of the expert systems built with this approach are directed toward diagnostic problem solving. INTERNIST [14] and KMS.HT [23, 24] are typical systems using this approach. For example, KMS.HT is a domain-independent expert system generator for diagnostic problem solving. In order to simulate hypothesize-and-test reasoning, the system employs a generalized set-covering model in which there is a universe of all possible manifestations (symptoms) and a universe of all possible causes (disorders). For each possible cause there is a set of manifestations which that cause can explain, and for each possible manifestation there is a set of causes which can explain the manifestation. Given a diagnostic problem with a specific set of manifestations which are present, the inference mechanism finds sets of causes which could "explain" (cover) all the manifestations. For a more detailed explanation of the theory underlying this approach and the problem-solving algorithms, see [23] and [18].

Advantages and disadvantages.   Frames are a good way of representing descriptive information. Information such as that from a text often centers around one concept or object at a time, so frames could provide an organized, direct, and natural mapping for this kind of knowledge. The organization allows for efficient searching because there is immediate access to relevant information. Frames also provide a natural method for representing hierarchies of information and allowing the inheritance of values through ISA and AKO slots. Also, the structure of the knowledge is modularized and readily apparent in frames, so this may make the knowledge base easier to modify and maintain. Finally, frames allow for focused questions concerning the particular topic they cover.

As with semantic networks, a drawback to using frames is that there are no formal ways of dealing with them yet. Also, many of the inference techniques used in conjunction with frames, such as frame-based abduction, are newer methods which are still being developed and tested more fully.

Scripts

Scripts [25] are frame-like structures which represent common sequences of events. Just as frames can represent stereotyped classes of objects, concepts, or events where certain properties are expected, scripts can represent stereotyped sequences of events where things are expected to occur in certain ways. Prototype scripts contain slots which can be filled in with details about a particular event when the script is instantiated. For example, when a person goes to a gas station to get gas, there is a certain amount of expectation as to the sequence of events. Details are missing, but the main sequence of events is predictable. Scenes within scripts can lead into other scripts as well. For instance, if the gas station attendant was particularly helpful and friendly in some way, the driver might call the owner of the gas station the next day to say so. This *compliment* script can come from any script where a person is dealing with another person who works for someone else, so it can be shared by several other scripts.

There are preconditions which should be met before the sequence in question takes place. For the gas station script, the person must have money and must perceive a need for gas. Once these conditions are met, he or she must drive to a gas station. Then, depending on whether it is full-serve or self-serve, the person gets the gas according to that description. A script to represent this event is the following:

Gas Station Script:

   Props:

      Car

      Gas Tank

      Gas Cap

      Gas Pump

      Meter on Gas Pump

      Gasoline

      Money

   Roles:

      Driver

      Gas Station Attendant

      Gas Station Owner

   Preconditions:

      Driver perceives that car needs gas

      Driver has money

   Results:

      Car has gas

      Driver has less money

      Gas Station Owner has more money

   Point of view:

      Driver

   Scene1: Enter gas station

      Drive to gas station

      If want self-serve, go to Scene2

      If want full-serve, go to Scene3

```
Scene2: Self-Serve

    Get out of car

    Remove gas cap

    Fill tank with gas

    Replace cap

    Read gas meter to determine cost

    Walk to gas station attendant

    Goto Scene4


Scene3: Full-Serve

    Wait for gas station attendant to come to car

    Tell attendant amount of gas

    Wait for attendant to put gas in tank

    Read gas meter to determine cost

    Goto Scene4

Scene4: Pay for gas

    Give money to gas station attendant

    Goto Scene5

Scene5: Leave gas station

    If not inside car, get in the car

    Drive away
```

Most of the terminology for scripts [25] is intentionally similar to the terminology for scripts for a play. Roles are slots for the people who appear in an instance of the script, while props are slots for the objects which appear in an instance of the script. The point of view is a slot for a person which shows that the sequence of events in the script is from that person's point of view. Scenes are ordered and represent the causal chain of events which usually take place. Entry conditions are the preconditions which should be satisfied to instantiate the script, and results are the conditions which should be true after the entire script is completed.

The reasoning applied to scripts allows for the inference of facts which were not explicitly stated. A script can be instantiated by matching on parts of the script, such as the preconditions, the roles, or the props. Then details can be filled in by looking at the script. For example, if we know that Tom went to the gas station and bought gas, then, by applying the script to the situation, we can assume that he had money and that he paid for the gas. The reasoning mechanism can also allow for the recognition of unusual experiences and can draw conclusions from that. For instance, the story may say that the gas station owner is Tom's father, and it may also say that Tom did not pay for the gas. Then the system can conclude that these two incidents are related. Furthermore, it can store the new, unusual information, so that it can handle future typical deviations from the script. In addition, instances of scripts can be saved, and generalization can be built into the system. For example, if there was another story of a person going to a store and not paying for goods because the owner was a relative, then the system can generalize that a person may not pay for goods or services at a store if a relative owns the store. The amount of detail allowed depends on the design of the script and the design of the inference engine. Certainly, the gas station example is simplistic, but it could easily be extended.

An example of a system which successfully employed scripts is SAM [9], a system that was used to understand newspaper stories.

Advantages and disadvantages.   Scripts provide a natural way of representing and organizing descriptive information which centers around common situations or events. The structure of the knowledge can be shown, and focused reasoning and questions concerning the particular topic covered by the script can be allowed. The one major drawback to using scripts is that they can only be used when dealing with common, everyday events, for otherwise there would be no experientially agreed-upon material for the script.

Hybrid Approaches

Often, a single form of knowledge representation is not adequate for the solution of an expert system task, so many recent systems have exploited the advantages of different representations by combining them in one system. We call this combination *hybrid representation*. In some cases one representation is at a higher level than the other, but in others the system might have different subsystems at the same level, where the different representations are used to solve different portions of the problem.

One purpose of using multiple representations is to allow the representation of both shallow and deep knowledge. Knowledge that has been transformed into the system is called *compiled* or *associative* knowledge and is deemed shallow in nature. Knowledge that is more basic or detailed and that is needed to prove facts and explain why decisions are made is termed deep knowledge. By having two levels of knowledge, if a rule appears to fail, then one has the ability to think or reason about why things are not working.

The most common combination of representations involves rule-based and frame or network representations. Within this mix, we might have one system "over" the other. With the rule-based system at the top level, the matching involves frames. Clauses in the LHS can be frames, working memory elements can be frames, and the RHS can add new frames to working memory or modify slots in the frames in working memory. This has been a popular approach and is useful in decision systems.

In a different approach, the frame or network might be at the top level. As shown in Figure 10–4, each node in this semantic net consists of an individual rule base. In a system like this, answering questions about objects is possible.

Upon triggering a procedure in a frame system (Figure 10–5), a rule set could be evaluated. If neither system is at the top level, then some top-level control would be necessary. In that case, the separate rule and frame systems would be called like subroutines, as shown in Figure 10–6.

Many popular expert system shells now allow for a mixture of representations. For example, ART, KEE, and LOOPS allow multiple representations of knowledge. Whether a hybrid approach is used for a particular system will of course depend on the domain and requirements of the knowledge to be represented. If the knowledge readily fits a single paradigm, then the use of a hybrid approach may overcomplicate the system.

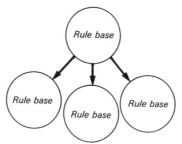

Figure 10–4 Semantic net of rule bases.

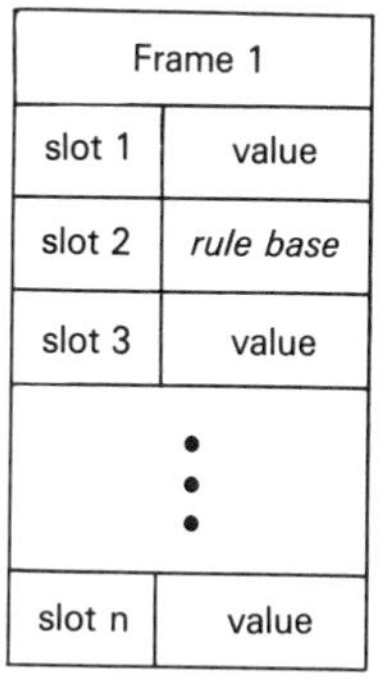

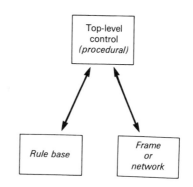

Figure 10–5 Rule base in slot of frame.

Figure 10–6 Two representations at same level.

SOME SAMPLE EXPERT SYSTEMS

The Fault Isolation System

The Fault Isolation System (FIS) is a second-generation expert system shell for diagnosing electronic or electromechanical systems [19, 20]. Developed as part of an ongoing research project at the Navy Center for Applied Research in Artificial Intelligence, FIS was designed to diagnose complex analog systems, isolating faults to the level of modules such as amplifiers and power supplies. The system can reason qualitatively from a functional model of a complex device. FIS is a hybrid system using both semantic net and rule-based representations. In the system, the device to be diagnosed, or the UUT (unit under test), is comprised of replaceable modules. Each module is represented by a rule base, each of which is a node in the semantic net. The network represents the relational dependencies between the modules.

Figure 10–7 illustrates a complex UUT. Each box is a module that has a rule base. The individual rule bases capture the knowledge of what it means to be that module in terms of cause-and-effect relationships between inputs of that module, outputs from that module, and the module itself. Notice that this is strictly local information so that modules, once defined, can be reused in other UUTs. The following two rules might be in a module's rule-base:

```
              Cause                          Effect
    IF I am defective     THEN the effect is my DC output is low.
    IF my DC input is low  THEN the effect is my DC output is low.
```

The first rule states that if the module is defective, then the effect might be that its output is wrong; the second rule states that the module is not defective, but just propagating a signal that was already defective.

At the next higher level, a network connects the modules and represents the dependencies between them. How modules connect, i.e., what inputs are connected to what outputs, is represented at this level. It is this knowledge that allows the local, rule-based knowledge of the modules to be related to each other.

At the highest level, a global rule base helps to prevent unnecessary problem solving. If certain facts are known about the system, we might be able to know immediately that a certain module is defective based on tests already made. The global rule base is then tested up front so that in some cases not all of the system has to be searched.

In the FIS system, instead of having just a "big pot" of rules, rules are attached to specific places in the network and only become active at a certain time. In this way, the system might be considered a distributed data base of rules or a model-driven rule base.

FIS also incorporates the use of certainty factors to allow the use of knowledge of *a priori* known failure rates for modules that exist in the system. In this way, if

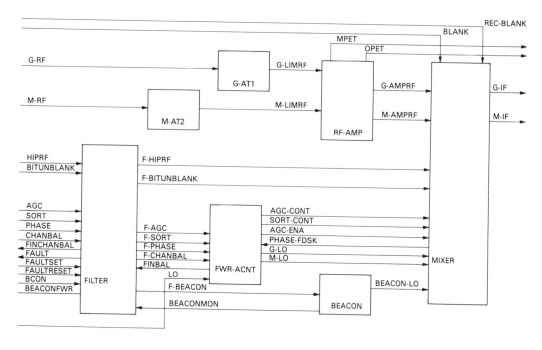

Figure 10–7   A complex unit under test (UUT)

two modules are suspected, and one has a high *a priori* failure rate and the other a low rate, the system would be able, with some certainty, to decide that the first module is the defective one. In addition to *a priori* failure rates, the system maintains a certainty factor for each module that indicates to what degree that module is currently suspected.

The following are sections from the knowledge base of FIS:

```
((nil g-rf g-at1)

(g-at1 g-limrf rf-amp)

(nil m-rf m-at2)

(m-at2 m-limrf rf-amp)

(filter f-beacon beacon)

(beacon beacon-lo mixer)

(beacon beaconmon filter)

(nil rec-blank mixer)
```

```
(nil blank mixer)

(filter f-hiprf mixer)

(filter f-bitunblank mixer)

(pwr&cnt agc-cont mixer)

 ...)
```

This section of the knowledge base captures the semantic network. Each expression in parentheses is a list of a module, connection, and module. The first entry, (nil g-rf g-atl), indicates that the line *g-rf* is an input line connected from nothing (actually, from the environment) and to the module *g-atl*. The second entry, (g-atl g-limrf rf-amp), indicates that module *g-atl* connects to module *rf-amp* by way of line *g-limrf*. Following the semantic net in the knowledge base are the individual rule bases for each module. Some of the rule bases are as follows:

```
(((name filter) (frate 0.02)

   (cert (0 6.0))

   (causal-rules

        ((t (hiprf logic bad)

         (f-hiprf logic bad))

        (t filter

         (f-bitunblank logic bad))

        (t (chanbal logic bad)

         (f-chanbal logic bad))

        (t filter (f-chanbal logic bad))

        (t filter (f-sort logic bad))

        ...

        (t (bcon logic bad)

         (f-beacon logic bad))
```

```
((name pwr&cnt) (frate 0.2)

    (cert (0 6.0))

    (causal-rules

        ((t (f-sort logic bad)

          (sort-cont logic bad))

        (t (f-agc logic bad)

          (agc-cont logic bad))

        . . .

        (t (f-agc logic bad)

          (agc-ena logic bad))
```

The rule bases are located one after another in the experience base. Each starts with the keyword *name* followed by the name of the module. Next in each rule base is the *a priori* failure rate, preceded by the keyword *frate*. This is followed by the keyword *causal-rules* and then the rules for the module. Each rule consists of three parts: a precondition, the *if* part (the cause), and the *then* part (the effect). The precondition specifies what must be true in order for the rule to be considered and usually has the default *t* (true), indicating that the rule is free to be considered.

The *if* part of a rule is either a single value or a triplet. If it is a single value, then it is the name of a module and indicates that the cause of the failure is the module itself. If it is a triplet, then it consists of a connection, an attribute that can be measured, and the result of the measurement, and this indicates that the cause is whatever the test result indicates. The *then* part of a rule can only be a triplet, and it represents the effect of the defect.

Looking at the first rule for the *filter* module, we have

```
((t (hiprf logic bad)

    (f-hiprf logic bad))
```

In English, we might read this as

```
IF the cause of the failure is a measurement of bad at point hiprf

THEN the effect is that at point f-hiprf we will measure logic as bad
```

The rule

```
((t filter

   (f-bitunblank logic bad))
```

Translates into English as

```
IF the filter is the cause of the failure

THEN the logic on line f-bitunblank will be bad
```

Each module, then, is represented by causal rules that explain that module's possible defects in terms of itself or its inputs and outputs. The module assumes no knowledge of what is outside of its bounds, and the network captures the knowledge of the relations and dependencies among the modules.

From a software engineering point of view, having each module as an isolated entity is an important capability. First of all, a module can be reused in other UUTs. Secondly, when a new module (rule base) is created, there is no concern about possible interactions between it and the other rule bases. Futhermore, since each rule captures one instance of cause and effect, the interaction among individual rules is minimal from a control standpoint.

The user interface of FIS uses the semantic net information to present the user with a graphical representation of the UUT. The user can examine and modify the rule bases with a module editor. The semantic net description can be modified with a graphics editor. This capability is also important from a software engineering point of view: entering and modifying rules or dependencies is easy and minimizes the chance of introduction of errors.

BaRT

Bayesian Reasoning Tool (BaRT) is a knowledge engineering tool which has been developed at the Navy Center for Applied Research in Artificial Intelligence [2, 3]. BaRT uses belief maintenance algorithms designed by Pearl [17] to perform classification problem solving which handles reasoning involving uncertainty.

The structural framework used in BaRT is a semantic network (more specifically, a *belief* network). Each node in the network represents a discrete-valued hypothesis which describes an aspect of the domain and contains information about the current belief in each value of the hypothesis. Each link between two nodes represents a direct causal dependence between two of the hypotheses, capturing the local relationship. An advantage of this representation is that it depicts the underlying structure of the domain knowledge.

Object-oriented programming is used to define the generic classes of objects for BaRT. The design of the BaRT class hierarchy allows different *methods* (which perform the reasoning techniques) to be associated with the different types of objects. Such a design is both modular and efficient: each object holds only the information relevant to its own operations.

The top-level class is *bart-object,* which contains slots for information needed by *all* objects defined in BaRT. There is a slot for the name of the object and slots which center around the particular system version of BaRT being used. One subclass of *bart-object* is *network.* The instances of this class are the individual networks representing different domains of information.

Another subclass of *bart-object* is *basic-node.* The slots of this class contain information relevant to all types of nodes, such as the particular network to which each node belongs. The class *basic-node* in turn has two subclasses: instances of *net-node* represent hypotheses of the domain, and instances of *evid-node* represent evidence influencing the beliefs in the values of particular hypotheses. The class *net-node* has two further subclasses: instances of *top-node* are network nodes which have no parent nodes, and instances of *leaf-node* are network nodes which have no child nodes. Both of these are *boundary* nodes, and this distinction is useful because there are specialized methods associated with such nodes.

A third subclass of *bart-object* is *basic-link,* whose slots contain information relevant to all types of links, such as the parent node and the child node of a given link. This class has the subclasses *lambda-link,* which contains slots for information passed from a child node or evidence node to a parent node, and *pi-link,* which contains slots for information passed from a parent node to a child node. The class *net-link* inherits slots and information from both *lambda-link* and *pi-link:* instances of *net-link* will send information from parent to child and from child to parent. It is necessary to make the distinction between *lambda-link* and *pi-link* for several reasons, one of which is that evidence nodes send information to their parent nodes through *lambda-links* but never receive information from their parent nodes, so it is inappropriate to have the information associated with *pi-links* here.

Inferences are computed using methods associated with the objects. One such procedure updates the beliefs in the values of a hypothesis. These inference techniques are described in detail elsewhere in this book.

CONCLUDING REMARKS

As we have striven to emphasize, there is no "best" method for knowledge representation. (Ramsey et al. [22] discuss the comparative advantages and disadvantages for expert systems methodologies.) With enough detail of knowledge, most knowledge representation formalisms can be mapped into each other and are therefore interchangeable. However, certain types of knowledge will be easier to encode and understand using one formalism as opposed to another. Also, the amount of space required to store the information will vary depending on the formalism, and the efficiency of the inference techniques will vary. For instance, we might represent the same facts in predicate logic and in semantic networks; however, the search strategy used may be much more efficient using the semantic network representation.

The reader is referred to Barr and Feigenbaum [1], Nilsson [16], Cercone and McCalla [7], and Brachman and Levesque [4] for further discussions of the subject.

REFERENCES

1. Barr, A., and Feigenbaum, E. *The Handbook of Artificial Intelligence.* Los Altos, CA: William Kaufmann, 1981.
2. Booker, L. B., and Hota, N., "Probabilistic Reasoning about Ship Images." In *Uncertainty in Artificial Intelligence 2,* edited by J. Lemmer, and L. Kanal, pp. 371–379. Amsterdam: North Holland, 1988.
3. Booker, L. B., Hota, N., and Hemphill, G. "Implementing a Bayesian Scheme for Revising Belief Commitments." *Proceedings of the Third AAAI Workshop on Uncertainty in Artificial Intelligence.* Seattle, WA, 1987, pp. 348–354.
4. Brachman, R. J., and Levesque, H. J. *Readings in Knowledge Representation.* Palo Alto, CA: Morgan Kaufmann Publishers, 1985.
5. Brownston, L., Farrell, R., Kant, E., and Martin, N. *Programming Expert Systems in OPS5: An Introduction to Rule-Based Programming.* Reading, MA: Addison-Wesley, 1985.
6. Buchanan, B. G., and Shortliffe, E. H. *Rule-Based Expert Systems: The MYCIN Experiments of the Stanford Heuristic Programming Project.* Reading, MA: Addison-Wesley, 1984.
7. Cercone, N. and McCalla, G., eds. *The Knowledge Frontier: Essays in the Representation of Knowledge,* New York: Springer-Verlag, 1983.
8. Chandrasekaran, B. "Decomposition of Domain Knowledge into Knowledge Sources: The MDX Approach." *Proceedings of the Fourth National Conference of the Canadian Society for Computational Studies of Intelligence.* Saskatoon, Saskatchewan, 1982.
9. Cullingford, R. "SAM." In *Inside Computer Understanding,* edited by R. C. Schank and C. K. Riesbeck. Hillsdale, NJ: Erlbaum, 1981.
10. Duda, R., Gashning, J., Hart, P., Konolige, K., Reboh, R., Barret, P., and Slocum, J. *Development of the PROSPECTOR Consultation System for Mineral Exploration, Final Report, SRI Projects 5821 and 6415, Technical Report 5821 and 6415.* Palo Alto, SRI International, 1978.
11. Gomez, F., and Chandrasekaran, B. "Knowledge Organization and Distribution for Medical Diagnosis." *IEEE Transactions on Systems, Man, and Cybernetics SMC-11* 1(1981): 34–42.
12. Hendrix, G. "Encoding Knowledge in Partitioned Networks." In *Associative Networks: The Representation and Use of Knowledge by Machine,* edited by N. Findler, New York: Academic Press, 1979.
13. Jacob, R. J. K., and Froscher, J. N., "Software Engineering for Rule-based Systems." *Proceedings of the Fall Joint Computer Conference, IEEE.* Dallas, 1986, pp. 185–189.
14. Miller, R., Pople, H., and Myers, J. "Internist-1: An Experimental Computer-based Diagnostic Consultant for General Internal Medicine." *New England Journal of Medicine* 307 (1982): 468–476.
15. Minsky, M. "A Framework for Representing Knowledge." In *The Psychology of Computer Vision,* edited by P. Winston, pp. 211–277. New York: McGraw-Hill, 1975.

16. Nilsson, N. J. *Principles of Artificial Intelligence.* Palo Alto, CA: Tioga Publishing Co., 1980.

17. Pearl, J. "Fusion, Propagation, and Structuring in Belief Networks." *Artificial Intelligence* 9(1986): 241–288.

18. Peng, Y., and Reggia, J. "A Probabilistic Causal Model for Diagnostic Problem-Solving." *IEEE Transactions on Systems, Man, and Cybernetics* 17 (1987): 146–162, 395–406.

19. Pipitone, F., "The FIS Electronics Troubleshooting System." *IEEE Computer* 19(1986): 68–76.

20. Pipitone, F., DeJong, K., Spears, W., and Marrone, M. "The FIS Electronics Trouble-shooting Project." In *Expert System Applications to Telecommunications,* edited by J. Liebowitz, pp. 73–100. New York: John Wiley, 1988.

21. Quillian, R. "Semantic Memory." In *Semantic Information Processing,* edited by M. Minsky. Cambridge, MA: MIT Press, 1968.

22. Ramsey, C. L., Reggia, J. A., Nau, D. S., and Ferrentino, A. "A Comparative Analysis of Methods for Expert Systems." *International Journal of Man-Machine Studies* 24 (1986): 475–499.

23. Reggia, J., Nau, D., Wang, P., and Peng, Y. "A Formal Model of Diagnostic Inference." *Information Sciences* 37 (1985): 227–285.

24. Reggia, J., and Perricone, B. *KMS Reference Manual, Technical Report TR-1136.* College Park, MD: University of Maryland, 1982.

25. Schank, R. C., and Abelson, R. P. *Scripts, Plans, Goals and Understanding.* Hillsdale, NY: Erlbaum, 1977.

26. Simmons, R. F., and Slocum, J. "Generating English Discourse from Semantic Networks." *Communications of the ACM,* 15 (1972): 891–905.

27. Sticklen, J., Chandrasekaran, B., and Josephson, J. R. "Control Issues in Classificatory Diagnosis." *Proceedings of International Joint Conference on Artificial Intelligence,* 1985, pp. 300-306.

11

Testing and Evaluation of Knowledge-based Systems

Patrick R. Harrison

INTRODUCTION

The purpose of this chapter is to bring together from a widely scattered and fragmented literature some of the major issues concerning the evaluation of knowledge-based or expert systems (KBS). First, a definition of evaluation and a definition of the basic method underlying the behavior of most current knowledge-based systems are used to bring a perspective to the discussion and to limit the generic classes of KBS operations discussed. The concept of generic operations is introduced as a language for abstracting and classifying evaluation strategies. Next, a model of development is proposed that brings together rapid prototyping and more traditional life-cycle development approaches. The development model provides a structure and perspective for viewing the central issues of evaluation. The relationship between knowledge base specification, evaluation, and representation and overall performance evaluation is explored within the framework of the model of development. Important issues are described and approaches to their solution are discussed.

Definition of Evaluation

Figure 11–1 shows two aspects of software evaluation that are commonly used in computer science [16, 31]. Optimization focuses attention on measurements of utility, efficiency, robustness, cost, and maintainability; the evaluation of KBS performance focuses attention on the reliability, validity, and certification of the software. In practice, the two aspects are not always separable; however, the

```
┌─────────────────────────────────────────┐
│              EVALUATION                   │
│  OPTIMIZATION                             │
│       1. Utility                          │
│       2. Efficiency                       │
│       3. Robustness                       │
│       4. Cost                             │
│       5. Maintainability                  │
│                                           │
│  EVALUATION OF KBS PERFORMANCE            │
│       1. Reliability                      │
│       2. Validity                         │
│       3. Certifiability                   │
│       4. Competence                       │
└─────────────────────────────────────────┘
```

Figure 11–1   Aspects of evaluation.

concepts of efficiency and correctness which encompass them are distinguishable. This chapter focuses on the correctness of the software. *Evaluation* is defined as the analysis of a knowledge-based or expert system in terms of consistency, validity, and certification. In common parlance, the question is, *Does it demonstrate the expertise or competence it is supposed to have in a consistent fashion? Consistency* addresses the question of whether the system does whatever it does in the same way under the same conditions, while *validity* addresses the question of whether it does what it is supposed to do. *Certification* can be thought of as *validity in context* and will be viewed as part of the validation process. It is possible to have a very consistent system that does the wrong thing in the same way every time or to have a system that does the right thing in the same way every time but in the wrong context.

Heuristic Classification

Heuristic classification is a method of solving a range of problems called classification problems [6]. Figure 11–2 shows the generic operations in KBS design that use this method [6]. It might seem that classification problems are a rather small subclass of KBS problems, but in fact, a very large percentage of existing KB systems deal with such problems and are made up of these components in some combina-

```
┌────────────────────────────┐
│  Construct                  │
│       A. Specify            │
│       B. Design             │
│               1. Configure  │
│               2. Plan       │
│       C. Assemble           │
│               1. Modify     │
│                             │
│  Interpret                  │
│       A. Identify           │
│               1. Monitor    │
│               2. Diagnose   │
│       B. Predict            │
│       C. Control            │
└────────────────────────────┘
```

Figure 11–2   Generic operations on a system.

tion. We shall restrict our comments concerning evaluation to systems that use this method. The basic method will help us understand how to approach evaluation within the prototyping loop. The various generic component operations will serve as a means for directing us to systems that have the same generic component structure so that the evaluation approach used in the past can become part of the current analysis.

A graphical representation of the general heuristic classification method is shown in Figure 11–3. Data and solutions are modeled as separate concepts. Data are used to define a data abstraction such as *typicality* [6]. Heuristics are then used to map the data abstraction onto a solution abstraction or class. This provides focus for the analysis. Direct associations between data and solution features are then used to refine the solution. For example, the data could be descriptions of the behavior, daily work done, and likings of an individual, descriptive of, say, a consumer model. Using information that relates consumer models to advertising approaches, the abstracted consumer model could be matched with a general advertising approach. This could then be further refined using data from the individual to refine the general approach. In a particular case, data might be mapped directly onto the solution space with no refinement needed. Thus, the solution class might be "wrestler" and the pertinent data might be "over 300 pounds," "limited vocabulary," "dyed hair," and "protruding stomach." For another application, the solution abstraction might become the data for another data abstraction, and so forth. The model is quite flexible and describes a methodological building block.

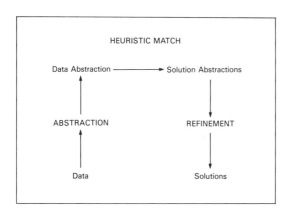

Figure 11–3 Model of heuristic classification problem from Clancey [6].

The taxonomy of problem-solving operations described by Clancey uses the heuristic classification method. These operations are assumed to be generic in nature and can be used to operationally define the characteristics of a KBS (see Figure 11–2). The importance of this from our point of view is that the operational classification of KBS components provides a means of classifying evaluation strategies. For each generic component, we could assume a general or typical approach to evaluation and a set of assumptions that might prove valuable in defining criteria for validation of the KBS. An example of this idea is provided by the Mycin system, which includes the generic components [6]

$$MONITOR + DIAGNOSE + IDENTIFY + MODIFY$$

Thus, the system monitors the patient for symptoms, diagnoses the patient's category, identifies diseases, and recommends therapy to modify the patient's condition.

The issues and criteria used in evaluation are more clearly seen in relation to the generic operational components of the system. For example, the operation DIAGNOSE involves expert judgments in the face of incomplete and ambiguous information. Similarly, the operation IDENTIFY focuses on the solution categories that are pertinent to the disease categories. The completeness of the disease categories, the correctness of the diagnostic process, and the ability of the system to map the diagnosis onto the disease classes can be seen as three different points of focus for evaluation. Furthermore, both of these, as well as the other operations, provide a basis for defining generic evaluation operations that will be required. What, for example, are the generic issues in evaluating the system component DIAGNOSE?

An important distinction in this model is between methods that involve analysis and those that involve synthesis. In general, it can be assumed that analysis implies that either the solutions are preenumerated or all possible solutions can be generated on an as-needed basis [6]. By contrast, synthesis problems involve constructed solutions, so that the solution space may be more difficult to bound. From our point of view, the most interesting problems in terms of difficulty of evaluation are those that are constructed or that have a very large solution space that cannot be preenumerated.

The Primordial Soup

In a symbol system such as Lisp, a distinction is made between knowledge and the representation of knowledge. Following Newell [25, 26], it is assumed that there is a separate system level called the *knowledge level*. The components of this level are goals, actions, and bodies. The medium is knowledge and the behavioral law is the principle of rationality. Behavior is goal-directed: the principle of rationality predicts that actions are chosen which accomplish goals. Bodies such as a human body provide a means for acting to achieve the goals. Below the knowledge level in the hierarchy of system levels is another level called the *symbol level* [25]. At this level, knowledge is translated into data structures that describe both the structural properties and the fundamental operations necessary to use the knowledge represented in the data structure. Finally, data structures are organized in programs for problem solving.

The importance of distinguishing the knowledge level and the symbol level is that a knowledge-level analysis can proceed without a model of how the knowledge is being processed. Representation in a symbol system such as Lisp muddies the water by introducing the problem of simulating processes that are not well understood (e.g., memory). The resulting simulations define constraints on possible problem conceptualizations. By separating the knowledge level from the symbol level, the formal analysis of knowledge and the representation of knowledge can be approached in a clear way. The conceptualization of the problem that results from the analysis of knowledge can then provide a verifiable specification for the evolving knowledge system [13]. Also, the isomorphism between knowledge and representation can then be verified as the representation is developed in the symbol system. These two separate activities are repeated as part of the prototyping loop. (The reader is referred to Brachman and Levesque [3] and Rich and Waters [32] for a more detailed discussion of knowledge representation problems.)

It should be noted that there is no intrinsic restriction on the symbolic representation system used for heuristic classification problems. The general vocabulary should include a means for representing definitions, facts, relations, heuristics, and type-subtype structures. Certainly, Lisp or some higher level abstraction sitting on top of Lisp could be used as a representational system. For an analysis or goal-driven problem, a system such as EMYCIN might provide an appropriate development environment. For a synthesis or primarily data-driven problem, OPS5 might provide a minimal development environment. For a more complex system involving nonmonotonic reasoning and complex inheritance relations, KEE or ART, which offer a sophisticated expert system development environment, might be the best choice. In any case, it is assumed that the developer has considered the ability of the development environment to represent the *conceptualized* problem. Kline and Dolins [19], Richer [35], Rothenberg [36], and Szolovits [42] provide criteria one can employ to evaluate development environments against conceptualizations.

KBS Development and Evaluation as a Developmental Process

In terms of input and output, a weak analogy exists between the behaving KBS interpreter and the behaving, inferencing human. This rather Skinnerian view of behaving suffices for conceptualizing evaluation, providing a first-order model of the meaning and place of KBS technology in replicating human performance. The three fundamental concepts upon which the analogy rests are experience, environment, and control. Experience includes the entire stimulus history of human beings, but for our purposes it is restricted to general and specific knowledge that could be used in reasoning about a limited and abstracted task. Environment is the complex, hierarchically arranged ecology in which behavior is expressed and is restricted by analogy to the KB interpreter and, through its symbols and structure, the context which it defines. Control refers to the rationality and logic that are applied to experience in affecting performance. It is the general inference engine, or *shell*, together with control knowledge, that defines the operating characteristics and constraints of the inferencing system. The relationship between these components is highly interactive. SOAR is an architecture that represents an attempt to define a *general problem-solving* KBS [20]. It describes the implementation of a general model of intelligent behavior and, in doing so, the general building blocks and levels of interaction that are required in such a model.

From this view, the KBS has an ontogeny with a long period of immaturity during which incremental growth occurs. Expanding, integrating, evaluating, re-integrating, abstracting, and refining the contents of experience (knowledge), development and change in the environment (the context), and the development of controls and control knowledge (the inference engine) continues well into maturity.

Evaluation is an integral part of the evolution of the system. Rapid proto-typing, incremental development, and the concept of growing complexity through successive prototypes constitute the assumed general model for development. The knowledge specification is developed within the prototyping loop through successive evaluations and refinements [12, 33, 34, 38, 44].

What Makes the Evaluation Problem Unique

Figure 11–4 shows a list of some of the factors that make it difficult to use standard software evaluation techniques and standard structured design for the development of a KBS. The fundamental issue is the nature of expert knowledge. Expert behavior is often based upon heuristic, incomplete, and uncertain knowledge. Expert behavior develops over a long period of time and is subject to continuous refinement. For this reason, the normal requirements-specification part of software development cannot be executed in the normal fashion. Both the requirements and the specification continue to be developed and refined as knowledge is acquired and analyzed. The initial system requirements are described primarily in functional terms—that is, in terms of their behavior. This is by nature incomplete and requires that the functional descriptions be reevaluated as knowledge acquisition continues.

---

1. Knowledge acquisition that corresponds to requirements phase.
2. Indeterminacy of control.
3. Combinatorial explosion of possible programs.
4. Uncertainty of knowledge.
5. Incompleteness of knowledge.
6. Constant need to tune and adjust.
7. Lack of validated tools or compilers.
8. Requirements are in functional terms.
9. Reiterative prototype building process.

Figure 11–4   Unique features of a KBS.

MODELS FOR DESIGN AND EVALUATION

Figure 11–5 shows KBS development as involving two major blocks of activity: requirements analysis/specification and prototype/evaluation [17]. This represents the overall development process as a highly interactive definition-and-refinement process. Figure 11–6 shows the general flow of evaluation. The knowledge level is developed and evaluated independently of a machine representation. Then the syntactic and semantic issues associated with machine representation become a focus for evaluation. Finally, performance evaluations commence. These are all repeated over the development cycles. A more detailed representation of this

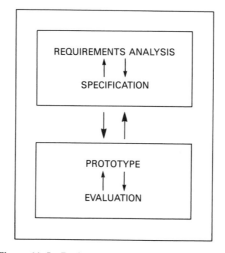

Figure 11–5   Basic flow of early KBS development.

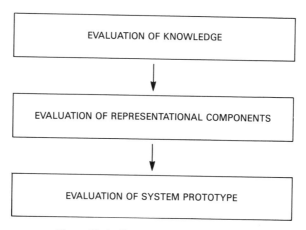

Figure 11–6   General steps in evaluation.

model is given in Richardson [33, 34] and describes the AI life cycle as having the following structure:

Requirements phase
Prototyping phase
KBS building phase
Testing phase
Delivery and monitoring phase

Richardson further describes the prototyping stage as an incremental loop with the following basic steps:

Knowledge acquisition
Building a prototype
Evaluation of results
Augmentation of requirements
Direction for next prototype

Most of the current development models represent an amalgam of proto-typing, structured design, and life-cycle software engineering [16, 17, 33, 34, 44]. Figure 11–7 shows the model of development we shall use in discussing evaluation. It is given in the form of an abstract algorithm. The requirements come first and are typically stated in functional terms. They usually result from an analysis of expert behavior and provide an initial focus for the system development. For example, Figure 11–8 shows a subset of the generic functions of the tactical officer on a P-3 aircraft. These functions were determined from an analysis of the workload of the tactical officer using the Zachary workload method [45]. The functions provide both a basis for determining what the KBS is supposed to do and a basis for more detailed analysis and development of knowledge structures to support KBS functionality [1]. Notice that the model starts with a requirements and needs analysis. The specification is developed within the prototyping loop.

REQUIREMENTS & NEEDS ANALYSIS

PROTOTYPING (SPECIFICATION)
    LOOP
        LOOP
            Knowledge acquisition
            Knowledge level analysis & organization
            Domain & control knowledge representation
        UNTIL TESTABLE LEVEL OF COMPLETENESS ACHIEVED IN KB
        Inference engine design & integration
        Evaluation and competency testing
        Augmenting requirements
    UNTIL PROTOTYPE IS COMPLETE

EMBED KBS IN LIFE-CYCLE MANAGEMENT PROCESS
    Integrated design, testing, certification, maintenance, etc.

Figure 11–7 A model for design and evaluation of KBS development.

COGNITIVE

1. Determine aircraft position.
2. Determine sonobuoy pattern.
3. Determine target course/speed/depth.
4. Classify contact.

EXECUTION / ACTION

5. Deploy buoys.
6. Display target fix.
7. Program weapon.

MANAGEMENT / COORDINATION

8. Coordinate acoustic sensor utilization with ss-1,2.
9. Stabilize tactical plot.

Figure 11–8 Some factors used in assessing an application (from Zaklad [43]).

The second major step in the development model is the prototyping loop. Actually, it is a loop within a loop. Knowledge acquisition proceeds until a testable level of completeness has been reached, and then the system is tested and the process repeats itself. This continues until a full prototype has been developed. Note that incremental development, refinement, reintegration and so on all imply that evaluation is continuous and inseparable from development. Note also, however, that evaluation of the knowledge base precedes evaluation of the KBS as an inferencing system. *The first major focus for evaluation is the consistency, completeness, and validity of the knowledge* [6, 7]. An inconsistent, ill-developed knowledge base precludes meaningful performance testing. As they say in computer circles, garbage in, garbage out (GIGO).

Once it has been established that the knowledge base is consistent, correct, and valid, evaluation of the knowledge base can be frozen and overall performance testing can begin. It should be remembered that a KBS is supposed to behave like a human being in a very limited problem context. So the tools that are used to evaluate human expertise are the same tools that will have to be adapted for measurement of the behavior of the KBS. Test problems, empirical test procedures, explanation facilities, and criteria for the evaluation of performance are the main issues [22].

Another important issue within the prototyping loop is the inference engine design. We shall finesse this problem by using a hybrid system that is commercially available. A system such as KEE or ART provides a variety of tools to speed up prototyping and has been tested enough that it can be assumed to operate correctly. This is an essential assumption, because it allows us to focus attention on the knowledge base [36]. If the KBS is to be tailored from the *ground up*, it will be necessary to develop the knowledge base to some point and then freeze the development of the knowledge base while development of the inference engine becomes the focus [17]. Such a process would continue through all iterations. The problem with it, however, is that effects are hard to localize: is there a problem with the inference engine, or is there a problem with the knowledge base?

In the third step, the prototype and the knowledge specification that has evolved become the raw materials for further development using a life-cycle software development model. It is at this point that certification, testing in operational contexts, and the like will occur. The tools and techniques of software engineering can be used to develop the system beyond the knowledge and inferencing sub-system. It should be noted, however, that modifications to the knowledge base or the control/inferencing system require that testing of both the knowledge base and the KBS prototyping loop be reinitiated.

KNOWLEDGE ACQUISITION

Reliability and Validity of the Knowledge Base

Reliability implies that the KBS behaves the same way under the same circumstances. The key to overall reliability is ensuring that the knowledge base is consistent, correct, and complete. Nguyen [27, 28] and Stachowitz [39–41] discuss some useful concepts for evaluating these characteristics while a knowledge base is being developed. Stachowitz in particular has developed a system that is fairly comprehensive in the syntactic and semantic analysis it performs. His system can analyze the range of data objects that can be developed using a KEE-like development environment. This includes both descriptions in the first-order predicate calculus and descriptions in the frame system KEE provides. The basic idea is to subject each rule or object to a series of tests which determines its suitability for inclusion in the knowledge base. Figure 11–9 lists some of the basic tests for consistency, including the following for rules:

> Redundancy
> Conflicts
> Subsumption
> Unnecessary conditions
> Unreachable conditions
> Cycles

Redundancy refers to rules that are equivalent in the sense that they trigger in the same situation and produce the same results. Or at least the results of one are a subset of the results of the other. Two rules that succeed in the same situation but produce conflicting results are in *conflict*. Thus, the rule $A \wedge B \rightarrow C$ and the rule $A \wedge B \rightarrow \sim C$ are in conflict. *Subsumption* refers to rules that produce the same result, but the LHS (left-hand side) of one is a subset of the LHS of the other. The rule $A \rightarrow B$ would subsume the rule $A \wedge X \rightarrow B$. *Unnecessary conditions* occur when two rules have the same LHS and RHS (right-hand side), except that one LHS condition is the negation of an LHS condition in the other rule. The condition Q is *unnecessary* in a rule when, for example, $A \wedge \sim Q \rightarrow B$ and $A \wedge Q \rightarrow B$. A rule has an *unreachable condition* if no other rule could assert the condition and if the condition cannot be a fact in the inital working memory (data base). *Cycles* refer to

```
┌─────────────────────────────────────────────────────────────────┐
│  KNOWLEDGE ACQUISITION, ORGANIZATION, AND REPRESENTATION          │
│  Knowledge-level evaluation to define generic models or components│
│       MONITOR(systems state) + DIAGNOSE(faulty component)         │
│       INTERPRET(sensor data) + IDENTIFY(platform) + MONITOR(tracks)│
│                                                                   │
│  Consistency, Correctness, and Completeness of Knowledge          │
│                                                                   │
│       Redundancy                                                  │
│           P(x) ∧ Q(x) → W(x) ≡ Q(z) ∧ P(z) → W(z)                 │
│       Conflicts                                                   │
│           P ∧ Q → R < conflictswith > P ∧ Q → ~ R                 │
│       Subsumption                                                 │
│           P(x) → Q(x) < subsumes > P(y) ∧ R(y) → Q(y)             │
│       Unnecessary conditions                                      │
│           P ∧ ~ Q → R < Q is unnecessary > P ∧ Q → R              │
│       Unreachable conditions                                      │
│       Cycles                                                      │
│           P → Q, Q → R, R → P                                     │
│       Incomplete classes                                          │
│       Incomplete or missing relations or definitions              │
│       Incomplete slot values                                      │
│                                                                   │
│  Control Knowledge and Strategies                                 │
│                                                                   │
│       Focusing                                                    │
│       Coherence                                                   │
│       Discrimination                                              │
└─────────────────────────────────────────────────────────────────┘
```

Figure 11–9   Knowledge-level evaluation.

rule chains that are circular. An example of such a rule chain is $A \rightarrow B$, $B \rightarrow C$, and $C \rightarrow A$.

Semantic Analysis

Stachowitz [39–41] has extended the idea of semantic analysis to include evaluation involving knowledge-base semantics and metaknowledge. The system he is developing at Lockheed called EVA checks for the above factors but along more dimensions. For example, the system can check for categories such as redundancy and reachability within a generalization hierarchy using inheritance information. Applying these checks across metalevel constructs such as generalization, synonymy, and compatibility ensures a more refined concept of organization in the knowledge base. EVA can also define and use constraints to do semantic checks involving cardinality, relations, subrelations, data types, and the like. The system is designed to be applicable to more than one form of knowledge constructed in a number of environments such as KEE, ART, or OPS5.

   EVA does more than consistency checking: it also has functions that contribute to the evaluation of the completeness and correctness of the knowledge base. EVA can collect information from instances of rules, inheritance relations, class structures, and form sets that show incomplete classes and relations and missing rules. It can also detect missing slot values. The representation of facts and rules as a connection graph with leaves that are input or output nodes provides a basis for defining a test case generator. Such a generator could be used as a basis for a more formal analysis of correctness. However, as the size of the rule base increases, the usefulness of the representation would diminish.

Fuzzy Decision Tables

Francioni and Kandel [11] offer an approach to knowledge-base development that does redundancy and contradiction checks on a rule base as it is being developed using a decision table approach to development. They present algorithms for representing rules in nondeterministic fuzzy notation. For example, the equivalent of *AND*ing two predicates *x1* and *x2* would first require defining an acceptance range for both predicates in the interval [0,1]. Suppose this range was [0.3] for both *x1* and *x2*. Then the action part would be taken only when the fuzzy switching function $MAX(x1,x2)$ produced a number within [0.3]. The idea is that if the maximum is within the interval, the minimum must be also. Fuzzy logic is also used to make redundancy (the intervals are the same) and contradiction (absorption axioms on the left-hand side) checks as the fuzzy decision table is being formed.

Completeness of Knowledge Bases

It is likely that knowledge derived from experts is not complete. In a project conducted by the author, the process of knowledge acquisition revealed "holes" in the military tactics used in a particular operational context. These were made explicit only because attention was paid to completeness. A secondary gain from this process is the definition and explication of inconsistent, incorrect, or incomplete knowledge. One may think of knowledge acquisition as a primary means of problem definition and refinement. Lack of completeness makes default problems explicit and may even turn out to be a reason for stopping a project.

Separating Control and Domain Knowledge

Another important consideration in developing the knowledge base is to separate domain and control knowledge. As Figure 11–10 shows, domain knowledge focuses on *what* while control knowledge focuses on *when* and *how* [10]. The *sensitivity* of the KBS to changes in the rule base can be in part attributed to the degree to which this separation has been achieved. One form of evaluation that measures this is achieved by first partitioning the rules into noninteracting sets or by goal/subgoal trees. Then, within partitions, rule behavior is tested under commutation. If the

```
THE KNOWLEDGE LEVEL
    DOMAIN
       What
    CONTROL
       When
       How
```

Figure 11–10   Separating domain and control knowledge.

rules produce different results when their order in the rule base is changed, they contain control knowledge.

Summary of Consistency Issues

Problems with reliability obscure problems with validity. However, a consistent KBS does not imply a valid one. The determination of validity requires finding good criteria to measure the predictive power of the system—that is, the power to predict the criteria within an acceptable margin of error. The questions are, *How well do the actual results of the KBS agree with the predicted results using the criteria?* and *How error free are the criteria?* Correctness addresses the question of validity in terms of a formal evaluation of the knowledge base and a manual test case evaluation. However, full validation typically requires both the knowledge base and an inference engine that generates results for comparison.

In sum, a critical, and perhaps the most important, step in evaluation is determining the consistency, completeness, and correctness of the knowledge base. This is a process that must be continued throughout the lifespan of the program. It must be considered a major determinant of the reliability of the rule base—that is, its ability to produce consistent results given the same basic conditions.

It should be noted that completeness may reflect an unachievable goal: it may not be possible and, if possible, may not be important. It is important, however, to specify the limits of the system in this sense anyway. Completeness constrains the interpretations the system is capable of making and specifies the practical boundaries of KBS behavior.

OVERALL PERFORMANCE EVALUATION OF THE KBS

General Evaluation of Suitability

The process of knowledge acquisition and refinement continues for some time, all the while feeding back to the requirements/specification task. As information is gathered and organized, a better picture of the knowledge domain appears. Prerau [30] has organized a set of factors important to the evaluation of the *appropriateness of a domain* for KBS development. These factors can be used as part of the reassessment of this issue as the knowledge acquisition process continues. Figure 11–11 shows a summary of the factors.

1. An algorithmic approach will not work.
2. The knowledge domain contains heuristic knowledge.
3. There are recognized experts at the task.
4. The task requires symbolic reasoning.
5. The task is restricted in scope.
6. The task takes no more than several hours to do.
7. The task has a bounded number of concepts (≤ 200).
8. The task is decomposable.
9. The knowledge is not shallow.

Figure 11–11 Some factors used to assess the applicability of a domain for KBS development.

In addition, metrics for analyzing the size and complexity of the task can be applied at this stage. As the knowledge base becomes bigger, natural partitions into tasks/subtasks or goals/subgoals appear. These partitions can be thought of as independent rule bases that can be loaded and used when needed and then removed when their agenda items have been completed. The metric involves determining how close the largest partition is to being complete. The expert is shown the knowledge base, and he or she estimates how much larger the partition or rule base needs to be in order to be able to do what it is supposed to do. The estimate can be cross-validated by looking at test cases and analyzing the behavior of the knowledge base in handling a range of test cases. With the help of an expert or by using the percentage of test cases that can be handled by the rules, we can make a qualitative judgment as to how big the KB partition will need to be.

The second dimension is the complexity of the KB as measured by the depth or number of levels it is likely to contain. One way to estimate the depth or complexity of a KB is to take a *vertical slice* approach to the analysis of a case. That is, one takes a typical case and develops it fully. If the knowledge base contains many levels for data abstraction, heuristic matching and solution abstraction, it is a good candidate for further development. If, on the other hand, the knowledge base has 1,000 rules on many levels and the rule base is less than 50 percent complete, we have a complex problem. The system is likely to be difficult to construct and refine, but it is also likely to be more interesting than a system with a "flat" knowledge base. If we have 1,000 rules and a flat rule base, then it is unclear whether the KBS approach is necessary; there may be more direct ways to map data to solutions, such as direct data base queries.

Overall Reliability of Prototypes

The reliability of the prototype becomes a matter of the consistency of its performance under what are judged to be situations that should produce the same results, as well as the ability of the system to produce consistent results in the face of incomplete and uncertain variants of the same situation. The basic approach to the analysis of overall reliability has a well-established empirical basis. Going back to the heuristic classification method, the basic idea is that data and data abstractions provide the fuel for analysis. Changes in data produce changes in data abstractions which, in turn, produce changes in the selection of solution abstractions. The KBS is reliable if it selects the same data abstraction given data that vary along unimportant dimensions. The analysis of reliability can focus on changes in data versus changes in the data abstraction first.

Reliability also involves the question of the consistency of the solution refinement process. If the system is consistent in the manner in which it builds data abstractions, is it then also consistent in the manner in which it refines solution abstractions? Is it paying attention to the right data? Does it use defaults correctly?

Yet another aspect of reliability involves measuring the behavior of successive prototypes on common problems. Presumably, each prototype will be more complete than the previous version. However, the basic solutions should be consistent.

Performance Evaluation

Figure 11–12 summarizes some of the issues in determining the overall performance of the KBS. Basically, three major tasks are involved in performance evaluation: the generation of test cases or problems that test the range of desired behavior, the development of criteria for the evaluation of performance on the test cases, and the actual testing procedure.

```
EVALUATION AND COMPETENCY TESTING
Test problem generation

    Typical cases
        Range of values and initial states
        Defaults
        Uncertainty
        Monotonicity
    Exceptional cases
    All cases or range of cases
    Unsolvable cases
    Sensitivity

Evaluation

    Criteria for evaluation
        Sui generis criteria
            Located fault? How many tests?
            Ask and tell, KBS versus expert
        Constructed criteria

    Measuring performance
        Judgments and the Turing test
        AIQ
        Competency testing
        Standard experimental designs
            Pretest-posttest control group design
            Single and double blind
```

Figure 11–12 Performance-level evaluation.

Test Case Development

Test case development can be divided into two categories: tests for systems that have preenumerated solutions and for those that have constructed solutions. An example of the first kind is the generic operation DIAGNOSE. Diagnosis implies a preenumerated set of solutions. The problem may be bounded such that a complete set of test cases can be enumerated, or, conversely, the set may be so large, as in a fault diagnosis problem, that only sample cases can be generated. An example of a constructed solution is the generic operation PLAN. For a plan generator, pre-enumerated solutions may not exist, so test cases have to be organized around input data and external and qualitative measures of the *goodness* of the constructed solution would be used for performance analysis. The measure of goodness might be based on expert judgments, might involve metalevel criteria as to the attributes of good and bad plans such as simplicity, or might rely on measurable outcomes of implementing the plan such as time savings, better task performance, and faster response time.

In the heuristic classification model, there are three major blocks to consider in generating cases regardless of whether the solution is preenumerated or constructed:

- Moving from data to data abstraction
- Heuristic matching of data abstraction and solution abstraction
- Refining solution abstraction

A basic test case would consist of a refined solution and initial data. The processes of moving from data to data abstraction, heuristic matching, and moving from solution abstraction to solution refinement would provide details of the solution process as well as an explanation of performance as regards a deeper analysis of the reasoning process. Normally, the solution set would be described first and the data that are supposed to map into it second. The questions of uncertainty, defaults, and unsolvable problems become testing issues in this system. They represent variants and constraints on KBS behavior once full test cases have been successfully tested.

Seek

A powerful technique for the development of test cases is illustrated by the SEEK system developed by Politakis [29]. SEEK integrates performance evaluation with design by integrating domain knowledge with test cases so that evaluation can proceed as part of the development process. Test cases can be invoked for the purpose of refining or developing the knowledge base. The designer is able to carry out experiments that generalize, specialize, or change the confidence level of rules. In this way, testing is integrated with development.

The SEEK system implements the generic operation DIAGNOSE. The data consist of clinical observations such as swollen hands, myositis, anemia, or pleuritis. These observations are organized into categories as major or minor factors in mapping the patient (as a data abstraction) into a disease class (mixed connective-tissue disease). Rules are frame-like structures that map data into disease categories as a function of the number of major and minor observations pertinent to a given disease class that have been made and the confidence that the diagnostician has in each observation. For example, a diagnosis of definite mixed connective-tissue disease requires four major observations, positive RNP antibodies, and no positive SM antibodies. For the diagnosis to be just probable, only two major and two minor observations are required as well as positive RNP antibodies and no positive SM antibodies. The diagnosis is possible in the case of only three major observations, with no further requirements or exclusions.

Cases used to test SEEK performance are maintained in a data base that is part of the system and entered through a menu-driven questionnaire. They are actually stored as a sequence of numbers that represent observations and a number that represents the resulting diagnosis. The case generation facility provides a means of extracting test data from the experts.

Performance analysis can be done using single cases or all cases. The first step is to run the cases and compare the SEEK conclusion with the expert conclusion. A table of results is generated that specifies the number and percentage of correct matches between SEEK and the expert. The developer can run this analysis with various cases and rules excluded so that the influence of the rules and flexible alternatives can be tested.

Rules can be generalized or specialized by changing their confidence values. If a condition (observation) is removed from a rule, the rule is easier to satisfy and is considered generalized. If a condition is added to a rule, the rule is harder to satisfy and is considered specialized.

Performance analysis proceeds by collecting statistics for a rule across all cases. These statistics are then used by heuristic rules to suggest experiments. An example of a heuristic rule is [29]:

```
IF:
    the number of cases suggesting generalization of the rule is
    greater than the number of cases suggesting specialization of
    the rule and the most frequently missing component in the rule
    is the MAJOR component
THEN
    decrease the number of major findings in the rule
```

The choice of which finding (observation) to remove requires an analysis of cases supporting the generalization. The finding most often missed across cases supporting the generalization is removed.

Determining which rules to change after a misdiagnosis requires that all partially satisfied rules that mention the expert's conclusion be backtracked using the rule's left-hand side. The purpose is to isolate the rule that yields the expert's conclusion which is closest to being satisfied. This is the rule that is to be modified. Once the designer has decided which experiment to run, the rule can be changed in a conditional fashion and the results analyzed statistically to see whether any improvement has been realized and whether any adverse side effects have occurred.

Establishing Criteria for the Measurement of Performance

To measure the performance of a KBS, criteria must be established that define the standard for competent performance. Criteria fall into two general categories: *sui generis* criteria directly reflect performance and can be used directly in assessing performance; constructed criteria are combinations of parameters that measure constructs which, taken together, in some sense indirectly establish a performance standard. *Sui generis* criteria are inherently less error prone than constructed criteria and are preferred when available.

Normally, criteria of both types are required to fully assess the performance of a KBS. For example, an electronic fault diagnosis system can be analyzed against various default combinations on an actual board. For each case, assessment may include whether or not the diagnostic system correctly diagnosed the fault, the number of tests required, the particular sequence of tests used, and which test was chosen first. This could be compared directly with the behavior of an expert on the same case. Or, depending upon KBS requirements, a correct diagnosis might suffice for establishing the case. Another example would be the evaluation of a KBS that PLANs a system. Suppose this system has no obvious behavior that directly reflects performance other than the fact that it either does or does not operate. How do we then fine tune the system so that it generates better and better plans? Criteria must be constructed that indirectly support a *goodness* construct. For example, suppose we have established a concept that says that functional plans that are small are to be preferred to functional plans that are large. Or perhaps, plans that are simple are preferred to plans that are complex. Then, for each construct or factor, a measurement or measurements must be constructed. Plan size is measured by the number of steps in the top-level plan; plan complexity is measured by the average length of the dependency chains in activities.

Conducting Experiments

Once criteria have been established, experiments must be run to test the system. This is the most difficult part of performance evaluation. At this point, sampling and experimental design become major activities. The process should start out with modest assessments of performance on constrained and specific cases and move successively toward assessment of extreme cases, cases with lots of defaults, highly ambiguous or low-certainty cases, impossible cases, and so on. Testing should first establish that the system is competent to handle specific cases and then show the robustness of the system as parameters are varied systematically. The major determinant of what constitutes adequate testing is what the system is required to do.

Using Judges

A common criterion used for establishing validity is the judgments of experts. The judges are given the output from the KBS and are asked to judge the adequacy of the results. This is actually the worst way to establish validity because there are as many criteria as judges and there is bias created by prior knowledge of the material being judged. The early evaluations of MYCIN had this problem [4, 37]. It is better to use *blind* evaluation techniques and to have judges establish criteria for evaluation that can be used consistently across cases. The use and evaluation of expert judgments has been studied extensively by psychologists, and the interested reader is referred to Torgerson [43] or Guilford [15] for more information.

Another way to use judges is to ask both experts and the KBS to solve some test problems that have been carefully developed. The results may be put in a standard format and the judges asked to evaluate performance without knowing whether the results are those of an expert or from the KBS. If the evaluations are the same [15, 43] for both the expert and the KBS, then the system has high validity. This is a variant of the Turing test [5].

Using Rating Scales

Klein [18] proposed what he called *AIQ* as a means of validation. This is no more than the development and application of performance rating scales to the KBS and to the expert. Rho, a nonparametric correlation coefficient, would be calculated to compare the performances of the KBS and the expert. This would provide a rather direct measure of validity. Rating scales could also be expanded as the prototyping cycle continued to include more measures that moved evaluation from the abstract to the concept of evaluation in context. Klein included the major categories of system effectiveness, user effectiveness, and organization effectiveness in his rating scheme. Psychologists have devoted much research to the development and use of rating scales for measuring performance [10].

Competency Testing

A key factor in determining the adequacy of an evaluation is the degree to which the criteria capture the essential elements of performance [2]. This is an art in itself. In a system being developed by the author, the initial data were provided by a detailed behavioral analysis of experts in the actual operational environment. The Zachary workload assessment methodology was used to assess the workload on the tactical officer (the focus of the KBS) [45]. The result was a detailed and comprehensive picture of the density and categories of generic activities performed by the officer and broken down by cognitive, execution/action and management/coordination (see Figure 11–8) categories. These were further analyzed relative to a time line which represented an unfolding operational scenario. Each functional activity, such as *stabilize tactical plot,* was decomposed into sublevels until measurable competencies (primitives) were defined. This process is a very powerful method to establish criteria for evaluation. The kind of detailed antecedent to KBS development that it represents provides the level of detail needed to establish unambiguous performance criteria.

Comparative Analysis

Each successive version of the system must be compared with the behavior of the previous version to ensure that the development effort is producing successive refinements in behavior. This concept is important throughout the lifetime of the system. The sensitivity of the system is measured by comparing results on standard problems before and after changes to the knowledge base. Changes to the shell at the same time can obscure the effects of knowledge-base changes. The relative-worlds capability of KEE makes it feasible to test different world models, called *what if* thinking, at the same time exploring changes in a more immediate way.

Simulation

Another source of validation criteria is from system simulations. Pilots Associate has used simulation for some validation criteria. If the system behaves properly in the simulated situation, it is more likely to behave correctly in the real world. If the simulation is complete, modules that have been developed can be installed in the simulation in place of the already simulated versions, and testing can be conducted in the partial context provided by the simulation environment.

A project currently being conducted by the author requires a very sophisticated simulator. The KBS is embedded in hardware and cannot be tested in any other way. The question is, How will the performance of the simulated system compare in terms of both reliability and validity with and without the embedded system?

CERTIFICATION

Ultimately, the system must pass beyond prototyping stages and be certified as field ready. This involves issues that are not addressed in this chapter, such as efficiency and maintainability. However, the incremental development approach described here makes these tasks easier and can have a major impact on the likelihood of positive outcomes.

A phenomenon discovered long ago called the *Heisenberg principle* must be assumed to operate when the KBS is placed in context. The Heisenberg principle says that when a change is introduced to a system, the very fact of change will produce effects. The KBS will change the behavior of the system in ways that might not be predictable. In any case, the Heisenberg principle would predict that the introduction of the KBS will perturb the system and that it will take some time before it returns to a steady state (if it does at all) in the presence of the KBS. After a steady state is established, the question becomes, How effective is the KBS in its operational context? and Is it mature enough to be considered fully operational?

An approach to the question of evaluation in context is to measure the distribution of functions and the overall functionality of the system with and without the KBS in place. For example, in a project currently being done by the author, a detailed analysis of all data flows in the system was conducted, including mapping the flows and measuring the rates of flow at specific points in the system. A second analysis was done to define the functions being performed by each human operator in the system and the distribution of these functions across platforms. The hypothesized consequence of introducing the embedded KBS is that the rates of data flow will increase in certain subsystems and that the distribution of functions across human operators will change. The particular KBS is totally transparent to the users, and the effect of the KBS is measured in terms of the impact of increased parallelism and increased hardware reliability on the functionality of the system.

CASE STUDIES IN EVALUATION

MYCIN

MYCIN is a rule-based expert system that uses the heuristic classification method to MONITOR patients, DIAGNOSE microbial infections, determine whether the infection is significant, IDENTIFY the organism, IDENTIFY appropriate antimicrobial drugs, and recommend the appropriate drugs for MODIFYING the patient's condition.

The MYCIN project was subjected to three major performance evaluations [4, 8, 37]. The first used five expert judges from the Stanford Division of Infectious Diseases. They evaluated 15 cases and were aware that they were evaluating data generated by MYCIN. They were asked to judge the performance of MYCIN in deciding whether a patient needed treatment (MONITOR and DIAGNOSE), in determing the significance of the isolated organism (DIAGNOSE), in identifying significant organisms (IDENTIFY), in selecting therapy (MODIFY), and overall [4]. MYCIN received a 75% approval rating across cases.

Several lessons were learned from this evaluation. The meaning of the 75% approval rating was unclear. In order to give it full utility, it would be necessary to know how the experts would have done with the same cases. Perhaps their performance would have been no better than MYCIN when judged by other experts. Also, the fact that the experts knew that they were evaluating MYCIN behavior biased the results, possibly producing a self-fulfilling prophecy. So a second study was initiated using experts from a nationwide sample to correct, as much as possible, the deficiencies of the first study.

The third performance evaluation corrected many of the shortcomings in the first two experimental designs. This study was divided into two phases. In the first phase, seven medical faculty at Stanford, a medical student, MYCIN, and the doctor actually caring for the ten patients used in the study carried out a case analysis based on the same data summaries. In the second phase, eight infectious disease specialists evaluated the results produced in the first phase by the ten evaluators of the ten patients. Based on the judgments of these specialists, MYCIN had the highest percentage of acceptable ratings (65%).

The foregoing evaluation demonstrates quite clearly the importance of using single- or double-blind techniques when relying on human judgments of performance. It also points out the importance of using independent judges to evaluate data, thus eliminating self-fulfilling prophecies. It would also be useful to measure interjudge reliability across the eight judges. This would provide a measure of the *expertise* of the experts.

Prospector

Prospector is a rule-based system designed to help a geologist evaluate the mineral content of a particular site to find out whether there are any interesting ore deposits on the site. The data are information about local sites, minerals, rock type, etc. The data are matched against a set of models that describe solution classes. Once a model is matched, the user is asked additional questions to refine the solution and determine the goodness of fit with the model.

Gaschnig [12] described several evaluations of the Prospector system. These evaluations relied on comparisons of the evaluation of site data by Prospector and by experts. What made the evaluation interesting was that solution abstractions (called models) were evaluated one at a time. In the reported evaluation, the RWSSU (western states sandstone uranium deposits) model was tested. Eight test sites were chosen and evaluated by a model expert and Prospector. The sites were chosen either as exemplars of the RWSSU model or as poor versions of the model. The data from each test site was gathered using a questionnaire that required numeric answers reflecting the degree of agreement or disagreement on a scale of -5 to $+5$. The results were converted into an overall score that reflected the goodness of fit with the RWSSU model again, (-5 to 5).

The resulting evaluation, based on difference scores, compared the scores from the model expert with the Prospector scores to determine the amount of agreement between them. Underneath the major model assertion as to the degree to which the site data supported the RWSSU model (scale of -5 to 5) was a complex set of subassertions that contributed to the analysis. What was interesting about the evaluation was that differences in the model and Prospector scores were further analyzed at these sublevels to pinpoint where the differences were occurring. The results showed that Prospector not only was reaching the same conclusions as the model expert, but also was reaching them for the same reason. This is a useful approach to evaluating and refining the knowledge structures.

In addition to the evaluation described, a sensitivity analysis was conducted by comparing the results of the actual data runs with the same analyses using data with certainties increased by $+1$ and with certainties decreased by -1. The results showed Prospector to be stable over seven of the eight cases using these variations in certainty values. A further analysis of the substructure of the unstable case showed where the greatest difference was occurring.

The evaluation of Prospector demonstrated the relation between the ability of the KBS to show its reasoning process and the depth of the various analyses. Systems that allow the inference process to be studied and queried in some manner or explicitly analyzed offer a critical datum for evaluation [24].

AM and R1

The AM project was designed to construct new mathematical concepts. AM consists of elementary set concepts such as substitution, equality, and identity, each with heuristics in the form of rules in concept slots. For example, the examples facet of the predicate concept has the heuristic [9, 21]

> IF, empirically, 10 times as many elements fail some predicate P as satisfy it,
> THEN some generalization of P might be more interesting than P

The idea behind AM was in the form of a question: given a set of prenumerical concepts with heuristics such as this, what could AM discover about mathematics? AM is driven primarily by an agenda of self-generated activities. The results showed that, among other things, AM discovered some elementary laws of prime numbers.

AM CONFIGURES (i.e., constructs) a solution. The goodness of the AM solution was determined by a set of evaluation questions that delve into the quality of the discoveries, the process of discovery, the degree of user guidance required, and the results of experiments made by modifying heuristics or concepts [9]. The answers to most of these questions require that expert judgments be made.

R1 (now called XCON) is a KBS designed to CONFIGURE VAX computers. It takes a customer order and produces an appropriate configuration for the customer's VAX system [23]. R1 is a rule-based system that was developed using the OPS4 and OPS5 programming languages. The initial system was given a substantial evaluation in 1979 to determine whether or not it could be certified for field use. The system was tested by giving it 50 orders to fill and then having the resulting configurations evaluated by six experts. The experts were able to pinpoint actual configuration errors via *sui generis* criteria. Based on their findings, R1 was judged expert and was integrated into field activities for further onsite evaluation.

EXPLANATION

One of the fundamental ways in which we learn from experts is to ask them questions concerning their behavior. Likewise, the development and execution history of a KBS provides a fertile resource for the evaluation of system performance. The ability to do real-time analysis, direct inspection of data structures, queries of the execution history for a problem, and partial executions of a procedure enhance the evaluation process. Neches [24] suggests that explanation should be part of the running KBS and that a KBS should be able to answer four classes of questions, pertaining to justification, timing or appropriateness, definition or function, and capabilities.

Justification questions would ask why the system is interested in particular parameters, goals, or actions, why a particular goal or action is necessary, or why a recommendation should be followed. Timing or appropriateness questions focus on why the KBS considered or rejected a particular goal, action, or conclusion under some set of conditions or with regard to some reference. Definition or function questions focus on the meaning and effects of and relations between terms, actions, goals, and parameters. Capability questions deal with what the system knows about concepts, what factors entered into conclusions, and what methods were used in the achievement of goals [24].

These questions provide a guide for considering an on-line evaluation facility that allows the developer to turn the attention of the KBS to itself for the purpose of self-evaluation.

SUMMARY

The reliability and validity of a KBS must continue throughout the lifetime of the system. Evaluation starts with knowledge acquisition and continues through prototyping and operational testing. KBS development requires both a developmental and systems approach. A KBS has a long period of immaturity during which it is developed, tested, and incrementally refined.

Development tools that have been thoroughly tested are preferred during early prototyping because they enable the developer to focus on the acquisition and development of knowledge. As the knowledge base begins to reach a steady state, it can be temporarily frozen and focus can be shifted to the development of the KBS prototype. This focus will shift from KB to KBS design as prototyping continues. Rothenberg [36] and Richer [35] have written excellent articles on the evaluation of expert system tools and their integration into designs.

Evaluating the performance of KBSs requires an understanding of the evaluation of human experts and expertise. There are no accepted general metrics for evaluating KBSs, although some work in this direction is beginning [22]. The same problems of reliability and validity that make behavioral and cognitive evaluations of people difficult make the evaluation of KBSs difficult. Actually, the KBS evaluations may be somewhat easier since the intervening processes between input and output are open for investigation.

The inherent lack of completeness in any heuristic classification problem can be seen in the model. In moving from data to data abstraction and from solution class to refined solution, the determination of where to put KBS boundaries is somewhat arbitrary. In human beings who make inferences, there is no reason to believe that abstraction and refinement processes do not use knowledge structures that we often refer to as common sense or general abstracted experience. The problem with KBSs is that when they are constructed, the relation between specific domain knowledge and general knowledge is severed. For this reason, the system is bound to be incomplete. In a weak sense, boundary conditions, defaults, and the default reasoning system help to define this incompleteness.

The general trend in KBS development is to build into the system facilities for generating test data and verifying knowledge (at least in the development environment). This includes enhanced facilities for explaining KBS structures and behavior [24, 46]. Even if a KBS has been thoroughly tested, the solution often includes satisfying the user that sound reasoning was used in the process.

REFERENCES

1. Borgida, A., Greenspan, S., and Myopoulos, J. "Knowledge Representation as the Basis for Requirements Specifications." *Computer* 18 (1985): 82–90.

2. Brachman, R. J., and Levesque, H. J. "Competence in Knowledge Representation." *Proceedings of the National Conference on Artificial Intelligence.* Pittsburgh, PA, 1982, pp. 189–192.

3. Brachman, R. J., and Levesque, H. J., eds. *Readings in Knowledge Representation*. Los Altos, CA: Morgan Kaufmann, 1985.

4. Buchanan, B. G., and Shortliffe, E. H. *Rule-based Expert Systems: The Mycin Experiments of the Stanford Heuristic Programming Project*. Reading, MA: Addison-Wesley, 1984.

5. Chandrasekaran, B. "On Evaluating AI Systems for Medical Diagnosis." *AI Magazine* 4 (1983): 34–37.

6. Clancey, W. J. "Heuristic Classification." *Artificial Intelligence* 27 (1985): 289–350.

7. Clancey, W. J. "The Advantages of Abstract Control Knowledge in Expert Systems." *Proceedings of the National Conference on Artificial Intelligence*. Washington, DC, 1983, pp. 74–78.

8. Clancey, W. J., and Shortliffe, E. H., eds. *Readings in Medical Artificial Intelligence*. Reading, MA: Addison-Wesley, 1984.

9. Davis, R., and Lenat, D. B. *Knowledge-based Systems in Artificial Intelligence*. New York: McGraw-Hill, 1982.

10. Dunnette, M. D., ed. *Handbook of Industrial and Organizational Psychology*. Chicago: Rand McNally, 1976.

11. Francioni, J. M., and Kandel, A. "A Software Engineering Tool for Expert System Design." *IEEE Expert* 3 (1988): 33–41.

12. Gaschnig, J. "Application of the PROSPECTOR System to Geological Exploration Problems." In *Machine Intelligence 10,* edited by J. E. Hayes, D. Michie, and Y. Pao, pp. 301–323. New York: Halsted Press, 1982.

13. Genesereth, M. R. "An Overview of Meta-Level Architecture." *Proceedings of the National Conference on Artificial Intelligence*. Washington, DC, 1983, pp. 119–124.

14. Genesereth, M. R., and Nilsson, N. J. *Logical Foundations of Artificial Intelligence*. Los Altos, CA: Morgan Kaufmann, 1987.

15. Guilford, J. P. *Psychometric Methods*. New York: McGraw-Hill, 1954.

16. Hayes-Roth, F., Waterman, D. A., and Lenat, D. B., eds. *Building Expert Systems*. Reading, MA: Addison-Wesley, 1983.

17. Keller, R. *Expert System Technology: Development and Application*. Englewood Cliffs, NJ: Yourdon Press, 1987.

18. Klein, G. A., and Brezovic, C. P. "Evaluation of Expert Systems." In *Defense Applications of Artificial Intelligence,* edited by S. J. Andriole and G. W. Hopple. Lexington, MA: D. C. Heath Co., 1987.

19. Kline, P. J., and Dolins, S. B. *Choosing Architectures for Expert Systems: Final Report, RADC-TR-85-192*. Rome Air Development Center, Griffiss Air Force Base, Rome, NY, 1985.

20. Laird, J. E., Newell, A., and Rosenbloom, P. S. "SOAR: An Architecture for General Intelligence." *Artificial Intelligence* 33 (1987).

21. Lenat, D. B. "The Nature of Heuristics." *Artificial Intelligence* 19 (1982): 189–249.

22. Liebowitz, J. "Useful Approach for Evaluating Expert Systems." *Expert Systems* 3 (1986): 86–95.

23. McDermott, J. *R1: A Rule-based Configurer of Computer Systems: Report CMU-CS-80-119*. Pittsburgh, PA: Carnegie-Mellon University, 1980.

24. Neches, R., Swartout, W. R., and Moore, J. D. "Enhanced Maintenance and Explanation of Expert Systems through Explicit Models of Their Development." *IEEE Transactions on Software Engineering* 11 (1985): 1337–1351.

25. Newell, A. "Physical Symbol System." *Cognitive Science* 4 (1980): 135–183.

26. Newell, A. "The Knowledge Level." *Artificial Intelligence* 18 (1982): 87–127.

27. Nguyen, T. A. "Verifying Consistency of Production Systems." In *Proceedings of the Third Conference on Artificial Intelligence Applications*. Kissimmee, FL, 1987, pp. 4–8.

28. Nguyen, T. A., Perkins, W. A., Laffey, T. J., and Pecora, D. "Knowledge Base Verification." *AI Magazine* 8 (1987): 69–75.

29. Politakis, P. G. "Using Empirical Analysis to Refine Expert System Knowledge Bases." Ph.D. dissertation, Rutgers University, 1983.

30. Prerau, D. S. "Selection of an Appropriate Domain for an Expert System." *AI Magazine* 6 (1985): 26–30.

31. Pressman, R. S. *Software Engineering*. 2d ed. New York: McGraw-Hill, 1987.

32. Rich, C., and Waters, R. C., eds. *Artificial Intelligence and Software Engineering*. Los Altos, CA: Morgan Kaufmann, 1986.

33. Richardson, K. "Workshop on Verification and Validation of Knowledge-based Systems: Part 1, Overview and Meeting Summary." *NASA Workshop*. Moffett Field, CA: NASA/Ames Research Center, 1987, pp. 285–296.

34. Richardson, K., and Wong, C. "Knowledge Based Verification and Validation as Related to Automation of Space Station Subsystems: Rationale for a Knowledge Based System Lifecycle." *NASA Workshop*. Moffett Field, CA: NASA/Ames Research Center, 1987, pp. 306–311.

35. Richer, M. H. *An Evaluation of Expert System Development Tools, Report KSL 85-19*. Palo Alto, CA: Stanford University, 1986.

36. Rothenberg, J., Paul, J., Kameny, I., Kipps, J. R., and Swenson, M. *Evaluating Expert System Tools: Report R-3542-DARPA*. Santa Monica, CA: Rand Corporation, 1987.

37. Shortliffe, E. H. *Computer-based Medical Consultations: MYCIN*. New York: Elsevier, 1976.

38. Smith, R. G. "On the Development of Commercial Expert Systems." *AI Magazine* 5 (1984): 61–73.

39. Stachowitz, R. A., Chang, C. L., Stock, T. S., and Combs, J. B. "Building Validation Tools for Knowledge-based Systems." *Proceedings of the Space Operations and Robotics (SOAR) Workshop*. Houston, 1987.

40. Stachowitz, R. A., and Combs, J. B. "Validation of Expert Systems." *Proceedings of the Hawaii International Conference on Systems Sciences*. Kona, HI, 1987, pp. 686–695.

41. Stachowitz, R. A., Combs, J. B., and Chang, C. L. "Validation of Knowledge-based Systems." *Proceedings of the Second AIAA/NASA/USAF Symposium on Automation, Robotics and Advanced Computing for the National Space Program*. Arlington, VA, 1987.

42. Szolovits, P. "Expert Systems Tools and Techniques." In *AI in the 1980s and Beyond: An MIT Survey*, edited by W. E. L. Grimson and R. S. Patil, pp. 43–74. Cambridge, MA: MIT Press, 1987.

43. Torgerson, W. S. *Theory and Methods of Scaling*. New York: Wiley, 1958.

44. Weiss, S. M., and Kulikowski, C. A. *A Practical Guide to Designing Expert Systems.* Totowa, NJ: Rowman and Allanheld, 1984.

45. Zaklad, A., Deimler, J. D., Iavecchia, H. P. and Stokes, J. M. *Multisensor Correlation and TACCO Workload in Representative ASW and ASUW Environments: Final Report, 1753A.* Willow Grove, PA: Analytics, 1982.

46. Zualkernan, I., Tasi, W. T., and Volovik, D. "Expert Systems and Software Engineering: Ready for Marriage?" *IEEE Expert* 1 (1986): 24–31.

Structural Considerations in Expert System Development and Implementation

Introducing AI into the Systems Development Model

Daniel A. De Salvo

INTRODUCTION

A reasonable definition of a knowledge-based system would be "an information system that uses design paradigms and software techniques derived from research into artificial intelligence." As Figure 12–1 shows, knowledge-based systems are a part of artificial intelligence and include natural language processing and expert systems but exclude robotics. This chapter discusses the practical implications of adjusting the systems development process to make use of these AI applications and addresses the need for different design tools, programming skills, and management methods.

One of the great paradoxes of the artificial intelligence world is its lack of a sound definition for either "knowledge" or "intelligence." For the purposes of this chapter, we could define knowledge as "an abstract problem-solving method that acts on information in the way an algorithm works on data." But it is more reasonable to admit that in practice knowledge is most often defined by the scheme—e.g., rules, frames, and objects—used to represent it.

We shall consider some examples of knowledge-based systems and walk through their effect on each stage of a simple software development model (SDM). For discussion purposes we view the SDM as a mechanism for controlling a software project, and we borrow control theory concepts to describe the dynamics of adopting this new technology.

It should be noted that we do not advocate any particular software development model. Rather, our purpose is to give a flavor of the changes that can occur when knowledge-based systems are introduced into an SDM in general rather than a specific SDM.

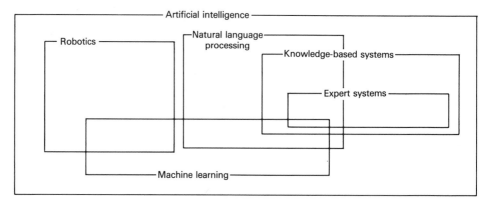

Figure 12–1   The artificial intelligence arena.

The Software Development Model

We can define a software development model as having at least three character-istics:

1. An ordered set of steps to be performed by a software development team.
2. An agreement between the development team and its customers as to what the software will do.
3. A schedule for completing each of the steps to the satisfaction of the cus-tomers.

In addition, we need to establish at least two kinds of guidelines for each step of the model:

1. *Transition criteria* [2] for deciding when to move from one step to the next.
2. *Development standards* that describe how the development team may complete each step.

In practice, the software development model becomes a *management* program for controlling the development of a *computer* program. Orr [1] describes the process of defining a computer program in terms of control theory.

Metzger [5] points out a list of changes that may alter the course of a software project, including requirements changes, design changes, new technology, changes in people, and the need to correct mistakes. As Figure 12–2 shows, we can use the concept of feedback to describe how a project team controls these changes. The simple feedback mechanism controls a step or substep of a software project. The project team repeatedly adjusts the execution of each step to bring it into line with the SDM's transition criteria and development standards. When it meets these standards, the project moves on to the next step.

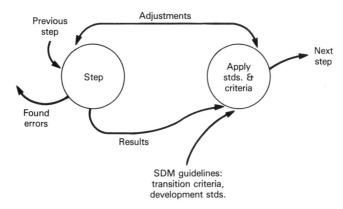

Figure 12–2   Feedback within the SDM.

Performing feedback in the manner shown in the figure requires a knowledge of existing SDM transition criteria and development standards. In many cases, existing guidelines may not apply to the new technology. For example, U.S. Steel benchmarks are ill suited to many AI applications. It follows that ill-fitting guidelines must be modified in order to properly control the course of a software project.

As Figure 12–3 shows, the introduction of a new technological tool, be it a design paradigm, programming language, or vendor product, also requires the software development team to adopt new skills. For example, AI's nonprocedural programming languages can seem alien to the programmer who encounters them for the first time.

Sample SDM

Almost any software development organization will construct a software development model or adapt one to its own purposes. Boehm [2] points out that the data processing industry has gone through an evolutionary progression of approaches to modeling software development.

The skeletal SDM we shall examine has three steps which, in one form or another, are common to most SDMs:

- *System specification,* i.e., determining what the system should do.
- *Software design,* i.e., defining the functions the system is to perform in order to satisfy the specification.
- *System implementation,* i.e., building the system.

Every SDM must have rules that govern its use. Let us assume the following rules for our small sample model:

- *Feedback between each step and a prior step.* For example, the system implementation step might reveal flaws in the system definition. The systems

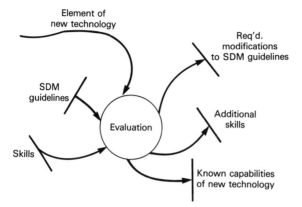

Figure 12–3   Evaluation of a new technology.

developers would then have to correct these flaws and consider their impact on the rest of the project.

- *Iteration of a step.* Iteration is often required to fix program bugs or to add increasing capability to an emerging system.
- *Validation of the product of a step.* For example, most system developers want their customers to agree with the system definition before starting on the system specification.

Such rules, of course, would be documented many times over on a real project. Since each change in the rules or their application multiplies the amount of documentation, we might safely measure the effects of a new technology in terms of the number of pounds of paper produced. However, for now, we can assume that such documentation exists and we shall describe it only in as much detail as is absolutely necessary.

New Tools For Building New Program Structures

Every step of the way, building a computer system is a balance between what we want to do and what we can do with the tools at hand. The AI community has given us a set of new conceptual tools, programming languages, and development environments that permit us to use new kinds of structures in building programs.

Design paradigms.   Webster's New World Dictionary defines "paradigm" as "a pattern, example, or model." Extending this definition, we can say that most KBS paradigms implement a *cognitive model*—that is, they reflect a theory of how human beings process information. Among the better known design paradigms are the following:

- *Rule-based programming systems,* also known as production systems, in which heuristics, i.e., rules of thumb, appear as IF-THEN rules.

- *Logic programming,* in which the syntax of the language implements predicate calculus.

- *Object-oriented programming systems,* or OOPSs, in which the basic elements are an object that combines a data structure, procedural programs that act on the information stored in the structure, and a syntax by means of which objects exchange "messages" as input and output.

- *Frames,* also known as frame representation languages, in which the basic element is a data structure with one or more slots (fields); each field may hold data of a complex type and, perhaps more importantly, may point to a program that calculates or binds data into the field at program run time.

- *Neural networks,* which model the adaptive behavior of neurons and are usually implemented as parallel systems of neurons with multiple, weighted relationships. Altering the relationships (connections) between the neurons and modifying their weights modifies the system's behavior.

Programming languages and shells. While applications have been written in almost every programming language, some languages have historically been associated with AI or KBS development projects, and others are simply convenient tools for their development. Lisp falls into the former category, while C falls into the latter. Languages like Prolog (for logic programming), Smalltalk (an OOPS language), OPS-5 (for production rules) and C++ (another OOPS language) were developed around specific programming paradigms.

Shells, on the other hand, are complete applications development environments, in the same vein as data-base management systems. Typically, they incorporate one or more AI languages, at least one major design paradigm, a programmer's workbench complete with editor, debugging tools and software utilities, and a large library of functions that the developer can include in an application. KEE from Intellicorp, ADS from AION, ESE from IBM, and KBMS from AI Corp. are examples of shells.

The freewheeling AI research environment has also developed some excellent development platforms. Lisp workstations, for example, led the market in providing programmers with windows, expanded keyboards, mice, and graphics. Some languages, such as Smalltalk, can be very hard to work with outside of their native environment.

KNOWLEDGE-BASED SYSTEMS AND SYSTEM DEFINITION

Our sample SDM defines the system specification step as the place where we identify what a system should do. Obviously, one cannot go on to the next step of designing a system until the right people agree that the system has been correctly defined. When they do agree, these agreements form the system definition's *transition criteria.* Most SDM implementations identify a series of documents that describe the agreements in detail and consider the system definition complete when the documents are finished and responsible individuals have signed them. The agreements typically start with a set of functional requirements—the users' information processing needs that the system should fulfill—and address at least (1) system behavior, including inputs, outputs, and performance; and (2) operational constraints, such as the host computer system for the application.

Each agreement, of course, rests on an organization's standards for systems development. The greatest impact of a new technology on systems definition may occur in the act of trying to identify or change the applicable systems development standards.

In theory, a system definition should identify what an organization wants a system to do. The system design step should define how a system will perform its functions. In practice, both the developers and their customers must understand the problem to be solved and, in a way appropriate to each of their roles, the capabilities of various data processing tools.

The application of AI—or, for that matter, almost any other new data processing tool—introduces uncertainty into the environment. The result can be an unbalanced, ineffective, or inefficient system. It is therefore wise to review a new technology in terms of its capabilities and to constrain its use in such a way as to limit the effects of its shortcomings.

System Behavior

A system's behavior is normally judged by at least three criteria:

- Performance, i.e., how fast it operates.
- Inputs and
- Outputs.

The performance of conventional systems can usually be addressed by measuring such things as keyboard response time, data throughput capability, and accuracy of data retrieval. Of course, these measures apply to knowledge-based systems as well. However, knowledge-based systems often use and develop much more abstract information than their conventional counterparts. As the following example shows, a system's performance measures should match the way it handles inputs, and a KBS application may require different performance measures than its conventional counterpart.

Example 12–1: A limited use of KBS tools

Figure 12–4 describes a real-time control system which manages an air conditioner, approximating a desired room temperature. The system samples the room temperature and responds once for every two samples taken. The response is a simple adjustment to the air conditioner.

As Figure 12–5 shows, the combination of air conditioner and control system permits the room temperature to oscillate within the range of comfort. Incidentally, the figure is for discussion purposes only; the external temperature gradient it shows

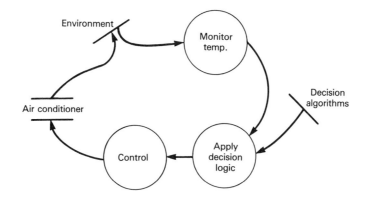

Figure 12–4   A simple control system.

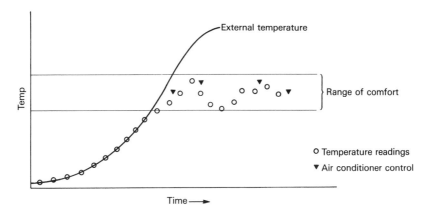

Figure 12–5   Behavior of temperature control system.

would imply, in a real system, either an absurdly slow sampling rate or a fire in the building.

The standards to follow in specifying a system like that of Figure 12–4 might read as follows:

- *Speed.* Sampling every *t* moments, issuing a control response every 2*t* moments.
- *Behavior.* A simple positive or negative feedback response to maintain temperature within the desired range of comfort.
- *Data handling.* Simple inputs at a low granularity.

Extending the example further, suppose that the system's users would like to improve the system's performance by narrowing its range of comfort. In other words, suppose they have changed their functional requirements for the system. And suppose also that they have identified heuristics—rules—for more accurately controlling the system by looking at temperature trends and implemented these rules in a prototype KBS, with results as shown in Figure 12–6. Thus far, the KBS tools have proven useful:

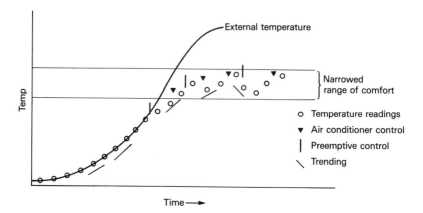

Figure 12–6 General controls interleaved with heuristic controls.

the system users were able to build a prototype that not only verified their assumptions, but also provided a working example of how to apply the assumptions. The effect on the system development process has therefore been positive, especially if—as is often the case—building the prototype helped speed up the job of defining the new requirements.

But now, consider the decision: the system developers have reviewed the heuristics and have determined that they can, with a reasonable level of effort, modify the existing system to incorporate the prototype's behavior. And they feel they can do it with conventional techniques. So, provided that they can maintain the heuristics in the system, the system developers can produce a conventional system which is indistinguishable from a true KBS. In that case, unless they want to drastically change their concept of the system—e.g., to add rules that would examine the temperature gradient and set off a fire alarm—the users should agree to a conventional implementation.

The point of the example is brought out effectively by Roger Schank [3], who makes an interesting case for distinguishing between software that has the same output as a cognitive process, such as numerical programs that play chess, and software that actually processes information in the same way as a human being. If all we need to do is create a system that performs a particular function—what Schank calls a "product" orientation—then the decision of whether to use a knowledge-based or conventional system comes down to picking the type that is both easiest to build and easiest to maintain. For example:

- Implementing a KBS may require some surface changes to an existing system—e.g., letting the KBS tap into its data sampling.
- Modifying an existing conventional solution so that it behaves in the same way as the KBS may require the developers to change large portions of the conventional system's code.
- Implementing a KBS could require a significant investment in training if the KBS tools are unfamiliar to the developers, whereas the developers probably have years of experience with the existing tools.

Operations

The system developer who wants to bring a new technology on-line has three options: ignore the current operational standards, change the standards, or make the new technology fit the standards. The first option almost always leads to a dead end: the prototype, which is potentially useful, may die because it ignored the standards. This was a common fate of early knowledge-based systems which were developed on specialized Lisp machines, especially where the organization's standard computing environment was, for example, an IBM mainframe with 370 architecture.

The second option is normal in the course of events: data processing groups constantly rearrange their standards to accommodate new technologies. Taken as a whole, the number of dollars invested in new computer technologies is very large and represents a substantial part of the corporate budget. However, much of this change adds to standards in order to fit technologies that have no prior organizational niches. KBS applications, on the other hand, tend to appear as evolutions of existing systems. The attempt to have existing standards evolve can pose particularly thorny issues in a number of areas, including the following:

- *User interface standards.* For example, the standard corporate terminal may not work with the shell that the developers feel they need.
- *Data-base access regulations.* In the real world, administrators are reluctant—and not without reason—to let an unproven application modify the data in their data bases. Even allowing an application to read an organizaton's data may require the system developers to prove that the new system will not injure the performance of the existing one.
- *Interprocess communication with existing systems.* A KBS may operate on a different time scale than does an existing system, making communication among processes slower.
- *Hardware and operating system platform.* In the computer business, this can be a monstrous problem. Any new software technology takes time to spread from its original platform to another, which means that an organization has to (1) have the right software technology and hardware, (2) buy the right software technology and hardware, or (3) wait in order to use a new software technology.
- *Programming languages.* Just about the time an organization settles on the programming languages it is willing to support, a new one comes along. Then programmers have to learn the new language, designers have to understand its limitations, the organization has to arrange for licensing of the language, and somebody has to pay for it.
- *Data-base standards.* This problem is actually diminishing in today's environment, as more data-base vendors develop standardized methods of accessing their data.

The system developer is almost stuck in a "black box" with these problems: existing standards go in one side, the developers' proposed solutions come out the other, and the whole thing starts all over again. In a slightly different context, Metzger [5] points out that the interactions between the characteristics of a system can be defined by

$$I = \frac{E(E-1)}{2}$$

where I represents the number of potential interactions and E is the number of characteristics. If the system under consideration is a system of standards, then E approaches $T(i)$, where T is a type of standard—e.g., program documentation—and i is a particular instance of that standard—e.g., a standard for the use of data-flow diagrams.

In practice, most organizations end up combining the second and third options. Both, however, take time and require compromise. For example, KBS applications written in Lisp did not enter the corporate world in any numbers until the language became available on standard business computers.

KNOWLEDGE-BASED SYSTEMS AND SOFTWARE DESIGN

Artificial intelligence has given us a number of new kinds of program structures with which to build software. Let us examine the interplay between these structures and our existing design tools.

We can start with the premise that a computer program is a model, in the same sense that a mathematical equation or a recipe is a model: known inputs produce known outputs, and we can examine the model to understand why.

Conceptually, a design is a higher level (more abstract) model than a program. If we build our computer program from a sound and verified design, we vastly improve the odds that the program will be successful. Also, it usually costs a good deal less to make a design than to construct an actual program. This being the case, we can treat the cost of the design as the price we pay for reducing the risk inherent in building the application. Boehm [6] clearly establishes the economics of this relationship.

Now, the economics make sense only if we are able to produce an accurate design. Unfortunately, however, not all knowledge-based programming techniques lend themselves to current design methods. For the rest, we have several options:

1. Don't use new structures that don't fit existing design methods.
2. Develop design techniques that apply.
3. Don't do a design.
4. Pretend to do a design in order to get funding for the project.

Obviously, option 1 carries the least risk but isn't very interesting, and option 2 is outside the scope of most software development organizations' charters. Option 4 carries the most risk: not only could the development fail, but the credibility of the design team could as well.

That brings us to option 3, which has to be evaluated on its economic merits. As the following example shows, this option is viable whenever the cost of a design approximates the cost of development.

Example 12–2: A deliberately difficult OOPS

Consider an object-oriented programming system (OOPS) that simulates a fairly complex hydraulic system. The basic module is an object, which consists of a data structure with fields (slots) to which programs (called methods) are attached. Some of the different types of objects of the system are pipes, valves, and pumps.

The individual programs consist of object definitions, each of which includes a description of the data structure, the names of the programs attached to each structure, and the scheme for executing the programs. Each object is accorded its own process.

Triggers (demons) execute programs based on a change of state in a data field. Allowable types of demons include those that fire methods when a slot value is created, modified, deleted, or used.

Objects communicate by sending each other messages, which are analogous to program calls. However, all objects are visible to all other objects, i.e., messages are not encapsulated.

To make the problem even more difficult, suppose that some of the objects are attached to asynchronous events. For example, a valve might respond to the user's inputs at the keyboard.

Being asynchronous, this system does not have a definable order to its events. Consequently, the number of states in which the system can exist may be permuted by the number of possible asynchronous occurrences. There would be, for example, a large number of possible combinations of fluid levels, valve settings, and pump cycles in the system at any given time.

If we were really foolish, we could let the objects dynamically clone themselves. That is, rather than queuing up to compete for an object, messages would automatically get their own copy of the object. Thus, the system might start generating new valves and pipes on its own. This, of course, could theoretically result in an infinitely large number of possible system states.

Even in this radical case, existing object-oriented design techniques can be effective. However, detailed descriptive techniques, such as structure charts, are only partially applicable. For example, the utility of a PDL (program description language) for describing an OOPS is minimal, since, in an OOPS, the description of the object is the program.

Finally, certain techniques that may be very useful may be outside the scope of the existing design standards. For instance, OOPS usually provide for inheritance. Thus, an individual object can inherit the characteristics of the class of objects to which it belongs. As an example, the description of the object "temperature gauge" would not have to specify that the gauge has a dial readout if that was already defined for the class "gauges." But the graphical and procedural standards for defining these relationships may simply not exist at a given organization.

We can limit the risk of option 3 by taking several preliminary steps:

1. Identify the knowledge-based tool that may be appropriate to the software application.
2. From these tools, separate the ones that are amenable to design techniques.
3. Define the components which would be built with the remaining tools.
4. Evaluate the risk of building the components without a design.

Again, Boehm makes a strong argument for prototyping, which we can consider to be a special case of option 3.

Some Theorization About the Designability of KBS Programs

Most of our available system design tools rest on the premise of structured programming that it is possible to build good programs with only three basic types of construct: *control, sequence,* and *repetition.* This works very well as long as we can predict at least the possible states of a system [7]. The concept is particularly dependent on the idea of *chronology,* that is, that processes begin and end in some order.

However, as Example 12–2 shows, some AI design constructs are basically *asynchronous* in nature: processes exist autonomously and may exhibit apparently random behavior, and programs may treat other programs as data. We cannot treat such systems exhaustively, although we may be able to understand their behavior empirically. For example, for anything except a very small OOPS, the process of exhaustively mapping out the possible system states would probably be impractical.

However, we can make use of empirical methods, particularly prototypes, to design nondeterministic knowledge-based systems. When an organization can afford to risk some development money, and the potential payoffs from the application are great enough, building a knowledge-based system incrementally may be worthwhile. Object-oriented programming systems in particular tend to have graphical interfaces that make prototyping both fast and effective.

We can also impose, if not a classical structure, at least some organization on these systems as follows.

- *Build small, discrete OOPS applications that can communicate with other applications and each other through "gateway" objects.* For example, a steam plant model might consist of a pumping subsystem, a heating subsystem, and a routing subsystem.
- *Limit the interface between the system and other software, particularly by defining a small number of "gateway" objects and limiting the number of states they can display.* For example, we might provide only one user-controlled valve and one gauge for each discrete application.

• *Rank system messages in order of their occurrence.* For example, an object can't tell the object called "printer" to print something unless "printer" has signaled that it is through with its last job.

These items combine to limit our risk. The basic rationale behind rapid prototyping is that it is easier, and therefore less expensive, to build some applications without a lengthy design effort.

Boehm [6] points out (in a somewhat different context) that we can apply Bayesian principles to evaluating prototypes. As we grow more certain—or at least statistically less uncertain—about the behavior of our OOPS components, we can make better decisions about using them and incur less risk in the process.

Even for those applications that are truly deterministic, the usefulness of a given design technique may be in question. The following example shows that, even when we can define a system exhaustively, some components of the system might be more properly defined with a combination of high-level design tools and a prototype.

Example 12–3: A conventional knowledge-based system

Figure 12–7 shows a proposed hybrid system in which the customers want to add heuristics to an existing data base. The existing system contains stored search queries which the users can access by referencing a label. Unlike the earlier example of a control system, the users do not have a small, stable area of interest for their heuristics.

In this example, we can see a typical problem with KBS shells. Even when they have facilities for communicating with other programs, such shells tend to be monolithic. That is, a KBS shell has a great deal of internal software that the user and even the developer never work with. Basically, a developer takes the facilities of the shell and works with or around them to the best degree possible. A similar problem exists with data-base management systems.

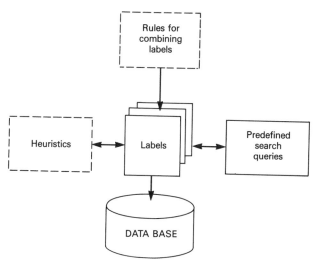

Figure 12–7 Customer requirements in Example 12–3.

The users' objectives for the new component are as follows:

- Continue to make use of the existing system's capability to store data-base queries under a callable label. For example, the command "hotpicks" might expand to "average_return better than n% for quarter > current_quarter − 4 to quarter = current_quarter."
- Add heuristics that are callable by label, and that can be used to influence the results of a stored query. For example, the command "bearish" might read "if current_gold_price > (110 ∗ dollar_pound exchange) then average_return = (.9 average_return)."
- Provide the ability to call any combination of labels to interact with each other during a given session.

For example, the customers would like to be able to ask the system for "hotpicks" with a "bearish" viewpoint—and yes, the query and the rule are both trivial examples.

The major constraints on the new component are the following:

- The system must run on a particular brand of computer and a given operating system. The customers simply cannot provide any other resources.
- The only KBS tool available on the given platform is a shell that provides a production-rule programming language. The rules of the language can be referenced by labels, and a rule can call a label. For example, the rule "bearpicks" might read

```
If hotpicks and bearish
Then <generate some report>
```

However, calling multiple (stored search query) labels within a single rule will cause multiple passes through the data.

After having reviewed the customers' requirements, the developers identified two critical factors which will determine whether they use a KBS or algorithmic approach to building the system:

- *Performance.* The developers have determined that they can afford the processing overhead of the KBS shell, but multiple passes through the data are unacceptable.
- *Maintainability.* The existing system is complex enough; the developers want to avoid increasing maintenance problems wherever possible.

The developers have also determined that the actual number of individual labels—for search queries and for heuristics—is fairly small.

We can extend the example by having the syntax of the shell's rule language force the developers to create one rule to call each label. This restriction is partially offset by the fact that one label can reference several other labels. Thus, by calling a compound label from a rule, the system can make multiple cuts against the data base in one pass.

With the preceding in mind, the developers face three classic alternatives:

1. Build as much of the new component as possible in the KBS shell.

2. Use the KBS shell for writing rules and an algorithmic approach for the rest.

3. Write the entire application algorithmically.

Let us examine each of these alternatives in turn.

Alternative 1: Use the KBS shell as much as possible

Figure 12–8 shows a brute-force KBS implementation with one compound label for each possible combination of individual labels. Even removing order as a consideration—in other words, "bearish‖hotpicks" would be the same as "hotpicks‖bearish"—the total number of individual and compound labels comes out to

$$T = \sum_{K=1}^{J} \frac{J!}{(J-K)!K!}$$

where T is the total number of labels, J is the number of individual labels, and K is the number of individual queries referenced by a given compound label.

For the purposes of this discussion, we can assume that the combinations of labels are all of the form ⟨label⟩ BOOLEAN ⟨label⟩, where BOOLEAN defines a relation like AND or OR. Otherwise, T becomes T^n, where n is the number of different allowable Boolean expressions.

Changing the contents of any one individual label—e.g., modifying the threshold value for "hotpicks"—would be a single coding change, since the compound labels

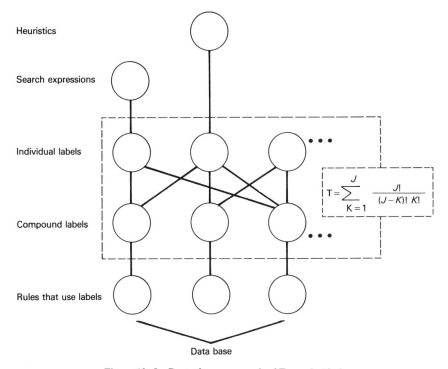

Figure 12–8   Brute-force approach of Example 12–3.

refer only to the name "hotpicks." Replacing or adding a new label, however, would require changes to every expression that referenced the label. This would be tedious, but require minimal skill with the KBS shell: generating the permutations of labels and their paired rules would be a relatively simple editing task.

Alternative 2: KBS rules with external query handling

Knowledge-based systems typically maintain a very complex environment in active memory that is hard to manage and must be painstakingly updated any time control passes between modules. This may put a performance price on moving from one function to another, particularly between a KBS module and an external, conventional program.

Figure 12–9 describes the interaction between the mostly KBS application, the stored search expressions, and a data base. Even though the application has some basic inefficiencies, it is probably as efficient as the KBS shells' compiler will allow it to be. By contrast, Figure 12–10 describes the interaction between the KBS shell and external search programs. Since we made the assumption that the KBS shell provides a direct interface to the data base, the hybrid of Figure 12–10 probably doesn't buy much execution speed.

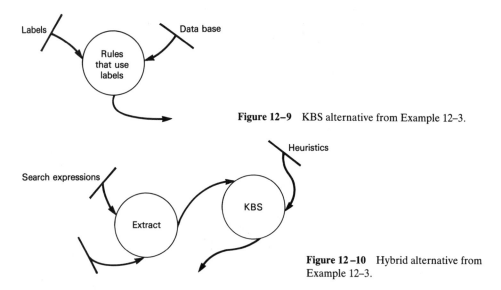

Figure 12–9   KBS alternative from Example 12–3.

Figure 12–10   Hybrid alternative from Example 12–3.

It could be argued that maintaining the hybrid system would be easier than maintaining a shell application and its attendant overhead and that it would be less space as well. Most of the space occupied by current KBS shells is fixed, and individual rules or objects take up very little room by comparison. In view of this, the decision between alternatives 1 and 2 comes down to maintainability, which is a function of (1) *complexity,* i.e., the number of associated elements that have to be changed anytime an individual element is changed, and (2) *difficulty,* i.e., the effort involved in changing each element. The comparison can only be made on an application-by-application basis.

Alternative 3: Re-create the KBS facilities for handling heuristics

The closer a system like this comes to the functionality of the KBS, the less likely it is that it will perform any better. In any case, it is axiomatic to good design to avoid reinventing the wheel.

In this example, then, regardless of the alternative, most of the software design can be accommodated with existing design tools. The behavior of the rules, for example, is deterministic, and the relationships between the various system components can be described in a structured manner—for example, with data-flow diagrams and structure charts. However, an attempt to exhaustively define each rule and expression in the design would not be a useful exercise. Consequently, the developers would have to get a waiver from any system design standards that call for such an exhaustive description of the system.

KNOWLEDGE-BASED SYSTEMS AND SYSTEM IMPLEMENTATION

So far, we have looked at three examples of knowledge-based systems. As Figure 12–11 shows, each has taken a slightly different path through the systems development methodology presented in this chapter. Tables 12–1 and 12–2 highlight the relationships between these three examples and the SDM. In combination, they demonstrate the basic issue that faces a system developer in implementing a new technology: at some point the familiar frame of reference breaks down. The fact that the examples all made use of prototypes shouldn't be surprising: people have used working models to figure out problems for a long time.

At this point, the implementer may still be a computer scientist but must behave as a craftsman. Therefore, the rest of this chapter looks at the implementa-

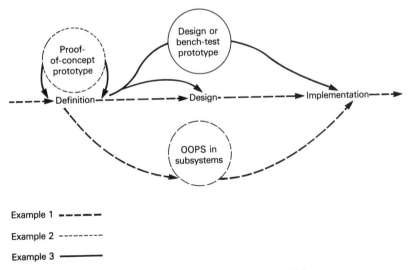

Example 1 ‑ ‑ ‑ ‑ ‑

Example 2 ‑ ‑ ‑ ‑ ‑ ‑ ‑ ‑

Example 3 ───────

Figure 12–11   Sample systems and the SDM.

Table 12–1   Definition-step effects.

	Definition		
	Example 1	Example 2	Example 3
Feedback from design	((Revised specifications))		Prototype
Critical technique	Prototype	Prototype	Description
Critical transition criteria	Prove prototype	Prototype is functional specification	Approval of functional requirements
Effect on development strategy	Augment requirements with prototype	Empirical acceptance	Broader functional requirements

Table 12–2   Design-step effects.

	Design		
	Example 1	Example 2	Example 3
Feedback from implementation	((Errors in design))		
Critical technique	Classical design	Subsetting of system	Mixed prototype and classical design
Critical transition criteria	Design acceptance	Empirical acceptance	Prove system's maintainability
Effect on development strategy	Use of proof-of-concept prototype	Waiver	Use of bench-test prototype

tion aspects of KBS tools and processing hardware and provides some comments regarding the use of prototypes as an empirical aid to systems implementation.

Proof-of-Concept Prototypes

As shown in Example 1, a proof-of-concept prototype is a tool for pinning down functional and design specifications. Figure 12–12 provides a typical checklist for evaluating a proof-of-concept prototype. Such an evaluation may seem trivial, but ultimately the systems developer will have to present some justification for the prototype and defend the conclusions based on the prototype. As the checklist shows, the key questions to ask are: (1) What specific problems are addressed by the

(1) Cost
- Time, personnel, computer resources, etc.

(2) Client
- Immediate (e.g., design team)
- Ultimate (e.g., for main project)

(3) Benefits
- Project to be supported
- Cost/time savings to be incurred from project
- Basic needs to be fulfilled by the prototype
- Validate key assumptions for a project, or validate/correct project resource estimates?
- Other projects affected

(4) Major concepts
- Working hypothesis
- Specific premises to be proven

(5) Major results
- Specific outputs required from project
- Specific criteria for evaluating project

(6) Approach
- Tool/language of choice
- Knowledge representation scheme
- Project team members and their duties
- Key management controls (e.g., change control board contacts)

(7) Action items
- Major deliverables
- Key deadlines
- Pressing issues

(8) References
  Pointers to other projects, documents, standards, etc.

Figure 12–12   Checklist for proof-of-concept prototypes.

prototype? (2) What is the scheme used to exercise the prototype and evaluate the findings? and (3) What are the business and design points supported by the prototype?

Bench-Test Prototypes

A bench-test prototype is a working but not optimized version of a major system component. A bench-test prototype can be used to validate design concepts and may evolve from a proof-of-concept prototype.

In Example 2, the entire system could be considered a bench-test, or series of bench-test, prototypes. Ultimately, to put the system of Example 3 into production, a major amount of empirical work—e.g., iterative refinement—would be necessary.

Bench-test prototypes have several key characteristics:

- They pay for themselves, typically by saving time on a project. Even in less radical circumstances than those of Example 2, a working model of one part of a final application can be used to reduce the amount of time needed to explain a system's design to the people who have to approve it.

- The inputs, outputs, CPU, foundation software, and other elements present in the final application are matched as closely as possible in the bench-test prototype. By comparison, the proof-of-concept prototype of Example 1 did not have to run on the same platform as the control system or use a real-time sampling device.

- Proven bench-test software serves at a minimum as a working model for the final code and, preferably, can be incorporated into the final code. Where it would be too expensive or time-consuming to do this, the bench-test software should accurately reflect the algorithms and parameter passing that will be used in the final product. For example, in Example 2, the developers might build and empirically test a series of prototypes in a "user-friendly" graphical OOPS like Smalltalk and then implement each component in C++ as it came on-line.

KBS Processing Hardware

Hardware constraints are rapidly disappearing as KBS software moves out of the AI lab and into commercial use. However, any new technology will take time to propagate from its original platform to other platforms.

KBS hardware constraints fall into two areas: constraints on the development hardware, and constraints on the delivery hardware. The vendors of KBS shells are still struggling to implement their products on a wide range of hardware. In particular, they are trying to get their products out of specialized Lisp environments and into conventional ones.

Until they finish this job, the KBS designer may have a difficult time matching a specific shell to a given CPU. For example:

- ADS from AION currently runs on IBM mainframes and PCs, but does not run on a number of popular workstations and minicomputers, including the VAX.

- KBMS from AI Corp. currently runs only on the IBM mainframe (under VM or MVS/XA).

In order to navigate this archipelago of related but not-quite-compatible products, the systems developer needs to identify at least two critical things:

1. *Whether the development and delivery platforms have to be the same.* For example, a KBS that will integrate with an existing system must fall under the

maintenance procedures associated with that system. The team responsible for maintaining the existing application may find it very difficult to incorporate the KBS into their plans unless both the delivered and prerelease versions are resident on the same CPU.

2. *Any change- or version-control procedures that the KBS software development project will have to accommodate.* For example, a KBS component might be included in the plans for a large application. The individuals responsible for integration and migration testing of new versions of the existing system might be very distressed to find that the only documentation for the KBS was a PC prototype.

KBS Tools

Knowledge-based systems solve abstract problems. Consequently, they are often built in languages designed to express techniques such as reasoning by analogy and heuristics. In general, there is no "best" KBS language, any more than there is a "best" computer language or even a "best" human language. As the following examples show, each has its vices and virtues.

Lisp is a language rich in symbolic constructs. Its run-time binding of variables makes it very easy for the programmer to establish indirections in great depth. Lisp is also a recursive language, and many of its basic constructs, such as the COND statement for looping, optimize this capability. Being about the same age as Fortran, Lisp has had plenty of time to mature, and, with the advent of the Common Lisp standard, any Lisp application may be easily ported to a number of different hardware and operating system platforms.

Nonetheless, current Lisp offerings have their drawbacks. At the top of this list are the large load modules they generate: almost all Lisp implementations require more memory than most data processing organizations are used to spending on a language. Also, the behavior of Lisp is foreign to many programmers who have been trained on languages like Pascal and PL/1.

Rule-based languages, or production rule systems, are explicitly designed to model data relationships. They also have the advantage of being nonprocedural descriptions. In theory, the programmer has only to define the relationship between two data elements, and the system's underlying inference engine will handle the rest.

In practice, however, the syntax of many production rule systems can be confusing to the programmer who is used to a procedural language. It can be difficult to remember that an IF-THEN rule implies a causal relationship, but will not necessarily execute a process. Also, most production rule systems may mix procedural and nonprocedural elements in such a way that the programmer has to take into account some implicit—and therefore obscure—semantics of the language. For example, many shells provide an arcane agenda mechanism for applying rules; the programmers' adjustments to this agenda combine with the arrangement of the rules to determine the order in which they are applied. This is a powerful capability, but it can cause a programmer to plead for a plain CASE statement.

Logic programming languages—and here we mean primarily Prolog—are data-base languages. They define relations, primary and subsidiary, between data elements. Prolog is an implementation of the predicate calculus in software. These languages are powerful, dynamic, and direct tools for solving many different kinds of problems.

On the negative side, logic programming languages arguably have a syntax which is foreign at best to most conventional programmers. Ultimately, they suffer from the same problem as rule-based languages: a theoretically nonprocedural construct is very difficult to implement on a computer with von Neumann architecture.

Frames, or systems that combine a frame data structure with a programming language, are a classical construct of artificial intelligence. Frames and such relatives as scripts are excellent tools for describing symbolic relations between data variables. They are also the basic data structure used in many object-oriented programming systems.

Perhaps the greatest problem with frames is that they are so much like conventional data structures. For example, they lend themselves nicely to entity relationship diagrams and other data design techniques. This, however, can mislead the implementer into wasting their capabilities, or worse, into misunderstanding some subtlety of their behavior. Also, frames basically came out of the Lisp environment, so that frame implementations in conventional languages tend either to be more limited than their Lisp progenitors or to require significant amounts of software to give them Lisp-like functionality.

OOPSs, or object-oriented programming systems, are truly powerful modeling tools when connected to a graphical interface, particularly for creating empirical models of mechanical systems. There are even some efficient OOPS implementations, such as C++.

Although an object-oriented system can be very difficult to map, it is not fair to characterize all OOPS applications as difficult to design or debug. In fact, with a proper regard for their capabilities, just the opposite may be true: OOPS systems just require a different approach from the system developer. Their biggest drawback may be the time it takes a conventional programmer to unlearn old thought patterns and learn new ones.

Neural networks implement one or more major paradigms for modeling the adaptive behavior of biological neurons. They can improve their ability to perform basic functions, usually based on pattern recognition. In effect, they are primitive learning devices. The various implementations now in use are based on mathematically sound principles and hold out a great deal of promise for future applications.

The current crop of neural net implementations present the system developer with two problems. First, neural networks are inherently parallel systems, but since most computers are not, the implementations must either simulate parallelism at some cost to resources or make use of specialized hardware. Second, the current implementations are based primarily on random connectivity between elements (individual "neurons"); as a result, the implementer may be able to verify a neural network's output but cannot trace a system's flow of control.

SUMMARY

In this chapter, we have used a small systems development model as the framework for discussing some of the practical issues involved in building knowledge-based systems. We have looked at some examples of how knowledge-based systems can escape our traditional design techniques and force the system developer away from the role of engineer or scientist and into the role of craftsman.

The sample SDM we used had three phases: *system specification, system design,* and *system implementation.*

While these do not alone constitute the SDM, they are basic tasks that occur and recur throughout the various real SDM implementations. In additon, we have examined the relationship of knowledge-based systems to the transition criteria that govern moving from step to step of the SDM and to the development standards that govern the execution of each step.

In the section covering system specification, we reviewed some issues involved in defining the behavior and operations of a knowledge-based system. In the section on system design, we outlined some arguments surrounding the use of prototypes and theorized about the "designability" of knowledge-based systems. Finally, in the section on implementation, we summarized the effect of some current KBS implementations on our SDM and covered key implementation aspects of KBS tools, processing hardware, and prototypes.

ACKNOWLEDGMENTS

To my colleagues, Jim Zucco, Gary Weesenborn, Art Benedict, Jock Embry, Jeff Grier, Mike Jones, Jay Liebowitz, Tom Onasch, Lee Scalzott, Brad Utz, and Stan Wozniak who helped, encouraged, and advised me: thanks. To the tireless Ed Moura at Prentice Hall, I owe you one. To my wife Elaine and boys Dominick and Robert, I owe you guys everything.

REFERENCES

1. Orr, Ken. *Structured Requirements Definition.* Topeka, KS: Ken Orr and Associates, 1981.
2. Boehm, Barry. "A Spiral Model of Software Development and Enchancement." *IEEE Computer* 21 (1988).

3. Schank, Roger. *The Cognitive Computer*. Free Press, 1986.

4. De Marco, Tom. *Structured Analysis and System Specification*. New York: Yourdon, 1979.

5. Metzger, Philip W. *Managing a Programmning Project*. Englewood Cliffs, NJ: Prentice-Hall, 1973.

6. Boehm, Barry. *Software Engineering Economics*. Englewood Cliffs, NJ: Prentice-Hall, 1981.

7. Dijkstra, Edsger W. *A Discipline of Programming*. Englewood Cliffs, NJ: Prentice-Hall, 1976.

13

Developing User Documentation for Expert Systems

Karen L. McGraw

INTRODUCTION

User documentation is an important component of any software system, especially when the software has been designed as a tool to help users accomplish work-related tasks more efficiently. Current literature decries the failure of much user documentation to accurately portray the software's capabilities, describe the procedures the user must complete to achieve expected results, or detail steps to solve problems or attain more information. To resolve these problems, documentation specialists are attending to specific implementation methodologies, instructional design techniques, and human factors guidelines.

Like any other software system, expert systems require effective, easily accessed user documentation. However, the nature of expert systems and their target audiences demands even more focus on user needs and abilities, as well as increased attention to documentation design efforts. Because expert systems are often developed from prototypes that are enhanced as they evolve, the corresponding development cycle for expert system documentation must be able to incorporate changes as they occur. Thus, the documentation methodology that is applied must reflect this iteration and must also accommodate intensified teamwork and ongoing testing procedures.

The purpose of this chapter is to present a systems-oriented methodology to guide developers in constructing user documentation for expert systems. First, we lay groundwork for understanding problems and techniques in the development of expert system user documentation by summarizing similar information regarding traditional user documentation. Second, in our discussions of user documentation for expert systems, we identify differences between expert systems and traditional software that affect the documentation process and suggest a modified waterfall model to guide the writer in creating expert systems user documentation. In the third major section we present detailed information on the requirements phase of the suggested methodology, including activities that documentation specialists can complete during this phase. Fourth, we discuss goals of the design phases and present information and techniques to help documentation specialists establish documentation structure and format. Fifth, we offer tips on implementing the established guidelines as documentation specialists write, edit, and evaluate user documentation to support the target expert system. Finally, we briefly address the issue of on-line, electronically presented user documentation for expert systems and present a set of basic guidelines for the design of this type of user documentation.

USER DOCUMENTATION FOR TRADITIONAL SYSTEMS

The Need for Good User Documentation

Good, effective user documentation is not an afterthought. It must be planned early in the development process of the software system (be it a traditional or expert system). Technical writers, analysts, knowledge engineers, or others tapped to write the user documentation must be skilled in the required writing style, learn about the system itself, and investigate issues such as format, contents, and design early in the development process. Approaching the task of software documentation for end users in an organized manner can yield numerous benefits, to both the user and the producer of the software. For example, a systems approach to user documentation, coupled with the application of instructional design theory, can increase user satisfaction, increase user efficiency vis-à-vis the software system, and decrease training requirements and costs.

Increased user satisfaction.   Greenwald [23] notes that mail-order software products with the highest rate of return are products whose customers were frustrated with the instructions. Documentation problems probably included errors of omission, inaccuracies, and faulty style and format (i.e., indirect, passive, paragraphs instead of numerated tasks) that did not enable users to formulate strategies for completing tasks.

Those responsible for designing user documentation for traditional or expert systems must realize that few users consult the documentation *prior* to actual system use. The majority of users consult the documentation when they do not understand (1) what to do next, (2) what their options are, or (3) how to solve a specific problem. Their degree of user satisfaction will be ascertained not simply by *what* was in the manual, but by how it was organized, how easy it was to find, its readability, its completeness, and its accuracy.

When interacting with traditional, tool-oriented software (e.g., software that serves as a tool to accomplish a specific task, such as a spreadsheet), users may not consult the manual because they have expectations for the task that they wish to perform with the software. For example, if they are using word processing software, they have expectations based on their work with typewriters. Expert system software may also function as a tool or job aid in the completion of a task; however, the original task may not provide a model that appropriately parallels its completion on the computer. The expert system that has been designed to include a high-quality user interface should allow users to interact with the system to accomplish typical tasks without consulting the documentation. Due in part to the open, complex nature of expert systems and their users, well-designed user documentation must be provided to enhance system use and user satisfaction.

Increased user efficiency. Productivity is often a vague concept measuring the results gained from resources expended. Ineffective documentation wastes resources. Wasted effort due to poor documentation means that the end user gets less accomplished in a given period of time. Wasted effort also results from increased amounts of time required by internal training organizations which design courses to teach the product to end users.

Brockmann [13, p. 15] notes that "inadequate user documentation can greatly increase human errors in computer systems." Bailey [3] investigated the major causes of human errors in working with computer systems and concluded that 60% of all human errors with software are related in some manner or other to the quality of the documentation. Controlling errors by designing the documentation from the perspective of a user can reduce the percentage of inefficient activities (e.g., quitting and restarting the system, losing data, and searching through printed materials to solve a problem).

Decreased training requirements and costs. Especially if the software system being developed is slated for introduction into a corporate environment, training requirements and costs must be considered. Computer training and support costs in large corporations are commonly greater than the initial hardware costs [17]. This is because, while hardware is a one-time expense, training and support costs are ongoing. Reducing or streamlining training requirements can result in increases in productivity (i.e., more people using the system productively instead of the corporation's incurring charges to overhead costs such as training) and in decreased costs (i.e., the cost of nonproductive time spent in training, instructor costs, etc.) [36]. The benefits to the receiving organization are obvious; the benefits to the company that is responsible for producing the software can include better customer relations, more follow-on work, and rates that reflect the additional worth of quality materials that meet corporate needs.

Traditional User Documentation

Types of user documentation. User documentation historically has taken one of two forms: reference documentation and instructional documentation (sometimes a combination of the two). *Reference documentation* includes technical information about the system and is often organized alphabetically or by function. *Instructional documentation* may include similar material, but presents it in a manner that enables the user to learn specific tasks in a more procedural (e.g., step-by-step) format. Typically, supplying only one type of documentation results in user complaints. Reference documentation may meet the needs of expert-level users or a more technical audience while ignoring those of novices. Manuals designed to be instructional meet the needs of the novice user but may be of little assistance to the more technical or experienced user. Researchers investigating this problem [4, 30, 32] suggest that designing two-part manuals with both an instructional and a reference section represents a useful compromise. Novices then can read as much material as they need and can use, while expert users may consult only the portions they need to solve a specific problem. This two-pronged approach is popular with designers of user documentation for application-oriented software. In fact, it is not uncommon for software publishers to package these two types of materials as separate, but supportive, manuals.

An accepted methodology for user documentation.   The *Standard Documentation Process* (SDP) is a model that describes an accepted approach to methodologically creating traditional user documentation [13, p. 38]. Using this model, documentation specialists proceed through the various steps of (1) designing document blueprints, (2) drafting the document, (3) editing the document, (4) reviewing the document, (5) field-testing the document, (6) producing and distributing the document, (7) maintaining the document.

Specific Considerations for Documentation Design

General principles of documentation design have been derived from research in the fields of technical communication, learning and instructional design theory, and human factors. Many of these principles or guidelines would appear to be common-sensical in their orientation. Regardless of how obvious they may seem, however, the percentage of time that they are ignored renders their mention here reasonable. Although initially compiled as guidelines for traditional user documentation, they are equally relevant to the development of expert system user documentation.

Among the general guidelines recommended by Sullivan and Chapanis [46] for traditional documentation that also are applicable to expert system user documentation are the following:

- Use simple, familiar language.
- Use short, active, positive sentences.
- Be complete and specific when describing actions.
- Describe one thing at a time.
- Use lists rather than long prose passages.

Information and procedural instructions should be presented (1) in a task-oriented format by hierarchy of use and (2) in the order in which the user must use the information [42]. If possible, the information should be grouped into logical sections according to function to facilitate recall and usability [6]. Additionally, Guymon [24] notes that documentation design should address the following issues:

- Is the text self-instructional to the greatest extent possible?
- Has the writer contended with the factor of readability, both by applying readability formulas and by assessing overall comprehensibility?
- Is the writing active and concise?
- Does the piece enable retention and transfer of learning?
- Has the documentation specialist contended with visual message design?
- Has the documentation specialist contended with alternative learning styles?
- Has a systems approach been implemented?

Common problems with traditional documentation.   It has been argued that software documentation for system users is consistently bad, for reasons ranging from the claim that it is not clear, simple, or easy to understand to the complaint that it is incomplete or incorrect. Documentation problems may result from a number of factors, including:

- Poor anticipation of reader/user expectations and needs.
- System revisions not communicated to the documentation specialist.
- A writing style that does not accommodate skimming or scanning, forcing the reader to move through the manual in a serial manner.
- Inability of the documentation specialist to act as a user advocate.
- Ill-conceived schedules and forecasts for time and personnel.
- Inadequate training in technical writing, documentation, and instructional design theory.

Incorrect or inadequate user documentation can have effects that range from vague user irritability to complaints and even legal action [13]. As noted previously, poor documentation can result in an increase in human errors, wasted time and equipment, higher training costs, and rejection of systems or programs.

USER DOCUMENTATION FOR EXPERT SYSTEMS

Good documentation is labeled as such based on the criterion of whether the user can consult and understand the documentation when needed, regardless of whether the system for which it was designed is traditional or expert system software. However, some differences do exist between traditional and expert system software that affect the development of supporting user documentation.

Differences Between Expert System
and Traditional Software

Traditional computer software requires that its user documentation address problems of a procedural nature. In fact, authors in the field suggest that the bulk of a piece of user documentation consists of "sets of operating instructions arranged in logical patterns according to the target audience's goal in using the software" [43, p. 50]. Further, each procedure that is identified generally presents a chronological sequence of instructions for completing that procedure.

Expert systems differ from traditional software in several ways that affect the complexity of the task of creating user documentation [33, p. 42]. Unlike most other software, which presents the user with only one view of the system at a time, expert system software generally has "windowing" capability. Windowing allows the user to have more than one view of the system at a time. Although this can greatly enhance the usability of the expert system for a proficient user, windowing can increase confusion and frustration for a less experienced user. The end result can be a user who feels lost in the system.

Second, languages in which expert systems are developed allow designers and programmers to produce programs which are object-oriented and highly graphical. Traditional computer software has been largely textual and sequential, allowing users to "find their way" more easily through the program. Expert systems, on the other hand, may require documentation that uses an increased number of screen images to support the text. These images serve as locational cues that can help users identify where they are in the system and the consequences of selecting from among various alternatives.

An Approach to Creating User Documentation
for Expert Systems

Organized, methodological development of expert system user documentation parallels what could be termed a modified systems approach to development. The methodology recommended here has its roots in an adaptation of the waterfall model for software development [7]. McGraw and Harbison-Briggs [36] suggested that an adaptation of the waterfall model could be used in the expert system development process in that this model makes it possible to denote iterations between phases. Also, while the SDP model for software development does not easily accommodate the iterations that are common in expert system development, a modified waterfall model could. The model that appears in Figure 13–1 illustrates the expert system user documentation life cycle. The following list briefly describes the tasks performed during each phase of the model:

FEASIBILITY

- Defining the product concept and focus.

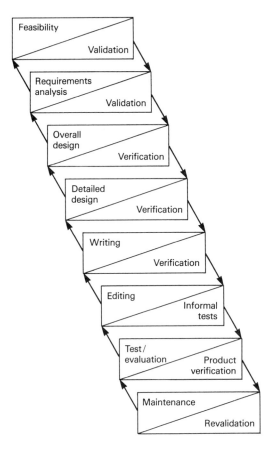

Figure 13–1 A developmental methodology for expert system user documentation.

REQUIREMENTS ANALYSIS

● Specifying the required content of the documentation, based on anticipated functionality of the system.
● Revising the required content of the documentation, based on the identification of end users and their capabilities.

OVERALL DESIGN

● Determining the general structure of the documentation.
● Completing an initial page or chapter map of the documentation.
● Detailing general specifications for the documentation based on task analyses and objectives.

DETAILED DESIGN

● Determining the specific requirements of each component (e.g., each chapter, reference material, the index, etc.) of the documentation.

- Specifying writing guidelines (e.g., style, voice, special vocabulary) to be used throughout the project.
- Determining design guidelines (e.g., grids, typography, notation of keys, etc.) to be used throughout the project.

WRITING

- Working with system designers, documents, and potential users to extract key information.
- Implementing various design specifications to complete progressively more accurate drafts.

EDITING

- Refining the initial draft based on system use and internal editing.
- Copyediting the draft.
- Initial (external) editing by end users.

TESTING

- Internally reviewing/refining the documentation components.
- Externally reviewing/refining the documentation components.

MAINTENANCE

- Planning for revisions.
- Managing the collection of suggested revisions.
- Compiling revisions necessitated by updates to the system.
- Rank-ordering and implementing changes through the life cycle of the product.

REQUIREMENTS FOR EXPERT SYSTEM USER DOCUMENTATION

The requirements analysis phase is one of the most critical in the development of user documentation for expert systems. Documentation specialists should expect to expend a high percentage of time in this phase of development, as it provides the foundation upon which later phases build. Once identified, requirements, should be monitored and refined in parallel.

Defining Requirements

User documentation requirements are dependent upon the specifications, functionality, and design of the expert system the documentation is to support. Thus, the first step in requirements analysis is to explore, in depth, plans for the system itself. Documentation specialists should acquaint themselves with all available documents describing the system functionality and design. This time-consuming exercise enables those who will be required to write about the system to "get the picture" of the system and to develop a mental map of its structure. System design documents and/or functional design documents allow the documentation specialist to view the expert system from the point of view of a designer as well as a potential user. In many cases, prototype demos of various display screens or system modules may exist and can be viewed to help complete this task.

Once the documentation specialist has obtained an overall view of the system's eventual functionality, he or she should sketch out a view of the system, including each module or component that will be viewed or used. While doing so, the documentation specialist should act as a user advocate, as he or she contemplates user needs relative to each display, module, or component.

Identifying users. Once the documentation specialist grasps the general functionality of the expert system, he or she should identify the user audience. End users of expert systems generally share specific characteristics that are important to user documentation efforts [33, pp 42–43]:

1. They do not necessarily have previous computer experience.
2. Because expert systems are often used to assist novices, end users may not be experts in the domain that the expert system represents.
3. End users need to retrieve information or advice from the expert system in an efficient, timely manner. *The sophistication of the system should not inhibit its ease of use.*
4. Expert system end users tend to think of the expert system as "seamless"; that is, they are generally unaware of the individual components, displays, or knowledge bases which interact to make up the expert system.

At this point in the requirements analysis process, documentation designers/ writers should perform an in-depth analysis of user needs and abilities. Important subtasks in this activity include the following:

1. *Identify the primary users of the expert system.* Try to anticipate the users' goals in using the system, the amount of training they will receive on the system, the environment in which the system will be used, and the impact on the user of successful and unsuccessful use of the system.
2. *Identify the primary users' characteristics that will affect the design of the documentation.* Consider such factors as general education, previous on-the-job training that relates to system use, prerequisites to using the system, and the user's reading abilities.
3. *Determine the users' previous experience with computer systems and documentation.* Try to draw analogies from a user's experience with other computer systems. Explore the design of computer documentation that the users have been successful with to determine whether any of the design techniques used in that documentation are applicable to your documentation. Typo-

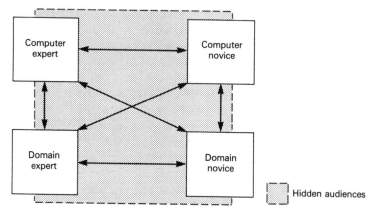

Figure 13–2 Complex audience model. (Adapted with permission from Rosenbaum and Walters, "Audience Diversity: A Major Challenge in Computer Documentation," *IEEE Transactions on Professional Communications* (1986): 49.

graphical cues and standards the users have already grown accustomed to may be more effective in your documentation than new design features.

Figure 13–2 illustrates an audience model for user documentation that we have adapted from Rosenbaum and Walters [43], who suggest that designers create an audience model to help target and focus user needs. In this model, the question of the target audience is more complex than that of whether a user is a novice or expert. A typical user may be a *computer* novice or expert and/or a *domain* (i.e., subject matter) novice or expert. (Rosenbaum and Walters also note that "hidden" audiences, such as prospective buyers of the software, may exist and must be accounted for.) Those who write user documentation for expert systems may find that they must provide varying degrees of the following types of material:

- Introductory technical and computer-related information to enable a computer novice to complete fundamental tasks (e.g., turning the system on, using the mouse, shutting the system down).
- Subject matter background to enable a subject matter novice to understand the system's purpose and usefulness.
- Procedural information to guide a novice or infrequent user through a session.
- Reference-oriented information to enable the expert user to maximize his or her use of the system.
- Case studies or examples of using the expert system to solve "real life" domain problems.

Establishing detailed requirements.   Once the audience has been identified, documentation specialists should investigate the tasks that users must complete to use the expert system software successfully. One method for accomplishing this is by conducting a task analysis. *Task analysis* is a methodological tool that can be used to (1) describe the functions a human performs and (2) determine the relation of each task on a certain dimension to the overall job (Shannon, 1980). Task analysis forces documentation designers and writers to consider the functionality of the system and the resulting user needs. It enables an identification of the types of tasks that the user must perform and the types of expertise the users who perform these tasks must have [11].

Information that is task-oriented is a "personalized, active voice form of information" [11, p. 1] that "describes step-by-step, how the user is to perform certain tasks" [40]. Odescalchi ([40, 41]) recently tested task-oriented and product-oriented information and was able to derive the following conclusions:

- Writers required 42% more time to develop task-oriented information.
- 79% of the users preferred task orientation.
- 41% of the users showed a productivity gain due to task orientation.

Woodson [52] states that there are no established rules for conducting a task analysis and implies that function should determine form. Miller [39] suggests that although there are no set rules that reduce the technique to a routine endeavor, there are guidelines. Among the primary determinants of the final form a task analysis takes are the purpose of the task analysis and the desired detail within it [34].

There are many different types of task analysis. One of the most appropriate for use in defining documentation requirements is the task/subtask analysis. Using this technique, the documentation specialist first identifies the major tasks involved in a potential user's interaction with the expert system to determine the tasks the user will attempt. These major tasks are then broken down to identify the subtasks that are necessary to complete each major task. For example, although selecting an item with the mouse seems to be a relatively simple task, to accomplish it success-fully requires that the user understand what a mouse is, how to use the button(s), how the cursor corresponds to mouse movement, how to know when an item is active for selection, and what triggers the selection. Figure 13–3 is an example of a partial task analysis completed for an existing expert system.

Functional component	Task	Subtask
1. Login to system.	1.1 Identify system state.	a. Recognize system on
	1.2 Initialize system if not on.	a. Press monitor button in. b. Press system toggle to ON. c. Observe screen prompts.
	1.3 Respond to verification prompts.	a. Type in user ID. b. Press RETURN c. Type in password. d. Press RETURN.
	1.4 Monitor system test.	a. Check display for malfunction code. b. Compare code with those in test table.

Figure 13–3 Sample of a partial task analysis.

One way to approach task analysis is to classify tasks according to types of human behavior [36]. Some authors ([5, 52]) have suggested that designers use process classifications (e.g., perception, mediation, communication, motor) and consistent terms for corresponding activities or behaviors (e.g., detect, inspect, observe, etc. for perception). For example, terms that could be used in a task analysis to describe typical motor and perceptual behaviors for an expert system user include the following:

TYPICAL MOTOR BEHAVIORS FOR EXPERT SYSTEM USERS

- Select
- Click
- Drag
- Move
- Align
- Log in
- Delete
- Retrieve
- Save
- Press
- Type

TYPICAL PERCEPTUAL BEHAVIORS FOR EXPERT SYSTEM USERS

- Observe
- Identify
- Scan
- Read
- Locate
- Listen

Using a Task Analysis. After the tasks have been identified, they should be analyzed to determine what type of material or information is required to support them [11, 33]. Can the task be described as a prerequisite skill that need not be mentioned in the documentation? Will the task require minimal training and hence a mention in the documentation? Will the task require extensive hands-on training and/or major coverage in the documentation (both on-line and printed)? Will the task require the development of special user interface prompts, messages, or on-line help?

Next, expand the task analysis by grouping tasks into user objectives according to each segment of the system. In compiling the objectives, the documentation specialist must consider the following:

- Activities and options the user can attempt in each portion of the system.
- The goals and purposes of each available option.
- The consequences of selecting (or not selecting) each option.
- Whether or not there is a logical sequence of use within the system.

Finally, the documentation specialist should use the preceding information to establish an initial outline for the user documentation. For example, during work on the FRESH system (an expert system for determining force requirements for battle management), documentation specialists were able to identify 47 individual tasks that users needed to be able to complete before they could successfully use the expert system [33]. Once identified, they were grouped together into behavioral or instructional objectives. *Behavioral objectives* are brief task statements that contain an action verb denoting observable behavior, and terms for the performance envi-

Objectives	Related task codes
1. The operator will be able to successfully complete a FRESH login.	001, 002, 005, 006, 010*
2. The operator will be able to use an alert notification message to choose an appropriate option from the notifications screen.	009, 010, 011, 012, 013
3. When presented with a sample natural language screen, the operator will be able to identify all of the active and inactive panes.	007
4. Given a sample FRESH screen, the operator will identify and demonstrate use of mouse documentation line.	006

*Task codes reference specific tasks on the task analysis done during this project. Listed codes denote tasks upon which the operator's success in meeting the objective depends.

Figure 13–4   Modified behavioral objectives compiled from tasks. (Used with permission from McGraw, "Guidelines for Producing Documentation for Expert Systems," *IEEE Transactions on Professional Communication* 29 (1986): 44.

ronment in which the objective's attainment can be tested, the resources used in completing the task, and in some cases, the criteria (e.g., two out of four attempts) for success.[1] The objectives appearing in Figure 13–4 were developed on the basis of a task analysis and were used to help confirm that users would need general information (e.g., on using the mouse, monitors, and the natural language interface), followed by specific information on using the expert system to solve problems. This determination helped in the planning of printed documentation, on-line system help, and training materials.

DESIGN TASKS: ESTABLISHING STRUCTURE AND FORMAT

In the adapted waterfall model, tasks involved in designing the actual documentation follow requirements analysis activities. Documentation design requires that the documentation specialist attend to (1) and the physical structure of the piece and (2) the design techniques (e.g., format and typography) that are to be used.

Defining Documentation Structure

According to Brockmann [13], organizing text materials in documentation must be done in such manner that the organization will both be apparent to readers and meet the reader's expectations. Thus, documentation specialists should structure the piece in a reasonable manner and should communicate that structure to the reader through the use of visual message design techniques (e.g., headings, graphics, and consistent chapter structures).

[1] For more information on behavioral objectives, see Robert Mager, *Preparing Instructional Objectives* (Palo Alto, CA: Seron Publishers, 1962).

The field of psycholinguistics defines reading as "bringing meaning *to* the text in order to get meaning *from* it" [51, p. 132]. Similarly, Goodman contends that "reading is a complex process by which a reader reconstructs, to some degree, a message encoded by a writer" [22, p. 5]. Using documentation successfully requires that the reader be able to make efficient use of his or her expectations or schemata [2] of text organization in order to reconstruct the intended meaning. Thus, researchers contend that to communicate effectively with readers, designers of the material must acknowledge and make use of the reader's expectations [47]. For example, McGraw [33] suggests that while compiling a user profile, documentation specialists should attempt to determine the users' previous experience with traditional software systems, expert systems, and any accompanying documentation. If designers cannot anticipate user's expectations, they must plan techniques (e.g., advance organizers or identification of general vs. specific information) that will communicate the document's structure and format to the reader.

Some typical documentation structures are to develop multiple manuals, each of which meets a particular purpose (i.e., reference or instructional), and to incorporate both types within a single manual. If the documentation is to be incorporated in a single piece, the following structure is suggested and is described in subsequent sections:

- Structured material
- Introductory material
- Individual chapters
- Reference sections

Structural material.   Structural material in documentation includes components that precede the major body of the documentation. In printed documentation (as opposed to on-line documentation), this includes title pages, the table of contents, copyright and preface pages, and a list of figures.

Introductory material.   The purpose of the introductory section of a piece of user documentation is to acquaint the user with the documentation. The introduction may be titled something along the lines of "How to Use This Manual." Within this section the documentation specialist tells the user what the overall purpose of the documentation is, how the document is structured, and what types of visual message design techniques (e.g., graphic or typographic cues, page format, etc.) have been used to help the reader scan and extract information and gives tips for using the manual.

Communicating Structure.   Researchers have noted that software users benefit from the use of diagrams and/or metaphors that communicate the overall structure of the product to the user [16]. For example, users find an illustration that conveys the organization of the manual helpful. From a functional view, a graphic depicting the overall organization of the system is a well-received component of the

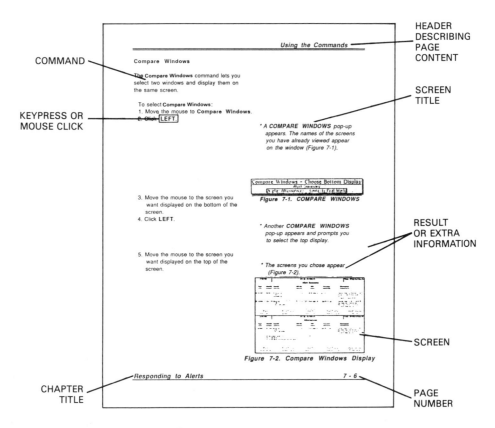

Figure 13–5 Sample page communicating design features.

introductory section of a manual that documents an expert system. Not only can the user gain a mental map of the system prior to using it, but he or she can also superimpose a structure for the documentation on top of this for increased ease in referencing the manual.

Communicating Visual Message Design. Figure 13–5 is an example of a page from an introductory section of an expert system manual in which the visual message design features are noted for the reader. The design features include *typographical cueing systems,* which are nonverbal devices for attracting and focusing the reader's attention. Typographical cues include the use of type font (e.g., boldface, italics, underlining, etc.), size, and color, as well as arrows, boxes, and *white space*[2] [2].

Suggestions for Use. Most manuals have a section that suggests ways to use the manual. Because of the diversity of expert system user audiences, this section is

___

[2] White space is the horizontal or vertical blank space on a page and can be used to differentiate between sections, frame tables, figures, examples, etc.

invaluable in expert system documentation. Information in this section may include the following, but will vary depending on the content of the expert system itself:

- Suggestions for use by those who are expert in the field, familiar with computers, and/or holistic learners (e.g., providing a high-level overview section at the beginning of each new section or chapter).
- Suggestions for use by those who are novices in the field (e.g., providing additional sources of information on the field, prerequisite information, the use of a glossary for key terms, and matching the desired objective with chapter objectives).
- Suggestions for use by those who are computer novices (e.g., following step-by-step directions to complete a specific task and reviewing introductory information on input devices).
- Additional useful references not included in the documentation.
- How to access available on-line information.
- Hotline numbers.
- How to note suggestions for revision of the manual.

Individual chapters.   Individual instructional chapters should reflect a consistent structure or organization to assist users in identifying, accessing, and extracting desired information. Chapters should be sequenced in a logical manner (i.e., a chapter describing system tools such as the keyboard, mouse, and user interface should precede chapters specific to applications within the system), but the documentation specialist must not assume that users will approach the manual in a serial manner. Thus, the design should incorporate some method to reference a definition or description of a key term (e.g., one column details specific steps while italicized notes in the supporting column refer the reader to the place where the concept was introduced).

Following are some suggested sections to include in each chapter, together with a brief description of their purposes or an example of the use of the information contained within them.

Introductory Sections.   The lead section in each chapter includes general information that can:

- Mold user expectations of the chapter's contents.
- Allow the reader to determine quickly which chapter he or she needs at a specific time.
- Provide advance organizers (e.g., chapter outlines and overviews) to convey a sense of structure of the chapter's contents and increase ease of learning.
- Provide top-level goals for individual learning.
- Present overviews (for holistic learners, expert users, and/or those who are familiar with computers) and information on how to obtain specific, step-by-step information (for novice users).

- Identify key terms (which are defined in the glossary) for user reference prior to their appearance in the text.
- Identify any prerequisites for successful completion of the chapter (e.g., being able to use an existing query language).

Instructional Sections. The design of instructional text has been the sole subject of a number of texts, such as Jonassen [28, 29] and others. The following guidelines summarize some specific suggestions from the fields of technical writing, training, and human factors research. Where applicable, examples appear in italics.

1. Use a step-by-step, action-oriented writing style.

Ex: *To quit the session and return to the parameters screen, press RETURN.*

2. Use consistent terminology throughout all instructional sections.

Ex: *Press the number of your choice (1–4) and press RETURN. (Not "press" in one instance and "depress" in another.)*

3. Differentiate input (what the user types in) from output or consequences (what the expert system feeds back or responds).

Ex: *Input may be shown in black* **Times Roman** *type. Output may be shown in a computer typeface or other* sans serif type, *in color, and/or surrounded by a frame denoting a computer screen.*

4. Use a consistent method for the display of special keys (e.g., RETURN) or key sequences that the user is to press.

Ex: *Special keys may appear in capital letters or boldface type, or surrounded by a small box denoting a key.*

5. Differentiate user actions (e.g., *Select EXIT to end the session.*) from explanations and justifications (e.g., *See page 1–7 for information on how to select an item.*) and from consequences (e.g., *The message "Are you sure you want to exit." appears.*). This allows the user to work through procedures uninterrupted by text that may be superfluous.

Ex: *User actions could appear in one column in a procedural format. Explanations, justifications, and consequences could appear in a different typeface in a supporting column directly across from the text they reference.*

6. Incorporate frequent use of graphics (e.g., screen images) that support procedural steps. Researchers such as Booher [8] have noted the importance of pictorial information in support of instructions that must be handled procedurally. These graphics are of particular importance in expert system documentation in that they serve as locational cues and help offset user feelings of being lost.

7. Apply a consistent method for the use of supporting graphics. Determine the use, size, and placement of figures or photographs in the document. Placement of supporting pictorial information is a key to the effectiveness of its use.

Ex: *A two-column format enables supporting screen images to be placed directly to the side of the text that describes their use or appearance.*

Additional Components.   In addition to the aforementioned guidelines, good instructional design includes opportunities for users to observe the system in use, practice using the system, and monitor their success. Because they are complex, powerful, and multifaceted, expert systems may affect the user's confidence in his or her ability to anticipate the extent of a system's usability or to use a system successfully.

Users often become aware of the power and capability of an expert system only after many interactions, substantial training, or observations of another user. Indeed, the very power of the system may leave the potential user nervous about interacting with the system. Some typical questions of the first-time user are the following:

> *What can I do with the system?*
> *What does a typical session with the system look like?*
> *How will I most often use this feature?*
> *How long will a session take?*
> *What will the end result of using the system be like?*

Instructional documentation for expert systems can be strengthened by the inclusion of well-placed, concisely reported case studies or brief practice/feedback activities. These components can "walk" a user through a simulated session and provide him or her with expectations and a sense of the system's structure and capabilities prior to actually using the system. Figure 13–6 illustrates a portion of a sample session. Descriptive text appears in the inner column, while supporting text, further explanations, consequences, and supporting figures appear in the outer column.

Reference sections.   The reference sections of a user manual often consist of a compilation of appendices, each of which has been designed to meet a specific user need and to support or extend a particular portion of the manual. The following items are useful components for a reference section of expert system user documentation.

Glossaries.   Since user documentation rarely is read serially (i.e., from front to back), defining a key term only once within the text is not acceptable. On the other hand, defining the term following each occurrence is redundant. Mini-dictionaries or glossaries offer the reader a single reference point for the definition of major terms that may appear throughout the text. Glossaries should be formatted and designed to allow easy access and user scanning.

Command Reference Guides.   Glossaries of terms are standard fare in most manuals for tool-oriented software. Glossaries of commands, which make up the structure of most reference-style manuals, are appropriate extensions of a reference section for expert system user documentation. Typical glossaries of commands are formatted in alphabetical order. While this structure is acceptable if the user knows

This system can be used for many applications. The instructional chapters in this manual describe single applications. In actuality, you will probably use several applications during a single session with the expert system.

This appendix provides you with a set of sample uses. The appendix has three sections. The first section details an initial use of the system. Section 2 describes using the system as a monitoring and decision-aiding device. Section 3 details the "What-If" capability and demonstrates using the system as a contingency-planning tool.

SECTION 1

Initial Login
   To begin a session, sit at the workstation and press the FUNCTION key, release it, and then quickly press the F key.

A pop-up LOGIN WINDOW appears.

   Type in your UserID and press RETURN. When the cursor appears beside "Password:", type in your Password and press RETURN.

The system verifies your access and checks your system mailbox for alert notifications.

   The SYSTEM MENU appears on the screen. If the screen is darker than you prefer, press the LOCAL key, release it, and quickly press the B key.

   To use the natural language screen to build a query that defines an alert, move the mouse to "Natural Language Menu" and click LEFT.

A natural language screen appears.

Setting Alert Thresholds
   You may use the system to set alerts based on acceptable and unacceptable parameters. The system notifies you at login if any of the thresholds you set have been violated since your last session.

   Set thresholds by building a natural language command, such as "Define a CASUALTY Report alert."

Figure 13–6   Excerpt from a sample user session.

the name of the command he or she needs, it is less useful when the software system is large and open, as is an expert system. In the latter case the documentation specialist may wish to design a command reference guide (Figure 13–7). In one expert system for which such a guide was designed, the availability of commands and their resulting subcommands and actions was dependent on the user's current activity and screen view. Thus, the guide was designed according to screens, which were given titles within the system. For any major screen, the user could consult the reference guide and skim the document to compare or review the available commands and their actions.

Commands	Function	Results	Notes
SAVE	Saves the content of the alert.	Alert is saved. Most recently viewed natural language screen appears.	Page 6–12.
DELETE	Deletes a defined alert.	Most recently viewed natural language screen appears.	Page 6–13.
START OVER	Clears alert definition screen of all inputs.	Empty alert definition screen is displayed	Page 6–14.
MAIN MENU	Displays the main menu.	The menu appears, listing 4 main options.	Page 3–5.
DEFINE ALERT	Displays alert definition screen.	You may input alert thresholds from this screen.	Page 6–15.

Figure 13–7   Portion of a command reference guide.

Prerequisite/Extended Information.   The reference section is a reasonable location for the inclusion of material that helps users acquire prerequisites and/or extends information presented in the instructional sections. For example, a number of expert systems reflect user interfaces that employ some type of natural language system, such as NLMenu™.[3] Supporting documentation for these components provides general instructional information on their use. Some manuals might devote an entire chapter to specifics, such as understanding the natural language menu itself (e.g., differentiating active from passive panes and scrolling within panes) and selecting items from the active menus (with a mouse or keyboard), and giving tips for building and executing queries. However, experience has shown that even with instruction on the use of the system, novice users have some difficulty formulating queries—that is, they know *what* they want to ask, but are not sure *how* to ask it.

In this situation, the reference section might include a set of sample queries that demonstrates what the user intended to ask and how the resulting query should be formulated to retrieve the desired information. This instructional extension may be referenced from the instructional text within the body of the manual, and those users needing more information could consult it as needed.

Troubleshooting Section.   The only time some users consult documentation is when they encounter a problem or a situation that they perceive as a problem. If the problem concerns not knowing how to do a specific task, users typically consult the index to find the appropriate pages of instructional text. In rare cases, however, users may confront other problems, such as system messages or lockups. When these problems are encountered, users should be able to interpret the problem and find a simple solution. A troubleshooting component of the manual, designed in a columnar format, can meet these needs. Actual screen images of typical messages in

[3]NLMenu is a trademark of Texas Instruments, Inc.

response to problems or brief descriptions of anticipated problems may be placed in the first column for easy identification. A second column can briefly describe the expected problem. A third column can describe procedural instructions for the user to follow to solve the problem.

References. This component of the reference section simply provides bibliographic information on sources noted within the body of the documentation itself. Whether in regular or annotated form, all the entries should be consistent in format and style.

Index. The index actually can be one of the most important components of the entire document. Users who consult the documentation to meet a specific need may attempt to look up terms that seem to describe their need, desired result, or current situation. The format of an index can be either run-in or nested. Run-in indexes display the term first, followed on the same line by the page numbers on which the term appears, is used, or is described. When the term is initially described or defined, it might appear in boldface type.

Nested indexes display the term (e.g., documentation) on one line. Beneath that line, each related use of the term in a particular circumstance (e.g., documentation methodology; documentation, problems with) appears with its page number on an indented line. Nested indexes, because they meet specific needs more appropriately, are preferred in user documentation.

Defining Design Guidelines

The adapted waterfall model for expert system user documentation suggests that, before beginning the actual writing task, the documentation specialist define detailed design issues. Such issues include typographical cues and standards, spatial cues and standards, and standard layouts.

Typographical cues and standards

Legibility of Text. Text legibility refers to the ease with which users can read the printed text. Legibility has often been associated with style of type. *Serif type* includes typefaces in which the primary strokes of each character have thin extensions projecting from them (e.g., Times Roman). These extensions help to add differentiation to individual characters. By contrast, *sans serif type* includes typefaces in which the primary strokes of each character have no extensions (e.g., Helvetica). Tinker reports that there is no difference in legibility of serif vs. sans serif type. However, the serif type extensions provide a reader with more "cues" as he or she is skimming and scanning down a page. Therefore, words printed in serif typefaces can be read more quickly than those printed in sans serif typefaces.

Styles of Type. Documentation specialists should establish a plan for the consistent use of type styles throughout a document. A limited number of type styles should appear in any one document to ensure that a reader is not distracted and that each type style communicates its message in the most effective manner. User documentation commonly reflects the use of at least a portion of the following features of type: lowercase, all uppercase, italic, boldface, underlining (and possibly combinations of these). Although some guidelines do exist (e.g., italic print and multiple type styles retard reading rate), we recommend that design specialists assist the inexperienced documentation specialist in establishing the use of type styles.[4]

Sizes of Type.   The legibility of type is also related to the size of the typeface. The size of type is measured in *points,* each of which approximates 1/72 of an inch. While point size may vary across typefaces (i.e., 10-point in one typeface may be a slightly different size in another typeface), the following standards seem to persist:

- The type size most commonly used for user documentation ranges from 8 to 14 points.
- The text body of most documentation pieces is printed in either 10 or 11 points.
- As expected, readers can more quickly locate words set in larger type (i.e., such as might be found in a header) than in smaller type.

Headings.   Headings, or headers, label sections and/or pages within the documentation and signal the structure of the documentation to the end user. The heading signals textual information that does not add new content on a topic but instead gives emphasis to certain aspects of the semantic content or points out aspects of the structure of the content [38]. User documentation displays various levels of headings, signaling both the overall structure and the structure within each chapter of the manual. Designers use both type size and style to signify the level of importance, generality, or specificity of text. The following levels are examples of what the designer and documentation specialist may define:

```
Level A (chapter title) = Uppercase, boldface, 20-point type
Level B (section title) = Mixed case, boldface, 12-point type, rule above
Level C = Mixed case, boldface, 12-point italics
Level D = Mixed case, normal, 10-point, underlined, indent, and run in.
```

The more levels of headings a designer uses, the more structure the user has to remember as he or she scans the text for information. Jonassen [28] found that readers failed to retrieve information any more quickly or accurately from a text with numerous levels of headings as compared to one with fewer levels. Although documents may have several levels of headings, we suggest the use of no more than four or five.

In addition to signaling structure, headings provide access to information in the text [26]. Waller [50] contends that the primary function of headings is to

---

[4] A word of caution: overuse of type styles is worse than no variation in type style and is a common beginner's error.

orient readers to the text, thus allowing them to locate the information they need. Jonassen and Falk [29] found that users located 50% more answers in the same amount of time using a version of the text with extensive, consistent, well-designed marginal headings.

It is important for the designer and documentation specialist to keep in mind that in addition to typography, heading content is also crucial to user efficiency. For example, designers are advised to refrain from the use of vague, concept-oriented headings [48] and instead design headings that focus on users' specific needs, such as "Saving a Scenario."

Spatial cues and standards. To address the use of space within the design of a document, the documentation specialist must consider the page size, packaging issues, and the desired binding. Defined early, these features make it possible to establish the general layout of the page. The margin width, justification of text, header placement, and the use of tabs must also be considered.

Writers should pay special attention to the use of *spatial cueing*. Spatial cues are visual signals throughout a document that are based on the use of space. Spatial cues include, but are not limited to, the amount of space before and after a heading, the spacing between lines of the text body, the spacing around figures or separating figures from text, and the designation of margins and line and column widths.

Visual cues are important when users scan for information. Hartley [25] notes that in list-type manuals, spatial cues are often more important than typographic cues. The appropriate use of space can enhance a user's ability to pick up on visual cues such as headings and special typographical conventions. In general, readers rate pages with a lot of "white space" as being easier to read than pages that are full of text.

Line and Column Widths. Line widths are discussed in terms of picas. A *pica* is equivalent to 12 points, and 6 picas are equivalent to an inch. The document designer uses picas to plan and measure the width of columns of type, the length of columns of type, the amount of space between a heading and body text, and the like. Overall, readers typically prefer medium-width lines (up to 36 picas). Very small widths (e.g., 10 picas) require that the reader scan back and forth excessively through the column and thus are inefficient for extracting information. Readers prefer two-point *leading,* [5] additionally.

Margins. The use and extent of margins are inextricably tied to the selected line length. Margins represent a use of white space and, if well-designed, can contribute both to retrieval time and reader comprehension. For example, margins can be used to help frame nearby text and to place headings. In addition, margins allow for the placement of *marginalia,* i.e., text elements that appear in the margins. Marginalia may include marginal notes, key terms, technical definitions, or any other information [33, 19] that aids users in finding, comprehending, and using

---

[5] Leading is the amount of space between lines of text.

text. Additionally, marginalia may describe the consequences of user actions or where the reader can find more information about the topic being discussed in the text.

Determining a standard layout.   A *grid* is a layout guide or frame that helps the documentation specialist structure the consistent placement of text and graphic elements on a page (for printed documentation) or screen (for on-line documentation). Figure 13–8 displays two basic grid or guideline systems. The

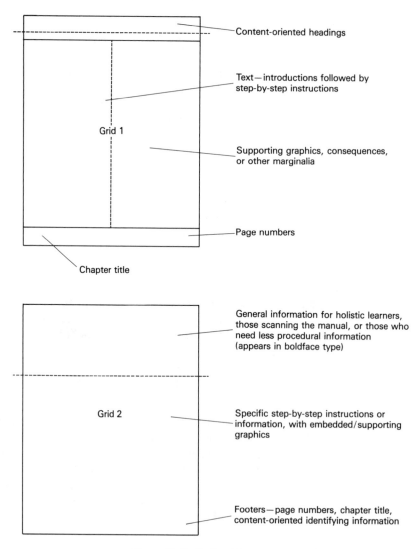

Figure 13–8   Basic grids.

cross-hatched lines denote major sections or areas of the page and guide the designer in the placement of headers, page numbers, the body of the text, graphics, and marginalia. Grid designs are numerous, and the selection of any one grid should depend on the type and purpose of the text, the size of the page, page limitations, and the intended audience. For example, to meet the needs of both novice and "expert" users equally, a grid may be designed such that general information appears in the top quadrant (for experts and holistic learners) and specific steps and supporting illustrations appear on the rest of the page (for novices and serialistic learners).

For a recent expert system documentation assignment, we chose a grid and page design that was based on a single column of instructional text, with supporting graphics and marginalia placed in a second column. These decisions were based on the way in which we anticipated that the audience would use the documentation. Single-column format is usually scanned significantly faster than a double column of text [15], and we expected that users of the expert system most often would need to scan for information. In addition, this format allowed ample white space at the side of each text column for the placement of marginalia (e.g., consequences, justifications, screen images, and readers' notes).

Color.   Color can be a cueing device, as it helps draw the user's eye to specific information. However, the use of color is not without drawbacks. First, it increases publication costs significantly. More importantly, unless it is used functionally (and sparingly) to signal specific types of information (e.g., computer output), it actually can detract from the message of the text. Documentation specialists are urged to consult designers for assistance in the selection and use of print and background colors.

IMPLEMENTATION AND EVALUATION

Upon the foundation that has been laid by previous efforts at requirements analysis and design, the documentation specialist drafts the expert system user documentation and supporting figures. The task is not unlike investigative reporting, systems analysis, or knowledge engineering efforts. It will require that the documentation specialist use a combination of methods to extract information about the expert system from system designers, content experts, and documents. Once the information is extracted, the documentation specialist is responsible for applying design guidelines as he or she "translates" and formulates the content from these sources into a readable presentation that is keyed to the identified audience.

Writing and Editing the Document

Documentation specialists should follow some specific organizational steps in preparing a preliminary draft. Following are some particularly useful examples [33]:

1. Read related sections of functional design documents before writing.

2. Meet with the designer of the given portion of the expert system to determine the completeness and consistency of the design document and to confirm what the major subsections or areas of interest to the user are.

3. Ask the designer to walk you through his or her portion of the expert system on the computer.

4. Draft an initial layout sheet showing the intended structure of the chapter, including major sections and subsections and anticipated length.

5. *"Storyboard,"* or plan out, the chapter before writing. The process of compiling a storyboard allows the documentation specialist to graphically lay out pages of the documentation in such manner as to move through the entire documentation. Storyboarding typically lays out the major sections and subsections of the document, possible pictorial information, and charts or tables (Figure 13–9).

6. Write to the storyboard, considering the design guidelines established earlier.

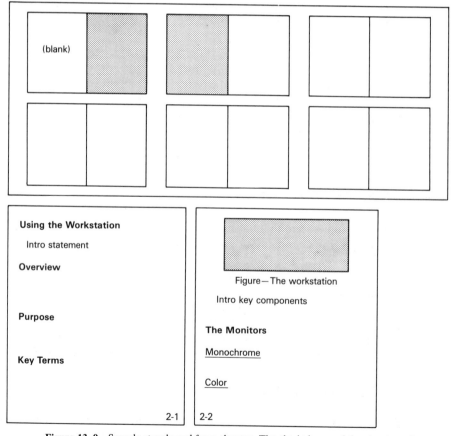

Figure 13–9 Sample storyboard for a chapter. The shaded area of the storyboard is enlarged to show the skeletal structure for the initial pages of a chapter.

Once writing and editing are begun, management, organization, and communication become crucial to the accuracy and consistency of expert system documentation [33]. The development of an expert system is cyclic: the system will change repeatedly before it is "finalized." Changes to the knowledge base cause cascading revisions throughout the system. The expert system actually evolves as displays are tested and the knowledge base expands. Development teams, made up of a writer and a system designer (e.g., a knowledge engineer), are essential to the production of documentation that matches the expert system in whatever evolutionary stage it happens to be in at the time. Weekly meetings should be held for the development teams. These meetings allow writers and designers to share information on upcoming changes to the system, delays on the design of displays or components that affect the production of specific chapters, and general information that impinges on schedules.

After the initial draft of a chapter has been completed, the documentation specialist should mark it as preliminary, identify it with a date and/or version number, and indicate whether or not it is to be released externally.[6] Then the editorial process proceeds as with any other documentation effort. It is useful to have the chapter edited by both the designer of that portion of the expert system the chapter covers and someone skilled in editing [33]. The assigned editors are responsible for technical as well as stylistic editing, and for making the document consistent with the design document and other established conventions, such as the appropriate use of special terminology.

Testing the Document

The systems approach to documentation design and production entails iterative testing and revision of the completed piece to estimate the extent to which the documentation meets its initial requirements (e.g., representing the expert system, meeting user needs, and the like).

Internal tests.   After the writer has completed each chapter or reference section, he or she should submit it to an *internal test*. Such a test need not be formal or monitored, but it should entail more than mere stylistic, grammatical editing. Initially, the designer of the portion of the expert system covered should review the "finished" version to ensure the accurate incorporation of previously edited material. Then, someone other than the original writer and designer should use the portion of the document with the system, testing the accuracy, flow, and comprehensibility of the writing. If it is possible to test a chapter with a cooperative member of the intended audience at this time, it is definitely worthwhile to do so.

External tests

Empirical Evaluation.   Upon completion and internal testing of the various portions of the documentation, the documentation specialist should begin *external*

---

[6] For obvious reasons, preliminary versions of expert system documentation usually should not be released to potential clients or customers prior to a complete internal review.

testing procedures for the expert system documentation. Although many such procedures exist for use with traditional computer documentation, empirical evaluation and subjective evaluation [33] are recommended for the external evaluation of expert system documentation.

Empirical evaluation involves formally testing the documentation with the expert system and actual users in the environment in which it is to be deployed and analyzing the results. Prior to testing, the documentation specialist should design several tasks that an end user may be required to complete during normal use of the expert system. Each task should require the use of information from a different portion of the user documentation. For example, one task might be to log into the system, another might involve using the system to view schedules for a specific entry in a data base, and a third might involve constructing a query for the expert system to answer. Each task should be tested beforehand to ensure that it can be completed within a 15–30 minute time period.

Users should be paired to form teams, and each team should be given one of the tasks to complete. Using the chapter(s) of the manual appropriate to the problem and any available reference sections (e.g., the glossary, quick reference charts, or indexes), the team attempts to complete the assigned task. It is advisable to videotape the team members and any screens or portions of the document they use as they work. The tape will provide much valuable information, showing team members discussing a problem, questioning one another, and talking about finding the information they need.

After the tasks have been completed, the documentation specialist should meet briefly with each team, replay the appropriate videotape, and question each user about verbal and nonverbal cues recorded during the completion of the task.[7] The resulting comments will address the appropriateness of the design and overall functionality of the document. If certain portions of the material appear problematic, probing questions can be used to elicit suggestions for changes.

Subjective Evaluation.   Subjective evaluation entails the use of discussions, questionnaires, and/or various scales, such as the Likert scale [31] or semantic differential assessment. The purpose of this type of evaluation is to elicit a user's personal reactions to the documentation. Some tools, like the open-ended questionnaire (e.g., "Tell me what you thought of the ___"), are highly subjective. They yield data on one user's personal response to the documentation, but the information is difficult to analyze and use in making changes that meet the needs of a wide audience. For this reason, variations on attitudinal assessment devices are often used to provide subjective information in a format that more readily enables analysis and extrapolation. A combination of scaled items with some open questions or comments allows the collection of useful data while encouraging users to openly express themselves in response to specific items.

Figure 13–10 shows one tool that has been used in testing a manual for an

---

[7] This procedure is known as *protocol generation and analysis*. More information is provided in [36].

Attitude Survey

Read each statement. Place a number in the blank beside each statement to show your degree of agreement or disagreement. Use the codes below:

6 = Strongly agree   3 = Tend to disagree
5 = Agree   2 = Disagree
4 = Tend to agree   1 = Strongly disagree

Please respond to each statement. If you would like to clarify a response or make other comments, feel free to use the Comments section at the bottom of the page, or the back of this sheet.

Table of Contents and Appendixes

Review the Table of Contents and Appendixes in the FRESH User Manual before you answer these questions.

____1. The Table of Contents has enough detail.
____2. The Table of Contents gives me a general idea of what the manual is about.
____3. I think I would use the information in the Appendixes.
____4. The Appendices seem complete.
____5. The Glossary of Commands is displayed in an easy-to-use format.
____6. I think I would use the information in the Glossary of Terms.

Instructional Chapters

Review one of the instructional chapters (chapters 2 through 11) before answering the following questions.

____1. I think I could use the step-by-step directions to complete a task.
____2. The Overview section on the first page of each chapter gives me a general idea of what the chapter is about.
____3. The Purpose and Key Terms on the first page of each chapter help signal what is important in the chapter.
____4. The typed information in the margin is useful.
____5. The instructions are easy to read.
____6. The manual seems to contain enough examples.
____7. The manual seems to contain figures that support the text.
____8. The location cues (headings, etc.) helped me to find information quickly.

Overall Assessment

Answer these questions about the manual as a whole.

____1. The manual appears to cover the various FRESH applications.
____2. The manual is specific enough to meet most users' needs.

Comments:

Figure 13–10 Subjective assessment tool for user manual evaluation. (Reprinted from K. L. McGraw, "Guidelines for Producing Documentation for Expert Systems," *IEEE Transactions on Professional Communications* 29 (1986): 46.)

expert system. Users are asked to respond to the scale and provide comments immediately after they have completed their assigned task. The results of both the subjective and empirical testing can be compiled and evaluated, and appropriate revisions planned.

Building in Modifiability

When all revisions have been incorporated into the manual, production will resume as with other computer system documentation. Even more than with traditional computer documentation, revision and refinements to expert system documentation will continue long after the installation of the system. Two suggestions can help make modification tasks more efficient. First, whenever possible, the document itself should be created and stored in an electronic format. Using a page layout program[8] to produce the actual user documentation enables designers to make prompt revisions when necessary and to produce the revised piece with less cost. Second, the documentation should include a form on which the user can note specific problems or needs for revisions and instructions for returning the completed form to the designers. Whether this component appears in an introductory section or in the reference section of the document is immaterial. However, a comment sheet should include enough information to help designers plan revision activities. Information typically appearing on comment sheets includes the following:

- Instructions for using the sheet
- Instructions for returning the sheet
- Name and contact information (optional)
- Date and time of occurrence of problem or need
- Affected chapter, page, and version of the manual
- Identification of what was attempted when the problem was noted
- Detailed description of what occurred and what the user expected
- Specific suggestion for revision
- Space for use by system and/or documentation designers (e.g., received by, date received, action suggested, priority assigned)

Suggestions for changes should be organized as to the date they were received, the source they came from, and specifics detailing the problem encountered. This enables designers to implement orderly, accurate revisions of the document and helps ensure that later versions of the documentation incorporate all the necessary revisions or enhancements. A well-designed comment sheet allows both the user to input information and the developers to track the request for revision and plans for its implementation. Whenever possible, electronic communication of the requests for revision between users and designers should be encouraged.

ON-LINE DOCUMENTATION

To this point, we have confined our discussion of expert system user documentation to printed efforts. However, current trends require that we mention the use of on-line documentation as a feasible addition (some would say an alternative) to printed matter. For example, many vendors (e.g., Microsoft) currently produce traditional software with on-line documentation in addition to printed documentation. Users who may be reluctant to consult printed documentation during a session may be more inclined to request on-line information about the topic pertaining to their current activity. Additionally, a government initiative (Computer Aided Lo-

---

[8] Such as Pagemaker, Quark XPress, and others.

gistics Support) specifies that software submitted after 1990 in completion of a contract with the Department of Defense be supported by on-line documentation. Finally, technological advances such as windowing (even for microcomputers) provide a mechanism for feasibly presenting on-line documentation without completely interrupting the view of the current screen.

Expert systems are often designed to emulate the problem-solving ability of an expert in a particular domain so that they can be used as a decision aid or tool by a less skilled individual. Based on input from the user, user responses to system queries, and data in the knowledge base, problems are diagnosed, resources managed, and complex data synthesized. Users working with an expert system to solve a problem in a particular domain may not be skilled computer users. When they reach a point in the system at which they feel unsure of themselves and their subsequent actions, they may have difficulty identifying what type of problem they are experiencing and how to label it in order to find it in the documentation. Because of the open nature of many expert systems (i.e., many different functions may be performed from a given point in the system because the system was customized to the user's needs), the user may benefit from context-sensitive documentation that is provided within the system itself. Santarelli [45] refers to a major benefit of on-line documentation in noting that "it allows people to instantly go to the screen without stopping what they were doing to go to a manual."

The on-line documentation approach, also called system help, or embedded training, seeks to provide the user with simple, concise, timely information in response to his or her needs. On-line documentation must be designed carefully and necessitates approaches and considerations that are different from paper-based documentation. Many of these differences are due to the difference in the nature of the media. For example, printed manuals allow users to skim easily back and forth through the text, compare one or more page at a time, dog-ear pages for later reference, and view a page while working through a problem. On-line documentation may cause users to feel lost because they expect a structure that is not present or obvious [10], i.e., they cannot "sense the structure" of the documentation. Other problems are due to the poor transfer of typography and display techniques from print to the screen.

While most instructional designers, documentation specialists, and expert system users agree that on-line documentation is appropriate as part of a total documentation approach for expert systems, care must be exercised in its design. Some of the basic guidelines that should be considered when designing on-line documentation are the following:

- On-line documentation should be based on a task orientation.
- The information displayed following a request for help should pertain directly to the situation (context) at hand.
- Initial information displayed may be of a general level, but should allow the user access to more specific on-line information. This technique, called "nesting" or "query-in-depth," customizes the response to the user's needs [9].

- Each window or display should be labeled (e.g., numbered) for reference and to communicate its location in the system.
- Users should be given the ability to "page through" and/or exit from the help system or on-line documentation and return to the initial task at hand.
- When printed documentation also exists that pertains to the assistance that the user requests, the on-line documentation should display relevant page numbers in the printed document for user reference.
- On-line documentation that is displayed in response to a user prompt should use windows or split screens [18] and should not completely overlay the user's current work.
- Designers of on-line documentation must attend to human factors research in the areas of the legibility and resolution of text on screens [27, 37, 44] appropriate cueing mechanisms, spacing and screen density [48], the effective use of "white space," discrete screens vs. scrolling, the use of grids, and writing style.

SUMMARY

This chapter has brought together information from a number of fields, notably communications and technical writing, instructional design, and systems analysis. User documentation for expert systems is a vital component of a user-centered product. Well-designed and implemented documentation yields benefits to both the end user and, eventually, the producer of the documentation. The process of producing user documentation for an expert system borrows from the well-established systems-oriented methodologies in use for producing traditional user documentation. These methodologies must be reshaped, however, to allow for the additional complexity of expert system software. This complexity is wrought not only by the diversity of the audiences and the newness of the technology, but also by the iterative cycle that is accepted for expert system production.

Documentation specialists working with traditional software frequently apply the SDP methodology in creating user documentation. We have suggested a development methodology for expert system user documentation that parallels the systems-oriented waterfall model, but allows for iterations between phases. The implementation of this model, from the feasibility and requirements analysis phases, through the design and implementation phases, to evaluation and modification efforts, has been discussed at length. While the emphasis has been chiefly on printed documentation efforts, on-line documentation has been briefly addressed and initial guidelines toward its design offered.

REFERENCES

1. *How to Plan Printing,* Chicago, IL: S. D. Warren Company, 1978.
2. Anderson, R. "Schema-directed Process in Language Comprehension." In *Cognitive Psychology and Instruction,* edited by A. Lesgold et al., New York: Plenum Press, 1978.

3. Bailey R. *Human Errors in Computer Systems.* Englewood Cliffs, NJ: Prentice-Hall, 1983.

4. Beard, R., and Callamars, P. V. "A Method for Designing Computer Support Documentation." Master's thesis, 1983.

5. Berlinger, C. "Behaviors, Measures, and Instruments for Performance Evaluation in Simulated Environments." Paper presented at a symposium and workshop on the quantification of human performance, Albuquerque, NM, 1964.

6. Blanding-Clark, T., and Cross, T. "Designing Effective User Interfaces and Documentation." *Journal of Information and Image Management* 17 (1984): 45–48.

7. Boehm, B. W. *Software Engineering Economics.* Englewood Cliffs, NJ: Prentice-Hall, 1981.

8. Booher, H. "Relative Comprehensibility of Pictorial Information and Printed Words in Proceduralized Instructions." *Human Factors* 17 (1975): 266–277.

9. Bork, A. "A Preliminary Taxonomy of Ways of Displaying Text on Screens." *Information Design Journal* 3 (1983): 206–214.

10. Bradford, A. "Writing and Using Online Tutorial Information." Paper presented at the College Composition and Communication Conference, New York, March, 1984.

11. Bradford, A. "Presenting Information on a Computer Screen: A Decision Process for the Information Planner." *Human Factors Society Bulletin* 30 (1987): 1–3.

12. Bradford, A., and Rubens, B. "A Survey of Experienced Users and Writers of Online Information." *Transactions of the IEEE Professional Communication Society* 26 (1985): 269–274.

13. Brockmann, J. *Writing Better Computer User Documentation.* New York: John Wiley & Sons, 1986.

14. Brockmann, J., and McCauley, R. "Does the Computer Affect the Writing Process?" *Technical Writing Teacher* 11 (1984).

15. Burnhill, P., Hartley, J., and Young, M. "Tables in Text." *Applied Ergonomics* 7 (1976): 13–18.

16. Carroll, J., and Thomas, J. "Metaphor and the Cognitive Representation of Computing Systems." *IEEE Transactions on Systems, Man, and Cybernetics* 12 (1982): 107–116.

17. Cayne, D. "Apple Computer and Its Macintosh." *Personal Computing Strategic Analysis Report.* Stamford, CT: The Gartner Group, 1987.

18. Clark, I. "Software Simulation as a Tool for Usable Product Design." *IBM Systems Journal* 20 (1981).

19. Duchastel, P. "Marginalia." In *The Technology of Text,* vol. 2, edited by D. H. Jonassen, pp. 167–192. Englewood Cliffs, NJ: Educational Technology Publications, 1986.

20. Gaines, B., and Shaw, M. *The Art of Computer Conversation: A New Medium for Communication.* Englewood Cliffs, NJ: Prentice-Hall, 1984.

21. Glynn, S. M., Britton, B. K., and Tillman, M. H. "Typographical Cues in Text: Management of the Reader's Attention." In *The Technology of Text,* vol. 2, edited by D. H. Jonassen. Englewood Cliffs, NJ: Educational Technology Publications, 1986.

22. Goodman, K. S. *Reading: Process and Program.* Urbana, IL: National Council of Teachers of English, 1970.

23. Greenwald, J. "How Does This #%$@! Thing Work?" *Time,* 18 June 1984, p. 64.

24. Guymon, R., and Gottfredson, C. *Writing Better User Manuals.* A course presented through Battelle by Guymon and Associates, 1984.

25. Hartley, J. "Eighty Ways of Improving Instructional Text." *IEEE Transactions on Professional Communication* 24 (1981): 17–27.

26. Hartley, J., and Jonassen, D. H. "The Role of Headings in Printed and Electronic Text." In *The Technology of Text,* vol 2, edited by D. H. Jonassen. Englewood Cliffs, NJ: Educational Technology Publications, 1985.

27. Hulme, C. "Reading: Extracting Information from Printed and Electronically Presented Text." In *Fundamentals of Human-Computer Interaction,* edited by A. Monk. London: Academic Press, 1984.

28. Jonassen, D. H. "Blocking and Types of Headings in Text: Effects on Recall and Retrieval." Paper presented at the annual meeting of the American Educational Research Association, Montreal, Canada, April, 1983.

29. Jonassen, D. H., and Falk, L. M. "Mapping and Programming Textual Materials." *Programmed Learning and Educational Technology* 17 (1980): 19–26.

30. Kleid, N. A. "IBM's Information Quality Measurement Program." *Proceedings of the International Technical Communications Conference.* Chicago, IL, 1984.

31. Likert, R. "A Technique for the Measurement of Attitudes." *Archives of Psychology* 140 (1932): 44–53.

32. Maynard, J. "A User-driven Approach to Better User Manuals." *IEEE Transactions on Professional Communication* 25 (1982): 216–219.

33. McGraw, K. L. "Guidelines for Producing Documentation for Expert Systems." *IEEE Transactions on Professional Communications* 29 (1986): 48–55.

34. McGraw, K. L., and Riner, A. "Task Analysis: Structuring the Knowledge Acquisition Process." *Texas Instruments Technical Journal* 4 (1987): 16–21.

35. McGraw, K. L. *Macintosh Productivity Benefits Research Summary Report.* Landover, MD: Falcon Microsystems, 1987.

36. McGraw, K. L., and Harbison-Briggs, K. *Knowledge Acqusition: Principles and Guidelines.* Englewood Cliffs, NJ: Prentice-Hall, 1988.

37. Merrill, P. "Displaying Text on Microcomputers." In *The Technology of Text,* vol 1, edited by D. Jonassen. Englewood Cliffs, NJ: Educational Technology Publications, 1982.

38. Meyer, B. J. F. "Signaling the Structure of Text." In *The Technology of Text,* vol 2, edited by D. Jonassen, pp. 64–89. Englewood Cliffs, NJ: Educational Technology Publications, 1985.

39. Miller, R. *Development of a Taxonomy of Human Performance: A User-oriented Approach.* Silver Spring, MD: AIR, 1971.

40. Odescalchi, E. K. "Productivity Gain Attained by Task-oriented Information." *Proceedings of the 33rd International Technical Communication Conference,* Washington, DC: Society for Technical Communication, 1986, pp. 434–439.

41. Odescalchi, E. K. "Documentation Is the Key to User Success." *IEEE Transactions on Professional Communication* 29 (1986): 16–18.

42. Palko, K. "Development of Human Factors Guidelines for Computer Software Quick Reference Guides." Unpublished master's thesis, Texas A&M University, 1986.

43. Rosenbaum, S., and Walters, R. D. "Audience Diversity: A Major Challenge in Computer Documentation." *IEEE Transactions on Professional Communications* 29 (1986): 48–55.

44. Rubens, P., and Krull, R. "Application of Research on Document Design to Online Displays." *Technical Communication* 32 (1985): 29–34.

45. Santerelli, M. "It's Not the Same Old Help Anymore." *Software News* April 1984.

46. Sullivan, M., and A. Chapinis. "Human Factoring: A Text Editor Manual." *Behavior and Information Technology,* 2, pp. 113–125, 1983.

47. Thorndyke, P. "Cognitive Structures in Comprehension and Meaning of Narrative Discourse." *Cognitive Psychology* (1977): 77–110.

48. Swarts, H., Flower, L., and Hayes, J. *How Headings in Documentation Can Mislead Readers, Technical Report No. 9.* Washington, DC: American Institutes for Research, 1980.

49. Tullis, T. "An Evaluation of Alphanumeric, Graphic, and Color Information Displays." *Human Factors* 23 (1981): 541–550.

50. Waller, R. H. W. "Typographic Access Structures for Educational Texts." In *Processing of Visible Language,* vol 1, edited by P.A. Kolers and M. E. Wrolstad, New York: Plenum Press, 1979.

51. Weaver, C. *Psycholinguistics and Reading: From Process to Practice.* Boston, MA: Little, Brown and Company, 1985.

52. Woodson, W. *Human Factors Design Handbook,* New York: McGraw-Hill, 1981.

Index

A

Analytic Hierarchy Process, 10–11

B

backward execution, 178
BaRT, 298
Bayes' rule, 248
belief functions, 252
belief networks, 258

C

certainty factors, 250
certification, 322
classification, 218
color, 110
computer graphics, 99
computer-supported collaborative work, 155
CSRL, 218

D

E

F

G

H

T

U

V

W

TEAR OUT THIS PAGE TO ORDER THESE OTHER HIGH-QUALITY YOURDON PRESS COMPUTING SERIES TITLES

Quantity	Title/Author	ISBN	Price	Total $
_____	Building Controls Into Structured Systems; Brill	013–086059–X	$35.00	_____
_____	C Notes: Guide to C Programming; Zahn	013–109778–4	$21.96	_____
_____	Classics in Software Engineering; Yourdon	013–135179–6	$38.00	_____
_____	Controlling Software Projects; DeMarco	013–171711–1	$39.00	_____
_____	Creating Effective Software; King	013–189242–8	$33.00	_____
_____	Crunch Mode; Boddie	013–194960–8	$29.00	_____
_____	Current Practices in Software Development; King	013–195678–7	$34.00	_____
_____	Data Factory; Roeske	013–196759–2	$23.00	_____
_____	Developing Structured Systems; Dickinson	013–205147–8	$34.00	_____
_____	Design of On-Line Computer Systems; Yourdon	013–201301–0	$48.00	_____
_____	Essential Systems Analysis; McMenamin/Palmer	013–287905–0	$35.00	_____
_____	Expert System Technology; Keller	013–295577–6	$28.95	_____
_____	Concepts of Information Modeling; Flavin	013–335589–6	$27.00	_____
_____	Game Plan for System Development; Frantzen/McEvoy	013–346156–4	$30.00	_____
_____	Intuition to Implementation; MacDonald	013–502196–0	$24.00	_____
_____	Managing Structured Techniques; Yourdon	013–551037–6	$33.00	_____
_____	Managing the System Life Cycle 2/e; Yourdon	013–551045–7	$35.00	_____
_____	People & Project Management; Thomsett	013–655747–3	$23.00	_____
_____	Politics of Projects; Block	013–685553–9	$24.00	_____
_____	Practice of Structured Analysis; Keller	013–693987–2	$28.00	_____
_____	Program It Right; Benton/Weekes	013–729005–5	$23.00	_____
_____	Software Design: Methods & Techniques; Peters	013–821828–5	$33.00	_____
_____	Structured Analysis; Weinberg	013–854414–X	$44.00	_____
_____	Structured Analysis & System Specifications; DeMarco	013–854380–1	$44.00	_____
_____	Structured Approach to Building Programs: BASIC; Wells	013–854076–4	$23.00	_____
_____	Structured Approach to Building Programs: COBOL; Wells	013–854084–5	$23.00	_____
_____	Structured Approach to Building Programs: Pascal; Wells	013–851536–0	$23.00	_____
_____	Structured Design; Yourdon/Constantine	013–854471–9	$49.00	_____
_____	Structured Development Real-Time Systems, Combined; Ward/Mellor	013–854654–1	$75.00	_____
_____	Structured Development Real-Time Systems, Vol. I; Ward/Mellor	013–854787–4	$33.00	_____
_____	Structured Development Real-Time Systems, Vol. II; Ward/Mellor	013–854795–5	$33.00	_____
_____	Structured Development Real-Time Systems, Vol. III; Ward/Mellor	013–854803–X	$33.00	_____
_____	Structured Systems Development; Orr	013–855149–9	$33.00	_____
_____	Structured Walkthroughs 3/e; Yourdon	013–855248–7	$24.00	_____
_____	System Development Without Pain; Ward	013–881392–2	$33.00	_____
_____	Teams in Information System Development; Semprivivo	013–896721–0	$28.00	_____
_____	Techniques of EDP Project Management; Brill	013–900358–4	$33.00	_____
_____	Techniques of Program Structure & Design; Yourdon	013–901702–X	$44.00	_____
_____	Up and Running; Hanson	013–937558–9	$32.00	_____
_____	Using the Structured Techniques; Weaver	013–940263–2	$27.00	_____
_____	Writing of the Revolution; Yourdon	013–970708–5	$38.00	_____
_____	Practical Guide to Structured Systems 2/e; Page-Jones	013–690769–5	$35.00	_____

Total $ _____

— discount (if appropriate) _____

New Total $ _____

AND TAKE ADVANTAGE OF THESE SPECIAL OFFERS!

a.) When ordering 3 or 4 copies (of the same or different titles), take 10% off the total list price (excluding sales tax, where applicable).

b.) When ordering 5 to 20 copies (of the same or different titles), take 15% off the total list price (excluding sales tax, where applicable).

c.) To receive a greater discount when ordering 20 or more copies, call or write:

Special Sales Department
College Marketing
Prentice Hall
Englewood Cliffs, NJ 07632
201–592–2498

SAVE!

If payment accompanies order, plus your state's sales tax where applicable, Prentice Hall pays postage and handling charges. Same return privilege refund guaranteed. Please do not mail in cash.

☐ **PAYMENT ENCLOSED**—shipping and handling to be paid by publisher (please include your state's tax where applicable).

☐ **SEND BOOKS ON 15–DAY TRIAL BASIS** & bill me (with small charge for shipping and handling).

Name _____

Address _____

City _____ State _____ Zip _____

I prefer to charge my   ☐ Visa   ☐ MasterCard
Card Number _____ Expiration Date _____

Signature _____

All prices are subject to change without notice.

Mail your order to: Prentice Hall, Book Distribution Center, Route 59 at
Brook Hill Drive, West Nyack, NY 10995

Dept. 1   D–OFYP–FW(1)

DATE DUE